The Notorious Georges

LAW AND SOCIETY SERIES

W. Wesley Pue, Founding Editor

LAW AND
SOCIETY

The Law and Society Series explores law as a socially embedded
phenomenon. It is premised on the understanding that the conventional
division of law from society creates false dichotomies in thinking, scholarship,
educational practice, and social life. Books in the series treat law and society
as mutually constitutive and seek to bridge scholarship emerging from
interdisciplinary engagement of law with disciplines such as politics,
social theory, history, political economy, and gender studies.

For a list of the titles in this series, see the UBC Press website,
www.ubcpress.ca.

The Notorious Georges

Crime and Community in British Columbia's Northern Interior, 1909–25

JONATHAN SWAINGER

PUBLISHED BY UBC PRESS FOR
THE OSGOODE SOCIETY
FOR CANADIAN LEGAL HISTORY

UBCPress · Vancouver

32 31 30 29 28 27 26 25 24 23   5 4 3 2 1

Printed in Canada on FSC-certified ancient-forest-free paper (100% post-consumer recycled) that is processed chlorine- and acid-free.

Library and Archives Canada Cataloguing in Publication

Title: The notorious Georges : crime and community in British Columbia's northern interior, 1909-25 / Jonathan Swainger.
Names: Swainger, Jonathan, 1962- author.
Series: Law and society series (Vancouver, B.C.)
Description: Series statement: Law and society series | Co-published by the Osgoode Society for Canadian Legal History. | Includes bibliographical references and index.
Identifiers: Canadiana (print) 20230483399 | Canadiana (ebook) 202304850X | ISBN 9780774869416 (softcover) | ISBN 9780774869430 (EPUB) | ISBN 9780774869423 (PDF)
Subjects: LCSH: Crime and race—British Columbia—Prince George—History— 20th century. | LCSH: Police—British Columbia—Prince George—History— 20th century. | LCSH: Criminal law—British Columbia—Prince George— History—20th century. | LCSH: Group identity—British Columbia—Prince George—History—20th century. | LCSH: Prince George (B.C.)—History— 20th century.
Classification: LCC HV6197.C32 B7 2023 | DDC 364.9711/82—dc23

Canada Council   Conseil des arts
for the Arts   du Canada

Canadä

BRITISH COLUMBIA ARTS COUNCIL

BRITISH COLUMBIA

UBC Press gratefully acknowledges the financial support for our publishing program of the Government of Canada, the Canada Council for the Arts, and the British Columbia Arts Council.

This book has been published with the help of a grant from the Canadian Federation for the Humanities and Social Sciences, through the Scholarly Book Awards, using funds provided by the Social Sciences and Humanities Research Council of Canada.

UBC Press
The University of British Columbia
Vancouver
www.ubcpress.ca

For David Harris Flaherty
(February 25, 1940–October 11, 2022),
editor of the first two volumes of
Essays in the History of Canadian Law
(1981/1983).

Mentor, friend, and unflagging supporter.

Contents

Illustrations and Tables

TABLES

Foreword

THE OSGOODE SOCIETY FOR CANADIAN LEGAL HISTORY

Jonathan Swainger's *The Notorious Georges* is a thoroughly researched investigation of crime, disorder, policing, courts, and community attitudes and responses in the Georges – South Fort George, Fort George, and Prince George – in the early decades of the twentieth century. The Georges were characterized as "rough and tumble" and "gritty" communities on the frontier of white settlement and expansion within. At the same time, many community members sought "respectability," as they defined it, wishing both to enhance the region's reputation and long-term economic development. Municipal leaders, the police, and magistrates routinely blamed crime and disorder on Indigenous peoples, those of mixed heritage, racialized Asian and Black residents, and transients, but Swainger shows this not to have been the case. White residents of European origin were responsible for most of the community's ills. In this sense, the history of the Georges mirrors that of British Columbia as a whole, which in this period was a society in which racism and cultural chauvinism dominated all aspects of social and economic life and the administration of the law. The Osgoode Society for Canadian Legal History is delighted to add to our growing body of work on western Canada.

The purpose of the Osgoode Society for Canadian Legal History is to encourage research and writing in the history of Canadian law. The Society, which was incorporated in 1979 and is registered as a charity, was founded at the initiative of the Honourable R. Roy McMurtry, formerly attorney general for Ontario and chief justice of the province, and officials of the

Law Society of Upper Canada. The Society seeks to stimulate the study of legal history in Canada by supporting researchers, collecting oral histories, and publishing volumes that contribute to legal-historical scholarship in Canada. This year's books bring the total published since 1981 to 118, in all fields of Canadian legal history – the courts, the judiciary, and the legal profession, as well as the history of crime and punishment, women and law, law and economy, the legal treatment of Indigenous peoples and ethnic minorities, and famous cases and significant trials in all areas of the law.

Current directors of the Osgoode Society for Canadian Legal History are Constance Backhouse, Heidi Bohaker, Brendan Brammall, Bevan Brooksbank, Shantona Chaudhury, Paul Davis, Linda Silver Dranoff, Timothy Hill, Jacqueline Horvat, Ian Hull, Mahmud Jamal, Rachel McMillan, R. Roy McMurtry, Waleed Malik, Dana Peebles, Linda Plumpton, Paul Schabas, Robert Sharpe, Jonathan Silver, Alex Smith, Lorne Sossin, Michael Tulloch, and John Wilkinson.

Robert J. Sharpe
President

Professor Jim Phillips
Editor-in-Chief

Acknowledgments

Given that this book began as an article that was to survey crime and policing history in the Georges, it is little wonder that I have accumulated a list of individuals who have assisted me in what has grown out of proportion. My family – Jennifer Sauvé, Matthew Swainger, and Thomas Swainger – has supported this and other research projects throughout the years: sincere thanks for their patience. A tip of the cap goes to Erin Payne, who, as a student in a senior undergraduate class in the January 1998 semester, introduced me to the Prince George city police. Erin, along with his partner, Carla, were early success stories of the history program at the University of Northern British Columbia.

Beginning in the January 2009 semester, I launched a project to combine, in an electronic archive, every newspaper story touching on policing, crime, the criminal courts, and the administration of justice found in the Prince George newspaper database. Relying on student labour as a component of course research, this archive included electronic scans of newspaper pages and searchable content summaries linked to each story. The "guinea pigs" of the first class were Blake Bouchard, Doug Boyes, Katerina Liss, Pritpal Minhas, Erica Moulton, Melissa Parks, Angela Wells, Andrew Ross, Jeff Slack, Kelsey Wiebe, and Randi Willmore. Subsequent years included Jennifer Cullen, Marlina Hawes, Kelsey Knowles, Stephanie Leong, Jillian MacMillan, Cyndie Yule, Mica Jorgenson, Troy Lee, Alauna Brown, Larisa Clotildes, Jasmine Kirk, Kathryn Louro, Ryan Peel, Wilson Willock, Matthew Barrager, Melissa Clement, Jenna Davis, Darin Kamsteeg, Christopher Larsen, David Lewis, Megan Macmillan, Ryan

McKenney, Devin McMurty, Emerson Pereira, Tannon Schmaltz, Morgan Wright, Lyndsey Bodgener, Emilo Caputo, Sarah Leach, Maria Martins, Hailey Massingham, Alison Matte, Kaitlyn Nebone, Claire Radford, and Rebekah Rustad. The still incomplete database spans from 1910 to the late 1950s (when the volume of daily newspapers swamped the project). Working with these student colleagues and engaging with their research illuminated aspects of local crime/policing history that I had not anticipated. That many of these students have gone on to successful graduate degrees and subsequent careers in education, the law, the civil service, and small business is, I know, testament to the real-world value of thinking historically and applying the historian's tools of empathy and imagination. For their efforts and dedication to the cause, as well as for enriching my own learning experience, I cannot thank them enough. A second group of students, who did not contribute to the database but employed it in support of local history research, included McKenna Blunt, Emma Conlon, Nicole McNeil, Alex Nielson, Reiley O'Brien, Elizabeth van Roode, Matthew Swainger, Jillian Pearson, Piper James, Rebecca Pinko, Lydia Kinesawich, Baylee McGillivray, Mikeila Oliveria, Racheal Holmes, Quinn Beblow, Nolan Thiffault, and Maddison Wesley-Plambeck.

Of the latter group, Jillian Pearson deserves mention for her labours with the British Columbia Provincial Police (BCPP) duty logs during the first plague summer (May–August 2020), when, thanks to SSHRC and university funding, she worked with me as a research assistant. Being able to task a second-year undergraduate with an assignment, and know that the work would be done well, is a rare thing. Her perceptiveness, work ethic, and good humour were splendid. To Jillian and my wife, Jennifer, goes the shared credit for early diagnosis of the cause leading to acting BCPP chief John Bourne's breakdown, the details of which appear in Chapter 2. That in 2023 Jillian is on the cusp of a career in education compels me to acknowledge that I would be hard-pressed to imagine someone better suited to inspire young minds.

Other debts incurred along the way include assistance provided by Susan Smith-Jospehy in Quesnel; Elizabeth Hunter, manager of the Quesnel and District Museum and Archives; Tracy Calogheros, chief executive officer, Exploration Place, Prince George; Alyssa Leier, curator, Exploration Place, Prince George; and Chad Hellenius, assistant curator, Exploration Place. Leslie Kellett, the legislative coordinator of the Legislative Service Division at Prince George City Hall, tolerated a series of inquiries about city council minutes, and, early on, Walt Babicz of Prince George City Hall, facilitated access requests to the city's historical records. Emily Harris, archivist at the Peace River Museum, Archives and Mackenzie Centre in Peace River, Alberta, took time to undertake an idiosyncratic newspaper search concerning Mr. Justice H.E.A. Robertson's journeys through the Alberta side of the Peace River country. Closer to home, Nathan Reinheimer, of the Prince George Public Library, fielded constant queries about the Prince George Newspaper Digitization Project, which houses electronic copies of the city's surviving newspapers, starting in 1910. Databases are wonderful tools, but Nathan continually demonstrated that these electronic marvels require steadfast human beings to sort out tangles. Further, the staff at the Northern British Columbia Archives at the University of Northern British Columbia (UNBC) were always available to lend assistance. They include the former head archivist, Ramona Rose; the current head archivist, Erica Hernandez-Read; Kim Strathers; and Flossie Smith. Former UNBC inter-library loan clerk Mary Bertulli chased down all manner of requests. Her shoes have since been filled by the equally resourceful Valerie Cantin. Reference librarian Kealin McCabe has tolerated all manner of nonsense from me for years and, despite it all, is still willing to chat. Wonders never cease. And in both an official and unofficial capacity, my splendid wife, Jennifer Sauvé, who, throughout this research journey, has been the reference librarian at the College of New Caledonia in Prince George, assisted my navigation of the local history records at that institution. These records are, I believe, one of Dr. Frank Leonard's legacies. That he continues to offer counsel on the Georges was and is appreciated. Dr. Ted Binnema, my colleague in the History Department at UNBC, has been a sounding board throughout this process. I acknowledge his collegiality and, indeed, his friendship during our shared years at UNBC.

I also want to make mention of the assistance provided at the provincial archives in Victoria. As was the case for countless other scholars, COVID interrupted my research. The provincial archives developed a plan to provide access while endeavouring to protect our collective health. For managing an awkward situation involving anxious researchers, my sincere thanks to everyone who found the means to make access possible, especially for someone, like me, who was physically distant from the archives. I also have to acknowledge the financial support, including a publication subvention, provided through the Research Office at the University of Northern British Columbia. Supporting archival research trips and the hiring of a student researcher once it became obvious that this project had grown into a book-length study was both timely and generous. Through these efforts, the staff in the Research Office continue to honour one of the university's founding commitments: expanding our historical knowledge of northern British Columbia, and, for that, I am grateful.

Abbreviations

EMB	*Edmonton Morning Bulletin*
ETR	*Evening Times Republican* (Marshalltown, IA)
FDL	*Fernie District Ledger*
FGH	*Fort George Herald*
FGT	*Fort George Tribune*
FGWT	*Fort George Weekly Tribune*
FMS	*Macleod Spectator* (Fort Macleod, AB)
GFDT	*Great Falls Daily Tribune* (Montana)
IJ	*Indianapolis Journal*
IN	*Interior News* (Smithers, BC)
IS	*Inland Sentinel* (Kamloops)
KS	*Kamloops Standard*
KSS	*Kamloops Standard Sentinel*
KT	*Kamloops Telegram*
LH	*Lethbridge Herald*
LP	*Regina Leader-Post*
MG	*Montreal Gazette*
MJ	*Minneapolis Journal*
MS	*Montreal Star*
NDC	*Nelson (BC) Daily Canadian*
NDN	*Nanaimo Daily News*
NP	*National Post*
NYT	*New York Times*
OC	*Ottawa Citizen*
OH	*Omineca Herald* (New Hazelton, BC)
OJ	*Ottawa Journal*
PGC	*Prince George Citizen*
PGH	*Prince George Herald*
PGL	*Prince George Leader*
PGP	*Prince George Post*
PGS	*Prince George Star*
PRBN	*Peace River Block News*
PRDN	*Prince Rupert Daily News*
PRJ	*Prince Rupert Journal*

PRO	Prince Rupert Optimist
PRR	Peace River Record
QCT	Quad City Times (Davenport, IA)
SC	Spokane (WA) Chronicle
SDS	Sault (ON) Daily Star
SFE	San Francisco Examiner
SP	Sandon (BC) Paystreak
SPG	Saint Paul (MN) Globe
SS	Similkameen (BC) Star
SSP	Saskatoon Star Phoenix
ST	Minneapolis Star-Tribune
TDME	Toronto Daily Mail and Empire
TG	Toronto Globe
TL	New Denver (BC) Ledge
TS	Toronto Star
VDC	Victoria Daily Colonist
VDNA	Vancouver Daily News Advertiser
VDP	Vancouver Daily Province
VDT	Victoria Daily Times
VDW	Vancouver Daily World
VNH	Vancouver News Herald
VP	Vancouver Province
VS	Vancouver Sun
VTC	Victoria Times Colonist
VW	Vancouver World
WBW	Weekly British Whig (Kingston, ON)
WFP	Winnipeg Free Press
WFPEB	Winnipeg Free Press Evening Bulletin
WS	Windsor (ON) Star
WSP	Winnipeg Saturday Post
WT	Winnipeg Tribune

The Notorious Georges

Introduction

Anxious at the Very Gates of Hell

S peaking before the Presbyterian Church of Canada Congress in
Toronto in early June 1913, Reverend C. Melville Wright had reason
to be nervous. A "boyish" curate just five years out of college, he
appeared to be on the verge of national prominence.[1] If this hometown
return proved successful, a leadership role might await him in the coali-
tion fighting for social reform and against vice. Here was an opportunity
to make an impression. Ministering to his congregation in Fort George,
in British Columbia's northern Interior, Wright fought for notice from
men for whom "the rattle of coins is so loud they cannot hear the voice
of conscience."[2] The flourishing Hotel Northern bar in South Fort George
was second only to local brothels in attracting customers. Sowing the
Lord's message required conviction. Despite the challenges, Wright assured
his audience that he would persist for it was "worth all the struggle when
we can defeat sin at the very gates of hell."[3] The young minister's call to
action was a sensation. Waves of applause circled Massey Hall.[4]

A day later, Wright momentarily retreated. Having seen the headlines,
he realized that trouble was brewing. "I did not mean to describe Fort
George as the very gates of hell," he claimed. "It's no worse than any
other place. Toronto for instance."[5] This balm for Fort George residents'
wounded pride proved temporary. Asked "what particular form of vice is
rampant," Wright returned to his familiar themes. "In the first place, the
liquor traffic is flourishing. There are two saloons with four to six bartenders each ... There is a segregated district, four big houses with thirty

women, in South Fort George, two blocks from Knox Church."[6] That he singled out South Fort George was no accident. Although he ministered across the immediate area, he was pastor of the Presbyterian Church in Fort George, a structure financed by and built on land gifted from George Hammond's Natural Resources Security Company (NRSC), the sales agent for the Fort George townsite, which was in competition with South Fort George.[7] Certainly, the minister's concern for the state of local morals was self-interested. After all, if desirable, upright Christian settlers preferred Fort George to the seething den of iniquity in South Fort George, both Wright's church and his benefactor, Hammond, would profit. Few in South Fort George missed this subtext. Having learned of the speech through the *Vancouver Province*, the *Fort George Herald* dismissed the depiction as "extravagant and ill-considered," adding that "we have had several examples of this weakness from the Rev. Mr. Wright to draw unto himself the fleeting attention of the public by methods which would indicate that he seeks reputation rather by notoriety than by more commendable actions."[8] Further, "Wright strives to obliterate sin from the surface. He would drive out houses of prostitution, he would close-up hotel bars, and would make religion compulsory. This sort of thing has all been tried before. It gives way to an illicit liquor traffic; to the erection of foundling hospitals for misbegotten children, and to atheism."[9]

The newspaper's dismissal aside, Wright's description was telling. Barely five years since its establishment as a white settler community, South Fort George had a tawdry reputation. While the minister had exaggerated, the portrait was uncomfortably close to the mark. Reports of dubious business practices, immorality, and vice in the settlements were already journalistic staples. Indeed, one of the reasons that Wright had been invited to speak at the Toronto congress was because the "Georges" – South Fort George, Fort George, and, in time, Prince George – had been "prominent in the public mind."[10] As early as the spring of 1910, the question of whether investors in the NRSC's Fort George townsite were being duped sparked a battle between *Saturday Night* magazine, published in Toronto, and Vancouver's *BC Saturday Sunset* that spurred on local competition over which of the Georges was the worthy destination for incoming white settlers. This war of words ultimately involved not only the two magazines but the *Fort George Herald* and the *Fort George Tribune* as well and fed newspaper and magazine copy elsewhere in Canada and beyond. For those hoping to attract settlers and capital to the Georges, the near-constant allegations and insults, many of which reached a national audience, were anxiety inducing.

And while Wright's speech had antagonized residents, even the region's most enthusiastic boosters would have to admit that the local setting was not one of well-ordered civility, families attending church services, and residents dutifully avoiding strong drink, games of chance, and personal indulgence. So, as the Grand Trunk Pacific Railway (GTP) inched closer to the new townsite that would eventually bear the name Prince George, locals and the railway company hoped that a fresh start was in the offing, free of the hard words, acrimony, and bruising legacy of earlier dust-ups. Inasmuch as Wright was wrong-footed by the repercussions trailing behind his Toronto comments, he regained his equilibrium when it was revealed that Irene Jordan, South Fort George's most prominent madam, had apparently secured permission to build a new brothel on Fort George's outskirts.[11] Having prided itself on being a "clean community," in contrast to its lewd and boozy neighbour, Fort George appeared poised to cash in on commercialized sex. W.R. Gordon, editor of the *Fort George Tribune,* was hard pressed to understand how Jordan's plan had remained undisclosed until a week before the new establishment's grand opening.[12] Was there skulduggery afoot or had the community changed its mind about tolerating the sex-trade? Surely, "Miss Jordan and her lady help" would be sent packing.

When the *Tribune* questioned local British Columbia Provincial Police (BCPP) chief Achilles O'Neill Daunt about Jordan's proposed expansion, he indicated that the police would "not allow any of these women to settle in any place other than the district now occupied by them at South Fort George."[13] Daunt, however, was about to resign, leaving the *Tribune* to wonder about the incoming police chief's disposition. Further, an interview with Jordan failed to clarify who had approved the construction of the two-storey, 111-square-metre house, with its fourteen rooms, electric call-bell system, gasoline-powered lighting, furnace, and substantial cellar. Jordan anticipated housing six "girls" once operations were underway. News of the expansion had allegedly inspired brothel keepers from South Fort George – Bee Baker, Bessie Peters, and Jean Starr – to consider similar moves, and Jordan worried that unrestrained expansion would "spoil the game."[14] Proposing to sell her adjoining lots to any women in the same line of work, Jordan hoped that a segregated district in Fort George would dampen opposition to the brothels. True to the simmering hostilities between the two communities, John Daniell, owner of the *Fort George Herald,* which defended South Fort George against all comers, gleefully wondered if Fort George's upright business leaders, seduced by a red-light district's "free money," had prevailed upon Jordan to build her new establishment.[15] Weeks later, and after speaking with Jordan, Daniell reported that she had, in fact, been approached by an unnamed Fort George businessman, but that, given the uproar, she was no longer interested in operating a new house.[16] Believing that the NRSC had been behind the affair, Daniell claimed that, once the dust settled, the company would reimburse Jordan for her expenditures.

In the interim, a telegram reached John McConnell at the *Vancouver Sun,* informing him of a petition protesting Jordan's planned expansion and stating that, because local men were too "feeble" to remedy the situation, women in Fort George had been compelled to act.[17] While the petition, with its sixty-five signatures, was directed to Attorney General W.J. Bowser, McConnell sought out Mrs. Peter McNaughton, who, as president of the Vancouver Local Council of Women, pledged the organization's support and assistance to its Fort George sisters. Mary Ellen Smith, who later became British Columbia's first female member of the Legislative Assembly and activist Helen Gregory MacGill voiced similar sentiments.[18] Following the petition, Bowser received a letter from J.H. Johnson, president of the Fort George Hotel, who opposed the segregated district's expansion.[19] Having been given orders by BCPP superintendent Colin Campbell, William R. Dunwoody, the region's new police chief, appeared on 7 August and shuttered Jordan's new brothel on its first day of business. Reportedly, "the chief arrived on the scene in time to receive a sweet invitation to help carry in the piano."[20]

Coming barely a month after Wright's appearance in Toronto, the episode reinforced impressions that something was awry in the Georges. And while local uplifters may have counted the pushback against Jordan as a victory, the episode gave the impression that most of the local male population – including self-identified "respectable" residents – considered the sex trade a necessary evil. For those residents emboldened with the possibilities of reforming Canadian society as a whole, and the Georges in particular, the "victory" against Jordan had to be pressed. For Reverend Wright, that opportunity appeared a month later, with the arrival of the intriguing Marie Christine Ratté.

Born in Quebec and raised a Catholic, Ratté converted to Presbyterianism before entering the Methodist National Training School in Toronto in 1911, a time when evangelical Protestantism and the Social Gospel were approaching their peak of influence in English-speaking Canada.[21] Upon graduation, Ratté became a Presbyterian deaconess and then launched her career as a social worker at Toronto's Redemptive Home. Hers was an "aggressive evangelism," dedicated to educating congregations about the degradations of the so-called white slave trade rather than converting souls. Invited to speak by Wright and the Fort George Presbyterian Church, Ratté delivered two talks. The first, for an afternoon meeting of the Women's Auxiliary on 9 September 1913, centred on the social evil of the sex trade, particularly as it concerned the district. She spoke of the ravaged lives of those women who were entrapped, their rapid deterioration and early deaths, and the widespread system of recruiting to fill the places of those who were abandoned, diseased, or dead. Such were the realities of the "entire business of prostitution."[22] Wright presided over the second talk, a men-only evening affair, where proceedings were opened with his announcement that the church would support any woman who wished to escape prostitution, pay her fare to one of the nation's nine reclamation homes, and support her until she obtained suitable employment. Having had his moment in the spotlight, the pastor surrendered the floor to Ratté, who "dealt with all the various arguments that have been presented in favor of the restricted district in towns and cities. She dismissed the idea that such areas were good for business, arguing that any benefit was short-sighted. Legitimate businesses invariably suffered. Further, defending prostitution as a 'necessary evil' was unworthy of human beings. It was an admission that men were lower than the beasts." The social evil "was a man's business," for it was men who were responsible for the existing conditions, and it was men who kept up the demand for prostitution. Therefore, the remedy was in the hands of Fort George's respectable men, who knew it was their duty to protect all women from such horrors. Beyond pleasantries, the *Fort George Tribune* did not record how Ratté was received, but, if the response to her comments six months later at the Social Service Congress at Ottawa was a fair indication, her listeners departed impressed with her eloquence and powerful presence.[23] Yet timing worked against Ratté's passionate call to action: when war erupted in August 1914, the call to arms submerged Fort George's appetite for reform.

Explored through local crime reports, policing history, historical newspaper commentary, and the dynamics of community building, the origins of the Georges' notoriety and the communities' self-perceptions and worries about how others imagined the region drive what follows. It is a conversation centred on a persistent unease over reputation at the heart of the Georges' pursuit of respectability in late Edwardian Canada and the years straddling the Great War. It is a dynamic understood, in part, by considering anthropologist Clifford Geertz's maxim that culture comprises stories that people tell themselves about themselves.[24] Yet, rather than emphasizing outward expressions – the celebratory claims of boosters – this book highlights how this sense of culture and these stories tinted the settler population's self-perception.[25] And while white voices dominate the historical record, I also take up evidence of the anxieties of racialized actors in the Georges – Black, Chinese, and Indigenous peoples.[26] Self-doubt and uncertainty also fed their angst.

While it was easy enough for a society that wore its racism with pride to attribute disorder, excess, and crime to those racialized others whom white settlers imagined were unsuited to a well-ordered community life, the evidence at hand suggests otherwise. Was it possible that "legitimate" citizens, desirable settlers touting a prized lineage, had contributed to the Georges' bad reputation? Could clean-cut, steely-eyed, northern white men and good-humoured, even-tempered, resourceful northern white women be sources of immorality, vice, and political radicalism?[27] Was it possible that, when commentators found the Georges wanting, white settlers were responsible for much of the disorder? Indeed, had the journey northward diluted their white privilege, their character, their claims to moral superiority? Did British Columbia's "wild and immoral netherland" inscribe them with an unanticipated and unwanted identity?[28] And did that reduction, that erosion of their standing, explain why distant governments, corporate enterprises, and well-heeled entrepreneurs looked askance when the Georges came calling, or why they overlooked the region's interests in favour of other communities that were seemingly more pressing, more urgent, and, perhaps, more lucrative? Was this why policy-makers in southern and urban British Columbia appeared as if they neither heard nor cared about concerns born beyond their own communities and constituencies? In the northern Interior, such suspicions accumulated, nourishing a hardening sense of being unappreciated, overlooked, and disregarded. What some had idealized as a call to bring Christian beliefs and white ordered space into the province's settlement frontier had, in a matter of a few years, been transformed into a regionalized identity that viewed the urban Lower Mainland and Vancouver Island with scepticism and distrust. True, there is nothing to suggest that the Georges were alone in holding such sentiments. But the persistence of this unease, throughout the twentieth century and into the twenty-first, speaks of a deeply etched historical identity.

There are dangers in my method. Concentrating on evidence of disorder and crime in the Georges may sensationalize rather than explain the cartoonish image of a northern Interior community once described as populated with loggers and prostitutes.[29] While such an image may have earned sly grins at local watering holes, the slight rankled northerners. And, over time, it credited locals' suspicions that their sensibilities and felt necessities carried little weight with opinion leaders and decision makers in the province's capital and the Lower Mainland. Acknowledging these possibilities exposes the caricature of local history and explains the disquiet that the image produced. After all, if the Georges could be dismissed as a motley collection of rough-and-tumble labourers cavorting with prostitutes, why should decision makers and opinion leaders in Victoria and Vancouver worry about marginalizing the region? As such, this conversation is not a voyeuristic tour of what was sometimes a tumultuous history. Yes, it will be populated with bad characters, hopeful newcomers, wary long-term residents, lay and trained judicial officials, schemers, complainants, legal counsel, the feckless, neighbours with axes to grind, the guilty and the innocent, witnesses, bystanders, newspaper editors, the unlucky, the confused, and the mad. Such a cast obliges us to remember that, while people found themselves entangled in the criminal law and were seldom presented in a light of their own choosing, they were nonetheless work-a-day settlers, Indigenous people, and entrepreneurs making do and hoping to emerge a little better off. We must be mindful to see them in the whole, and not just as a witness, a constable, a complainant, an accused, or an interested party. Indeed, we must rely on our imagination to treat them with as much empathy as we can muster and to acknowledge their humanity. Then we may glimpse something familiar, something recognizable, in their actions and responses, while acknowledging their distinctiveness, peculiarity, and sometimes quixotic behaviour, marking them as residents of a particular region and era.

Answering to these ideals obliges me to be clear about my approach and method. This work aspires to be an accessible and engaging book seeking a wider audience than may be typical for scholarly research. My motive is simple. As a reader, I have been frustrated when jargon-laden language and performative writing obliterates the human centre of legal and crime history. This is not to suggest that the field should aspire to pot-boiling "true-crime" narratives. But surely scholarship can offer compelling narratives that retain their humanity while holding to rigorous standards. We can seek readers beyond the academy – we can be engaging *and* serious. My hope is that this book finds an audience among general and non-specialist readers, while providing students of local, British Columbian, western Canadian, and settlement history, as well as police and crime historians, with an argument about community reputation and sense of self rooted in historical print media and primary archival evidence.

Seeking this balance has involved substantive and stylistic challenges concerning scholarly conventions. Deciding which themes warranted an extended discussion, while trying to limit lengthy asides and digressions, has been an ongoing labour. Should a sentence, paragraph, or anecdote be elaborated, trimmed, or eliminated entirely? Does a point need a citation demonstrating my scholarly bona fides? Is it prudent to spare the general audience another elongated (and likely unread) explanatory note while leaving the inferred interpretative associations to those readers who are immersed in the literature? Indeed, how best should I manage a diverse readership's expectations? In this, I am reminded of Michael Dawson's stealthy comment, in *The Mountie from Dime Novel to Disney*, that, if, as some critics claim, the experience of reading "recodes" half of a book's meaning, surely those same readers are responsible for their half of the work's "errors."[30] This is not to suggest that my approach and its execution have been flawless, but I take comfort in the knowledge that "there is a crack, a crack in everything / That's how the light gets in."[31]

While I have attempted to wear lightly my engagement with the literature, this does not mean that my thinking has been unaffected by theoretical and interpretative perspectives. The central interpretative point of departure for this research was sparked by the percolation of an idea from Lisa Helps's master's thesis and a conference comment delivered by geographer Nicholas Blomley. Helps explored how the labelling of "disorderly" people – vagrant bodies – relied upon their occupancy of public space, which subjected them to regulation.[32] Specifically, such people were arrested because "their bodies took up public space in particular ways by being a certain kind of person and/or doing a certain action."[33] For his part, Blomley observed that the straight lines and surveyed boulevards of townsite grids created the authority to exclude, given the associated expectations of an ordered space that, in turn, defined the substance and meaning of disorder.[34] This process was, and remains, a violent act.[35] The imposition of a surveyed grid is also bound up in the late Allan Silver's question of whose interests were furthered or thwarted by such demands for order.[36] That the Lheidli T'enneh had to be dispossessed before self-identified "respectable" white people were beleaguered by their own inability to impose order in the new settler community is a striking irony.[37] That failure to regulate their community, detailed in my treatment of the Prince George police force's difficulties, generated its own anxiety, reflected in the white community's leaders discomfort that, despite their pretensions, they would be found wanting. Their subsequent efforts to explain away the community's notoriety held true to their preferred identity and the demonization of Indigenous peoples as well as racialized Chinese and Black residents. This storytelling aligned with that found in Kenton Storey's *Settler Anxiety at the Outposts of Empire* and Robert Hogg's *Men and Manliness on the Frontier: Queensland and British Columbia in the Mid-Nineteenth Century*.[38] Comparing colonial Vancouver Island/British Columbia and the Antipodes, Storey and Hogg explore the meanings of manliness and white superiority on the British Empire's distant edges. While the supposed threat of Indigenous violence in the northern Interior had largely dissipated by the years straddling the First World War, the unease created by metropolitan surveillance, measures of late-Edwardian masculinity, and white superiority remained.[39] That subscription to these notions failed to assure the northern Interior's "respectable" people that they would be counted among the province's natural leaders added to the region's disquiet.

Karen Dubinsky's discussion in *Improper Advances,* which offers a captivating exploration of reputation and place in rural and northern Ontario, also highlights the theme of anxiety.[40] While British Columbia's northern Interior functioned differently than Dubinsky's northern Ontario, her work influenced my book's genesis. "The complex and multifaceted process of nation building," mirrored in gender and sexual relations and a "manly north" populated with men of "real metal with no tinsel," was certainly present in the northern Interior's construction.[41] Like Ontario's northland, British Columbia's middle north was, after the turn of the century, increasingly rendered as "a dangerously immoral, uncivilized place of vice." In Dubinsky's phrasing, as rural areas got "cleaner," the north became "dirtier." And, akin to what transpired in northern Ontario, the Georges grew concerned that such images resonated with an unfavourable "opinion from the outside" that stigmatized the region.[42] In a similar fashion, Lynne Marks's wonderful *Infidels and the Damn Churches: Irreligion and Religion in Settler British Columbia* was another constant companion during my research, despite ending just as the white settlement frontier beyond Barkerville was opening. For me, Marks completed the circle started by Storey and Hogg. In a colony and, later, a province where irreligiosity was dominant, virulent anti-Asian and anti-Indigenous racism "allowed many white working-class men to define their social respectability and inclusion in racial and class terms alone, without needing to affirm Christian connection and respectability."[43] To be racist was to be "manly." That such attitudes were on display in the Georges belied residents' belief that they were and remained distinct from the rest of the province and the nation. Locally, these attitudes targeted all racialized peoples – Indigenous, Asian, and mixed-heritage people, as well as Prince George's small Black population – and, in doing so, fed into their anxieties centred on establishing and maintaining their own place in the Interior. To understand the Black community's "complicated" Canadian history, I turned first to Robin Winks's classic text *The Blacks in Canada,* Barrington Walker's edited collection *The African Canadian Legal Odyssey,* and Sarah-Jane (Saje) Mathieu's insightful *North of the Color Line: Migration and Black Resistance in Canada, 1870–1955.*[44] Mathieu writes that, in the years preceding the First World War, "Canadian hysteria over Black immigration was specifically rooted in language, stereotypes, and anxieties with powerful purchase during the nascent age of segregation. The arrival of Black men in particular sparked groundless white paranoia, especially among some women's groups."[45] That, after the Great War, Prince George city council blamed the Black community for the city's notorious reputation was simply racist scapegoating. Again, this research reminds us that, despite its relative isolation, the Georges and the northern Interior reflected broader Canadian attitudes and behaviours that compelled Black citizens to live "in spaces carved out by liberal racism, between legal equality and pervasive forms of societal discrimination."[46] As was often the case with the city of Prince George and its police force, efforts by the "respectable" white population to absolve themselves of responsibility for the city's ill repute by placing the blame on racialized people ignored the demonstrable fact that white residents were responsible for the lion's share of local disorder.

My engagement with the British Columbian histories of Asian peoples, and in particular the Chinese, most of whom considered themselves Guangdong, was informed by Patricia Roy's *A White Man's Province,* Peter Ward's *White Canada Forever,* Kay Anderson's *Vancouver's Chinatown,* and Timothy Stanley's *Contesting White Supremacy,* with the Georges' context drawing on Lily Chow's narrative treatment in *Sojourners in the North.*[47] Having arrived in the region no later than the last quarter of the nineteenth century, the Guangdong's local history was often one of remaining inconspicuous in the face of persistent hostility and prejudice. And while Stanley centred his inquiry on Victoria's students' strike of 1922–23, his argument also applies in the Georges:

> Anti-Chinese racism shaped the lives of people racialized as Chinese and those of all others living in British Columbia ... It shaped where and with whom people could live, where and with whom they could work, where and with whom they could go to school ... It determined people's relationships

to the people they encountered in their day-to-day lives and also shaped their relationships to the institutions of the Canadian state and whether those institutions were on their side.[48]

A similar dynamic infused the lived experiences and anxieties of mixed-heritage and Indigenous peoples, who, despite their long tenure in the northern Interior, were often viewed as an obstacle – surplus to requirements – for a region experiencing the modernizing impulses of expanding governmental bureaucracies in Victoria and Ottawa. As yet, neither the Lheidli T'enneh nor local mixed-heritage peoples have received a through-going scholarly treatment, but glimpses of their early twentieth-century history are found in local newspapers and in Margaret Whitehead's *They Call Me Father: Memoirs of Father Nicolas Coccola,* theses by Brenda Ireland and Robert Diaz, and David Vogt and David Gamble's excellent treatment of the Grand Trunk Pacific Railway's acquisition of the First Nations Fort George Reserve No. 1.[49] In my attempts to engage with the Lheidli T'enneh history, I have benefited from periodic conversations with Yvonne Pierreroy, a founding staff member of the University of Northern British Columbia in Prince George, who, by marriage, is related to "Johnny" Pierre Rois, whom we meet in Chapter 2.

The opening chapter begins in the first decade of the twentieth century, with the establishment of white settlement at what became the Georges. Although the region had drawn mixed reviews after the mid-nineteenth century, its prospects changed with the announcement in late 1903 of the construction of the Grand Trunk Pacific Railway.[50] The confirmation of a Pacific terminus at Kaien Island and the understanding that construction of the British Columbian leg would begin on the coast made the undertaking seem more real. While several points along the proposed route attracted speculative interest, the confluence of the Nechako and Fraser Rivers was favoured as a likely junction point where the east and west GTP might intersect, with prospective rail lines snaking northward from the Lower Mainland to the fabled Peace River country and beyond. Yet as much as the flats overlooking the two rivers drew interest, enthusiasm was blunted by the fact that 500 hectares of what had become prime real estate had been set aside in 1892 as the Lheidli T'enneh First Nation's Fort George Reserve No. 1. While the reserve's fate became the subject of ongoing conjecture and worry, its existence forced early arrivals to alter their plans, with rough log buildings huddled south of the reserve and the adjoining Hudson's Bay Company property. By the time paddlewheel service arrived at South Fort George in June 1910, residents and businesses were arrayed on streets and lanes whose names commemorated early residents James Bird, Sousa (Joseph) Thapage, Alexander Hamilton, and entrepreneur Beach Lasalle. Boasting the Barnard Express (BX) office, the original Northern Hotel (which eventually received the region's first liquor licence), a sawmill, and multiple churches within easy walking distance of the red-light district, South Fort George stood as the dominant white settler community in the years preceding the First World War. At the same time, George Hammond's Natural Resources Security Company townsite of Fort George emerged on the reserve's western flank, setting the table for a decade of competition over which was to be the primary destination for incoming white settlers.

The first chapter also explores the emergence of the Georges' bad reputation, rooted in the considerable press coverage detailing the friction created by the competing townsites and the uncertainties about the GTP's plans.[51] The antagonism between South Fort George and Fort George ignited a war of words between hometown newspapers that, in turn, was swept up into a national press battle. Fuelled by press and personal rivalries, this feud placed the Georges at centre stage in a journalistic mud-slinging match of farcical proportions that depicted the communities as a seething jumble of blind-pig liquor joints, gambling dens, and brothels, populated by a range of dubious characters, all willing to cajole and seduce rubes and greenhorn investors. The embroidered stories and exaggerations cemented the Georges' identity as a tawdry example of "frontier" excess and moral depravity. Time has revealed this identity to be especially tenacious.

The second chapter concentrates on the British Columbia Provincial Police, following its 1910 arrival in the Georges. While enforcing the law was the force's primary function, its arrival signalled the reinforcement of provincial authority in the region and, through that, confirmation of white dominance on the settlement frontier. Created as a rural police force in an era when the police functioned as peacekeepers, the BCPP, by the early twentieth century, straddled an urban/rural divide in responding to an array of policing and administrative challenges. Indeed, shouldering an expanding assortment of regulatory duties, everyday policing emphasized patrolling, station duty, and maintaining a visible presence, with precious little time devoted to pursuing villains. The outbreak of the First World War and the incorporation of Prince George as a city with its own police force signalled changes for the BCPP, although, in practice, the provincial force remained an active presence throughout the region from 1910 to 1925. The war ushered in new methods shaped by various factors, including a shortage of constables; responsibility for enforcing the Game Act; the surveillance of enemy aliens and deserters; public health concerns, including the Spanish influenza pandemic; and the extension of the modern regulatory state. The significance of the last is difficult to overstate. In the space of less than a decade, the region went from being the domain of Indigenous peoples and a handful of traders, missionaries, and adventurers to one with an unincorporated white settlement obliged to rely on the provincial capital for every conceivable matter of public policy, and then to one having an incorporated municipal government navigating settler obligations and expectations. Provincial statutes embraced the regulation of public health, trade, schooling, the registration of firearms, the oversight of hunting and trapping, and the regulation of railways and automobiles. For anyone who had been in the region in 1900, its metamorphosis over just two decades must have been bewildering. As such, while Albin Miller's declaration in November 1918 that he was not of a mind to obtain either a hunting or a firearms licence because "he had not seen a policeman for years" may have won him warm support in some quarters, his declared principles merely invited scrutiny from the local BCPP. The result was predictable. Aided by a constable, Acting Chief Constable John Bourne spared no efforts to prosecute Miller for trapping without a licence and carrying an offensive weapon.[52] Fined $200 on the first charge and $50 on the second, Miller was being schooled in the modern state's regulatory reach. Along with like-minded individuals, Miller undoubtedly found the experience unpalatable. Nonetheless, the lesson was clear. Despite the relative lightness of the modern state's touch in these years, no one, in the northern Interior or elsewhere in the province, would escape its grasp.

Chapter 2 also explores what the public invariably thought of as "real" policing – that is, pursuing criminals. This public expectation did not align with the BCPP's approach of being peacekeepers who attempted to prevent law-breaking in the first instance while employing a pragmatic approach to disorder when it did occur. The result was an emphasis on identifying situations and individuals tending toward trouble while not expecting constables to change what most observers at the time considered to be "human nature." Constables were to rely on sound judgment to recognize and defuse trouble before it became law-breaking. The action of a single constable was not going to alter the fact that the Georges – and, indeed, the province as a whole – were boozy and truculent in the early twentieth century. Thus, even though the provincial police attempted to suppress the importation and distribution of illegal liquor in the northern

Interior, no one believed that such actions would stop the traffic. While some constables may have harboured genuine worries about the moral and social costs flowing from the liquor trade, local opinion favoured regulating the business to provide safe alcohol in place of a local version of moonshine. And while such a perspective fails to align with exaggerated accounts of rough-and-tumble, hard-drinking, card-playing men kicking over the traces, the evidence from the police duty logs is clear. Not only was there little to distinguish the realities of everyday peacekeeping in the Georges from what occurred elsewhere in the province, but most of the "real" policing in the region concerned relatively minor thefts, infractions of the Game Act, and enforcing provisions of the Public Health Act, which, when combined, far outweighed occasions when constables corralled outlaws and hard men.

Chapter 3 shifts to the decade-long history of the Prince George city police. Shaped by provincial statutes that obliged yearly municipal elections – a system that effectively guaranteed short-sighted and often inefficient local leadership – Prince George city council created the city police force in 1915. What that council failed to do was articulate how the force was supposed to occupy its time. The city police were governed by a local police commission that theoretically protected the police from political meddling but, in reality, produced an environment where flawed oversight was the norm. Part of the problem rested in the relationship between city council and the commission and whether the former could direct the latter on how and when to act. So, while the existence of city police implied local independence from the provincial government's expanding regulatory reach, that force's lack of clear mandate and its regulation by the commission resulted in its functioning as little more than a municipal dogsbody, supervising electoral polls, assisting with firefighting, and performing various bureaucratic services that mirrored the modernizing state. The force was supposed to generate income through the collection of business licences and bylaw enforcement, although the latter expectation was not spelled out until early November 1916. Consequently, except in isolated instances, the city force was barely visible for much of its early history. Equally, its existence raises an intriguing question at the heart of our concern with reputation and community identity. Forming a city force implied policing residents. Was this understood and embraced, or was policing something that concerned only disreputable and disorderly people? Sharpened by the announcement of a statutory obligation for city police to enforce the provincial prohibition law, the point ceased to be merely academic. Everyone was to abide by the law, even the Georges' self-identified respectable white population. For the city force, the result was an exercise in frustration. Caught between the provincial statute and a local government that was ambivalent about the liquor law, the force was damned, regardless of how it acted.

As much as the years before 1919 were aimless, those that followed were calamitous. Chapter 3 examines the storm of trouble for the city police from 1919 to its 1925 decommission. Hobbled by intrigue, egos, and inconsistent and sometimes dubious priorities on the three-man police board, the city constabulary was unable to answer more mundane expectations, let alone enforce provincial liquor regulations. The latter failure brought the force to its knees. Given that bootleggers and other schemers knew every constable by sight, catching villains unawares was a rare thing and necessitated undercover operations employing outside help or cooperative civilian allies. Both approaches involved drawbacks. A particularly grim point for the city was reached when Theodore M. Watson, a former city councillor and, at the time, police board commissioner, was tried for attempting to bribe a city constable to facilitate protection for an illegal liquor racket in the early spring of 1920. Not long after the dust settled, another scandal erupted over the tolerance, if not active support, of the police commission for prostitution in the city. In response, Mayor R.W. Alward launched confidential negotiations to disband the city force and replace it with the BCPP. The degree to which council was onside with Alward's plan is unclear. The arrival of the BCPP in 1925 signalled both the begrudging acceptance of provincial oversight of local affairs and the impress of what entailed modern governance in British Columbia after the First World War.

Chapter 4 turns to the stipendiary magistrate's court and its role in shaping what the local community thought about crime and the courts as well as the meanings of order. Like lower courts across North America and beyond, this court catalogued familiar human failings. In the Georges, it mirrored the modernizing state's imposition of white, middle-class respectability and restraint in the face of residents' sometimes stubborn resistance. In the Georges, the First World War appeared as a dividing line in terms of disorder and criminality. Prior to the war, the local scene echoed the real and imagined excesses of the North American "Wild West," characterized by excessive liquor consumption, gun play, brawls in the street, and the ongoing operation of a local red-light district. This era ended in 1914. The relative quiet of the years from 1914 to mid-1918 was consistent with the exodus of single men answering the colours as well as a diminished police force as a result of enlistments. At the same time, the arrival of provincial prohibition brought new law-enforcement pressures to bear on residents' seemingly insatiable thirst. Echoing a process that occurred across the nation, prohibition statutes created a new class of criminals and fostered an environment where skirting the law took on the form of a game of cat and mouse. This chapter examines the fraught relationship between the police, the lower courts, and the community, which centred, in part, on Stipendiary Magistrate C.B. Daniell, whose rulings from the bench attracted a flurry of confusion and criticism.

The chapter also takes up the evolution of the provincial County and Supreme Court systems in the region and the roles they played in shaping local crime history, the community's self-image, and the Georges' identity. From the outset of white settlement at South Fort George, the Georges' opinion and political leaders looked to local policing and judicial responsibilities as emblems of permanence and stature. At a minimum, the coveted role as a judicial centre would advertise Prince George as more than just a business and commercial centre. Some residents no doubt hoped that the court function might enliven business for hotels and restaurants while cultivating a community of legal talent to serve the Interior's needs. In practice, hosting County Court sessions provided an initial taste of greater respectability. The long-anticipated arrival of regular Supreme Court assize was imagined within the community as another badge signalling that the city had arrived. Once regular County and Supreme Courts were secured after the armistice, efforts turned to convincing the provincial legislature that Prince George needed appropriate government buildings, including centralized office space, a courthouse, and a police station, to replace the "temporary" firetraps that housed these services. After all, if provincial lands minister Duff Pattullo could secure "an elaborate and permanent courthouse costing some hundreds of thousands of dollars" for Prince Rupert, surely Prince George might be provided with "modest but urgent conveniences" rather than being "spurned by the ruler and all his entourage."[53] At the same time, one of the unanticipated consequences of both County and Supreme Court hearings was a steady drumbeat of crime reportage detailing cases making their way to the docket. In the least, such reporting suggested that the notion of the northern Interior offering an escape and a second chance for newcomers was a fiction. Rather, the news reports reinforced a sense that the northern Interior, like the immoral north in Ontario, rested on a line between the thinly settled wilds and the supposed law-abiding comforts of white settler communities.[54] For local newspaper readers, as well as those consuming accounts reprinted throughout the province and beyond, criminal trials in the Georges (as well as those involving northern residents tried elsewhere in the province) hardened the impression that the region was plagued by crime, disorder, and alcohol-infused excess and violence.

Chapter 5 focuses on the elements of front-page crime and how slow-building notoriety, the construction of an association between race and crime, and two similar homicide trials involving women fed the Georges' poor reputation. That a constable's discretionary gaze relied on racist and class-based notions of who was apt to be at the centre of disorder and tumult is unsurprising. Be it the alleged proclivities and excesses of Indigenous and mixed-heritage peoples, the moral and economic threat posed by the racialized Chinese, the dangerous ideological presence of non-preferred European immigrants, and the sexualized menace of Black residents, these assumed "attributes" saddled racialized groups with the responsibility for creating the Georges' troubled reputation. These assumptions linking race and crime remained constant throughout the years straddling the First World War. This was nowhere better displayed than when, in April 1921, a riotous "affray" in Prince George's "Chinatown" dovetailed with city council's baldly racist assertion that Prince George's ongoing struggle with disorder and criminality was rooted in the city's Black community.[55] Suffice it to say that the measure of who belonged in the Georges and who represented trouble was layered with assumptions about race, class, and disorder. Equally, and echoing the suspicions of the provincial police force's senior administration about labour unions, constables in the northern Interior "visited" labour organizers in anticipation of unionization drives and fears of labour disruptions.[56] To the extent that the peacekeeper role might appear pragmatic, it is certain that racialized and class-based notions drove decision making about who were potential lawbreakers, whose property and values were to be protected, and whose definitions of order and disorder influenced discretionary policing in the Georges. That these ideas aligned with notions about the source of local disorder and crime was unsurprising in British Columbia, a self-described white man's province. Chapter 5 closes with two similar marticide investigations that fed into the existing narrative that something was awry in the northern Interior. After all, if conditions in the region posed such stress on those seeking a second chance at the good life that women were driven to murder their husbands, was it at all surprising that the region was notorious?

The epilogue offers a survey of events after 1925 that, to some observers, confirmed the broader region's notoriety. Examples include trouble with unemployed men in the mid-1930s, the National Resources Mobilization

"Zombie" troop protests near the end of World War II, a divisive and violent strike in late 1953 and early 1954, an outbreak of juvenile delinquency and "gang" violence in 1953 and 1957, labour unrest in the 1980s, Prince George being labelled Canada's crime capital, and the national shame of the Highway of Tears. Rendered as evidence of disorder, violence, and crime bred in the region's bones, these events – and particularly the Highway of Tears – have cemented the Georges' dubious reputation, despite the fact that all such events were products of factors that extended well beyond the northern Interior. Nonetheless, for some, these events confirm that the Georges have a well-earned notorious reputation for resting, perhaps with some licence, at the very gates of hell.

I

Establishing the Georges and
the Birth of a Bad Reputation

T he early twentieth century reimagined British Columbia's northern Interior. Once dismissed as having limited potential for white settlers, it became a promised land where they could burn their boats in anticipation of a boundless future. This transformation was attributable to Charles M. Hays, president of the Grand Trunk Pacific Railway (GTP), and his confidence that the region had the ingredients to ensure the profitability of his proposed railway.[1] Not only would the line and northern British Columbia prosper, but unlike the Canadian Pacific Railway, would do so without the company nurturing industries to generate traffic. Further, the GTP would thrive, it was imagined by Hays, thanks to a ceaseless tide of land-hungry settlers, despite British Columbia's nascent political parties disavowing land grants as a strategy to attract railway construction. Time revealed that both propositions were flawed. Still, in the summer of 1903, Richard McBride's new Conservative administration, which won another term in a razor-thin electoral victory on 6 October, may have given the impression that land grants might still be had.[2] After all, the provincial government's enthusiasm for railway expansion remained undiminished. Despite a shortage of funds to support such ventures and the absence of an articulated provincial railway plan, McBride's insistence that the GTP construction begin on the Pacific Coast hinted that an accommodation remained possible.[3] Indeed, that secret negotiations secured Kaien Island as the terminus, in exchange for the railway paying $10,000 into provincial coffers, lent weight to Hays's hope that the provincial government might eventually grant the railway company lands, which would then be sold on the open market. That the terminal on the northwest coast remained distant from central and eastern North American markets (while being closer to Asia), failed to dent Hays's enthusiasm, and the company's boosting of the rail line continued. While his predictions proved to be woefully inaccurate and set the GTP on course for receivership in 1919, Hays's confidence meant that, between 1903 and 1911, settlers turned their eyes to the imagined promise of British Columbia's northern Interior and what, in time, emerged as a three-way battle for supremacy between townsites at the confluence of the Fraser and Nechako Rivers.

This contest is central to the current chapter. Not only did the competition between these settlements consume an exhausting amount of energy, while contributing to uncertainty about the predominantly white settlement in the region, but it also encouraged fractiousness as a trait of local character in and around the Georges. Experience taught residents that certainty was evasive. Guided by their own interests, those with financial, economic, and political power managed and, all too often, manipulated local necessities. The arrival of railways, the development of timber resources, the establishment of pulp mills, and the expansion of mining were determined by interests outside the region. Indeed, the location of settlements for both Indigenous and white residents and the physical layout of communities invariably answered to forces beyond the local, though neither the Lheidli T'enneh nor the newcomers acknowledged this shared experience of finding themselves on the margins of decisions made elsewhere. The resulting settlement history in the morning of the twentieth century nurtured scepticism about schemes hatched by outsiders and by distant and all-too-fickle provincial and dominion governments. In turn, this early history produced an enduring regional reputation for mulishness in the disinclination to accept what others had determined was best for the northern Interior. The result was a legacy of anxiety rooted in the contrast between how residents imagined themselves and how they imagined that they were perceived elsewhere in the province and beyond.

This fractiousness was evident along the white settlement's cutting edge. As a group, the founders were "colourful." They liked their poker and their bootleg liquor. Their business practices were sharp, they were fearless in rounding off the law's edges, and, when circumstances demanded, they would evade, obscure, and lie. Their behaviour created tension in the telling of local history. Most early accounts depict the founders of white settlement in adventuresome tones. A less celebratory, but more accurate, image would be of individuals who could not be trusted with the family silver. This was certainly the case with the consortium linked to early South Fort George; with George Hammond, the Natural Resource Security Company (NRSC), and its Fort George townsite; with the GTP men overseeing the purchase and development of the Prince George townsite; and with a cast of supporting characters including John Houston of the *Fort George Tribune,* John Daniell of the *Fort George Herald,* and his nemesis J.P. McConnell of the weekly magazine *BC Saturday Sunset.* To a man, they dressed up self-serving business and partisan manoeuvres as serving the public good. Press accounts of their behaviour lent credence to the growing suspicion that everyone associated with the Georges was on the make. In the shadow of such impressions, potential newcomers found it near impossible to discern who, if anyone, was being honest about the conditions, opportunities, and challenges in the province's northern Interior before the First World War.

LOCATING SOUTH FORT GEORGE

Long before the Grand Trunk Pacific Railway was confirmed, observers identified the confluence of the Nechako and Fraser Rivers as prime real estate. Why? Many believed that it was here that the east/west GTP would intersect, with railways cutting through the province's Interior and onward to the Peace River country at the northwestern edge of the Great Interior Plain. Such speculation collided with the reality that a misshapen triangle of land wedged between the two rivers – some 500 hectares – was one of four Lheidli T'enneh reserves set aside on the Nechako and Fraser Rivers.[4] While not an unbridgeable obstacle to potential development, Fort George Reserve No. 1 obliged newcomers and speculators to adjust their expectations. The most common response was to take up lands on the southern or western boundaries of the reserve in the expectation that land close to the rivers' junction and probable rail crossing would increase in value as development progressed.

The region's oldest white settlement, South Fort George grew up around Alexander G. Hamilton's mercantile store, which began operations in 1906. Built south of the reserve and the adjoining Hudson's Bay Company (HBC) holdings, Hamilton's store sat on Sousa (Joseph) Tapage's eighty-acre preemption – and, no doubt, Hamilton hoped to squeeze every cent of profit out of his neighbouring sixty acres. Although both men remained

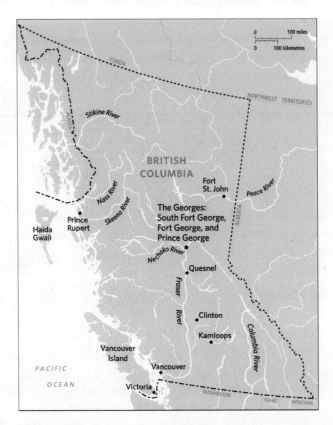

FIGURE 1.1   Map of British Columbia. | Cartography from Eric Leinberger.

FIGURE 1.2   Map of the Georges, 1906–13. | F.E. Runnalls, "Boom Days in Prince George, 1906–1913," *British Columbia Historical Quarterly* 8, 4 (1944): 286–87.

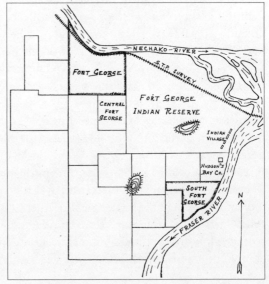

in the region until after the First World War, it was Hamilton who was tied to local development.[5] A bluff Irishman connected to the Orange Lodge and the Conservative Party, Hamilton in early 1897 came to the Kootenays in southern British Columbia, where he had a brief and scandalous career as a British Columbia provincial constable, first in Sandon and then in Silverton.[6] Drummed out of the police service following allegations of consorting with gamblers and frequenting brothels, and charges of attempted blackmail, Hamilton went to ground in the autumn of 1897. He later reappeared, first as a merchant in Stuart Lake, and then at South Fort George, where he fashioned himself as an informal legal adviser, owing to his claims of experience with the North-West Mounted Police.[7] Along with later claims he had been involved with Colonel Garnet Wolseley's suppression of the Red River Resistance of 1869–70, the military response to the North West Rebellion in 1885, service with the British Army in the first Zulu War, and a stint in camp with General George Custer, these stories were likely nonsense, although the penchant for reinvention was a common attribute on western Canada's white settlement frontier.[8]

Hamilton's imprint on what became South Fort George is difficult to miss. Not only was "Hamilton Avenue" the centre of the community's growing business district, but his term as president of the South Fort George Board of Trade and secretary of the school board kept him in the public eye. At the same time, he was known for the six cottages he built on the corner of Hamilton and Second Street, his winter mail contracts, an eighteen-horse stable constructed in late 1910 as part of his haulage operations, his Fort George Hardware Company (established in May 1911), and his ten-hectare farm across the Nechako River from the Fort George townsite. Ultimately, his reach exceeded his grasp. Nominated and then elected as the party's candidate after five ballots at the local Conservative convention in late March 1915, Hamilton was packaged as a Canadian pioneer – a "Dean" of western settlers – with a military bearing well suited for a nation at war.[9] Yet as the September 1916 provincial election neared, he withdrew in favour of Premier W.J. Bowser's land minister, William R. Ross, who was seeking a safe seat away from his home riding in Fernie, where he had lost touch with the region's working men while currying favour on the coast.[10] Perhaps, Bowser's knowledge of events in Sandon and Silverton encouraged Hamilton to fall on his sword.[11] The retreat signalled an end of his ambitions. After selling his Nechako farm, he withdrew first to his store and property at Stuart Lake before finally retiring to Vancouver in the summer of 1921.[12] His death went unrecorded in Prince George.

FIGURE I.3A   Tents near A.G. Hamilton's store, South Fort George, 1910. |
Alaska Highway News.

FIGURE I.3B   A.G. Hamilton's store, 1910. | *Alaska Highway News.*

Linked with Hamilton was Nick Clark of Vancouver, who arrived in
Fraser Lake in June 1908. An exploratory canoe voyage along the Nechako
and down the Fraser, during which the men met, convinced Clark that a
riverboat could be piloted along the Nechako from Fraser Lake, eastward
along the upper Fraser, and southward to Soda Creek. Returning to Vancouver, he allegedly incorporated the Fort George Lumber and Navigation

Company and arranged for the construction of the paddle-wheeler *Nechaco* – later renamed *Chilco* – which was launched on 12 May 1909.[13] Although what occurred next is muddled, Clark acquired an option on Hamilton's land in late 1909, sold it to mining entrepreneur Beach Lasalle, who, along with William C. Fry and M.C. Wiggins, were fronting the Northern Development Company.[14] Within a month, the company's advertisements marketing business lots in South Fort George appeared in the *Vancouver Province,* despite the company not being incorporated until September 1910.[15] That Clark's Fort George Lumber and Navigation Company and the Northern Development Company shared the same 614 Hastings Street address in Vancouver thickened the plot. Still, in the spring of 1910, land sales in South Fort George were underway, and a brood of tents, log cabins, and rough-planed shacks appeared near Hamilton's store. Soon, a barber shop, a second mercantile, branches of the Bank of British North America and the Trader's Bank of Canada, two restaurants, the BC Express (BX) office, and the *Fort George Herald* populated the business district. Albert Johnson and Michael Burns's Hotel Northern was under construction by October, destined to become the raucous epicentre of licensed alcohol consumption in the region.

One of the townsite's greatest advantages was Clark's waterfront mill, which provided local settlers with timber and planed lumber.[16] As its operations were expanded and upgraded, the riverboat trade grew to include the *Fort Fraser* and the *Chilcotin* in May and June 1910, in competition with BX steamers the *Charlotte,* the *Quesnel,* and the *BX,* all set afloat in late 1909 and early 1910. Clark's business was pushed into receivership in late 1910 by the termination of timber contracts to the perennially delayed Pacific Great Eastern Railway and by tightened margins owing to competition on the rivers from the BX Company and on land from Russell Peden's Northern Lumber Company sawmill. Valued at $58,000, Clark's company faced liabilities of over $80,000. Having been present in South Fort George since late October 1910, a Winnipeg-based consortium that included F.A. Thompson, R.L. Hay, C. McElroy, Dr. J.K. McLennan, J.D. McArthur and Company, and A.J. Adamson acquired Clark's assets in March 1911 and rechristened the enterprise the Fort George Timber and Transportation Company.[17] Clark eventually divested himself of shares in the new company and relocated to Vancouver. He later returned as part of an exploratory interest in oil sands development in Haida Gwaii and the Athabasca country.[18] Like Hamilton, Clark's eventual passing went unacknowledged in the local press.

Locating Fort George

While South Fort George's backers fashioned the region's predominant community, another entrepreneur, Ontario-born George J. Hammond, had his own plans. He began his career as a drug store clerk, a station agent on the Canadian Southern Railway in southern Ontario, and then a train dispatcher for the Chicago, Milwaukee & St. Paul Railway company. The latter led to a position with Western Union Telegraph and the Postal Telegraph-Cable Company in 1884.[19] Trouble found him four years later when he was charged with wiretapping. Hammond and partner O.M. Stone were accused of attempting to defraud a Terre Haute, Indiana, pool room operator by delaying the transmission of a horse-race report while a confederate placed a winning bet before the results arrived.[20] Although Hammond escaped prosecution, the case was his initial clash with the criminal law. Attracted to the dark arts of the late nineteenth-century North American stock market, he moved on to become a "bucket-shop operator," where investors were manipulated to wager on individual stocks rising or falling. By pumping up the apparent value of a stock or, conversely, suppressing its true value, Hammond bilked investors under the guise of the Combination Investment Company in Chicago and the Minneapolis-based Coe Commission Company.[21] Whether through good fortune or sheer luck, Hammond eluded convictions in Chicago, Minneapolis, and North Dakota. Perhaps suspecting that his luck south of the border was exhausted, Hammond returned to Canada for a vacation with his brother in southern Alberta. There, Hammond was felled by appendicitis. He was rushed to Lethbridge, where, while recuperating in the Gault Hospital, his room was struck by lightning.[22] How Hammond interpreted what a local newspaper characterized as a near-death experience is guesswork, but, after recuperating in southern California, he returned to Ontario, married Margaret Jean Cameron in Sault St. Marie before relocating to Nelson, British Columbia. There, he dabbled in real estate while working as a land sales agent for James J. Hill's Great Northern Railway and cultivated a personal interest in the province's northern Interior.[23]

Hammond's interest took form in early September 1909 when his NRSC acquired three parcels of land overlooking the Nechako River west of Fort George Reserve No. 1.[24] Having acquired the rights to the name "Fort George," Hammond launched a come-hither sales blitz of newspaper advertisements and brochures detailing a government ferry crossing, local post office, telephone exchange, town hall, library, hospital, hotel, board

GEORGE J. HAMMOND

FIGURE 1.4   George J. Hammond, police photograph and details, 1898. | Lincoln Book Concern.

of trade, "city" newspaper and printing office, and mercantile store, as well as an enormous Presbyterian church and manse, and riverfront wharfage occupied by the Bogue and Browne sawmill. Hailing the moment as singular, Hammond spared little in his inaugural advertisement of 20 October 1909. Here was the "golden opportunity" of founding North America's "last great metropolis."[25] In reports placed in the *New York American,* the *Seattle Times,* and an assortment of Vancouver newspapers, Hammond declared Fort George's emergence a topic of international acclaim. The future city's prospects warranted comparisons with Vancouver, Seattle, Washington's Inland Empire, and Winnipeg's commanding position on the Canadian Prairies. Claiming to offer a select opportunity for astute investors, the company announced that on 22 October 1909, the first 890 lots in Central Fort George would be released to the market for $100 per lot, with available terms of $10 cash down and $10 monthly payments. Single investors would be limited to five lots. So great was the occasion that the NRSC claimed that "every newspaper of consequence from the Pacific to the Atlantic" was detailing the sure-fire opportunity that was attracting buyers from across the continent and beyond.[26] A day

FIGURE 1.5   Map of Central Fort George and Fort
George, 1910, with the NRSC lots circled. | *Victoria
Daily Colonist.*

later, the fourth in the series of advertisements breathlessly announced
that telegraphed purchase orders were pouring in and that shrewd investors
needed to act immediately. "Title to these lots is indefeasible, guaranteed
and insured by the government of the province of British Columbia. It is
an absolute certainty that inside of one year, Fort George will be a bustling
city, and will increase in population and realty value several times faster"
than cities such as Seattle, Winnipeg, Vancouver, Calgary, or Edmonton.[27]
The final instalment on 26 October carried a sting for South Fort George's
backers when one of their own, Nick Clark, manager of the soon to be
bankrupt Fort George Lumber and Navigation Company, was quoted as
having preached Fort George's virtues for over a decade.[28] That Clark had
undoubtedly been referring to "old" Fort George – that is, South Fort
George – escaped notice. Having made the desired splash, Hammond and
his company settled down to business, maintaining a drumbeat extolling
the townsite's virtues.

The combative *Fort George Herald* in South Fort George acknowledged
the results. The NRSC had "required oceans of money, spent in advertising and exploiting in ways too numerous to mention here, to keep it
before the public and make its sale a success. And no one will deny it has
not been a successful sale. Thousands of lots have been traded to the

OUR MEN OF AFFAIRS

Mr. George J. Hammond, President and Managing Director Natural Resources Security Co., Ltd.

FIGURE 1.6   Cartoon of George Hammond, one of "Our Men of Affairs," 1912. | *Vancouver Daily World.*

public. Almost superhuman strength has been necessary to keep it going, and we must take our hats off to the gentlemen who have steered its career since the fall of 1909."[29] If his claims are to be credited, by Christmas 1910, Hammond had invested $100,000 on advertising and townsite improvements.[30] The *Victoria Daily Colonist*'s reprint of a *Winnipeg Post* report clarified that, by the end of July 1911, $131,000 had been spent building roads, clearing lots, grading streets, and laying sidewalks. This amount eventually rose to $171,000.[31] Buyers did, in fact, come from across the western world.[32] True, most were speculators without any intention of visiting the region, let alone relocating there. Nonetheless, in time, genuine settlers arrived, and their presence provided an air of permanence to the moonscape of tree stumps and muddy trails of the early Fort George townsite.

Despite initial laurels, curiosity about how Hammond financed the effort remains. Certainly, given the amount of money that "vanished" when the Combination Investment Company and the Coe Commission Company collapsed, it is conceivable that Hammond arrived in the northern Interior with a thick bankroll. Indeed, as he later struggled to convince

the GTP Railway to locate its station in Fort George, Hammond reportedly offered $1 million to lubricate negotiations. Whether the claim was
accurate is uncertain, but the blotted copybook of his American career
testified to a bottomless reservoir of duplicity. Another possibility is that
lot sales financed the advertising campaign and the local improvements.[33]
The difficulty with this explanation is that the campaign and sales began
simultaneously in October 1909. Of course, it is possible that he borrowed
money in anticipation of future profits, although this raises the question
of how, given his record, he could have secured such loans. The enterprise's
moving parts remain shrouded. What is certain is that his operations were
less than they appeared. To succeed, Hammond needed to convince the
railway company that building the station in Fort George offered greater
possibilities than locating it at the GTP townsite. This unlikely possibility
rested on Hammond's townsite boasting a population base and an established economic foundation allowing legitimate comparisons with Vancouver, Seattle, and Winnipeg. Therefore, populating Fort George with
thousands of residents *before* the GTP reached the confluence was central
to winning over the railway.[34]

Even this attempt to sway the railway company does not reveal the
whole story. Despite local lore, Hammond's company did not actually
own its townsite land. Lots 937 and 938 – comprising the Fort George
parcel – were initially owned by William Campbell of Winnipeg, who,
in mid-May 1910, sold 412 acres to unnamed parties for $300,000.[35] The
purchasers were probably John Hugo Ross, a Winnipeg real-estate promoter, and George Barbey, of Paris.[36] Five months later, they sold the lots
back to Campbell, who, in turn, sold them to Hammond in small incre-
ments of six to twelve lots at a time. The Hammond-linked Fort George
Townsite Company acquired Ross's holdings following the latter's death
on the *Titanic*.[37] Therefore, as Hammond acknowledged in his promotional literature, his company only *partly* owned Fort George.[38] Further,
mining promoter Frank Hammond (no relation), of the Pacific Securities
Company, owned lot 1429 of the Central Fort George townsite. Upon
completion of the township survey, the NRSC was obliged to market a
set number of business and residential lots within a specific period to meet
scheduled payments and to trigger the release of a fresh set of lots.
Hammond was gambling that he could stay one step ahead of Pacific
Securities. While the *Victoria Daily Colonist* reported that sales were brisk,
with 5,815 of 6,506 lots having been sold by the autumn of 1911, it was
uncertain which – or whose – lots had been sold.[39] Eight months later,
amid criminal libel proceedings against John Daniell of the *Fort George*

Herald, it was reported that the NRSC had sold 12,316 lots out of 20,145.[40] Yet, despite the campaign's apparent success, Hammond was just keeping his head above water.

He proved to be his own worst enemy. Perhaps owing to a desire to appear as a steely-eyed businessman or because he was drinking his own bath water, Hammond declared in the spring of 1910 that the GTP train station was destined for the Fort George townsite. This drew the attention of "Gold and Dross," a financial advice column in Toronto's *Saturday Night* magazine. Having inquired into Hammond, the NRSC, and the Fort George townsite, the column warned off readers and potential investors. The magazine's concern was simple: the company's advertisements did not "accord with the facts." Specifically, and despite the NRSC's inferences, the GTP was unaffiliated with any land companies in the region, and, until the Lheidli T'enneh surrendered their reserve, the railway company's plans remained fluid. Any claims to the contrary were without substance.[41] Over the ensuing months, the magazine continued to pour cold water over the townsite scheme. Its efforts represented such a threat to Hammond that he launched legal proceedings to prevent *Saturday Night* from commenting on either the NRSC or its Fort George townsite. Mr. Justice W.E. Middleton of Ontario's High Court of Justice dismissed the application.[42] Having secured its pound of flesh, *Saturday Night* departed the stage, but not before publishing a parting blow, with a full-page advertisement extolling South Fort George's virtues. The feature carried the names of the businessmen on that community's board of trade (which had sponsored the ad), including A.G. Hamilton and Nick Clark.[43]

The fracas that started between Hammond and *Saturday Night* eventually involved the *Fort George Herald,* the *Fort George Tribune,* and Vancouver's *BC Saturday Sunset* magazine. Rooted in the question of whether the Fort George townsite scheme had been a swindle, the notion of the Georges' early notoriety hardened by late 1910 as the dispute echoed through local newspapers acting as surrogates for the competing communities. Had the effect not been counterproductive, it would have been comical. Over the ensuing five years and in contrast with how the white settlers imagined themselves – confident, independent, hard-working, forward-looking, and fair-minded individuals who neither asked for nor expected more than their due – depictions of the Georges reduced the community to a cartoonish jumble of rowdy liquor joints, gambling dens, and brothels that were frequented by "scarlet women," card sharps, drunks, "wily Indians," and conniving businessmen, all of whom would gladly separate honest settlers and investors from their hard-earned money.[44]

And it is here that we again encounter the anxiety, a mercurial unease, produced by the tension between how local leaders and opinion makers – invariably white residents – saw themselves (and how they wished to be seen) and their disquiet in imagining how others viewed the Georges.[45]

Hammond's desperation following his judicial setback produced an offer to pay the GTP Railway $200,000 to build its station within 400 metres of Fort George's eastern boundary. This offer stemmed from the guarantee, included with lot sales agreements, that the property at issue was within a specific distance of the station. Having inquired into Hammond's reputation and found "disparaging reports" of the entrepreneur's reliability, a month before his fateful voyage on the *Titanic*, GTP president Charles Hays allowed negotiations to drag on, letting the NRSC "stew in their own juice" before withdrawing, given Hammond's inability to provide cash payments.[46] When the townsite promoter offered $1 million to allow the NRSC to market lots on the GTP townsite, the company's silence spoke volumes. Yet another cash offer in exchange for a public statement that the railway would locate its station within a four-kilometre corridor running along the Nechako River (corresponding to the width of the Fort George townsite) failed to gain traction. Finally, and without having reached an agreement, Hammond claimed that the railway company's station would be within 400 metres of Fort George's eastern boundary.[47] It was then, in January 1912, that Hammond petitioned the Board of Railway Commissioners (BRC) to compel the GTP to build its station at or near the NRSC townsite. The dispute dragged on until 1921.

In the interim, Hammond's campaign withered, as did Fort George. It may have felt as if events were conspiring against him: the tortuous station-site dispute, the financial jitters of 1913, the uncertainty caused by gathering war clouds, and, soon, the exodus of men to the frontlines all had their effect. And while the fire of 13 November 1914, which consumed much of Fort George's Central Street, may have symbolized the collapse of his aspirations, the GTP's acquisition of Fort George Reserve No. 1 in November 1911 had, in truth, sounded the death knell of the NRSC townsite.[48] Hammond exchanged his dreams for ashes. True, he battled onward, but his moment had passed. Homes and businesses relocated to the new Prince George townsite in mute acceptance of the inevitable. While some might romanticize Hammond and his struggle against "interests more powerful than himself and associates," his was always a con man's gamble.[49] Because the GTP had deeper pockets and political clout, it could afford the longer game. Left with little choice, Hammond retired from the stage, first to Vancouver and then, after a brief role in the provincial prohibition fight, to South Pasadena and, finally, El Monte, California, where he was still alive in 1943, when his only son, Robert, was killed in a mid-air collision while training RAF pilots in Mesa, Arizona.[50] Hammond died on 7 September 1950, and, akin to Hamilton and Clark, his passing escaped notice.[51]

LOCATING PRINCE GEORGE

Unlike South Fort George and Fort George with their chancers and confidence men, the Prince George townsite's origins were prosaic. Aided by idiosyncratic contributions of a Methodist minister and two Roman Catholic priests and the Department of Indian Affair's (DIA) presumptuous manner, moving the Lheidli T'enneh from Fort George Reserve No. 1 was a clumsy affair. From the outset, the GTP Railway company mistakenly assumed that events would wait on them. Yet even before the railway's confirmation, speculators such as Hamilton, Clark, Hammond, and others acquired land near the anticipated route. Consequently, by the time discussions turned to the question of station locations, Hammond possessed lots 937 and 938, where the GTP had anticipated building its station.[52] Denied its first choice and the opportunity to profit from sales in anticipation of the railroad's arrival, the GTP turned its attention to Fort George Reserve No. 1. Revealing a generous sense of entitlement, company assistant solicitor D'Arcy Tate thought that the Ottawa-based Board of Railway Commissioners would secure the entire reserve acres for "railway purposes."[53] Although dealing with the board seemed an attractive alternative to negotiating with the Department of Indian Affairs, chief engineer B.B. Kelliher thought it unlikely that the commissioners would acquiescence. Historian Frank Leonard dismissed Tate's hope as "a foolish suggestion from an experienced railway lawyer."[54] The company approached Frank Pedley, the deputy superintendent of Indian Affairs, with an official request to acquire the reserve for the company's townsite. This began almost two and a half years of pursuit – detailed first by Leonard and then by David Vogt and David Gamble – during which the Lheidli T'enneh gamely defended their reserve and their rights against priests, ministers, the DIA, and the GTP.[55]

Once the railway finally acquired the reserve in November 1911, the company turned to the business of settling scores. An initial goal was to impose its own stamp – its sense of order – on the townsite by choosing a new name. With historic links to the fur trade and the HBC post overlooking the Fraser River, "Fort George" may have seemed the obvious choice. The problem was that Hammond and the NRSC had been advertising "Fort George" and "Central Fort George" since October 1909 and had established a legal claim to the name in 1911 by registering one of its lots as the Fort George townsite. Given the already poisonous relationship between the GTP and Hammond, there was little reason to believe that the company's townsite would become "Fort George." Moreover, the war of words between those backing South Fort George and Fort George had sown so much confusion that the railway company had good reason to be leery of any association with "Fort George." In contrast, the name "Prince George" had been reserved for the GTP's exclusive use since 1912. It served a dual purpose of distinguishing the new community from its battling neighbours and fashioning a promotional link with the Pacific terminus at Prince Rupert.[56] So, when GTP president E.J. Chamberlain confirmed in January 1913 that "Prince George" would be the townsite's name, few were taken by surprise.[57] That the choice antagonized Hammond was merely a bonus. Despite the announcement, the name question remained unsettled, entangled in the battle over community incorporation and the railway company's desire to reduce the Hammond properties to scrublands west of the new city.

Thanks in large part to historian Frank Leonard's account of the GTP's "thousand blunders" in northern British Columbia, both the incorporation saga and the associated station-site battle have been told.[58] Motivated by the financial and administrative benefits of incorporation – increased local autonomy, a wider tax-base to distribute the costs of local improvements, and access to both provincial and dominion funding for development – the rationale for South Fort George pursuing incorporation as a city was understandable, particularly given the GTP's ham-fisted behaviour. For Fort George, while the same benefits also pertained, avoidance of irrelevance loomed large in the NRSC's thinking. The hard reality facing Hammond's community – and the railway company's objection to incorporating Fort George – was laid bare in a December 1913 letter from GTP solicitor Hugh H. Hansard to Victoria barristers Pooley, Luxton and Pooley:

> It is pretty well admitted now that all residents in the District will in a very short time reside in the Railway Company's townsite, South Fort George, and on the Hudson Bay Company's lot, and that there will be no or hardly any residents on the original Fort George townsite and the subdivisions added to that townsite by Mr. Hammond and his interests.

> In view of the fact that lots sold in the Fort George townsite and in the
> subdivisions added thereto by the Hammond interests will be in the near
> future abandoned, and the lots become valueless, this Company objects
> very strongly to its townsite being incorporated or in any way connected
> with the Fort George townsite and its subdivisions.[59]

The railroad company was committed to thwarting Hammond at every
turn by cutting him out of any new incorporated entity. Therefore, when
South Fort George's incorporation campaign spurred Fort George in a
similar direction and floated the idea that all three communities might
be incorporated together as the expanded community of "Fort George,"
the GTP rejected the initiative and chose to go it alone.[60] Despite sustained
opposition from both outlying communities, the provincial legislation
incorporating the new community – ironically, named "Fort George" –
received third reading in the early morning of 6 March 1915. In the town's
first municipal election, on 20 May of that year, it elected a mayor and
council. And, with a plebiscite tally of 153 to 13, it chose the name "Prince
George."[61]

All that remained for the railway was to navigate the conflict over its
station. With the GTP pitting its corporate interests against the NRSC,
the dispute hinged on the BRC's duty to ensure that the location of such
facilities reflected the common good. Motivated by self-interest in oppos-
ing the railroad company's plans, Hammond portrayed himself as the
people's champion in a struggle against the GTP's corporate might.[62] The
situation was more complicated than such an assertion admitted. Settlers
at the confluence were not of one mind when it came to the station. Some
residents subscribed to the notion that a station built at the end of George
Street, Prince George's high street, represented a sound business decision.
Others, including the city's first mayor, W.G. Gillett, who owned land
nearer the NRSC townsite, hoped that his holdings might profit from a
more westerly station. Still others, who had made their peace with the
townsite battles and had moved homes and businesses to Prince George,
absented themselves from the ongoing belligerence. With both Hammond
and the GTP stirring the pot while the latter ignored BRC rulings as well
as dominion cabinet edicts, the affair stretched from November 1912 to
March 1921, twice the length of the Great War. By the time the BRC
finally ordered that the station be located three blocks west of George
Street, the community's business centre was already well established and
the short journey to meet the train hardly mattered.

Birth of a Bad Reputation

The founding of the three Georges and the subsequent battle for supremacy proved central to local self-perceptions as well as to how others imagined the region. As was often the case in communities on the settlement frontier, white newcomers saw themselves as central to the progressive spread of civilization and order. This idealized sense of self was first articulated by newspaper man John Houston, who, in referring to the region's administrative designation, juxtaposed the "Old" and "New" Cariboo. Long before his October 1909 arrival at the confluence of the Nechako and Fraser Rivers, Houston had established himself as an irreligious crusading journalist, a pro-union man, prospector, entrepreneur, white supremacist, mayor, and a two-term member of the BC Legislative Assembly (MLA) for Nelson, before abandoning his political aspirations to oversee, first, the *Prince Rupert Empire* and then the *Fort George Tribune*.[63] Addressing an audience drawn to unadorned remedies, Houston unveiled his blueprint for the Cariboo in a rambling editorial covering two-thirds of the second page of the *Tribune* on 27 November 1909.[64] The "Old Cariboo" centred on 150 Mile House and was

> wedded to the old days, when Cariboo with Victoria was the "whole thing" in British Columbia. Its people live in the past, for few of them have lived in the district less than twenty years. They are good-natured when telling stories of the past glories of Williams Creek and of the millions that will yet be taken out of Slough Creek. They talk of railways; but only know of the Cariboo wagon road, on which a million dollars have been spent to kept it in repair. Over-represented in the legislature and in parliament for years, they like power, but do not know how to use it. They are in a rut, from which they will have to be jolted.

On the other hand, the "New Cariboo"

> is a wilderness. Its center is the Indian village of Fort George at which there is now a circular saw and a printing press in operation. Scattered from Fraser Lake to Giscombe [sic] rapids, along the Nechaco [sic] and Fraser Rivers for a distance of 150 miles are individual pre-emptors and small settlements in which pioneers are making homes. All told, they number about 100 white men, few of whom have wives and children with them. Few of these men are of Old Cariboo. They know if they must depend on the Cariboo wagon road for future transportation facilities that they might

FIGURE 1.7A   John Houston. | KootenayHistory.com.

FIGURE 1.7B   The *Fort George Tribune* office, 1909. | KootenayHistory.com.

as well pack up and leave the country. They know they are without representation in the legislature, for the tail does not wag the dog in Cariboo.

In Houston's reading, the New Cariboo boasted a distinctive people who were sceptical of distant centres of government, possessed a keen eye for the future, and were unafraid of the challenges it might bring. True to his own legislative experiences, he voiced a regional suspicion that contact with the provincial capital was corrupting. Indeed, expecting Victoria to champion the Interior's interests was foolhardy. Although the Lower Mainland and Vancouver Island were unreliable, Houston unapologetic-ally embraced the province's mainstream culture with its racist attitudes toward Asian immigration and labour. If the northern Interior was to thrive, it would do so only through white labour invested in the region's long-term development: the very nature of non-preferred immigrants, he argued, prevented them from holding the New Cariboo's best interests at heart. Finally, and as a legacy of his own personal battle with alcohol, Houston favoured abolishing the barroom and implementing a policy that liquor should be available only in "rooms in which well-cooked food is served." It proved a difficult pledge to maintain, and, shortly before his own physical collapse and death, Houston offered an amended policy favouring the sale of provincially produced spirits, wine, and beer (as opposed to imported beverages), with a local option for determining if a community wanted liquor sales.[65]

Having mapped this regional identity, Houston founded the Progres-sive Liberal Party (PLP) of British Columbia at a Fort George "convention" on 22 January 1910. Owing to the absence of surviving copies of the *Tribune* for any dates in that month and the *Cariboo Observer's* thinly veiled hostility, there are no accounts of the gathering. The *Observer* editor, John Daniell, dismissed the "egotistical" Houston as the "Great I am of Fort George" whose platform was nothing more than a simple-minded "pipe-dream" that ignored the efforts of the region's representatives in the provincial capital.[66] It fell to John P. "Black-Jack" McConnell, editor and part owner of the *BC Saturday Sunset*, to wax lyrical about Houston's "Moses-like policy."[67] In McConnell's telling, Houston possessed the means to peer through the fog of BC politics:

The policy that John has made contains much that is good and timely. It is the product of the straight-thinking man whose life has been mainly lived upon the far-flung frontier. Untrammeled by the exigencies of petty party considerations it deals two-bitted axe blows at the roots of political evils, it makes a full-throated, deep chested demand for reform and straight dealing in public affairs. If there were enough argonauts in British Colum-bia – not only of the pilgrims traveling through or sojourning in nature's fastnesses – but of those who in the busy "roaring streets," yet find their mental vision unclouded and turned towards the glistening peaks of pol-itical ideals, one might hope to see some of the principles become political actualities.

But the average voter denies himself the privilege of contemplating political ideals, we all grope in the smoke and dust and grime of expediency and the love and need of lucre which breeds graft and the interminable mazes of intrigue in politics.[68]

McConnell's rapturous swoon ended with a point-by-point account of the PLP's founding principles:

- all legislation involving the province's credit be ratified by voters;
- that financial aid provided to railroad projects be conditional on the province owning a majority of stock in the company and that, if such conditions were met, railways in central and northern Interior be built through lands capable of producing foodstuffs to replace those currently imported from outside the province;
- that the rural population be enlarged and that settlers on the land be provided with a $2,000 loan at 5 percent interest; that staking public land should be abolished and that all existing pre-emptions be surveyed at government expense;
- that legal, medical, and dental professionals, along with land surveyors, be required to pass competency exams before being allowed to practise;
- that liquor be sold only in districts that expressly agreed to its sale, and that alcohol of any sort be available only in licensed dining rooms;
- that the provincial voters' list be renewed every two years; that "undesirable" and non-assimilative peoples be barred entry to the province, and that those already present be restricted to specific forms of employment;
- that anyone performing policing duties in urban or rural areas be obliged to pass a physical and mental examination;
- and, finally, that the party commit itself to contesting every election and by-election in the province.[69]

The platform proved to be Houston's parting declaration: he died of exhaustion and congestive heart failure on 8 March 1910 after being delivered by sleigh to Quesnel in search of medical care.[70]

Houston's death inadvertently set the stage for months of mudslinging between South Fort George and Fort George in the columns of *Saturday Night,* the *BC Saturday Sunset,* the *Fort George Herald,* and the *Fort George Tribune.* Although *Saturday Night's* financial advice column "Gold and Dross" cast the first stone by questioning the virtues of George Hammond's Fort George townsite, it was John Daniell, whose presence in the district was noted in a 20 May 1908 HBC post journal entry, who emerged as the lead combatant. Three months after that initial notation, HBC clerk James Cowie recorded that Daniell was establishing the *Cariboo Observer* newspaper in Quesnel.[71] Following Houston's death, Daniell shifted the *Observer*'s daily management to H.L. Stoddard, upped stakes, and dedicated his own energies to a new enterprise, the *Fort George Herald* in South Fort George. The war of words that followed continued until mid-October 1912, when, after being found guilty of libelling Hammond, Daniell temporarily withdrew.[72] With the backing of the GTP in the midst of its contest over the station site and with war clouds gathering over Europe, Daniell returned as editor of the *Prince George Post* in March 1914, but his newspaper career was interrupted by the war.[73]

After having been summoned to Esquimalt for a military physical in mid-September 1915, Daniell revealed his enlistment as a naval air service candidate.[74] The *Post* suspended operations a month later. By May 1916, Probationary Flight Sub-Lieutenant J.B. Daniell was in England.[75] Eventually attached to Naval Squadron No. 3 under Commander R.H. Mulock, Daniell was gunned down by a German Albatross on 11 May 1917 as his Sopwith Scout was on the homeward leg flying escort to 18 Squadron RFC (Royal Flying Corps) bombers.[76] Crashing sixteen kilometres behind enemy lines, he was taken as a prisoner to Épinoy aerodrome and then to Karlsruhe, Trier, and finally to the Schweldnitz prisoner-of-war camp. At the latter, he edited *The Barb Magazine*, an English-language POW newspaper.[77] Returning to the northern Interior after the armistice, Daniell took up the editorship of the *Prince George Citizen* in January 1920.[78] He stayed on for three years before leaving in the second week of April 1923 for Venice, California, where he became editor of the *Venice Vanguard*. In time, he became an executive officer with McCarty Advertising Company in Los Angeles.[79] Daniell died on 31 December 1964, and, like Hamilton, Clark, and Hammond, the local newspaper offered no mention of his passing.[80]

Before he left for the war, Daniell's main opponent in the townsite war of words between South Fort George and Fort George was John McConnell, an Ontario-born journalist and former editorial writer for *Saturday Night* magazine. McConnell relocated to Vancouver, where, on 15 June 1907, he launched the *BC Saturday Sunset*.[81] While commentators noted similarities between *Saturday Night* and the *Saturday Sunset*, the subsequent vitriol over the Georges suggested that his departure from the former had not been amicable.[82] McConnell's Liberal politics meant that he clashed early and often with Richard McBride's provincial Conservative

FIGURE 1.8   *The Barb Magazine,* edited by John B. Daniell. | ScholarWorks at WMU.

administration. McConnell was also a founding proponent of Vancouver's Asiatic Exclusion League, indicating his embrace of racist assumptions about the undesirability of all Asian immigration – a stance that most white residents in the province considered sound policy.[83] Having established a foothold in the province through the *Sunset,* McConnell and his brother-in-law, Richard S. Ford, launched the *Vancouver Sun* in February 1912 as an enterprise dedicated to resurrecting the Liberal Party's fortunes in the province.[84] Despite later remembrances of having fearlessly "served the cause of Canadian journalism faithfully and well" and having scorned "the trivialities and little jealousies of politics," McConnell's columns in the *Saturday Sunset* suggest a truculent editorialist whose appetite for battle appeared limitless. A veteran of four marriages and uncounted libel suits – the latter a point of pride – McConnell lost control of the *Sun* in the early 1920s before returning to Ontario and his brother's Toronto-based advertising firm, McConnell and Ferguson.[85] Four years later, at the age of fifty-one, John McConnell died following a gall bladder operation.

FIGURE 1.9   John McConnell and daughter Edith, 1925. |
Vancouver Sun.

The third participant in the local name calling was the *Fort George
Tribune.* Upon John Houston's death, his nephew Harry Houston took
over the newspaper. The succession was barely in place before George
Hammond, threatening litigation over allegations made by the late editor,
assumed control in exchange for abandoning any potential suit. With
Albert Dollenmayer as manager (his association with Hammond dated
back to the Coe Commission Company), the *Tribune* became a NRSC
mouthpiece and began trading insults and accusations with John Daniell
at the *Fort George Herald.*[86] Because only a handful of the *Tribune*'s issues
have survived, impressions of that newspaper are captured mostly in the
arsenal of insults exchanged with the *Herald.* The tail of a *Herald* column
summarizing local and provincial news captures the tone:

The Nechaco [sic] townsite dribbling-bib, alias the *Fort George Tribune,*
printed an inch or so of disparaging remarks, levelled at the *Herald* editor,
last week. The Natural Resources Security Company, owners of the dribbling-
bib, apparently can't find anything worse than an "ex-deck hand" to call the

Herald scribe. We don't blush at all before the accusation. Yes, the *Herald*'s editor and owner did serve his apprenticeship in the British merchant marine. 'Tis not like being dubbed in the public print [as] a "get rich-quick swindler, wire tapper and jail bird," is it – George Hammond? To either the moon-faced type-picker who feeds the townsite company's organ to their multitude of dupes, or to the Albino manager of the townsite company, who has supervision of its columns, we attribute the "attack" of last week. Oh! you fools. Both those promoters-bell-hops are ex-employees of the Northern Interior Printing Company Limited [Daniell's company], and we have their mental gauge which is microscopical. The editorial end of the *Tribune* is not definitely allotted to any one man. The columns are for the purpose of inducing long distance investment, and any contributions, by the gamboling crowd of townsite puppets, which help in any manner to serve this end, are seized with avidity, and published in its columns. Go-to-it, you editors all. The *Herald* cares less than the value of a Hammond townsite lot for the squeakings of the townsite organ, or the persecution of its promoters.[87]

Hardly an even-handed exchange on the finer points of community life. The war of words was barely underway.

The final player was *Saturday Night* and its "Gold and Dross" column, which, within days of John Houston's passing, staked its position by casting doubt on Hammond's Fort George townsite proposition. The magazine's sniping continued into the summer of 1910 before approaching a crescendo with the photographic essay "Shacks and Forest at Fort George."[88] Researched in late June and early July, the article and photographs depicted "rough board shacks" and the surrounding "thick clump of virgin forest," and pointed out that, while its precise location remained undetermined, the GTP train station would be between one and a half and three kilometres away from the settlement. With this measure of things, the magazine reiterated that the NRSC was grossly misrepresenting the situation and that potential investors should be wary.[89] On the same day of *Saturday Night*'s photographic essay, John McConnell announced in the *Saturday Sunset* that "the world wants to know something about Fort George and the hinterland of the Northern Interior." And since "certain eastern newspapers" had heaped doubt on conditions in Fort George, McConnell was already en route northward to investigate the situation in person.[90] A collision between the two magazines appeared to be a near certainty. The unknown was how well the Georges would fare once the dust settled.

HOSTILITIES ERUPT

McConnell's first report during his northern adventure, offered under his pen name "Bruce" – after the Ontario county of his birth – was published on 6 August, detailing his journey through the southern Interior and into the Cariboo.[91] A week later, he dedicated an entire front page to photographs, a dismissal of *Saturday Night,* a narrative description of the Georges, an argument that the NRSC owned the Fort George townsite, a racist depiction of why the local Indigenous population would not sell their reserve to the GTP, and a boosting description of Fort George and its agricultural resources.[92] A week later, John Daniell responded to both *Saturday Night*'s "Shacks and Forests" treatment as well as McConnell's account of what he depicted as the Fort George townsite's inevitable rise to regional dominance. Wondering whether *Saturday Night*'s reporter had gone on a bender while visiting the Georges, Daniell argued, with some annoyance, that both the magazines had erred. On the one hand, *Saturday Night*'s correspondent had confused South Fort George's developing business district for the desolation of Hammond's Fort George townsite.[93] As much as the magazine's error was maddening (and one that dogged the Georges), McConnell's argument was even more misguided. His claim about South Fort George's distance from the rail line was groundless, as the railway's actual route was undetermined. Further, Hammond's ownership of the name "Fort George" foreordained nothing, since there was no reason to suppose that a prospective community's location or amenities would necessarily bear that name. Finally, in racist language matching McConnell's, Daniell argued that, regardless of what Chief Quaw, a "wily old red-skin," claimed, the GTP would acquire the reserve. Rather than invest in these groundless speculations, the *Herald* was on hand

> to tell the people all the facts. We will not manufacture carefully worded articles for the protection of rich companies whether they need them or not. The editor of this paper has lived in or near Fort George for the past five years and doesn't give a damn for the seven-day opinion of that forceful writer, Bruce, on this particular subject ... If *Toronto Saturday Night,* the Natural Security Resources Company, the Grand Trunk Pacific Railway, and Bruce want to "start something" over the merits or demerits of Fort George we want to referee, but let them beware of involving South Fort George, a town that is rapidly building up in spite of conflicting interests, on its own merits.[94]

Given Daniell's prominent role in the name calling that was about to erupt, the assertion that South Fort George was well placed to referee is amusing, although Daniell himself may have believed it. But the confusion over what distinguished Fort George from South Fort George and the anticipated GTP townsite meant that neither community would allow others to determine the northern Interior's image. And, as it turned out, Daniell emerged as a dogged, if not obsessive, competitor. He was, in a phrase, a good hater.

Returning to the contest at the end of July, *Saturday Night* acknowledged that John McConnell had taken "up the cudgels" in favour of the NRSC and had used the butt end on the magazine. Nonetheless, the attack had failed to bolster the NRSC's claim that Fort George would be home to the railway company's station and yards. *Saturday Night* also concluded that, given the *BC Saturday Sunset*'s dubious recommendations of speculative and unsavoury ventures in the past, its endorsement of Hammond's scheme was meaningless.[95] In response to this, McConnell dedicated two front-page columns to characterize *Saturday Night* as a "muck-raking publication" edited by "a bunch of irresponsible ignoramuses," who, in a seeming attempt to blackmail the NRSC, were exposing that magazine's own "prostituted standards."[96] This harangue proved to be one of the last between the two magazines, as, two weeks later, Mr. Justice W.E. Middleton dismissed George Hammond's request for an injunction preventing *Saturday Night* from commenting on the NRSC or its Fort George townsite.[97] Summing up why the matter was before the court, Middleton pointed to Hammond's allegation that *Saturday Night* had acted with ulterior motives that reflected "a deep-laid plot" in which the magazine was behind an undisclosed land company and thus was an active competitor of the NRSC. There was, however, no evidence to support the claim. The court could not grant an injunction to restrain publication of libel generally, and, further, Middleton doubted that any jury would find that anything reported by *Saturday Night* concerning Hammond's townsite scheme was libelous. If a jury did rule that it was, the court would set aside such an unreasonable verdict. Costs were awarded to *Saturday Night*.[98] With victory in hand, the magazine withdrew, leaving the *Saturday Sunset* and the *Fort George Tribune* to continue an increasingly personal battle with the *Fort George Herald* over the Georges' fate.

This realignment sharpened the barbs. Daniell was first out of the gate. Referring to McConnell's editorials preceding the Ontario High Court ruling, the *Herald* editor wondered if his *Sunset* counterpart had suffered a "brain-storm," for which "any reliable physician would advise complete darkness and ice bags for his present form of mania." McConnell retorted that Daniell's drunken enormities as editor were known to the police, a comment leading Daniell to question McConnell's masculinity as a "pink-tea editor" who was so full of half-truths and lies that he was a drunk.[99] At this point, McConnell's insults and allegations became entwined with masculine morality, suggesting, through the use of insults such as "tin-horn," "frisker," "four flusher," "piker," and "bootlegger," that his opponents lacked manly honour and self-control.[100] It proved to be an enduring theme in McConnell's attacks. Finally, McConnell dismissed South Fort George as a "wildcat" townsite, a financially risky and unsound proposition. This, too, became a recurring theme, despite a cease-and-desist letter from Vancouver lawyers Russell, Russell and Hannington, representing Beach Lasalle, one of the owners of the South Fort George townsite, who was seeking a "full and complete retraction of the article." McConnell responded by naming Lasalle, Nick Clark, A.G. Hamilton, and W.F. Cooke as the primary movers behind the South Fort George "wildcat" townsite.[101] Peppering his response with a litany of slurs, McConnell alleged that the cabal was damaging the region's reputation by attacking everything connected with George Hammond. And by being in league with *Saturday Night,* the schemers were broadcasting their "knocking" of the district to a national audience. There was more than a grain of truth in the charge, although McConnell himself was hardly blameless. He added more fuel to the fire by teasing that "spicy reading" and "illuminating information" about local MLA John Fraser would reveal him as a party to the skullduggery. This innuendo came to nothing. Nonetheless, the *Sunset* editor offered a hard truth to South Fort George's backers. Given its location almost two and a half kilometres south of the anticipated GTP rail line, the community was ill placed to maintain a prominent role in the region's immediate development. Once the GTP arrived, the hoped-for prospects would evaporate, an assessment that proved crushingly accurate.

On the same day that the *Sunset* was released, the *Fort George Herald* returned to the battle with two columns of small type headed by the accusation "LIES, LIES, LIES," in which Daniell vented his spleen at McConnell and the alleged string-puller Hammond.[102] Daniell's venomous outburst described the *Sunset* as "a prostituted 'independent' weekly" operated by a journalistic "pimp" peddling his columns to the highest bidder. "Bruce" was "a mountebank," a princely liar, "a white-livered ass" whose commentary was akin to a dog returning to its "vomit."[103] Yet, in defending South Fort George's founders, Daniell was in an awkward position. He too had once labelled Hamilton as a bootlegger. Further, by December 1910, rumours were swirling that Clark's company was in dire financial straits.[104] The best the *Herald* could offer was the tepid assertion that neither Hamilton nor Clark were actually involved in promoting the townsite (despite operating businesses there), that the "oldtimer" Clark had been one of "the liveliest" promoters in the region, and that "we have always found his word good."[105] Not exactly a daring rush to the barricades.

The editorial war raged until Christmas 1910 and then cooled until March 1911, after which Daniell signalled a new round of belligerence. Both men certainly relished the fight, with McConnell keen to goad his opponents. Conflict, recrimination, and libel proceedings made for good sales in the crowded Vancouver newspaper marketplace. In McConnell's telling, Hamilton was "a notorious bootlegger who peddled poisonous rotgut to Indians. The Indian chief at Fort George told me several of the young men of his reserve were killed by whisky sold to them by A.G. Hamilton last winter."[106] Nick Clark was a "tinhorn gambler who repudiates cheques which he issues to settle gambling losses" and who excused his behaviour by claiming to have been drunk at the time. Although Beach Lasalle was the first of the South Fort George clique to threaten legal action, tracing which went beyond legal counsel's brandishing complaints is difficult. Despite constant baiting, Clark seems to have been alone in bringing "Bruce" into court on a criminal libel complaint and filing a civil suit for an injunction to prevent McConnell from mentioning the South Fort George businessman.[107] In light of Hammond's setback in Ontario, Clark's decision to press the matter was ill considered. When it came time for depositions on the criminal side and discovery on the civil, the *Sunset* gleefully reported on Clark's confused account of events and his admission that his company's records were in disarray. When Clark's company initiated its winding up in early 1911, McConnell crowed that the proceedings "got to show that Nick Clarke [sic] is not only the tin horn gambler which I have accused him of being, but he is as well, a flim-flammer, a bogus cheque artist and the poorest kind of a businessman." The editor also paraded a series of dubious cheques and overdue accounts that required settlement before the new owners could acquire their assets.[108] When Clark's cases were dismissed, McConnell consigned "my interesting friend Nicolas Samuel Clark" to the scrap heap. Meekly acknowledging the defeat, Daniell charged the *Sunset* with scapegoating Clark because the South Fort George Board of Trade had raised legitimate questions about the NRSC's business methods.[109]

These legal tangles, both real and imagined, may have been little more than theatrics designed to sell copy. Regardless, the involvement of *Saturday Night* and the *Saturday Sunset* meant that the story, with its confusion, innuendo, name calling, and litigation, had a national audience. It was highly significant that hostilities began in Toronto, where backers of both South Fort George and Fort George undoubtedly hoped to attract investment capital, and in Vancouver, British Columbia's largest city, which boasted a newspaper advertising centre with a natural audience for opportunities in the province's northern Interior. That the participants failed to recognize the self-inflicted damage is striking. McConnell, for example, chose to blame *Saturday Night* for a confused article on the Georges in a London, England-based magazine. Further, the *Sunset's* editor claimed that the article "The Gentle Art of Selling Townsites" had purposefully distorted its portrayal of the Georges because of a squabble with McConnell over his magazine's advertising rates and circulation figures.[110] What especially attracted his ire was the British magazine's criticism of everything in the northern Interior except the South Fort George townsite, a position indicating that "this London writer has never been closer to Fort George than Dr. Cook ever was to the North Pole."[111] Inasmuch as McConnell blamed his opponents for the circulation of such falsehoods – a game in which he had been an active participant – the complaint was a selective version of events.

As 1910 turned into 1911, the enormities associated with the Georges lived on as half-remembered echoes in the public mind. A tone had been set and, with it, a note of disquiet – an unsettling "something" – about the region and its inhabitants. And while the name calling and the fallout continued into 1912, a libel suit brought by Hammond against Daniell and the *Fort George Herald* signalled that perhaps an end was at hand.[112] The case was brought before Chief Justice Gordon Hunter in Clinton on 1 May 1912. Legal sword play over the intricacies of a private prosecution, the question of whether the Crown could or ought to be involved, and procedural nuances associated with the terms "barrister," King's or Queen's counsel, and "Crown counsel," consumed the first day.[113] Once these topics were exhausted, Daniell entered a not guilty plea. The case centred on three assertions printed in the *Herald:* that Hammond and the NRSC continually misrepresented the content and character of the Fort George townsite; that he had manipulated newspaper reportage concerning Fort George's development and GTP efforts in the region; and that he had been held up to contempt and ridicule owing to Daniell's abuse and harassment, which included Daniell's libelling of Hammond by describing him as a "get-quick-rich" schemer and a "jail-bird" whose photograph was found in a "rogue's gallery."[114]

Representing Daniell, Stuart Henderson argued that the alleged libel was "true in substance and in fact" and that it had been uttered "for the public benefit."[115] His was a justification defence, seeking protection on the grounds that the comments were true. In support of this defence, Henderson sought a commission to examine witnesses in Chicago and Minnesota, including John Hill Jr., who had authored the bucket-shop exposé that featured a chapter on Hammond. After another bout of procedural wrangling, the commission was set to be held before a Vancouver judge presiding in chambers. Owing to the necessity of securing witnesses in the United States and providing for travel time to Vancouver for the hearing, the libel trial was rescheduled for the next available assize in the Cariboo Judicial District.

It was at this point in the proceedings that the tide turned against Daniell.[116] Owing to claims that any Cariboo jury would be antagonistic to his client, Hammond's counsel, Sidney S. Taylor, requested a Vancouver venue.[117] Mr. Justice Aulay Morrison thought the suggestion excessive but agreed to moving the trial to Kamloops, where, in mid-October, proceedings reconvened.[118] Obtaining sworn statements in Chicago for the commission in chambers in Vancouver failed, owing to a Vancouver court official being unable to prepare and dispatch the documents with sufficient time for the statements to be sworn and returned for the trial's new date. Although Daniell implored John Hill Jr. to travel to Vancouver and then Kamloops to testify, the American's insights on Hammond's early career were beside the point. While Hill provided testimony as to Hammond's exploits, the information did not affect the question of whether Daniell had libelled the townsite promoter.[119] After deliberating for just over an hour, the jury found Daniell guilty. While he escaped with a sentence of time served in custody before the trial, Daniell nonetheless had to face Morrison, who, drawing on common visions of the beneficial British Empire and fictions about a free English (Canadian) press, scorched the editor for having done "a cruel, cruel thing," an unmanly thing, and for acting in a fashion that would cause any decent Englishman (and his family) to stagger under a burden of shame.[120] The *Vancouver Daily World* detailed Morrison's withering condemnation:

> I am very sorry to see you, an Englishman, in the position you are. If there is one thing the great English people have been noted for, it is keeping their

press free from that of which you have been found guilty. If there is one thing that we Britishers in the colonies are proud of it is the English press. As an Englishman, I am sorry, I am ashamed, that you, an Englishman as you said you are, on the very threshold of your career, and I might say on the threshold of your existence in this province, should be responsible for such a thing as that.

Offered the opportunity to apologize, Daniell refused, accepted his judicial thrashing, and returned to South Fort George, where he boldly reprinted Hill's letter reiterating the details of Hammond's inglorious career in Chicago and Minnesota.[121]

Daniell's loss – when he had accurately portrayed Hammond's bucketshop career, when the NRSC's self-inflicted wounds in reference to the station site were on the public record, and when the company's exaggerated sales pitch for the Fort George townsite was widely known – suggests that the case turned on the unprovable. Specifically, while Daniell believed that Hammond had paid off Hay Stead of the *Winnipeg Saturday Post* (where the libelous statement was original published) so that the newspaper would reverse course and label South Fort George a "wildcat," – a fly-by-night townsite without legal standing – was the only evidence sustaining Daniell's claim. Effectively, Daniell lost because he believed his own propaganda and stood by it regardless of the consequences. It was irrelevant that John Hill Jr. could testify to Hammond's early misadventures; the point was of no account to the *Post* libel and the accusation that Hammond had attempted to purchase Daniell's silence. Having lobbed uncounted gibes and accusations at Hammond, Daniell was undone by those that did not or could not stick. Yet by the Christmas season of 1912, it hardly mattered. The NRSC advertising campaign had run out of fuel, the GTP had secured the Lheidli T'enneh reserve and was beginning to clear the townsite, and, while never claiming to foretell the future, Daniell no doubt knew that Hammond did not possess the means to defeat the railway company.[122] Still, Daniell's own loss was costly. While presenting his readers with a brave face and committing himself to battling onward, he had accumulated over $7,000 in debt while fighting his corner. Within a year, he sold the *Herald* to Russell R. Walker and effected a temporary escape from the newspaper business.[123]

These prewar years offer complicated versions of the stories that the Georges' white settler society told themselves about themselves. While the self-congratulatory appeal of the New Cariboo, with a population of independent, fair-minded, white, Christian people, was unquestioned, the townsite war's hard words and the images it painted suggested an unsettling counter-narrative. Indeed, for others – mostly outsiders – the region remained a foil for mid-nineteenth-century Vancouver Island's self-appointed role as an exemplar of the province's preferred identity on the eve of the First World War.[124] In that context, the Cariboo illustrated an absence, an unfinished and disorderly community. And even for those unaware of the province's history, who knew nothing of the northern Interior's initial promoters, confidence men, sharp dealing, and exaggerated sales pitches, something lingered on the edge of recollection. Here, in a nearly forgotten something, we find a persistent anxiety about reputation. For as much as early settlers and their families clung to an ideal of the New Cariboo and stood steadfast in their defence of their choice in turning their eyes and their aspirations toward the northern Interior, they too wondered about what the mean-spirited braggadocio of the newsprint war said about them. Was it possible that, despite their claims to respectability and order, they were somehow a party to that excess? It remained an unsettling possibility.

2

The British Columbia Provincial Police, Regulatory Policing, and Keeping the Peace

For a seasoned British Columbia Provincial Police (BCPP) constable stationed in the Georges in the 1920s, the policeman's lot held few mysteries. While the posting may have whispered of manly challenges and adventures in a rough-and-tumble community on the white settlement frontier, ordinary duty in the Georges trimmed such expectations. Burdened with the tedium of paperwork, office duty, and often uneventful patrols, constables might be pardoned for having the quiet hope that "something" might occur. Not that anyone wanted a local crime spree, but a little excitement would not be amiss. A brief search through the constables' monthly reports reveals how rarely duty in the Georges corresponded to notions of valiant police officers bringing villains to justice. The lion's share of police duty was administrative and regulatory, tasks associated with British Columbia's expanding modern state.

What, exactly, did the BCPP in the Georges do on a daily basis? Typically, the most experienced policeman in the station, the chief constable, spent his days behind a desk, answering a rising tide of correspondence from Victoria, organizing the station's duty roster, and ensuring that constables kept up with their paperwork. His policing skills, as distinct from his managerial talents, were called upon for "serious" investigations, communications with senior police officials, and maintaining diplomatic relations with local government, neighbouring police forces, and politicians from Victoria. For men in the ranks, ordinary duty fell into two broad categories. Constables assigned to the elastic category of general police duty in the station spent their days issuing various licences, registering firearms, guarding prisoners, collecting poll taxes, and fielding inquiries from the public. Once freed from desk work and dispatched on patrols, constables shouldered regulatory duties such as checking on pool rooms and theatres; inspecting nearby sawmills, railway worksites, dairies, and butchering operations; inquiring into reports concerning the physical and mental health of individual residents; greeting the train; and generally maintaining a peacekeeping and preventative-policing presence in the community. This latter role was especially important. The public accepted the presence of the police with varying degrees of enthusiasm. Their administrative duties as well as their physical presence in the community symbolized the government's regulatory grasp at a time when the provincial bureaucracy was coming into its own. Regardless of whether they liked it or not, police constables were, first and foremost, civil servants whose work centred on managing the public.

The Makings of a BCPP Constable

Until the 1920s, becoming a BCPP constable was similar to seeking membership in an English, middle-class, white men's fraternity. The police regulations of 1895 provided that applicants had to be Crown subjects by birth or naturalization, a provincial resident for one year, literate, "generally intelligent," between twenty-one and thirty-five years of age, in good physical and mental health, able to perform police duty, and of good moral character and habits.[1] Disobedience, drunkenness, insolence, immorality, and incapacity, as well as entering brothels or taverns unless on duty, were potential grounds for dismissal. Essentially, being white and a clubbable Crown subject represented a winning combination. While senior administrators looked askance at anyone who suggested that such a position was a patronage opportunity, the truth was that only those with the right pedigree were considered suitable. For the officer class, the force favoured white, "respectable," middle- and upper-class men who had military or policing experience elsewhere in the empire, while the ranks were populated with white, literate, and rising working-class or aspirant middle-class men with "steady" political inclinations. The result was a force populated with Anglo-Celtic Canadian men.

If queried, most constables would have self-identified as independent-thinking, manly white men. Few, if any, would have recognized that self-image as a defence mechanism, shielding them from the uncertainties of life on the settlement frontier. As Robert Hogg notes in his study of manliness on the mid-nineteenth-century frontier of Queensland and British Columbia, by constructing non-white, non-British masculinities as inferior and uncivilized, British men affirmed a version of masculinity that they had absorbed elsewhere in the empire.[2] Shielded by a preferred identity, their sense of rightness offered psychological armour in British Columbia's northern Interior, a land providing a fresh start and where questioning the rules was common. Whiteness offered an anchor when everything else seemed up for grabs. It was part of an "immutable ladder of merit and achievement ... It became a condition of humanity ... a universal that no other race attained. All other races were inferior, falling short of the universal, and therefore, of humanity."[3] Brandishing this supposed racial superiority and confident masculinity, constables expected to impose themselves on any challenge. Writing to BCPP superintendent William McMynn in September 1918, Acting Chief Constable John Bourne illustrated this thinking in a single page typed letter under the heading "Alien Enemies and Firearms."[4] The title exaggerated an overwrought case involving a shotgun with a broken butt that was, in Bourne's estimation, "absolutely useless as far as shooting is concerned."[5] After the outbreak of the First World War, Ed Clarke, a local man, had asked Charles Sager, a barber, to look after his shotgun, as he had accepted a job on an ocean-going tanker and was relocating his wife to Winnipeg. Clarke perished when a German submarine sunk the vessel in the Atlantic. His family contacted Sager, asking him to sell the shotgun and send the proceeds to Clarke's destitute widow. Sager unknowingly sold the gun to a man later identified as a German, warranting a charge of selling a firearm to an alien enemy. Bourne harboured no doubts that Sager was above reproach and that the "well-respected" and "very religious" barber had been performing a good deed. Nonetheless, the complaint stood, and Sager was arrested, found guilty, fined, and subjected to "a very strong talking-to from the bench." Bourne, who hoped that his "leniency" would meet with McMynn's approval, waited until the report's penultimate sentence to add that Sager was "a nigger barber in town." The slur cast new light on the situation. For the acting chief constable, his actions testified to his own "common-sense" (as well as that of the two sitting justices of the peace) in sparing the good-hearted but foolish Black man from the consequences of his actions. While this result may have legitimized the chief constable's adherence to the letter of the law, surely Sager's actions did not warrant him being hauled into public court and exposed to sly ridicule in addition to a dressing down from the bench.[6] But no, there was a white man's point to be made. What could have disappeared discreetly became a performance of Bourne's mastery of the situation, determined, in large, by his whiteness and Sager's Blackness. No instruction manual or training regime outlined such thinking – it was integral to the white policeman's mindset on the settlement frontier.

Bourne's racism combined with the circumstances of his passing in early February 1921 remind us that as much as he bore the markings of a conscientious officer, he was an ordinary man with flaws akin to all members of the BCPP. He had been stationed at Ashcroft in August 1918 when he was offered the position of acting chief constable at South Fort George to replace Chief A.C. Minty.[7] Bourne and his new bride, Ruth, packed up their household effects, shipped them northward on the CNR via Lucerne, and then travelled up river via 150 Mile House and Quesnel before arriving in South Fort George on 13 August. A day later, he threw himself into his duties. A driven officer who personally patrolled the district, assisted constables with arrests and investigations, regularly worked for a week with constables in Vanderhoof and Lucerne, he spent more time in the field than behind his desk. In October 1918, he orchestrated the initial responses to the Spanish influenza outbreak before Inspector T.W.S. Parsons mounted his efforts to counter the pandemic. In the summer of 1919, Ruth Bourne gave birth to the couple's first child. Months later, in early November, the tireless acting chief constable quite unexpectedly took ten days' sick leave. He returned to duty to provide an escort to the New Westminster asylum for a man diagnosed as insane by local physicians.[8] Returning home to South Fort George, John Bourne sought out local physician Dr. Carl Ewert, to whom the acting chief confided that he was suffering from "spells," numbness in his left arm and leg, and an unshakable tiredness. Ewert noted that Bourne's speech was laboured and confused. While the physician may have had suspicions, it is uncertain if tests were ordered or if he expressed his concerns to his patient during subsequent office visits. Bourne returned to duty and, save for his increasing reliance on the detachment's police car, he attempted to maintain his usual brisk pace.[9] On 8 and 9 January 1920, Constable Mansell noted Bourne's absence from duty; and on 21 January, the police car had to be sent to bring Bourne to the station. How often he was working or if he submitted duty logs for January or February is unknown. The office's other duty logs indicate that, while Bourne was occasionally present during those two months, Mansell had become acting chief constable.

It must have been blindingly obvious that something was wrong. In fact, Constable A. McNeill in Victoria was making ready on 1 March to travel north with the intent of relieving Bourne.[10] On the evening of

2 March, as Mansell completed a patrol to Prince George and was tidying up official correspondence, Constable Avison reported that Bourne had become violent. Avison stood guard over his superior officer for the remainder of the night.

Dr. E.J. Lyon was immediately summoned to examine Bourne, and Dr. Ewert arrived the next morning. Lyon produced the diagnosis, with which Ewert agreed: Bourne's body was at war with itself. He had contracted syphilis eighteen years earlier before departing from England. His was a hopeless case.[11] Following Ewert's examination on 3 March, Mansell wired BCPP superintendent W.G. McMynn, who, given McNeill's travel plans, knew something was amiss.[12] Responsible for filling out the paperwork to confine Bourne in the New Westminster Mental Asylum, Mansell wrote that, while Bourne had not been suicidal, he had demanded his revolver when in a "maniacal state." None of the constables speculated about Bourne's condition but Ewert did note that, while under guard, Bourne had threatened to shoot Constable Long.[13] The comment remains confusing. Former constable David Long had left the force in the summer of 1919, and it was Avison who sat with Bourne during that worrisome evening. Had the chief constable thought Avison was Long and threatened to shoot him, or had the doctor misheard? Regardless, on the following morning, both Mansell and Avison escorted Bourne to the train, where Constable W.R. Henley of Vanderhoof took charge of his former chief to begin the dispiriting journey south to the New Westminster mental hospital.[14] Appearing haunted and a decade older than his thirty-six years, Bourne was checked into the hospital on 5 March. Seven days later, a Wasserman test confirmed Lyon's and Ewert's diagnosis.[15] Ruth Bourne left South Fort George on 16 March for Ashcroft.[16]

John Bourne's health continued to collapse in the following months. Visits from two of his brothers left him confused while also raising false hope in his family that he might improve.[17] Medical superintendent Dr. C.E. Doherty left no room for doubt: "there is absolutely no possible chance of ultimate recovery, while the chances are that Mr. Bourne will not outlive two years at the very most."[18] Ruth Bourne appeared unaware of the finality of her husband's illness. Having returned to Ashcroft and her family, she attempted in late April to get her affairs in order and requested her husband's signature on their bank account and blank cheques; a month later, she inquired as to how well he was getting along and if he was "better." Perhaps recognizing that the prognosis had not been explained or that Ruth had not grasped the nature of her husband's condition, Assistant Medical Superintendent Dr. A.L. Crease reported to her that John had failed "a little both mentally and physically," that his gait was unsteady, and that his speech affected, though he had not recently suffered any seizures. Skirting what awaited, Crease closed by observing that John did "not appreciate the visits" he has had from family members.[19] Ruth retained hope, asking if her husband would respond if she wrote. Again, Crease indicated that John was failing, that, owing to his difficulty standing, he was confined to bed, noting that "he does not talk and I am sure would not be able to write you a letter."[20] After softly mooting the idea of a visit, Ruth acknowledged in late November that it would be pointless: "I guess he wouldn't know me if I were to see him."[21] Finally, on 21 January 1921, she wrote asking if "there's any hopes of him recovering," to which Crease acknowledged the unavoidable end: "Your husband is gradually failing both in his mental and physical condition. I do not hold out any hope for his ultimate recovery. He is not suffering [and] is taking his food fairly well and is sleeping well. He is unable to enter into conversation and each faculty is gradually leaving him."[22] Two weeks later, John Bourne suffered several seizures. He died in the early morning hours of 5 February.[23]

The zeal that Bourne had demonstrated for policing was a personal attribute rather than the result of training: indeed, a formal police-training regime did not exist within the BCPP until the early 1930s.[24] As a result, while some applicants could draw on previous experience, others had to rely on what they imagined to be "common sense." This latitude served to reinforce a combination of contemporary prejudice and rashness founded on misplaced confidence. The BCPP regulations warned constables about interfering "idly or unnecessarily" yet encouraged them to act "with decision and boldness" while maintaining a calm disposition that would invite "well-disposed bystanders" to provide assistance.[25] This formula worked in many situations but failed miserably in others, and it assumed that officers and men in the ranks were blessed with the innate skill to navigate any situation. At the same time, though, the more seasoned constables schooled newcomers in daily tasks and expectations.[26] A common method in the South Fort George office typically entailed a new recruit spending the first week in the station familiarizing himself with local routines and peculiarities before being sent out on patrol. This approach continued at least until 1924, when the *BC Provincial Police Regulation Constable's Manual* became available as a pocket-sized summary of duties, procedure, and general deportment.[27] The manual nurtured an ethos of professionalism in place of on-the-job experimentation. Combined with the long-awaited issuance of uniforms, thanks to the Police and Prisons

Regulation Act of 1923/24, the changes provided the BCPP a sharpened sense of identity and esprit de corps.[28] The combination placed the force near the forefront of modernized policing in the nation.

A Policeman for the New Cariboo

Save for a flash of interest as a potential divisional point on a proposed route for the Canadian Pacific Railway in the late 1870s, the confluence of the Nechako and Fraser Rivers attracted little attention in the last quarter of the nineteenth century. Absent reliable links to the continental interior and British Columbia's southwest corner, the Hudson's Bay Company (HBC) post at Fort George was too remote to occupy a significant place in the provincial imagination. Exceptions fed into established narratives about the dangers of the distant north country while playing upon concerns about the province's racial composition and the imagined threat associated with it.[29] For example, in 1901, "bad Indians" at Fort George had allegedly run HBC clerk E.L. Kemper and his "Chinese" cook out of the post, forcing them to regroup in Quesnel.[30] Reportedly, Special Constable William McLaren's arrival in the area re-established a measure of order. A few months later, reports alleged that, while under the influence of opium and alcohol, Louis Tsan, a young Saik'uz man, had killed Ah Mook (aka Ah Muck) and wounded Ah Foo (aka Ah Chew).[31] The drawn-out pursuit of Tsan concluded with him in custody and McLaren claiming that the local Indigenous people were an "unreliable, untrustworthy and troublesome tribe."[32] Tried at the Clinton assize on 3 October 1902, Tsan was found not guilty, owing to the jury's conclusion that he "had not fired the fatal shot which killed Ah Mook."[33] Commentators may have sought a reassuring lesson in the verdict – one centred on the supposed evenhandedness of British justice – that confirmed the portability of the Crown's legal order. At the same time, it was easy to conclude that while "justice" had prevailed, the episode dovetailed with a feeling that there was "something" amiss in the northern Interior.

The approaching settlement frontier and the impracticalities of providing any governmental service, or administering justice, from Barkerville, 183 kilometres to the south, sparked agitation to locate a permanent BCPP constable at Fort George. Rumours of an illegal trade in liquor swirling around local merchant A.G. Hamilton in the autumn of 1907 hinted at the prudence of such an appointment. Initially, nothing was done. In

May 1909, BCPP superintendent F.S. Hussey alerted Constable David Anderson of Quesnel that seventy-five cases of whisky, secreted inside fifteen beer barrels labelled "merchandise," had been dispatched from Victoria to South Fort George. Anderson was directed to either make a patrol northward or appoint "a suitable man" for the task of ensuring that the shipment, likely intended for Hamilton, was intercepted. While Anderson recommended Frank Aiken, nothing further was done.[34] That Hamilton subsequently obtained a liquor licence, only to have it pulled owing to protests from people he characterized as "malicious and lying individuals," reveals a great deal about the province's chaotic oversight of the liquor business. By the time his licence was withdrawn, Hamilton had obtained more alcohol. With no legal means to sell it, he "disposed of the liquor" and became, in his version of events, a bootlegger only by circumstance.[35] Newspaperman John Houston, who arrived in South Fort George in the autumn of 1909, sided with Hamilton, arguing that a hotel liquor licence had been granted – despite Hamilton owning a store, not a hotel – and the fee paid before the licence was withdrawn, and without the fee being returned. "A stock of liquor, to the value of several thousand dollars, was ordered and shipped and paid for. The liquor was in Fort George. It has been sold. If illegally, is the government free from blame?"[36] That thousands of dollars in liquor was delivered to a store in a region where Indigenous people outnumbered whites by a considerable margin and where the fur trade remained a primary economic activity, failed to trouble Houston. The attorney general's office, on the other hand, headed by W.J. Bowser, who knew of Hamilton's inglorious police career in the Kootenays, had reason to be sceptical.[37]

Hamilton's activities and rising settler interest indicated that the Georges warranted attention in the form of law enforcement and contributed to accumulating "knowledge" about the region. These reports invariably coloured popular impressions. Further, we have the contributions of a publicist for the Grand Trunk Pacific Railway (GTP), Frederick A. Talbot, who, in 1910, passed through the Georges while exploring the company's route to the west coast. Talbot's eight columns appeared in the well-subscribed magazine the *World's Work,* before being combined in *The New Garden of Canada: By Packhorse and Canoe through Undeveloped New British Columbia,* published in 1912.[38] In the summer of 1910, months before the arrival of South Fort George's first BCPP constable and a year before the Hotel Northern acquired its first liquor licence, Talbot offered a sodden portrait of British Columbia's northern Interior. While it was supposed to be "dry," in reality it was "wetter" than a licensed community bristling with gin palaces. Drink was freely smuggled in, while "rock-cut" was brewed extensively in a certain quarter and vended as "Hudson's Bay Rum" to secure a ready sale, this being the most famous drink in the West. It was as much like Hudson's Bay Rum as salad oil is like Chartreuse. The opium or nicotine juice with which it was saturated provoked intoxication in the shortest possible space of time, and the Indians were to be seen on every hand staggering and reeling under its baneful influence. The larger, well-ordered section of the community endeavoured to check this abuse, but in vain. There was no policeman within a hundred miles, so the law could not be invoked.[39]

Echoing Wild West tales populated with heroic white men resisting liquor's "baneful influence" while "Indians" bowed down under the influence of onrushing white society and its temptations, Talbot characterized hard drinking as a measure of manliness and an integral element of life on the settlement frontier. Amateur historian Reverend F.E. Runnells followed suit decades later. He described the Northern Hotel as boasting

a ninety-foot bar, and a staff of twenty-four bartenders who worked twelve on a shift. Hundreds of men crowded in to be served and frequently stood five or six-deep behind the bar. As much as seven thousand dollars was taken in one day, and it is said that the average throughout the season was two thousand dollars a day. The soft-wood floor was soon worn out by the hob-nail boots of construction men and had to be renewed frequently. Behind the barroom was the snake room for victims of the "D T's." Many young men who arrived with their pockets full of money and high hopes of visiting their homes back East would wake up to find their stake "spent."[40]

Such impressions of the Georges corresponded with the devil-may-care exploits of South Fort George's founding fathers and the frontier capital-ism of the Grand Trunk Pacific in an environment where men strove hard and played harder. It made for a good yarn. Here we imagine pros-titutes playing stud poker by the stairs, men leaning into their drinks in the crowded, hazy bar, and constables wrestling drunken "bohunks" into the cells at South Fort George. Here were the foul-mouthed drunkards who "cause embarrassment and anxiety to the women and anger and re-sentment amongst the men" for spoiling a family outing at an afternoon baseball game. Here too were scenes populated with immigrants such as Greek merchant Teddy Pappas, who allowed drinking in his store; Mah Moon, the laundry man, who prepared "a complete line of Oriental edibles with unpronounceable names to accompany the five cases of rye for thirsty customers"; and William Bellos, whose Royal Hotel attracted police attention for liquor and gaming offences.[41] Whether in newspaper columns suggesting who belonged in the community and who could be chalked off, or in populating depictions of how far the Georges had progressed, this was the stuff of caricature. For while William and Arthur Bellos appeared in daily police duty logs along with Moon, Pappas, and others, their clashes with the law said more about discretionary policing and the modern state's impositions than it did about a community alleged to be on a perpetual bender. True, such storytelling about the Georges might align with "knowledge" about the region, but when these overdrawn images supposedly representing everyday life are compared with the reports of constables keeping the peace in the northern Interior, these scenes become less a reflection of reality and more a product of the imagination.[42]

For example, two newspaper articles from before the First World War illustrate how newsprint versions of the Georges emphasized what were allegedly sorry conditions. The first, from the *Fort George Herald* of 2 September 1911, ran alongside an erroneous story detailing the sale of the Lheidli T'enneh Fort George Reserve No. 1.[43] Purporting to reveal the inadequacies of the provincial Liquor Act while criticizing the provincial government for its failure to build a jail in South Fort George, the article offered a racist commentary on "the seeds of violence and crime in the poor bestial brains of the Indians." They were apt to drink away "the lottery" of the reserve sale rather than purchase food and clothing for

> the swarm of hungry brown women and children on the rancherie ... A disgraceful scene was enacted on Hamilton Avenue last Tuesday night, when a crowd of drunken Siwashes brawled and fought like a pack of sleigh dogs, within hearing distance of private residences, and families that had to suffer the indignity of waiting [for] the termination of the red men's orgy or send forth volunteers to take a hand in subduing the frenzied mob.[44]

Of particular concern were the "half-breeds" who, once "they come into possession of a bottle, they hie themselves away to their Siwash tillicums and get the whole crowd drunk. Then the particular hell demon that sleeps in the cranium of the Indian awakes and twists the brain of the red-man until he sees red – and crime stalks abroad." The originating culprit was "the 'notoriously bad character' of mixed-blood people," who "would corrupt vulnerable 'Indians' by supplying them with liquor."[45]

The second incident occurred in late May 1913. Again, according to the *Fort George Herald,* a "giant" of a man named Kilpatrick had refused to leave the Northern Hotel's bar, despite the efforts of Charlie Wylie, hotel "policeman." Editor John Daniell narrated the eruption: "Wylie, who is also a big man, closed with the scow-man and a battle of giants opened fast and furious." Bounced from the hotel, the over-refreshed Kilpatrick turned on BCPP chief constable Achilles O'Neill Daunt and Constable Joseph Jackson "and a free-for-all fight started." The two policemen "had great difficulty in preventing a serious riot amongst the foreigners who closed in on them, and they were forced to draw their guns, but handled the difficult situation with credit. Kilpatrick was taken to the lock-up. He was fined fifty dollars or three months in jail, on a charge of creating a disturbance."[46] Authored a day later, Daunt's account offered a deepened version of the ruckus and its implications:

> We require good men here, and lots of them. Only last night we got rushed and pretty roughly handled by a crowd of 150 or so toughs, while arresting a man who reckoned he was sober when Johnson's manager considered he wasn't. We got him after being kicked and rolled in the mud for 15 minutes and came back and got three of the ringleaders afterwards, but it was a pretty hard looking proposition for three men to take on. It must be remembered that we cannot get good "Specials" here, and as long as this latest brand of tough is going to keep coming from the upper river, and the hotels are open[,] we need six real good men right in this town. I am not blaming the hotels, for the trouble starts when the drink is stopped by the bartenders. The bottle business is also a hard thing to handle, as parties of these fellows buy bottles, and pack them off, getting drunk outside of private homes, and scaring the women out of their senses.[47]

While other disturbances were reported during these years, these are notable because they contain what the newspaper portrayed as the most common elements – liquor, bootleggers, Indigenous and mixed-heritage people, transient labouring men, the police confronting long odds, and gendered and chivalric hopes that local white women would be spared exposure to such behaviour. Here was "real policing" in a community with a liquor problem, all feeding a tawdry reputation.

From a distance, it all "fits." Closer inspection suggests otherwise. First, such incidents and opinions were not peculiar to the Georges. Most British Columbian (and Canadian) communities had their own racist version of Indigenous and mixed-heritage people's supposed depravity and examples of labourers, buoyed with their pay packets, appearing in the local hostelry committed to the proposition that liquor was a solvent for life's worries and a lubricant for sociability. For many, sharing a jar, a ribald story, and a hand of cards was the best way to shake off weeks of camp life, the perils of working a river scow, or the din of saws and pickaxes. Indeed, the province's liquor history testifies to alcohol being a constant element in its philosophical, economic, and social make-up. Renisa Mawani's exploration of race and liquor notes the influence of both on "common-sense racial truths" at the heart of British Columbian identity.[48] Douglas Hamilton reflects on the province's "loose and forgiving frontier standard of behavior" producing a "wide-open" reputation that rivalled that of the American west.[49] Lynne Marks's splendid study of irreligiosity in prewar British Columbia makes a similar point: "this male drinking culture existed elsewhere in Canada, in local and fraternal halls, but was far stronger, more visible, and unregulated in much of British Columbia, especially the Kootenays."[50] John Belshaw's treatment of Vancouver Island coal miners acknowledges that "drinking was almost a universal avocation in these distinctly male communities, and the British miners had come from a tradition that had mixed both recreational and ritualistic drinking with pit work."[51] As historian Craig Herron has stressed, economies that were reliant on the extraction of natural resources – like mining and forestry – have historically brought together a large collection of young men working at some distance from population centres. And "both the intensity of the work experience and the tight regulation on public drinking undoubtedly encouraged drinking as much as possible as quickly as possible."[52] Simply put, the whole of British Columbia was a boozy, truculent, and unapologetically racist place well into the 1930s. Given such a setting, policing alcohol, dealing with the public-order challenges linked with excessive drinking, and enforcing the province's legislative attempts to manage liquor were regular features of BCPP duty and, in the Georges, underlay the call for stationing a constable at the confluence of the Nechako and Fraser Rivers.

The campaign for such an appointment began in the spring of 1907 and dragged on until late November 1910, when thirty-three-year-old Frederick Gosby, boasting seven years' experience with London's Metropolitan Police, service in South Africa, and two years' work with the Canadian Pacific Railway, was appointed to the Georges.[53] The details of his posting are tangled: his name appears on the BCPP pay sheet for South Fort George in mid-September 1910, followed by a seven-day leave of absence in early November, while the *Fort George Herald* reported that "special constable" Gosby arrived in late November from his previous posting on the Skeena River.[54] His presence was a sharp reminder that the community lacked any government facilities. This circumstance obliged him to use the newly opened Hotel Northern as an unofficial office, while the Barnard Express (BX) warehouse substituted as a jail. The latter proved to be an embarrassment when, in June, a government teamster stabling his wagon inadvertently released three men confined on liquor charges.[55]

As the efforts to secure a constable played out, an allied campaign was launched to construct a provincial government building. The project again set South Fort George and Fort George at odds, since the office's location represented a stamp of approval in their battle for local supremacy. Therefore, when government land agent Reginald Randall of Barkerville arrived in the third week of July 1910 to declare that the offices and government ferry facilities would be built at Fort George, howls of protest from South Fort George soon echoed through Victoria's halls of government.[56] Acting on his own authority, George Walker, gold commissioner and government agent (also of Barkerville), halted work on Randall's chosen site and declared that a local vote would determine the government office's location.[57] Reporting from Quesnel, the *Cariboo Observer* concluded that the tally would favour South Fort George, since it was the largest community. "This will decide the question, but too much hard feeling has apparently been aroused over the matter for it to let loose the dove of peace between the two townsites."[58] Held on 30 July, despite allegations of a faulty electoral process from the Fort George townsite backers (who boycotted the contest), the near unanimous vote favoured South Fort George.[59] Chastened, Randall returned to scout a location in South Fort George after the provincial secretary in Victoria had seemingly given the go ahead.[60] This impression proved to be mistaken.

Rather, officials in the capital were uneasy, and with good reason. Building a permanent office anywhere in the Georges was premature before the Grand Trunk Railway negotiations for purchasing the Lheidli T'enneh reserve had concluded (which would not be the case until November 1911), and the new townsite was laid out. Still, since South Fort George was the most populous settlement, establishing a *temporary* office there appeared reasonable. Perhaps hoping to smooth ruffled feathers and provide some clarity, Conservative premier Richard McBride journeyed northward with an entourage that included C.H. Lugrin, editor of Victoria's *Daily Colonist;* F. Carter-Cotton, former editor of the *Vancouver News Advertiser;* John Norton-Griffiths, British member of Parliament and railroad contractor; Harry Brittain, organizer of the 1909 Imperial Press Conference; and Lord Dunmore of the House of Peers.[61] Yet, rather than confirm the construction of temporary government facilities in South Fort George, McBride equivocated. What once had seemed logical was no more. By late October, the *Fort George Herald* claimed that the delay was because backers of the Fort George townsite had been twisting arms in the provincial capital. Even John Daniell, with his unalloyed Conservative Party credentials, thought that special interests had hoodwinked the McBride government.[62] The message was unsettling: South Fort George's sense of itself as the region's pre-eminent community, and thus deserving a privileged voice in shaping its future, held little currency in Victoria.

The matter festered until the spring of 1911. With all the necessary building materials, including steel jail cells, waiting in the local BX warehouse, the *Fort George Herald* conjured up images of *Alice in Wonderland* and declared that "the time had come" for the McBride administration to act.[63] Denied a local office, settlers would have to trek to Barkerville to complete government business. Finally, on 1 April 1911, J.A. Fraser, the local MLA, announced that, with Solomon-like wisdom, the government would split the difference. Temporary offices would be built on the HBC property, one and a half kilometres north of South Fort George and two and a half kilometres east of Fort George. The compromise offended both communities.[64] Accompanying the news was a *Herald* editorial harkening back to John Houston's vision of the "New Cariboo," which was "grouped within its confines under pressure of discomfort, merely because a provincial unpaternal government is not clothed with the spirit of enterprise."[65] Simply put, the New Cariboo could not rely on a provincial government that was open to the highest bidder's entreaties.

Further, that the tentative facility lacked a police office was consistent with the ongoing fiasco.[66] Apparently, the jail had been "lost" while "Victoria diplomatists" navigated through the claims of rival townsites while nonetheless recognizing that the proposed location "was too remote" from South Fort George to serve as a community jail:[67] "If it be absolutely compulsory a man will walk half a mile to transact his business with a government agent, but it is a hard matter for a solitary policeman to coax a drunk and disorderly 'bohunk' to stagger with him over half a mile of trail, knowing that he is to be put away in a rusty steel cage at the end of his meanderings." Moreover, in the summer, the trek would involve crossing the HBC slough on an ancient log construction "likened to a pontoon bridge minus its end sections." Was a constable supposed to ferry lawbreakers across in a canoe or, lacking that, "must [he] swim the creek with his prisoner?" Exasperated, Daniell was left wondering how South Fort George's interests might attract fair representation: "What have we done? – Most everybody voted right!!" [68]

SOUTH FORT GEORGE DUTY

The experiences of the first two BCPP constables posted to the Georges reveal the substance of ordinary duty. As much as the absence of an office, jail, and quarters was worrisome enough, Frederick Gosby was crestfallen to learn that his monthly pay packet, $86 per month when stationed on the Skeena River, had been reduced to $82 with his transfer to South Fort George. Writing to Superintendent Hussey in search of a raise to $100 per month – a salary that constables had received when posted in the Chilcotin District in 1897 owing to allegations of Indigenous lawlessness – the constable detailed that for a nine-hour day, common labourers earned $5, while local skilled labour secured between $7 and $10. For Gosby, who was effectively on duty around the clock and whose responsibilities were weightier, his salary amounted to less than $3 a day. Given the district's cost of living, the comparison was especially galling. "Having regard to the excessive high price of all food commodities, I find my present salary barely sufficient to enable me to eke out a very meagre subsistence, and I find it absolutely impossible to save a cent." [69] Even if Hussey were sympathetic, no raise was forthcoming. Suggesting that Gosby's return to policing had been half-hearted, he named Andrew Forrest special constable at $5 a day, resigned, and left the Georges to become a fisheries inspector. [70] His departure moved editor John Daniell to argue that the police deserved decent salaries to perform their duties. Gosby had indicated that "he could earn more money driving nails than as a representative of law and order." [71] Unwilling to acknowledge that circumstances in the Interior were unusual and avoiding a precedent that would increase the cost of policing in the province's thinly settled districts, there was little chance of a thicker pay packet for anyone assigned to South Fort George.

Shortly after his arrival in late November 1910, Gosby had received a directive revealing that officials in Victoria possessed only a vague sense of the geography of the northern Interior. Specifically, he was told to investigate troubles at Stoney Creek, approximately 128 kilometres to the west of South Fort George. After inquiring as to the means of travelling to his destination, Gosby hired "Johnny" Pierre Way – a "half-breed" guide – along with a dog team, in anticipation of a five-day journey, which involved breaking a winter trail to Stoney Creek. "Johnny Way" was Pierre Rois, whose family name was later adapted to Pierreroy. A man of local consequence, Rois along with his extended family played recurring roles as witnesses, suspects, and sometimes tragic figures, documenting the re-silience of the region's old originals. Both Stoney Creek investigations, one involving hard words between an Indigenous man and a local store-keeper and a second concerning allegations that unattended dogs from the Saik'uz First Nation were worrying white settlers' livestock, spoke of simmering tensions and understandable Dakelh resentment at finding themselves disadvantaged in the competition for the New Cariboo's re-sources. Neither case augured well for future relations.[72] Tallying the constable's final expenses, the *Fort George Herald* estimated that the in-vestigations had cost ratepayers about $160.[73] Introducing the modern state to the northern Interior was going to be an expensive undertaking. Gosby's brief tenure suggests that, despite its boisterous reputation, the Georges offered few challenges that were not evident elsewhere in the province. Sorting the Stoney Creek troubles, managing a dispute over wages following the failure of Nick Clark's Fort George Lumber and Navigation Company, and investigating an accidental death at the Fort George Trading and Timber Company camp on 20 April 1911 entailed his workload.[74] Having completed his paperwork, Gosby submitted his resignation, turned his "office" in the Hotel Northern over to Special Constable Andrew Forrest, and departed by canoe on 25 April.[75]

Gosby's eventual replacement, Constable John MacAulay, continued from where his predecessor left off. Characterizing the local conditions as "unsatisfactory," the new constable felt "at a disadvantage," noting that, while the number of settlers continued to grow, he lacked quarters, a lock-up, proper office supplies, and a place to file letters and forms.[76] As had been the case with Gosby, MacAulay's concerns were both personal and professional. While his monthly pay of $82 in South Fort George represented a raise from the $75 he had earned in Vancouver, accommo-dation of $2 a night consumed more than two-thirds of his salary.[77]

From the community's perspective, of greater import than the BCPP's lack of supplies and facilities was the fact its constable had the authority to grant the Hotel Northern a liquor licence.[78] While authorizing liquor sales might appear a peculiar response to worries about policing alcohol and keeping the peace, for John Daniell of the *Fort George Herald*, the licence reflected the responsibility and civility of local white residents and South Fort George's maturation. Quoting a mid-nineteenth-century temperance pledge and referring to a prominent BC prohibitionist, the editor argued that "there is no chance on earth for Dr. [Daniel] Spencer making a hit hereabouts, so he had better stay away. A well-regulated licensed house is a necessary adjunct to a real live town, inhabited by men who can take a drink and leave it alone."[79] As Lynne Marks has argued, British Columbia's distinctive settlement frontier rested on a well-lubricated mixture of masculinity, British white privilege, and a preference for the social benefits of clubs and fraternal societies rather than Christian churches.[80] Daniell's view aligned with those of Premier Richard McBride, who, as historian Robert Campbell noted, was "indifferent, if not hostile" to any efforts to curb liquor sales or consumption in the province.[81] The editor was arguing that the community and its well-ordered white male residents – the *real* citizens of South Fort George – possessed the means to govern themselves and their consumption of liquor.

Granting the Northern a liquor licence meant that the hotel soon became the epicentre of local alcohol consumption. Predictably, the legalizing of drinking – or, more accurately, of overindulgence – contributed to the ongoing debate as to whether South Fort George needed a jail in addition to that proposed for the former HBC property alongside the government offices. MacAulay lamented the absence of a community lock-up. It was worrisome for a constable whose labours included delivering over-lubricated denizens of the Hotel Northern bar to a cell where they could sleep off the evening's exertions. He retained the hope that a jail and police quarters might be constructed in South Fort George.[82] In this he was disappointed.[83] As the provincial government dithered, the *Fort George Herald* offered the solution that perhaps MacAulay could shoot the prisoners "full of holes" and bury the bodies. A tongue-in-cheek option involved confining prisoners in out-of-doors cells and issuing them with umbrellas.[84] As it turned out, concerns about the hotel being in South Fort George proper while the police office and jail were, potentially, on the other side of the HBC slough proved to be short-lived, because, after midnight on 1 July 1911, the Hotel Northern burned to the ground.[85] As some townspeople battled the early morning flames, others devoted their energies to looting the liquor stock, despite special constables having been appointed to prevent such efforts.[86] Almost immediately, the question was asked whether the Northern's liquor licence could be transferred so that the proprietors might continue sales from a hastily constructed temporary building. The answer was no.[87] Thus, with the hotel's destruction, proprietors Al Johnson and Michael Burns lost their licence, and South Fort George was, once again, officially dry.

The decision to deny the request and the reopening of the process of awarding a new liquor licence triggered alarms in South Fort George. Within weeks of the fire, the Fort George Hotel on George Hammond's townsite circulated a petition in support of its application to operate a licensed facility.[88] Predictably, newspaper editor and South Fort George booster John Daniell opposed the application:

> We do not know what effect this petition will have upon the license question as it applies to the Nechaco [sic] townsite, but the *Herald*'s opinion of the matter is that whilst the size and appointment of the Natural Resource Company's hotel [Hotel Fort George] would warrant this license being issued, no action should be taken by the Attorney General's Department pending the re-building of the Northern Hotel in South Fort George, as it appears to be the intention of the department to restrict the number of licenses to be issued in this section to the narrowest possible margin, and as the department appears to consider all the subdivisions hereabouts as part and parcel of the one town, discrimination will naturally have to be in favor of the most populated area thereof.[89]

Further, if a licence was issued without their input, the Conservative Party supporters in South Fort George would lose advantage and patronage to Fort George. The threat was genuine, and having been denied in the past, the Fort George Hotel's application was reconsidered in the capital.[90]

Absent a licensed facility, the re-emergence of the illegal liquor trade was likely. Indeed, government agent Thomas Herne informed both Victoria and Constable MacAulay of illegal sales in South Fort George. For this, the constable adopted a peculiar explanation. Claiming that, while he was unaware of the alleged breaches, he knew that on one occasion persons had received "a case or two of liquor for their own private use. Am at a loss to know how to deal with such and will await your instructions regarding same."[91] That acquiring liquor for personal consumption remained legal, while unlicensed sales were not, lent the constable's version of events a gloss of plausibility. Nonetheless, his more fulsome report a week later confirmed that he had been wrong-footed by events. He admitted that "things were rather upset here" and acknowledged violations of the provincial Liquor Act. Still, he claimed that the situation was in hand, though his own account suggests otherwise:

> The liquor belonging to Johnson & Burns, the late proprietors of the hotel, has been put under lock and key and the key put in the hands of

a disinterested party whom I know is not selling any. There are several
parties who get a case now and again for their personal use and so far, I
have been unable to find out if they are selling. But if I see anything which
looks suspicious, I will get a special to assist me for a few days as you suggested in your letter. Everything is quiet at present and there is no drunkenness or other lawlessness.

Had MacAulay surrendered the liquor to someone else because he was
unwilling, as a constable, to dole out "an occasional case" of liquor to
those he believed to be social drinkers? Possibly. In the end, he was anxious to learn the identity of the individual who had reported irregularities
in South Fort George.[92] One suspects Reverend C. Melville Wright of the
Methodist church in Fort George, who was then establishing himself as
the bottle's staunch foe. Despite MacAulay's handling of the situation
causing furrowed brows, Acting Superintendent Colin Campbell concluded at month's end that everything in South Fort George was in hand.
Further, thanks to the 1910 Liquor Act, the constable possessed the authority to inspect hotels and provide them with liquor licences based on the
number of adult white men within a mile radius of any hotel applying
for a licence.[93] This amendment brought the incident full circle. Because
the Fort George townsite was thinly settled, its population was insufficient to warrant a licence being issued to the Fort George Hotel. In late
October 1911, the rebuilt and rebranded Northern Hotel secured a new
liquor licence, with the *Herald* happily declaring that the district was no
longer dry.

When the dust finally settled, stipendiary magistrate and acting government agent Thomas Herne wondered if local conditions warranted the
addition of another constable. Specifically, could "an old constable" join
MacAulay? It appeared that "there will be more work than one man can
possibly handle on account of [the] way the two towns are situated being
so far apart and the police headquarters being on the Hudson's Bay Co.
land." Herne hastened to add that the constable was "all right and absolutely trustworthy." He was, however, inexperienced. Probably recalling
MacAulay's actions in the aftermath of the hotel fire, Herne allowed that
he too was also "new to any police work[;] consequently it is sometimes
awkward for both of us."[94] The nudge produced results. MacAulay was
promoted to Hazelton, while Constable Alfred Grundy, having served as
a guard at the British Columbia Penitentiary for fifteen months before
applying to become a constable, and Constable Thomas Higginbottom,
a Boer War veteran, arrived in mid-July to take up local policing.[95] By

then, a temporary jail had been constructed alongside the government buildings on the Hudson's Bay Company land, while plans for permanent facilities remained in draft form. Answering the need to house troublesome toughs among the men employed in the approaching railway construction, "detention sheds" appeared in both Fort George and South Fort George.[96]

Duty Logs and Regulatory Policing

The arrival of new personnel in June 1912 was followed by the introduction, in January 1913, of duty logs, obliging individual constables to provide daily three-line summaries of their activities. These summaries remained a requirement until the end of 1921. A product of Colin Campbell's appointment as BCPP head following F.S. Hussey's retirement, the logs spoke to the new superintendent's "reputation for brisk efficiency" and, through that, for encouraging constables' accountability and succinct record-keeping.[97] While the need to keep logs may have sharpened the constables' work ethic, the records themselves are maddeningly idiosyncratic. Given the absence of standardized descriptions of what duties entailed, the logs defy comparative analysis. For instance, until shuttering South Fort George's red light neighbourhood/segregated district in the third week of February 1917, the police relied on the brothels as hubs for distributing and gathering information, including notifying the women and their customers of stolen goods, circulating descriptions of suspicious characters, and inquiring about missing individuals. These visits also allowed the police to warn-off new working women or underage girls who arrived with the intention of selling sex.[98] As such, the patrols to the brothels potentially accomplished several tasks that were not easily reducible to a brief summary in the duty logs and thus, despite being integral aspects of local policing, the visits were referred to in myriad ways that obscured more than they illuminated.

The result is frustrating. It is likely that, at month's end, the chief constable mined the logs for data and reconciled them with other documents before headquarters received a district tabulation. These daily summaries were several steps removed from the annual crime statistics provided by the BCPP and the dominion government, but they capture a sense of the pace of police work and the flavour of ordinary duty, revealing that constables settled minor disputes, enforced provincial and dominion statutes, and reminded the public that rules existed, even on the white settlement frontier. Most summaries reduced routine tasks to pat descriptions, providing a minimum of detail while confirming that the author had been active. Absent a standard of how to report – beyond the required brevity – the summaries hid as much as they revealed. When assigned desk work, constables wrote of "police duty," "office duty," and "station duty," although the first may have covered community patrols. Office and station duty may have been distinct, with the former referring to bureaucratic labour whereas the latter captured answering public inquiries and guarding prisoners. Still, while one might tabulate the number of times a constable referred to "office duty" or mentioned provincial liquor regulations, the Public Health Act, the provincial Game Act, or the Dominion War Measures Act (even if arrests did not follow), the impressions are indistinct. In the end, the logs provide only a glimpse of the policeman's experiences – the "feel" of duty – rather than a quantifiable measure of the police presence.

References to guarding prisoners illustrate how idiosyncrasies in record keeping provided markedly different versions of duty. They also illuminate the reality of short-term hard-labour sentences. While most constables simply recorded "guard duty," Constable Henry Avison catalogued the prisoners' assigned tasks, such as splitting and stacking firewood, building sidewalks, planting and tending the government garden, cutting grass at the local recreation grounds, restocking the root cellar, shovelling snow, cleaning the office and cells weekly, building fences, putting up or removing storm windows, refreshing the ice house from the Fraser River, setting up the furniture for the Supreme Court assize at Prince George's city hall, washing their own clothes, and, when necessary, burying abandoned dead animals. Judging from Avison's record, hard labour was daily physical work that paused only when the weather rendered it too wet or cold to work.

Appointed as a special constable in March 1916, Avison had been Stanley Park's first ranger, zookeeper, and landscape gardener, a gold miner in the Yukon, a provincial sanitary inspector from mid-June 1910 to 1915 – a role in which he orchestrated South Fort George's battle against typhoid in 1913 – and South Fort George's sanitary inspector.[99] He appeared to be a no-nonsense individual whose enforcement of provincial public health regulations encouraged a by-the-books approach that, when combined with his love of gardening, produced a documented adherence to the seasonal rounds of planting, tending, gathering, and storing produce as a feature of hard-labour sentences. The result was more insightful than that produced by his less-exacting colleagues. However, while it is tempting

Figure 2.1   Constable
Henry Avison (standing),
Deputy Inspector T.W.S.
Parsons, Chief Constable
A. McNeill, circa 1920/21. |
City of Vancouver Archives.

to point to Avison's regime as being representative of what hard labour
meant at South Fort George, the daily logs' idiosyncratic character counsels
caution: it is unclear whether he recorded a routine that was already in
place but had gone unremarked in others' logs, signalled a change by
recording the details of how the prisoners worked off hard labour, or
ushered in a new regime.

These daily accounts offer a panoramic view of ordinary duty. At South
Fort George, the combined references to office or station duty and patrols
in the Georges were, by far, constables' most common duty descriptors.
Specifically, there are more than 3,300 references to "police duty," over
5,300 to "office" or "station duty," and over 9,600 references to "patrolling"
in South Fort George, Fort George, and Prince George from 1913 to 1921.
The descriptor "police duty" retreated after 1913, perhaps because of its
failure to distinguish between office and field work. From 1914 forward,

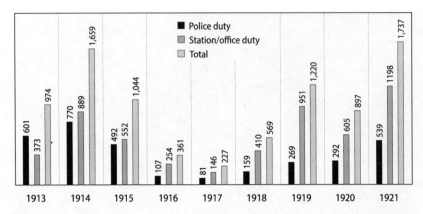

FIGURE 2.2 BCPP duty descriptors, South Fort George, 1913–21. | Compiled from BCA, GR 445.

"office" or "station work" became the most common short-hand summary describing duty in the headquarters at South Fort George. Given variables such as the changing number of men stationed at the South Fort George detachment, alterations in the geographic area covered by that office, the establishment of the Prince George city police in 1915, and constables' idiosyncratic phrasing, figures referencing "duty" and "patrols" are suggestive rather than definitive. Nonetheless, they lend themselves to an unanticipated conclusion about policing in the years straddling the First World War. Despite the Georges' reputation, policing in the northern Interior was generally a sedate affair, in which most of a constable's day was filled with bureaucratic obligations and the performance of a peace-keeper role. The latter suggests the belief that, by being present and visible (even before the advent of uniforms), constables discouraged disorderly and criminal behaviour. Akin to every other community in the province, while occasional eruptions and incidents shattered the relative calm, the Georges were not, in terms of policing challenges, a particularly riotous assignment.

The location of patrols is intriguing. At no point between 1913 and 1921 did the number of patrols of the Hammond townsite at Fort George – overseen by a resident single constable until December 1915 – near those undertaken in South Fort George.[100] Further, by 1914, the Prince George townsite, which at that time was not yet open for occupation, attracted more patrols than did Fort George. Why? South Fort George was the largest community in the district, and it boasted the region's only liquor licence. These factors resulted in constables patrolling in South Fort George more than anywhere else in the region, even if those patrols did not produce an avalanche of arrests and prosecutions.

For the most part, references to patrolling in the Georges drop off sharply after the outbreak of war in August 1914. The exodus of enlisted men combined with the corresponding reduction in the number of constables stationed at South Fort George meant that there were fewer people to police and fewer constables to shoulder the labour. And, while launching the Prince George city police in 1915 theoretically reduced the necessity of patrolling that community, the provincial force nonetheless maintained a presence there, reflecting the vagaries of the city constabulary's ambit. It was, as the occasional meeting between the BCPP chief constable and his counterpart in Prince George attested, a relationship that had to be nurtured.[101] BCPP historian Lynne Stonier-Newman claims that, when the provincial police performed their duties near a community with a local police force, ordinary procedure was to leave prosecutions to the city police. The South Fort George duty logs and the indifferent state of the early city police throw doubt on Stonier-Newman's generalization and suggest that such procedures created their own challenges.[102] According to Acting Chief Constable John Bourne, at 1 a.m. on 20 June 1919, he was informed by city police chief H. Alexander Stewart that a group of Indigenous people were being disorderly in Central Fort George. Bourne and Constable David Long patrolled the townsite but found nothing to warrant their attention. Reflecting on the call out, Bourne concluded that the city police ought to have arrested the intoxicated group in the city, where, he reasoned, the liquor originated. "From my investigations these Indians had been causing trouble and were drunk in the city all night and [there was] no excuse for letting them into [the] Provincial Police district before trying to arrest them."[103] Although relations with the city police had been amicable both for Bourne and his predecessors, the diagnosis of what had occurred on that particular evening was no doubt accurate. Indeed, as will become apparent, Stewart had his own troubles and appreciated the appeal of letting the provincial police deal with the revellers. Although an annoyance to the acting chief constable, the expectation that the BCPP would quell the disturbance said something about the force's success in establishing its authority within the local community as well as the degree to which its presence reflected British Columbia's expanding modern state.

While the duty logs confirm that enforcing provincial liquor laws was a regular obligation in policing the Georges, the data indicate that we must guard against exaggerating the importance of such duties. While

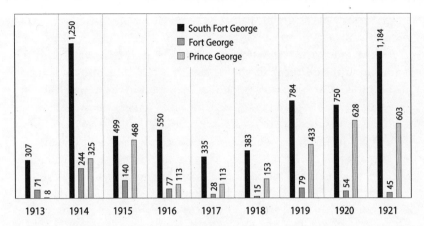

FIGURE 2.3   BCPP patrol references, South Fort George, 1913–21. | Compiled from BCA, GR 445.

the northern Interior of the early twentieth century was undoubtedly a masculine environment that encouraged drinking, and perhaps excessive drinking, the duty logs document that references to policing liquor were a distant third behind office/station/policing duty and patrolling. The most frequent descriptors employed between 1913 and 1921 were police duty (3,300), office and station duty (5,300), and patrolling (9,600), while policing liquor amounted to just under 970 entries. As with patrolling in general, the number of liquor-related duty and patrol references dropped off sharply during the war years, reflecting, as noted above, the departure of men to the armed forces and the reduction of provincial police patrols owing to wartime staff shortages. Yet even if the numbers for the years straddling the war were more typical for the Georges, the year with the greatest total – 1913, with 282 liquor references – trailed, by a considerable distance, station duty and general patrols. While policing liquor and managing those who overindulged undoubtedly involved genuine challenges and coloured the perceptions of the Georges as the tumultuous edge of white settlement, alcohol's *imagined* influence far outstripped its actual effect on the daily work of local constables.

If office duty, patrolling, and policing liquor were the main occupations of constables keeping the peace at South Fort George, what else filled their days? As was undeniably the case elsewhere across the province and the nation, while there were occasional examples of derring-do, the truth was that most "real" policing involved individuals burdened with a tin ear for trouble.[104] Constables policed vice (gambling, the sex trade, illicit drugs), responded to distressed family members' inquiries

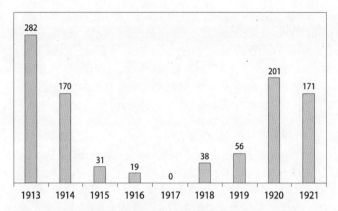

FIGURE 2.4   BCPP patrol and duty references to liquor, South
Fort George, 1913–21. | Compiled from BCA, GR 445.

about missing relatives, investigated alleged criminal wrongdoing, arrested individuals named in warrants, attended preliminary hearings and local court sittings, escorted prisoners to distant Supreme Court assizes or provincial institutions, kept an eye on worrisome labour organizers and activists, provided aid to settlers, pursued alleged enemy aliens and deserters, and, infrequently, investigated serious crimes. The war disrupted these patterns, with enlistments triggering relocations, the closing of South Fort George's segregated district in late February 1917, and the decision to keep the shrinking population of BCPP constables behind the desk at the police office rather than patrolling. Following the introduction of provincial prohibition on 1 October 1917, this low-profile approach ended, although the duty logs indicate that the local detachment did precious little enforcement until the following year.[105] In addition, the force was involved in the orchestration and provision of care during the Spanish influenza pandemic between mid-October 1918 and early 1919. A combination of postwar concerns, the continued expansion of the modern state, the arrival of Supreme Court sittings in Prince George, and emergent ideas about professionalism and policing created novel challenges as the public grew accustomed to the province's growing regulation of everyday life.

An unusual example of the postwar adjustment occurred in the early spring of 1921, when Constable W.R. Henley of Vanderhoof informed Inspector Parsons of a story passed on by A.G. Hamilton from his store at Tachie on Stuart Lake. Two Saik'uz men, Eugene Bull and David Joseph, had confessed to killing a man seven years earlier, in the autumn of 1914.[106] Attempting to elude confinement as an enemy alien, a former

Austrian army officer named Max Pospich (aka Popovich) had ventured north from Kamloops before disappearing into the bush around Trembleur Lake, northwest of Fort St. James and Prince George. Bull and Joseph happened upon the armed Pospich, who immediately opened fire. They responded in kind, killing Pospich. Fearing the consequences of their actions, they dumped the body in the middle of thirty-two-kilometre long Trembleur Lake. Seven years later, Hamilton learned of the story. Following a negotiation facilitated by Father J. Allard OMI from the Catholic mission on Stuart Lake, Bull and Joseph surrendered to Parsons and led the inspector to Middle River, where the shooting had occurred.[107] They then travelled in custody to South Fort George to await word from the attorney general's department.[108] According to W.P. Ogilvie, who was retained on behalf of Indian Affairs to represent the two men, if the prosecution proceeded, the rationale was to bring home the message to the Indigenous community that, regardless of the circumstances, shooting people would not be tolerated.[109] Having received his instructions from Victoria, Magistrate Herne proceeded with the preliminary hearing, with Bull and Joseph held over for trial, a decision that obliged Parsons to drag Trembleur Lake for remains.[110] The trial, convened before Mr. Justice Francis B. Gregory at the Supreme Court assize, began in Prince George on 16 June 1921. After hearing the evidence, which rested entirely on the men's confessions, Gregory assured the assembled audience and the jury that "it was only right that such matters as that occupying them should be cleared up in court before a jury."[111] Commending Parsons for his diligence, the judge indicated to the jury that

> in view of all the circumstances, it would not be necessary for them to leave their seats, and suggested that a verdict of not guilty was the only one which should be brought in [and] turning to the two Indians, who are within the confines of civilization for the first time in their lives, and who had never seen a train until brought in by the police on this charge, he told them that they must not be afraid of the police, who were disposed towards friendly feeling to the Indians. When an unfortunate occurrence of this nature took place, be explained to them, that it was their duty to go at once and notify the police.

The jury acquiesced in the directed verdict, closing what the newspaper described as "one of the most interesting criminal cases in the annals of crime in Northern British Columbia."[112] The *Interior News* of Smithers, in republishing the *Citizen*'s early coverage of the case, offered a distorted, if telling, lesson concerning British Columbia's modern state: "Arm of Law Reaches into Far North to Grab Indians Wanted for Murder in 1914."[113]

Unfortunately, few BCPP annual district reports survive to illustrate the more typical combination of ordinary duty and peacekeeping in the northern Interior. One example covering 1922 confirms the broad nature of police work while also delivering a message identifying who was responsible for local disorder. Two local newspapers covered Inspector Parsons's 1922 report, with the *Citizen*'s account quoting the original at length, while the *Leader* took more liberties. Both included the inspector's comments on the lumber industry, mining, and farming prospects, which were reminders that the police remained an important governmental witness of local development.[114]

The two accounts mentioned the positive relationship between the provincial force, the RCMP, and the city police, with the *Citizen* quoting Parsons's praise of city police chief Ezra Carlow: "At no time has the municipality been so well supervised and I feel quite safe in saying that through his efficiency our own area has been relatively free from crime. In the very nature of things urban, criminals of fixed location exercise an adverse effect upon the surrounding countryside, if successful they find imitators, and by removing the habitual municipal offender, Mr. Carlow has rendered a great public service."[115] The *Leader* offered a slightly different take, with Parsons stating that Carlow had been so efficient that the incidence of crime in the district "has been practically nil." Both noted that provincial constables had patrolled over 186,000 kilometres in the district, which included the Peace River country, inspected sixty-four camps, and attended fourteen inquests. "There were practically no violations of the Narcotic and Drug Act, [with] only nine convictions being secured during the year, and no houses of prostitution were reported. At the spring assize there were no criminal cases, and at the fall sitting one man was acquitted on a murder charge and one sentenced to one year for forgery."[116]

The *Citizen*'s report quoted the inspector as indicating that "Indians gave the police very little trouble during the year" and included specific comments concerning arrests across the region of "Chinese," Indigenous people, and, more than any other group, white men.[117] The newspaper commented that, "three decades ago Kitikshan rituals included the devouring of corpses — today the regenerate sons of those old-time savages either work on sections or drive taxi-cabs," a strikingly odd observation that was offered as evidence of "younger Indians" conforming to their surroundings.[118] The *Leader* also commented with considerable specificity on ethnicity and crime: "Two most serious crimes, attempted murder, and attempted rape, were committed by continental Europeans, and in the city of Prince George nine convictions against foreigners under the Opium and Drug Act and 20 under the Government Liquor Act, show it is the alien who gives more trouble to the police. In proportion to numbers, they are less law-abiding."[119] These conclusions appear to have been unique to the *Leader*.[120] Still, the *Citizen* noted that, in connection with the illegal drug traffic, "Orientals were chiefly concerned, and as a result it is stated that this part of the province has never been more free from drug peddlers or addicts."[121] Given that some observers might have exploited the Bull and Joseph case and the annual report to "prove" that the region was especially disorderly, while adhering to racist constructions of criminality, the newspapers nonetheless offered the impression that the region faced challenges similar to those elsewhere in the province.

PROVINCIAL GAME LAW

Upholding the provincial Game Act and overseeing the provincial Health Act occupied local constables more than any other areas of provincial legislation, with the exception of the liquor regulations. The novelty of wildlife and game regulation was yet another example of how the BCPP facilitated the extension of British Columbia's modernizing state. From the provincial government's perspective, the effort spoke to dual motivations: generating revenue to strengthen the enforcement of hunting and fishing regulations while encouraging conservation policies aimed at reducing what was alleged to be wasteful and destructive behaviour, particularly by Indigenous hunters.[122] Although the obligation of securing a hunting licence already existed, provincial game warden Bryan Williams acknowledged that his department lacked the resources to enforce the requirement.[123] Under those circumstances, introducing a new requirement that all hunters should possess a firearms licence might appear to be counterintuitive, but the rationale was that licences would generate revenue that, in turn, would bolster enforcement and thereby protect the province's wildlife resources. Further, Williams saw tightened enforcement measures as a device to attract European and British game-hunting enthusiasts, who, he argued, would contribute to the province's coffers and to local economies.[124] Incidentally, requiring a firearms licence offered the public some protection from careless hunters carrying or discharging weapons in a dangerous fashion, since they could have their hunting and firearms licences pulled for such behaviour. The amended Game Act of 1913 not only established four categories of hunting licences but also provided constables with a convenient pretext to seize revolvers without having to rely on the Criminal Code.[125] Despite the amended legislation, there was not, in fact, a flurry of activity around local constables dealing with firearms offences. Rather, excepting 1918, with a total of fifty-nine local arms-related references – possibly a product of the BCPP assuming sole responsibility for enforcing the Game Act, the circulation of wartime trophies, or the ongoing targeting of enemy aliens – duty log mentions of concealed weapons or the failure to possess a firearms licence in the South Fort George district averaged fewer than eight instances per year from 1913 to 1921. When compared with overall provincial numbers, there is no reason to conclude that firearms offences in the region, at least as governed by the Game Act, were significant. Once again, the evidence does not sustain the image of the northern Interior as a Canadian or British Columbian version of the mythical Wild West. Therefore, to the degree that the provision in the Game Act offered a convenient device for disarming pistol-toting toughs intent on villainy, constables wielded the authority lightly and did so without undermining the appeal of hunting as an activity entwining masculinity and imperialism as laudable counterweights to the perceived threats of modernity and urban life.[126]

The game law's core intent was managing wildlife as a commodity to benefit the province in the future. This goal unapologetically favoured white recreational hunters over those individuals whose lives and community economy relied on wildlife. Consequently, the enhanced game regulations aggravated an already strained relationship with Indigenous peoples, who, thanks to the rising popularity of recreational hunting and fishing, faced an increasingly competitive environment for foodstuffs. In 1905, almost five years *before* the first significant influx of white settlers to the northern Interior, Indigenous leaders from Stuart Lake, Stoney Creek, and Fraser Lake raised the alarm that provincial game regulations threatened local peoples with starvation.[127] The response to such claims varied. Reporting on the environment leading to the formation of the Provincial Game Department, game warden Williams alluded to Indigenous hunters as being among the worst despoilers of provincial wildlife and claimed that, if the situation remained unaddressed, British Columbia would lose out on attracting wealthy foreign big-game hunters. In supporting these claims by quoting directly from the correspondence that he had received, Williams distanced himself from an openly racist argument. Indeed, he advocated for a six-year moratorium on beaver trapping in northern British

Columbia to allow stocks to recover, while suggesting that an Order in Council excepting Indigenous trapping would counter local destitution.[128] His empathy was short-lived. A page later, he mounted a withering attack on the Indigenous population, which, he claimed, was slaughtering wildlife: "it is certainly true that some white men are doing their best to kill the game off, but the number killed by them is small compared with what the Indian kill."[129] Allegedly, Indigenous camps near Lillooet were "veritable Golgothas" – an execution hill – where the locals were supposedly too lazy and indifferent to track down the game that had been wounded but not killed. His was a privileged white man's lament:

> Surely the time has come when the Indians can make a living as well as Chinese, Japanese, or even the white man. They have the best of the land and do not pay any taxes. What will they do when the game is all gone, as it soon must be, at the present rate of slaughter[?] ... They had better make up their minds to make a living in the same manner as anybody else, and hunt only in the open season, as otherwise there will soon be no game for them to hunt at all.[130]

Although Williams shied away from similar racist assertions in subsequent reports, he held to the view that Indigenous hunting in the Interior would remain an enforcement challenge until Indigenous people began to make a living "by the sweat of his brow just as well as anyone else."[131]

Legislative changes in April 1918 ushered in a new regime of game law enforcement by BCPP constables. Not only was the provincial Game Conservation Board created and the Game Department amalgamated with the BCPP, but the superintendent of police became the ex officio provincial game warden and all constables were designated as game officers.[132] Williams opposed the changes for replacing knowledgeable deputies with police constables, whom he depicted as neither suited nor trained for the work.[133] His concerns did not win the day, and he soon found himself surplus to requirements. While specific constables may have lacked the woodman's skills or ability on horseback, the increase in local duty log entries referring to the Game Act – jumping from 92 in 1918 to 200 in 1919, 158 in 1920, and 301 in 1921 – suggests that the men stationed in the South Fort George district did not skimp on enforcement.[134] For example, Deputy Inspector T.W.S. Parsons, Constable Carl Johnson, and dog-sled wrangler Morris Quaw mounted a mid-February 1919 patrol through the outrageous snow and devilish cold of the Fort George game reserve. A second patrol followed weeks later. Elsewhere, while Constable W.R. Henley of Vanderhoof had to warn Stoney Creek Reserve residents in February 1918 not to take more deer than allowed by law, he also stressed that rounding up deer in the deep snow was also contrary to the law. Such concerns with Indigenous hunting were a rarity. In fact, the constable clarified that, while he had received hearsay reports that such methods had precipitated a "slaughter," investigation failed to produce any leads or reliable evidence.[135] And while the experiment of appointing Constable Reginald Johnson to patrol within the Fort George game reserve lasted for only two months in late 1919, the effort demonstrated that the BCPP were keen to enforce the Game Act.[136]

The force's responsibility for the Game Act also provided further evidence of an increasingly prominent trend within the provincial government: reliance on statistical analysis to demonstrate efficiency. While the interpretation of data had long played a role in both the BCPP's and Game Department's annual reports, following the Great War and the emergence of the ethos of professionalism and expertise in the modernization of governance, the use of statistics breaking down revenue generation per district, the number of firearms and hunting licences, salaries juxtaposed with revenue, and yearly accounts of prosecutions and fines in game law enforcement mirrored police data on driver's licences, staffing, crime enforcement, and patrolling, and, in time, on the number of automobiles in the province. The inference was plain: data enabled efficiency and effectiveness, and therefore such information was a valuable tool in the constant struggle to secure budgetary increases.

In addition to providing evidence of constables enforcing the game law, the view on the ground suggested that some local officials recognized that, regardless of what had been intended, the legislation had created hardship for Indigenous people. For Deputy Inspector Parsons, who had started his career with the BCPP in northeastern British Columbia's Peace region before rising through the ranks, the imposition of the game law on the country's "original inhabitants" was problematic. The Indigenous peoples "nourish the belief that all game is theirs and every white man's trapline [is] an encroachment on vested rights."[137] A case in point occurred in the aftermath of the Game Regulations introduced in late June 1921.[138] Specifically problematic was the decision to close the beaver-trapping season in northern British Columbia, to allow the animal population to recover from over-trapping, while simultaneously permitting Indigenous trappers to sell beaver skins to licensed fur dealers at public auction. When called on to defend the measure, the Conservation Board argued that the arrangement would undercut unscrupulous fur buyers who had been encouraging Indigenous trappers to continually harvest beaver, regardless of legitimate needs.[139] In practice, the policy had the opposite effect. As detailed in an editorial in the Smithers *Interior News,* the exemption for Indigenous trappers had fashioned a system of fur bootlegging. Licensed fur buyers were skimming fur profits from the region through Indigenous trappers, without bothering with auctions. The illegal furs were subsequently marketed in Alberta or Alaska. This practice

> is a field day for the outlaw trader who will take a chance, with the result that the government is deprived of the royalties, the Indian trapper gets filled up with bad booze, while the bootlegging trader waxes fat ... The Indian is the natural source to seek in an effort to protect or increase beaver, and were the trapping of beaver left with the natives they would see to it that in their own particular grounds there was no such thing as depletion of beaver. They know the number of beaver in their hunting preserve infinitely better than any government official and they take no more than will guarantee replenishment, but with the entry of transient whites into the trapping game, who kill without thought of tomorrow, the Indian has no incentive to do other than follow a similar course. Only by putting trapping of beaver exclusively in the hands of the Indians will the government ever get results from an endeavor to protect beaver.[140]

This editorial, including its untroubled racism, captured a regional interpretation of the legislation. Local MLA H.G. Perry harboured additional concerns after learning of the illegal trade in Alberta and Alaska. The suspected dealers were several individuals who had acquired licences from the head of the Game Conservation Board, Dr. A.R. Baker.[141] Confronted with swirling allegations that he had already resigned or was about to step down because of the charges, Baker dismissed the rumours and indicated that the matter had been taken up by local officials in the northern Interior as well as those in the Omineca and Peace districts.[142]

Despite these investigations, a provincial royal commission began in November to inquire into allegations concerning Baker's administration of the Game Act and, specifically, the process whereby beaver pelts were obtained from Indigenous trappers.[143] Following sworn testimonies, Commissioner H.C. Shaw concluded that, while Baker had committed some "injudicious" personal acts, he had not broken the law. When it came to Baker's oversight of the Game Conservation Board and the acquisition of pelts from Indigenous trappers, the commission opined that "there seems to have been no definite system" that was exploited by Baker's apparent favoritism toward certain fur buyers. Shaw concluded that, "while there is no evidence of any profit or gain to Dr. Baker, there was absolutely no check on the buyers except their own honesty, which, in the case of some, was very questionable, and there is today no means of ascertaining how many of the skins in the possession of the Indians reached the Game Board or how much the trader actually paid to the Indians." The finding was damning: that the plan adopted by the Game Conservation Board

> was a bad one as it allowed a dishonest man full opportunity to be dishonest; that there was no means of checking them; that it encouraged the Indians and others for this very reason to kill beaver and sell the pelts; that it made unfair discrimination and perhaps encouraged the Indian to lose respect for the law, all of which ... might have been avoided by having the Indians deal only with Government officials.[144]

Less than a week later and after being reinstalled as the Game Conservation Board chair, Baker resigned, despite having been cleared of criminal wrongdoing.[145]

PUBLIC HEALTH

Public health and sanitation were the final areas of provincial legislation that loomed large in the BCPP's peacekeeping efforts. For most of the period between 1909 and 1925, these responsibilities included camp inspections to ensure that outhouses and refuse pits were located at a safe distance from kitchens and quarters. Constables also checked that local eateries, butchers, and livery stables adhered to cleanliness standards and that, when ordered by a local physician, homes and businesses were placarded to prevent outbreaks of infectious diseases. Beyond the occasional grumble, there was little evidence of resistance to such efforts, which locals tended to view as reasonable restrictions imposed by the provincial government in aid of community well-being. Unsurprisingly, the Spanish influenza pandemic, which raged in the area from October 1918 to January 1919, represented an entirely different challenge, one that spurred on Deputy Inspector T.W.S. Parsons as if he bore personal responsibility for ensuring that the Georges weathered the outbreak.

News of influenza in Naples, Italy, and Montreal first appeared in the *Prince George Citizen* on 27 September 1918. Two weeks later, as reports of the pandemic in central and Atlantic Canada appeared, the provincial secretary briefed Parsons on what to expect.[146] Parsons then met with Prince George mayor Harry G. Perry and local physicians before investigating rumours of seven cases in South Fort George in addition to concerns at Lucerne, near the Alberta border. The *Citizen* of 15 October denied the presence of local cases, while an editorial assured readers that "provincial and civic authorities have done and are doing everything in their power to prevent the spread of the influenza plague." The newspaper was whistling past the graveyard with its claim that the "high point of the epidemic" had passed and that "there is no particular ground for serious apprehension if reasonable precautions are taken."[147] Through much of late October, the *Citizen* held the line, suggesting that the influenza was not particularly grave and inferring that the northern Interior could be spared the worst. Parsons's labours demonstrated otherwise.

After securing the Connaught Hotel as a temporary hospital, the deputy inspector began placing patients in beds before contacting dominion police constable W.F. Manson to take charge of four Indigenous people who had arrived from Aleza Lake.[148] Parsons also posted a notice in the *Citizen* banning public meetings, secured fifty-two blankets from the Northern Hotel for $8, collected additional sick people and delivered them to available beds, and orchestrated volunteer assistance.[149] Schools, theatres, and all public meeting places were closed. He rented the Union Rooms for $40 per month to serve as another temporary hospital, dispatched Acting Chief John Bourne to Aleza Lake on 22 October with medication, located more helpers, and paused to note the first death of a patient at the Connaught hospital. Bourne returned a day later, reporting that there were twenty-seven sick people at Aleza Lake. Both Hutton and Aleza Lake emerged as hot spots.[150] To the west, Constable Henley of Vanderhoof, who, on 17 October, had warned the Indigenous population to stay away from the community owing to influenza, ordered the local schools to close. Soon, he too was stricken. He unsuccessfully attempted a return to duty on 28 October and had to return to his sickbed.[151] Before the pandemic subsided, most constables stationed in the South Fort George detachment spent time on the sick list. Back in Prince George, Parsons met each train to gather sick passengers and shuttle them to the hospital.

Manson indicated in early November that eight people at Stoney Creek had died and "that practically every native resident of the village is down with the disease."[152] A week later, readers of the *Citizen* learned that the Lheidli T'enneh community had lost Chief Louis Stanislaus, who had played a central part in the surrender of Fort George Indian Reserve

No. 1, and that his fellow chief, Joseph Quah, was mourning the loss of both a daughter and a son.[153] While the newspaper insisted that the threat was retreating, deaths mounted. On 12 November, the paper reported that, in the United States, the death toll from influenza had surpassed that nation's Great War losses.[154] By mid-month, forty-two people had died at Stoney Creek, forty-five at Anyox, sixty-seven in Prince Rupert, and forty-six in Prince George, although the newspaper did not specify if the latter included Indigenous deaths.[155] Nonetheless, it is certain that the toll on Indigenous peoples was out of proportion: the *Citizen* reported that, in the province's southwest corner alone, there had been 714 fatalities among Indigenous peoples.[156] Indian Agent W.J. Allan later indicated that 154 Indigenous people, out of a district population of 1,400, had died.[157]

By mid-November, the crest had passed, and the Union Rooms were cleared of its last patients. The Connaught Hotel continued as the community's second hospital, with the *Citizen* acknowledging that, while Parsons's and Dr. David B. Lazier's labours had lessened, they were "by no means over."[158] Three days later, the ban on public meetings was lifted, and schools and churches were reopened.[159] Although duty logs revealed that outbreaks continued into the spring of 1919, by mid-January the worst had passed. According to the police, the final tally showed that approximately 1,800 people between Lucerne in the east and Kitselas in the west had been ill, with 220 known deaths. Given Allan's report on the number of deaths in the Indigenous community, First Nations people accounted for 70 percent of regional fatalities.[160] Parsons maintained a frenetic pace throughout, despite being sickened by the serum injection he received in mid-November. He reported that, between 22 and 31 December, he was "unfit for service," yet he remained on duty every day.[161] His had been a compelling demonstration of peacekeeping, consistent with the expectation that, as an arm of a modernizing provincial government, the police were obliged to act in the public interest. The provincial police and, through them, the state oversaw all efforts during the epidemic, even if medical personnel lacked an effective treatment beyond bed rest, nourishment, hydration, and fever management.[162]

ORDINARY DUTY

Parsons's effort in responding to the Spanish influenza pandemic, constables' daily patrols and regulatory policing, their enforcement of the

Game Act and myriad other small decisions and actions comprised ordinary duty and keeping the peace. Traced through daily duty logs, correspondence between local chief constables and headquarters in Victoria, and reports in local newspapers, where crime and policing often made good copy, these labours during the years straddling the Great War glimpsed both the past and the future. Reflected in the details of the white settlement frontier, the bureaucratic tedium of filed reports and licences issued, the obligations and benefits of the expanding modern state, and the alarm of midnight blazes and missing persons, the constable's lot touched on almost every aspect of life lived in the Georges. Securing a firearms licence, receiving orders to clean up a business or residential lot in South Fort George, or having a constable patiently explain that one's boozy enthusiasms were apt to result in spending the remainder of the evening in the lock-up all became common experiences, as residents grew accustomed to the BCPP as an arm of the modernizing state. There is little to suggest that residents felt aggrieved by such impositions – if they did, most limited their complaints to grumbles. There were few examples of residents actively resisting the police. Hubris, after all, had a price.

Ordinary duty went a great distance in normalizing the police presence and, excepting contrary individuals who believed it was their "right" to do as they pleased and those who were oblivious to the potential for trouble, most residents found little to fault in the BCPP's regulatory reach. Such acceptance was not inconsequential. The combination of it ushering in the modern state and its performance of what the public believed was "real" police work went a great distance toward legitimizing the BCPP. A similar effect had been true a generation earlier when the North-West Mounted Police marshalled a litany of services on the Prairies after the early 1870s and again in the Yukon during the turn-of-the-century gold rush.[163] Here we are reminded that police forces actively fashion their own public image. For in performing these roles the police defined elements of what the public might expect from the modern state in British Columbia. After all, for many citizens, the provincial constable was the primary point of contact with the government.[164] At the same time, while the duty logs revealed that most of the constable's day was taken up with the business of the modernizing state, law enforcement remained symbolically and practically important "to show that order and discipline were alive, were real – and to show this both to those who made the rules and those who broke them."[165] During these years, such assertions were rarely countered in the northern Interior, and the provincial constabulary had little reason to wonder if its collective authority was going to be questioned.

Indeed, the postwar years witnessed a re-casting of sorts for the BCPP for as much as the faith in the incorruptibility of the force and its British, Christian, male, white, aspirant middle-class self-identity remained, the early 1920s saw the issuance of uniforms, the introduction of new regulations, the institution of a province-wide communication system, and the production of a Constables' Manual that all spoke of an increasingly modern police culture.[166] The regulations articulated broad themes centred on organization, general instructions, administrative functions, and roles of both senior officers and detectives. At the same time, the Constables' Manual set out duties and enumerated the intricacies of criminal investigation for suspected arson, assault causing bodily harm, carnal knowledge, concealment of birth and child murder, fraud and false pretenses, and murder, among other offences. Constables were tutored in ascertaining facts, motives, and proof, as well as in the elements distinguishing, for example, assault, assault causing bodily harm, and domestic assault. The manual tacitly acknowledged that the older reliance on on-the-job training was insufficient for modern communities. In the new manual, the traditional makings of a constable armed with common sense and doggedness collided with a "modern" emphasis on methodology and the schooled distinctions between facts, evidence, and proof. True, the romanticized idea of the steady constable continued as an ingredient of the popularly imagined police, but the reforms of the early 1920s meant that, as the force looked to the future, it did so armed with a police culture anchored in professional policing approaches and discipline. That the BCPP annual report for 1924 lamented "the want of a department dealing exclusively with criminal investigation" underlined the new priorities.[167] The future was going to be about solving crimes. The age of the police detective was about to dawn.[168]

3

City Governance and
the Prince George City Police

Speaking to the inaugural Fort George City Council meeting on 22 May 1915 – the community had yet to officially change its name to Prince George – newly elected mayor W.G. Gillett raised the matter of creating a city police force.[1] The appeal was simple. Along with a city police magistrate, a city force would generate revenue through fines for bylaw infractions. Further, constables could shoulder "other" duties and save taxpayers the cost of an extensive city payroll.[2] Here was local governance on the cheap. This ad hoc spirit was evident in the city's Water, Light and Power Committee's suggestion that the fire chief could also act as the night policeman.[3] Having turned the matter over, and with Councillor E.H. Livingstone suggesting that "it would be better to take a little time to consider these matters," the discussion ended without a vote.[4] Perhaps local politicians thought it prudent to await the appointment of the city police commission. Nonetheless, a week later, Chief Constable William Dunwoody of the South Fort George detachment of the British Columbia Provincial Police (BCPP), who had just returned from a leave of absence during which he had successfully sought a bride in Ireland, met with Gillett to discuss arrangements "for the city to take charge of police work in the city."[5] True to Gillett's bullying manner, a city force would be established regardless of council's hesitancy.

The following decade revealed that city fathers were ambivalent about city constables policing the public. This hesitancy revealed a quandary. Did self-identified "respectable" residents – those invested in the community's long-term success – "need" policing by the BCPP *and* a municipal force?

FIGURE 3.1   Mayor W.G. Gillett, circa 1914. |
S.J. Clarke Publishing Co.

Did these residents think that *they* ought to be policed? Should their tax dollars be spent on city constables enforcing bylaws while the provincial force was on hand to police disreputable people and non-preferred immigrants? Answering these questions was complicated by a provincially regulated regime of yearly municipal elections, which produced an annual churn of mayors, councillors, and police commissioners, whose understanding of local policing was, on occasion, found wanting.

Moreover, when the city constabulary drew the attention of the mayor and council, it often appeared that self-serving, if not mercenary, thinking guided the discussions. Indeed, elected officials who thought of police constables as fetchers and fixers were all too common. Mayor Gillett's two terms in office (1915–16) were fractious affairs highlighted by ongoing budgetary challenges and other controversies. While two years in the mayor's chair by his successor, Harry Perry, established a measure of calm, a wave of Social Gospel rhetoric more commonly found on the Canadian Prairies latched onto issues of local sanitation and worries about vice within city limits, which paralleled sustained efforts to unseat the chief of the city police, James Dolan. Reform zeal reached a pinnacle with the introduction of provincial prohibition on 1 October 1917, and the city police force, hobbled by insufficient resources, struggled to enforce a poorly conceived and locally unpopular law.

Worse still and viewed from a century's distance, the antics of the years between the municipal election of 1919 and the decision in 1925 to abandon Prince George's city police almost defy belief. Beginning with the election of former city clerk Hiram Carney as mayor in January 1919 and closing with Dr. R.W. Alward's two years in office, local voters witnessed incompetence, corruption, the criminal prosecution of two prominent city employees, two riots, seven different police chiefs, the dismissal and rehiring of the entire city police force, persistent troubles centred on enforcing provincial liquor law, and recurring scandals over prostitution. Challenges managing the police were constant, and they revealed some hard truths about the ability of the community's privileged white men to fashion a competently governed and well-ordered city. Over-matched local leaders and self-interested commentators retreated to finger-pointing and evading responsibility.

CITY GOVERNANCE AND THE POLICE COMMISSION

The Municipal Clauses Act, the Municipal Elections Act, and the Incorporation of Municipalities Act, which were all passed by the provincial legislature in 1896, governed the form and function of city government in British Columbia until after the First World War.[6] The first (and by far the lengthiest) of the three acts set out the framework, terms of office, and limits of local governmental authority; the second detailed who could run for local office, voting rights, and the timing of the yearly election for mayor and councillors; and the third established the nuts and bolts of incorporating towns, cities, and municipalities. The Municipal Clauses Act also provided for the appointment of local police magistrates and the creation of local boards of police commissioners, which, initially, were populated by the mayor, the police magistrate, and an individual appointed by the lieutenant-governor in council.[7] Police board membership remained contentious, as local governments pushed back against a provincially named individual interceding in local governance. An 1899 amendment provided for the mayor and two persons nominated by the lieutenant-governor in council to form local police commissions, with the proviso that one commissioner had to be an elected member of the city council.

The change shifted the balance of power on police commissions to the municipalities, since two individuals were locally elected and represented a quorum.[8] By 1917, local voters acquired full control over police commissions with the passage of the Act to Amend the "Municipal Act," providing for board membership to be wholly determined by local elections while also extending the term of office to two years.[9] The longer term theoretically provided a greater measure of continuity in the oversight of the city police, although mayors and councillors, who were not elected solely as police commissioners, remained subject to yearly elections, which reinforced local government's instability.

The evidence from city council elections between 1915 and 1925 demonstrates the situation. Over the course of the city's first decade, six men held the mayor's office while thirty-nine different men were elected as councillors. Only Harry G. Perry served more than two mayoralty terms. A.M. Patterson was a five-term councillor during this period while Barney Keegan also served five terms; W.G.D. Harper, T.M. Watson, and F.D. Taylor all served four. Council was slightly less stable than the mayoralty: 59 percent of the time, new councillors were elected to office, while, for the mayoralty, the victor was new to the position 54.5 percent of the time. The mayor was automatically on the police board, and that office thus lent the board some sense of continuity. But, over the years, 78.5 percent of the time at least one new man took up responsibilities for overseeing city police. Exceptionally, T.M. Watson – an individual to whom we will

TABLE 3.1   Prince George City Council, 1915–25

Year	Mayor	Councillors
1915	Gillett	Eagel, Ellis, Lambert, Ruggles, Livingstone, Parks
1916	Gillett	Eagel, Armstrong, James, Lewis, Watson, Harper
1917	Perry	Brynolson, Armstrong, Cluff, Keegan, Watson, Harper
1918	Perry	Kerr, Porter, Campbell, Keegan, Watson, Harper
1919	Carney	Wilson, Porter, Campbell, Keegan, Watson, Harper
1920	Perry	Wilson, Baird, Wimbles, Keegan, Livingstone, McMillan
1921	Wilson	McKay, Patterson, Wimbles, Keegan, Feren, McMillan
1922	Johnson	Alward, Patterson, Taylor, McKay, Bunton, McLean
1923	Johnson	Ogilvie, Patterson, Taylor, Saunders, Lockyer, McLean
1924	Alward	Opie, Patterson, Taylor, Guest, Fraser, Lambert
1925	Alward	Opie, Patterson, Taylor, Guest, Fraser, Lambert

Source: F.E. Runnalls, *A History of Prince George* (Vancouver: Wrigley, 1945), Appendix A.

return – maintained a presence on the police board for a total of four years. Ultimately, then, despite its two-year term, representation on the police commission was *less* stable than that on city council.

Excepting Perry, who served three terms as mayor (1917, 1918, and 1920) before representing the riding in the provincial legislature (1920–28 and 1933–45), and Patterson, who was a six-term councillor (1921–26) before being mayor for seventeen years (1927–44), none of these representatives were career politicians. For most, council responsibilities likely lay on the desk corner while the office holder ran a small business or worked with larger concerns linked to railways or regional resource exploitation. Consequently, when presented with the challenges of discussing the local police force, the first response of both councillors and commissioners was invariably to inquire about what had been done in the past before considering new initiatives. Therefore, and despite the commission's responsibility for overseeing the city force, the inclination to think of a city constable as shouldering a broad assortment of municipal functions (in addition to those imagined to be "policing" duties) provided commissioners with absolution for their own inept administration of public affairs. Combined with the structural instability created by yearly municipal elections, such timidity from commissioners provided a wobbly foundation for Prince George's experiment with city policing.

Predictably, both the provincial franchise and local sentiment all but guaranteed that the appointed, and then the elected, representative on the police commission mirrored privileged white residents' expectations about who was best suited for public office. The Municipal Elections Act provided that "any person being a British subject of the full age of twenty-one years, and a freeholder, homesteader, or pre-emptor within the boundaries of the municipality, and who has resided within the boundaries

TABLE 3.2   Prince George police commissioners, 1915–25

Year	Commission members	Year	Commission members
1915	Gillett (mayor), Eagel, McLaughlin	1920	Perry, McInnis, Watson
		1921	Wilson, McInnis, Sibley
1916	Gillett, McLaughlin, Watson	1922	Johnson, Opie, Sibley
1917	Perry, Blair, Harper	1923	Johnson, Opie, Rush
1918	Perry, Campbell, Watson	1924	Alward, Garvey, J.D. MacLeod
1919	Carney, Fisher, Watson	1925	Alward, J.D. MacLeod, R.W. MacLeod

Source: F.E. Runnalls, *A History of Prince George* (Vancouver: Wrigley, 1945), Appendix A.

of such municipality for one year immediately preceding the date of the letters patent incorporating the municipality, shall be entitled to vote at the first municipal election."[10] Following the inaugural vote that obliged eligible voters to have been a local resident for at least a year, anyone, male or female, who was registered as a ratepayer, who was a British subject, twenty-one years of age, who had paid their municipal rates and taxes (not including the water rate), and who had been resident for one year, was eligible to participate. Exceptions included "Chinese, Japanese, or Indians."[11] Although ingrained racism and economic inequities ensured that such instances were unlikely, these qualifications theoretically enfranchised Black and South East Asian men and women. Unsurprisingly, contemporary realities meant that those who ran for local public office and those who voted to shape local government were, overwhelmingly, Anglo-Celtic, white, male, and property owners.[12] They held and exercised local power, and any failure to exert the political will to quell worries about local disorder, and any consequences for community reputation, would be theirs.

Despite council's inconclusive discussions in May 1915 concerning a city police force, in late June Charles B. Daniell (father of newspaper man John Daniell) was named the city's first police magistrate, and local lumber businessman George E. McLaughlin, Councillor E.A. Engel, and Mayor Gillett constituted the first police board. By that point, creation of a city police force was all but certain.[13] In early July, the *Prince George Post* reported that eighteen applications had been received for the position of police chief and that deliberations on who would fill that position awaited Gillett's return from city business on the coast.[14] BCPP chief constable Dunwoody noted in his duty log on 9 July that the mayor had indicated that the force would be established that evening.[15] The mayor's plans were delayed by fireworks over the question of whether a temporary city hall should be built or if accommodations might be rented. Having scouted prospective buildings with sufficient accommodations for councillors' offices, the mayor's office, and council chambers, and in light of potential construction costs, Gillett concluded that Irene Jordan's former brothel – originally built on the western edge of Fort George, padlocked by Dunwoody on his first day of duty, and later moved to Third Avenue on the Prince George townsite – was the best option. The rent would be $30 a month. Councillor F.M. Ruggles made the motion in support of the plan, and F.A. Ellis seconded. Once they recovered from their collective shock at the proposition, Councillors J.B. Lambert, H.E. Parks, and E.H. Livingstone erupted. Livingstone protested that the idea was an affront to Prince George citizens who had voted for the mayor and council on a platform of running "a clean city." It was outrageous that, in one of city government's first actions, Jordan, a brothel keeper, was effectively put on the city payroll.[16] The claim was in error for, as council minutes noted, local businessman S.H. Senkpiel, and not Jordan, was renting out the building.[17] Echoing divisions that were already apparent on council over the Grand Trunk Pacific (GTP) Railway station site – a dispute in which Gillett threatened to resign and withdraw the $15,000 personal loan he had arranged to float city government – the mayor rebuked Livingstone and demanded an apology for casting aspersions on the council.[18] It is uncertain if Livingstone retreated.

Once the mayor's deciding vote pushed through the city hall question, local newspapers waded into the fray. The *Prince George Herald* detailed the dispute before summarizing the brothel's brief career and commented on how the "house of many chambers" might be renovated. The newspaper slyly added that patrons could walk right in without using the electric buzzer system to summon a preferred councillor.[19] A day later, the combative John Daniell, who had already dismissed the suggestion of renting the former brothel as "amusingly impossible," reported surprise that the "council at last night's meeting choose the ex-bawdy house for the municipal headquarters." Daniell argued that, despite the modest rent, the building "should not have been considered at any figure." He then wondered if his father's police court would be allotted space in the new city hall. If it did, "and ghosts walk, then it is a merciful thought that the Goddess of Justice is blind."[20]

The pearl clutching was nonsense. Jordan's brothel had been shut down on the day it first opened, and it was unlikely that it had seen any customers. There were neither ghostly women in red stalking the boudoirs nor had there been sounds of nighttime revelry to quell. Reminiscent of the earlier newspaper war between South Fort George and Fort George, the manufactured controversy provided fodder for the three struggling weekly newspapers to lampoon each other, criticize Gillett, and claim the moral high ground in an appeal to right-minded residents.[21] A less contrived response to housing city government might recognize that the suppression of bond capital one year into the First World War had undermined the city's fiscal viability, and that, with little tax and licensing revenue flowing into municipal coffers, straitened budgets were the order of the day. Nonetheless, local businesses and residents expected potholes to be filled, roads graded, electrical services established, a dependable fire service for the business section maintained, reliable water wells drilled and kept up, and a recreation ground built.[22] The wish list trailed on. Simply put, the city's perilous financial situation meant that, despite the finger pointing on council and the press histrionics, paying inexpensive rent for a building that could be adapted to serve as city hall was a sensible proposition.

Having settled the city hall question, Gillett and the other police commissioners reported to council that R.P. Bosworth, with a background in policing in Derby, England, five years on the local force in Regina, and a stint as a special policeman for the GTP, had agreed to become Prince George's inaugural police chief.[23] While Bosworth's efforts in Derby had attracted a handful of positive news stories, his record in Regina was worrying.[24] The prospective chief had been one of two sergeants implicated in attempting to blackmail a city constable who had allegedly beaten and possibly robbed a local labourer. The incident had led to Bosworth's dismissal from the Regina force.[25] Three months later, he was again in the spotlight, when the police commission refused to swear in Bosworth and several other former policemen as special constables for duty during races at the Regina Turf Club.[26] It was shortly after this setback that he was offered the post of Prince George's police chief. Perhaps rationalized as a decision necessitated by the outflow of men answering the call to military duty, hiring the disgraced former sergeant reflected needs-must thinking.[27] The morning following his appointment, Bosworth was visited by BCPP chief constable W.R. Dunwoody, who handed over the city police cells and "two sets of spare equipment," to be returned once the city's own police equipment arrived. Four days later, the two men met once again, to discuss plans for dealing with the district's alien enemies.[28] After that, Bosworth all but disappeared from local newspaper reporting for the next eighteen months. Exceptions were the observation that he and Constable E.B London, the fire chief, were "keeping the Peace effectively"; the report that Bosworth's wife and family had escaped death on 6 September 1915, when rescued from the torpedoed Allan liner the *Hesperian;* and an account of the chief's appearance as he strode in his new uniform in the Fall Fair parade.[29]

Despite the hiring, Prince George's city council minutes and bylaws reveal that the council possessed only a vague notion of the role that the chief might play. There was but one city bylaw – Bylaw No. 4, from June 1915 – that referred to his enforcement duties, and it concerned the authority to compel property owners to clear the snow from sidewalks before 11 a.m. after a snowfall.[30] Subsequent discussions reflected an ad hoc approach: he was to undertake sanitation inspections, carry out the census, ensure that local club constitutions were followed, and supervise stalls and sideshows during the local agricultural exhibition. That Bosworth was not hard pressed can be inferred from newspaper reports that a former provincial constable, Harold "Red" Gaunitz, would be acting police chief while the chief was on holiday. The announcement drew a quip from the *Post* that "the lawless element of the local population (if there is such a class) is hereby warned to be very careful about starting anything when Chief Bosworth leaves on his hunting trip. Red Gaunitz who will officiate in the Chief's absence, is some husky."[31] The *Post* also promised that, "if there are any race riots, affrays, or desperate deeds pulled off whilst 'Red' Gaunitz is officiating, someone is going to get bruised, mangled, or torn, and it will not be 'Red.'"[32] While Gaunitz could hold his own in a ruckus, the imagined possibilities of a crime wave or race riots were slight. One wonders if the comments contained a veiled scepticism about the necessity of a city police force, especially since the BCPP remained close at hand. Had Bosworth's low profile reflected his objections to the role of dogsbody for city government? We are left to speculate, given an unfortunate gap in the record. Absent local newspaper accounts – some papers closed, while there is a gap in the extant copies of others – and with the selectivity of council minutes, there is a fourteen-week near silence in reporting between the end of January and mid-May 1916.[33]

The close of Gillett's second and last term as mayor and the election of merchant Harry G. Perry in January 1917 on a platform of economy and "clean city government" signalled a shift in the tenor of local affairs.[34] Coloured by a Social Gospel reform ethos more common on the Prairies, Perry's successful candidacy suggested that Gillett's conflict-prone methods had alienated local voters who were influenced by the desire to refashion Canadian society and had spurred on local conversations about improving the city's reputation. As a headline about Reverend C.H. Daly's call from the Knox Presbyterian pulpit declared, it was time to "Let Us Clean-up the Georges."[35] A month later, Daly repeated his call to action. Along with Reverend W.M. Scott, he informed the police commission "that vice of various descriptions was prevalent" in Prince George, including the continued operation of at least one brothel within city limits.[36] Accordingly, the police commission directed Chief Dolan to notify the unnamed madam that she was to leave town by 13 March.[37] At the same time, the arrival of slot machines in local establishments captured attention and moved council to impose a $20 per year fee for every machine.[38] Daly and Scott thought the policy ill advised, demanding that the chief of police enforce the law against all games of chance within the city's boundaries.[39] The mayor offered the deft assurance that the chief of police had been instructed to stop dice games, in the hope that the city would be free of that form of gambling.[40] The licensing of slot machines sat poorly with some councillors, and, when the subject rose again in mid-March, Acting Mayor T.M. Watson argued that the collection of such a fee was wrong, that the money already gathered should be returned, and that the machines should be ordered out of the city. With city councillors likely aware that such a move meant that the slot machines would relocate to South Fort George, the subsequent discussion proved inconclusive. Keen to maintain the uplifting tide, Reverend Scott persisted on another front, pressing local hoteliers to ensure that, in accordance with the law, a clear view of their licensed establishments' interiors was maintained. At the same time, he also hoped that the issuance of wholesale liquor licences in the community would be banned.[41]

Daly's and Scott's efforts resonated within a wartime environment that championed reform as a fitting tribute to overseas troops sacrificing their lives for Canada. They were part of a movement focusing on issues such as urban renewal, vice and the white-slave trade, immigration, worries about the well-being of the traditional family, political corruption, and expansion of the electoral franchise. Chief among the concerns – perhaps second only to suffrage for "respectable" white women – was temperance and prohibition, the latter of which, as we have seen, was embraced by British Columbia in 1917. The province's legislative brake on the public consumption of liquor was an awkward affair for all concerned. The statute was shot through with exceptions. Rather than implementing a dry regime, the act barred public drinking while allowing consumption in private dwellings.[42] Further, physicians, dentists, veterinarians, scientists, ministers, and hospital administrators were allowed to possess and administer varying amounts of alcohol while also permitting individuals to access alcohol for "medicinal purposes."[43] Both the manufacture and the exportation of liquor remained legal. Therefore, if one had the means or contacts to import alcohol for personal consumption, prohibition initially amounted to little more than an irritant.[44] It was only with the end of interprovincial and international importation, effected by a dominion Order in Council on 1 April 1918, that British Columbia was officially "dry," although "near beer," with an alcohol content of less than 2.5 percent, remained legal.[45]

The gaps in the original legislation, the ingenuity of thirsty drinkers, and, as Douglas Hamilton points out, examples of cooperative non-enforcement meant that the dominion importation bans merely encouraged cat-and-mouse contests that pushed alcohol consumption underground.[46] Further, when demand could not be supplied with brand-name spirits, committed drinkers turned to moonshiners operating stills secreted in back rooms and laid-low among the tall trees. A glimpse of the Prince George city magistrate's court in June 1917 – months *before* the prohibition legislation took effect – hinted at the enforcement challenges to come. Having already reported that the city police chief logged only a single alcohol-related conviction for the entirety of March, the *Prince George Citizen* noted that successive police court sessions had been awash in liquor. Three cases heard by Magistrate Daniell on 5 June all involved liquor offences: Andrew Lemp and A. Otis were both found guilty of being drunk and disorderly, while fur dealer Teddy Pappas was convicted of allowing drunkenness in his shop and having intoxicating liquor on hand. Each offence netted a $100 fine.[47] A week later, another case of drunk and disorderly behaviour was heard, during which the accused lamented that an incident of breaking a window was attributable to "too much beer."[48]

Gaps in the local newspaper record during 1917 and 1919 hobble efforts to capture early public accounts of prohibition's arrival and its effects in and around the city.[49] The BCPP duty logs offer some insight, albeit from a South Fort George perspective. The depleted detachment pursued no liquor-related investigations, let alone convictions in 1917. That is an astonishing statistic, given the community's raucous reputation. There were seventy Government Liquor Act (56) and Indian Act (14) liquor-related investigations recorded at the BCPP office in South Fort George a year later, although most of these were pursued by constables stationed in Lucerne to the east and Vanderhoof to the west. This near silence in South Fort George was broken by the work of BCPP constable James Mead, who, as acting chief constable in anticipation of Constable John Bourne's transfer from Ashcroft, launched an investigation of the illegal liquor traffic. He was likely prompted to act by headquarters. Mead concluded that, despite the virtual absence of any liquor-related prosecutions in 1917 and the first half of 1918, "the city of Prince George is apparently the distributing center for liquor, [and] complaints from outside points have all been traced down to places where liquor is kept and sold from this city." Allegedly, the business was driven by whites and the "Chinese," who, Mead understood, were supplied from Edmonton and Vancouver.[50] Confirmation of a sort arrived on the train delivering Acting Chief Constable

Bourne, who was on hand to assist Mead in arresting passenger Chow Lee, a Prince George storeowner, on a charge of trafficking liquor. The subsequent investigation produced an additional charge for opium trafficking.[51] While Mead had reported that whites and "Chinese" were behind the traffic, duty log entries suggest that, in the Georges, "Chinese joints" attracted most of the discretionary police gaze.[52]

Deputy Inspector T.W.S. Parsons met with Mayor Perry on two occasions to discuss prohibition infractions. On 21 August, one of the Bellos brothers – the report failed to indicate whether Arthur or William – was suspected of using his car to transport illegal liquor to outlying districts. Two days later, the "Bothwell" house (the context suggests the name should have been Bellos) was raided and liquor seized.[53] The following month, Parsons again discussed liquor infractions with Mayor Perry, but that conversation signalled the onset of fading attention to prohibition in favour of pursuing non-reporting enemy aliens and military service defaulters or evaders.[54] Save for a handful of stories from elsewhere in the province, liquor disappeared as a newspaper topic as grim war news, word of plans to dispatch Canadian troops to the Siberia Expeditionary Force, the Spanish influenza outbreak, and the armistice dominated front pages and editorial columns.[55] Indeed, as Douglas Hamilton has argued, with the end of hostilities in late 1918, support for prohibition evaporated, and the public largely ignored the law.[56] In mid-December, headlines erupted with news of a scandal involving Walter C. Findlay, the province's prohibition commissioner, who was arrested for his role in a whisky-smuggling operation centred in Vancouver and Victoria.[57] News of the sensation sparked a small column in a local paper, noting that it was rumoured that genuine whisky on the coast was selling for $2.50 a bottle whereas local bootleggers had "been retailing their vile concoctions for from $10 to $15."[58]

Riot

The municipal election of January 1919 was an anemic affair. The unopposed Hiram Carney, a former land speculator, telephone company promoter, and city clerk, was gifted the mayor's chair, and, through that position, he joined T.M. Watson and war veteran George R. Fisher on the police commission. Their first act was to suspend Police Chief James Dolan, based on the claim that the city's "Chinese" district – housing an estimated 500 new residents following an early January influx of labourers – was allegedly teeming with gambling dives.[59] While the *Citizen* published the "official" rationale behind Dolan's dismissal, the newspaper hinted that other reasons were at play. "Somewhat alarming statements in connection with police administration in Prince George the past year have been heard during the past few days. In justice to the fair name of our city it is hoped that a complete investigation into these reports is made."[60] Two days later, it was revealed that fifty-two quarts of whisky and seven cans of opium had disappeared from the city lock-up.[61] With the police commission arguing (not for the last time) that the city was to be cleaned up, Henry Alexander Stewart replaced Dolan. Without any police experience, the Great War veteran was to be paid $1,500 a year.[62] Local businessman Joseph Tadin was sceptical about the appointment. He claimed that "the past un-savory conditions existing since this moral reform movement began are still existent," but that the new chief's response was limited to walking up and down George Street while smoking his pipe.[63] Not only was gam-bling unabated, but rumours claimed that gamblers were being tipped off about impending raids. Unruffled, council directed Tadin's letter to the police commission.[64]

Given western Canada's unsettled postwar atmosphere, Tadin's observa-tions were apt to spark a reaction. Specifically, he had criticized a returned veteran and implied that Stewart was corrupt. Further, Tadin's business partner, Martin Zadelovich, had been recently acquitted on a charge of using seditious language, but only after receiving a stern lecture from Magis-trate C.B. Daniell.[65] Thus, when the local Great War Veteran's Association (GWVA) met in April 1919 to discuss the allegation directed at Stewart, trouble was in the works. After agreeing to bar Dolan and Tadin from the GWVA's rooms, the veterans adjourned their meeting, formed rows of four on George Street, and marched off in search of the two men, intent on ordering them to leave town.[66] Failing to bag their quarry, a crowd of veterans and civilians gathered outside of Tadin's Arcade Building, where Mayor Carney later alleged that the scene erupted when an un-named German resident threw the first stone. According to the news-paper, in response "a perfect fusillade of rocks and missiles of all kinds followed and the destruction of the interior of the building was rapid and complete." That the crowd was milling about armed with rocks and missiles failed to draw a comment. The crowd then gutted Max Schenk's real-estate office and Conrad Reinharz's land-location business. Dolan, Tadin, Schenk, and Reinharz were "ordered" by the rioters to leave town in the early morning, along with "a number of suspicious characters be-lieved by the police to be bootleggers."[67] The latter claim rang hollow.

FIGURE 3.2   The Arcade Café following the riot of 24 April 1919. | British Columbia Provincial Archives.

The *Citizen*, the mayor, and the GWVA quickly distanced themselves from "the indiscriminate ordering from the city of responsible residents irrespective of nationality."[68] According to the newspaper, those association members who had usurped civil authority would be taken in hand by the veteran's group, while the mayor confirmed that the orders to leave town had no basis in law. Reflecting on "the regrettable occurrence," the *Citizen* editorialized that "there can be no reasonable excuse for the destruction of property even under aggravated circumstances." Skirting several lingering questions, the newspaper concluded with some indulgent thinking:

> Residents of Prince George will have every protection of the authorities and any further activities on the part of troublemakers and riot agitators will meet with swift punishment. Which is what the peace-loving and law-abiding residents of the city demand. As to those troublemakers and undesirables who hurriedly left for other parts – under advice – there can be little general regret over their departure ... The city administration is determined to make this a safe, law-abiding British community. Let the people do their part in assisting the officials in this laudable ambition.[69]

The *Citizen*'s assessment is uncompelling. First, the supposedly "peace-loving and law-abiding residents" revealed no appetite for pursuing those responsible for the initial damage, which seemed to belie the claim that "further activities" would be met with swift punishment. Second, despite the fact that ordering "troublemakers and undesirables" out of town was illegal, the alleged "riot agitators" who ordered specific citizens to pack their bags escaped having to answer for running roughshod over civic government and for destroying property. Their comeuppance was limited to a lecture in the GWVA rooms, where, no doubt, a measure of backslapping and sly grins spoke with greater authority. Third, although veterans had recently been lionized as representing the best of Canadian society, several of the lawbreakers were returned soldiers, and their participation in the riot betrayed mythic notions of British fair play and respect for the rule of law – notions that, for some, the war had symbolized. Rather, they had been bullies whose behaviour fell well short of an idealized British manhood. Finally, the newspaper did admit that "the policy of permitting certain latitude in questions of public morals can never be carried out to public satisfaction, as has been amply demonstrated in this city during the past year. Administrators would save themselves endless worry and anxiety were they to rigorously enforce the statutes with regard to gambling and kindred evils. We believe the lesson taught during the past week will not go unheeded."[70] Here was the sting in the tale: Tadin's criticisms had been on the mark. Not only had Dolan and Stewart been playing favourites in policing the city, but they had done so with the connivance of the commissioners and council.

The tumult of early 1919 obscured the fact that, for the first time in the city police force's history, it had quietly gone about its business. Despite the city constabulary's limitations, several vice and liquor investigations were successfully prosecuted. In one instance, Stewart had been on hand to greet "a quartette of lady entertainers from Prince Rupert" who planned to establish a cabaret catering to the "best class of people" and "tired" businessmen. "Gently but firmly our guardian of the peace informed the ladies that the businessmen of this thriving center were receiving many and varied kinds of entertainment and that anything additional in this respect would be likely to bring on nervous prostration not to speak of domestic complications."[71] The women were advised to pursue their opportunities in Alberta. A column in the same edition of the *Citizen* congratulated the city police for their ongoing efforts to stamp out bootleggers peddling moonshine that, it was feared, would before long kill an unsuspecting drinker. "No punishment short of hanging fits his crime

FIGURE 3.3   The Alexandra Hotel in Prince George, which provided offices for the RNWMP. | Exploration Place, Prince George.

and the time is now ripe for a round-up of this delectable bunch. The police can depend upon the support (and assistance) of the decent element in rounding up the purveyors of liquid poison."[72]

Days later, the Royal Northwest Mounted Police (RNWMP) arrived in Prince George with a corporal and two constables, adding yet another actor to the city's police history.[73] A product of the decision to have the mounted police enforce dominion statutes in the four western provinces, the force in Prince George took up residence in the Alexandra Hotel on the corner of Third Avenue and Brunswick Street, from where it tracked down Bolshevik propaganda as well as evaders and defaulters under the Military Service Act.[74] The RNWMP worked alongside the provincial and city police, and there was little in the way of jurisdictional friction. Still, it is arguable that the Georges were overpoliced following the war. The region saw the occasional appearance of private detective agencies pursuing bootleggers; undercover operatives from the attorney general's office, who were also seeking those who defied provincial prohibition and the provincial government's later monopoly on liquor sales; mounted police beating the bushes for narcotics violations and alleged labour agitators; "provincials" enforcing a growing assortment of modernizing statutes in the countryside as well as within the Georges; and the city force, which minded local and provincial regulations. Whether the presence of so many law-enforcement personnel contributed to the area's disorderly reputation is difficult to gauge, but, given the tumult characterizing the years between 1919 and 1925, commentators may have imagined a connection.

The municipal election in mid-January 1920 testified to Carney's fraught term as mayor. Referring to the "lot scandal," in which insiders had picked up tax-delinquent properties for pennies on the dollar, and "the carnival of vice existent here," the *Citizen* hoped that the voting public would demand that elected representatives stand beside their oaths of office, "protect the city's interests and fair name," and "clean-up the mess" of city governance.[75] The decision of popular former mayor Harry Perry to re-enter municipal politics ensured that Carney would not be re-elected. And Henry Wilson was the only incumbent councillor who dared stand for re-election.[76] The vote provided the clean sweep hoped for by reformers. At the first council meeting, Mayor Perry announced, without explanation, that George Fisher's services as city clerk were no longer needed. Further, the *Citizen* reported that the police chief had been instructed to "go out after the law-breakers."[77] Chief Stewart admitted that enforcing the new interprovincial ban on liquor shipments represented a challenge. He added, however, that "there were not many undesirables in the city at the moment ... and with a stringent campaign there would soon be very little to find fault with."[78] This anticipated crackdown motivated T.M. Watson – police commissioner and former councillor – to approach Stewart about seeking police protection for an illegal liquor ring, in exchange for a split of profits. The scheme was explained by Chief Stewart to Constable Alex Sinclair who then feigned cooperation with Watson in anticipation of arresting the commissioner.[79] The constable later charged the commissioner with attempting to corrupt the administration of justice, not with a liquor offence. Following a preliminary hearing, the case was scheduled for the spring assize in Prince George. Days later, it was revealed that an audit of the city's accounts had unearthed "discrepancies totaling a considerable sum," suggesting that former city clerk George Fisher had misappropriated funds. The newspaper noted that inquiries suggested that the errors had resulted from poor bookkeeping rather than villainy.[80] The subsequent jury trial ended in Fisher's acquittal, with Chief Justice Gordon Hunter stressing that Fisher's difficulties were the result of "stupidity and incompetence."[81] This diagnosis of Fisher's abilities was confirmed a month later when he was convicted of obstructing Chief Sinclair who was arresting the former city clerk for having alcoholic drinks at the Brook, a soft-drinks café. Fisher was fined $75 on the liquor offence and $50 for interfering with the chief.[82]

FIGURE 3.4   Alexander F. Sinclair, 1918. | FamilySearch.com.

Unsurprisingly, the charge against Police Commissioner Watson featured at the spring assize before the chief justice and jury. Defence counsel William P. Ogilvie alleged that personal animosity shared by Stewart and Sinclair toward Watson stemmed from his criticism of their on-duty performance, which had motivated their scheme to frame him.[83] Watson's alleged criminal behaviour, his counsel maintained, was consistent with an attempt to catch the policemen in a trap of their own design. The evidence suggested otherwise. Charged by Chief Justice Hunter to leave matters of law to the court and concentrate on questions of fact and reasonable inferences, the jury deliberated for over three hours before foreman Ed Hall indicated that its members were split 10–2.[84] Following an exchange between Hunter and Hall, the jury retired for an additional forty-five minutes before confirming the deadlock. Left with no alternative, the chief justice dismissed the jury, indicating that the case would be tried anew in the autumn.[85] The retrial, which involved a single charge of attempting to bribe Police Chief Stewart, was held before Mr. Justice Denis Murphy and jury on 22 and 23 October 1920 in Prince George.[86] After a fresh presentation of the evidence, Murphy – a product of Lac La Hache in the South Cariboo and the provincial Supreme Court's first British Columbia–born judge – delivered a strongly worded charge imploring the jurors to defend provincial and national interests in considering the seriousness of the alleged offence. Cast against a backdrop of the Bolshevik Revolution, the armistice, the Winnipeg General Strike, and the break-up of the Union government in Ottawa, Murphy's charge was unstinting:

> This world is at present in a state of upheaval and unrest and the only confidence that a country can have in its future [and] the only reliance that its citizens can have in their protection and the protection of their rights is in the Courts of law and the men who administer them. Once you shake the confidence of the country in the Courts of law or in the men who administer law then at once you introduce anarchy, so that this is a matter of most serious import, firstly, to your community, and secondly, to the province at large.[87]

The judge cautioned the jurors against using their verdict as a statement on prohibition, but, in this regard, he was fighting an uphill battle. Three days earlier, in a province-wide plebiscite, British Columbia's voters had rejected the ban on liquor in favour of government-controlled liquor sales.[88] Murphy emphasized that the trial concerned neither prohibition nor its enforcement: "It is a question of corrupting the officers of the law ... If you are going to corrupt the Peace officers, then no man is safe in this country. Your lives may easily be put at stake and certainly your liberty and that of your families."[89] Left with little doubt as to the gravity of the matter, the jury returned in under two hours with a not guilty verdict. Watson reportedly broke down on hearing the decision.[90] The sensational Watson case, in which Prince George once again drew "upon herself some undesirable notoriety," had run its course.[91]

Reflections on what the charges against Watson meant appeared immediately after the complaint was sworn. The *Citizen* argued that, regardless of misplaced sympathy for the accused, "the time has arrived when this city must redeem itself in the eyes of people whose faith in the future has been shaken by long and bitter wranglings, overt acts of willful negligence, and the toleration of corrupt practices."[92] Daniell hoped the prosecution would deter the bootlegger, compel "the tinhorn gambler" to tread warily, and discourage the man seeking public office for personal gain. Despite these cautions, he concluded with his favoured warning:

We are not of the opinion that a western city can be conducted upon a high moral plane. We leave such opinions to the vainglory of the impractical idealists whose efforts to this end so often lend themselves to the manipulation of unscrupulous politicians. We believe that certain evils must exist. They always have, and they always will. They are not the so-called "necessary-evils," but they are indelible, deep-seated and as old as sin.

It was a world-weary diagnosis. Daniell claimed that the case turned on "the miserable laws now governing the liquor question in this province," a reading that Mr. Justice Murphy later dismissed.[93] Rather, the case concerned the administration of justice and the character of those holding public office. In laying his emphasis elsewhere, the editor failed to acknowledge that the imagined threats to a well-ordered community that had been conjured up in the past – racialized Chinese, Indigenous, and mixed-heritage people – played no part in this affront to the Georges' good name. And while he emphasized that "certain evils" were inherent in the human condition, a more honest assessment was that, despite having attempted to corrupt the administration of justice to shield his bootlegging operation, Watson escaped because he was a white, respected, public figure in a community anxious to forget about an unpopular and badly flawed prohibition regime.

That Watson benefited from a white man's privilege was further demonstrated when, as he awaited the October retrial, he became entangled in a bizarre incident confirming his unsuitability for public office.[94] Counted among the participants in a game of poker in an unnamed "licensed" club on George Street, the police commissioner was present to witness an incident in which a man named Prather, after losing a hand, attempted "to break up the place" before being ejected.[95] Armed with a pistol and forcing his way back into the premises, Prather jammed the gun into Watson's ribs before discharging a round into the floor. The *Citizen* was incredulous when, despite his damaging the club, the gun play and rough-handling of Watson, and then discharging the weapon, no charges were laid against Prather. Moreover, here was a police commissioner, frequenting a near-beer club and gambling parlour while being out on bail "pending his second trial on a charge of having bribed the police of this city to protect him in a syndicate to sell liquor illegally, being held up by some demented gambler."[96] That Watson remained a commissioner defied belief.

For Chief Stewart, who testified against Watson in his first trial and would do so again at the second, the scene spoke volumes. Having served just eighteen months, and not needing a weatherman to know which way the wind blew, he submitted his resignation while speaking of a desire to "enter private life."[97] Despite the newspaper's claim that "a complete stranger" would fill the vacancy, Constable Sinclair became acting chief and was confirmed in the position a month later, with Neil McMillan, a former Canadian Pacific Railway policeman and hotel detective, appointed as the night constable.[98] Fortunately for both, reporting on local policing was pushed off the *Citizen*'s pages for most of the next six months by bigger stories: the 21 October 1920 plebiscite on government liquor sales; the provincial vote of 1 December, in which John Oliver's Liberal government was returned; rumours of a pulp mill slated for Prince George; and the mid-January 1921 municipal election.

MORE TROUBLE

The respite came to a crashing end in the second week of April 1921, when city council issued a racist directive that police clamp down on supposed "undesirable" Black residents. This was paired with a provocative query in council as to whether the magistrate was providing the police force with sufficient support. The question took on additional urgency four days later, when the city's "Chinatown" erupted in a riot. The scapegoating of racialized groups in the city will be discussed in Chapter 5: they are mentioned here only to provide context for the fresh worries about local policing that enlivened notions that the community was plagued by disorder and crime while feckless elected officials dodged responsibility. This tangle of innuendo and accusation began when city council, headed by Councillor Barney Keegan (Mayor Henry Wilson was absent on city business in the Lower Mainland) penned a resolution pressing the police commission to "take active immediate steps to clean up the city in respect of drunks, driving at an excessive rate of speed; driving cars while under the influence of liquor; driving cars by persons underage; selling of liquor by bootleggers."[99] The commissioners were also asked to indicate whether the magistrate was supporting the police, and, if not, whether the "police department" – an organization that included the magistrate – needed a renovation. Specifically, the commissioners alleged that it was almost impossible to secure convictions before Magistrate Daniell. Consequently, the city had become a "dumping ground" for underworld figures, who overmatched the city's small police force. While the *Citizen* reported that

Mayor Wilson agreed with the assessment and stood behind the current police chief, the *Leader* recorded Wilson calling for "a reorganization of the police force" because it "would not or could not cope with the situation at present existing in the city."[100] Ultimately, the mayor's actual position hardly mattered. The city might no longer be a "municipal cesspool," but its penchant for self-administrated embarrassment remained.[101] While the introduction of government-controlled liquor sales might impose a measure of order, it remained an open question whether locally elected leaders were capable of cleaning up their act.

As had occurred in the past, budgetary pressures compelled a search for savings, with the suggestion that the fire and police departments might be combined. The scheme was rejected as unworkable.[102] Days later and despite the concern over city expenditures, Mayor Wilson arranged for the services of two Field Detective Agency operatives from Vancouver, whose arrival, according to the *Citizen*, was pegged by individuals whose business required such vigilance. Unable to secure any convictions for liquor violations, the detectives fled but billed the city $800.[103] The cost attached to such a failure reinforced what previous councils had learned: managing a city police force offered few certainties. Still, Wilson persisted in the belief that police services could be had on the cheap. Thus, without consulting his fellow police commissioners, he issued termination notices to Chief Sinclair and Constable McMillan, supposedly "to give the 1922 police commission a free hand in policing matters."[104] The bizarre explanation had been an attempt to camouflage other suspicions. Over the Christmas and New Year's holidays a quantity of seized liquor had again disappeared from the city hall vault. While the janitor admitted his involvement, the mayor suspected that Sinclair and McMillan had been complicit. Rather than dismiss them outright and leave the city without a police force, Wilson thought that giving them notice was prudent. This sleight of hand failed because, as was pointed out by the police board, he had exceeded his authority by effectively discharging the entire force.

Sinclair and McMillan had both been aware of the theft, but the chief believed that the janitor's statement was inadmissible – "there was no evidence against anyone" – and the city would be liable for the seized (and now stolen) liquor if an eventual prosecution failed. Sinclair reasoned that, if the janitor replaced the stolen bottles, all would be forgiven. This solution was fatally flawed: if the liquor were replaced, any prosecution of the offence arising from the seizure of the original bottles was doomed, because the replacement liquor, having no connection to those charges, could not be used as an exhibit. The police commission deferred further action, and, after a brief suspension, the unnamed janitor was reinstated.[105]

The elections in mid-January 1922 resulted in a new council and police commission. The first order of business for the commission was accepting Police Chief Sinclair's resignation.[106] Sinclair had been with the force for about two years. He had been a constable for barely half a year, from his appointment on 23 December 1919 until July 1920, when he became acting chief of police, and then chief in his own right a month later.[107] Constable Neil McMillan was elevated to the role of acting chief until the end of May, when it was concluded that a one-man force was insufficient.[108] Hoping to keep the pressure on bootleggers while McMillan was sidelined with a sprained ankle, the police commission hired T.B. Todd as a special constable. The mayor agreed that Todd would be paid $5 a day and be eligible for the commission's reward of $50 per conviction against any bootleggers. Coordinating his efforts with the BCPP, Todd quickly arrested three suspected bootleggers, who were prosecuted and fined.[109] The early June raid earned plaudits from both local newspapers, but congratulations extended only so far. When Todd sought his wages and the accumulated reward money, councillors balked and trimmed the total owing by $150. With Mayor Johnson arguing in favour of Todd receiving his full wages and the reward, the matter was referred to the city solicitor, who also recommended paying the full amount.[110]

Even though Johnson had been on the side of angels in the Todd matter, reports surfaced that, on another front, he had overstepped his mark. Relying on his imagined authority as police commission chair, the mayor interrupted the police court, wanting to interrogate Special Constable George Smith and demanding to know who had authorized the proceedings.[111] Magistrate Daniell explained to the mayor that, unless he could show some valid reason to curtail it, the hearing would proceed. The prosecutions at hand concerned motorists who had breached a city bylaw requiring that motor vehicles carry front and rear reflective lighting. Smith's insistence that his oath obliged him to lay the charges elicited a snide comment from newspaperman Daniell, who quipped that Smith's diligence fated him to become the scourge of local villains. Magistrate Daniell found all the accused, which included his own son as well as city councillors McKay and Alward, guilty. No one, it seems, questioned the appropriateness of the police magistrate presiding over a case involving his own son. For his trouble, Smith was dismissed by the commission following the prosecution.[112] As to the mayor's behaviour, the *Leader* offered that the mayor or chairman of the police commission may have wide powers, but he certainly has no power or authority to act in the manner he did in the case referred to. It is his sworn duty to uphold the police officers in the exercise of their duties, and to not interfere with enforcing the law. It is not the duty of police to ask him for authority to prosecute when there has been an infringement of the law, as would appear to be the attitude taken by the mayor in these cases. The attitude is certainly not in accordance with the ethics of Canadian court procedure.[113]

Johnson's notions about his authority did not mark him as the first Prince George mayor to act in a high-handed manner. Similar petty contests likely played out across the province's municipal landscape. Likewise, that editor Daniell could mutter about Constable Smith's diligence, and caricature him as an officious plod, was testament to the editor's sense of self-importance. Yet he was not the first newspaperman to confuse reporting with having a bully pulpit. And that the police commissioners concluded that Constable Smith, whose officiousness had irritated both Johnson and Daniell, was ill suited for employment on the city force illustrated something about small-town power and privilege that was not limited to Prince George.

While not the stuff of high drama, the mayor's behaviour suggests how the eccentricities of local power and influence coloured municipal government and its oversight of city policing. This was especially evident given the absence of provincial legislation concerning town and city planning before 1925, which meant that the idiosyncrasies of mayors and councillors exerted an outsized influence.[114] The scandal-plagued Carney administration was one example. Another can be found in the growing influence of Prince George's property-owners' association following the armistice. Backing candidates pledging fealty to an austerity agenda, the association found a true believer in councillor and future mayor R.W. Alward.[115] The association's influence was felt in local politics and every facet of city finance, including the police department and its statutory expectation that it should play a front-line role in battling illegal liquor. At one point Attorney General A.M. Manson chided municipalities over their uneven fulfilment failure of their enforcement duties. Although most had answered the call, he warned that those who backed government sales needed to support the act and its obligations, concluding with a veiled threat: "up to the present we have not entered any municipality to take over complete control."[116] While this may have been theatrics, the message was not easily laughed off. Failing to enforce liquor regulations risked the provincial government taking direct action. Whether this meant that the attorney general's office would dispatch undercover operatives, take over local policing, or, perhaps, assume control over municipal government was unsaid.

For Prince George city council, with its perennial difficulties managing the city police, Manson's comments must have given pause. After all, through government-controlled sales, municipal governments received a share of local liquor profits, with a percentage of those revenues earmarked for schools and city hospitals. Figures on liquor revenues released by the attorney general's office – likely intended to allay wariness over the modern state's regulatory reach – had the opposite effect, stoking suspicions that local government was being shortchanged. According to the *Citizen*, it was a poor policy that took "thousands of dollars a month out of such towns as Prince George, McBride, Vanderhoof, and Smithers and return so small a portion of this sum."[117] After examining the figures, the *Leader* denied that the city was being fleeced. In fact, Prince George received a larger share of liquor profits than it deserved, since customers from the outlying districts also contributed to sales figures and to the percentage returned by the province to the city.[118] Still, for those nursing doubts as to whether the provincial government cared about the strictures faced by interior communities like Prince George, the numbers were unlikely to convince those ill-disposed to the new regulatory state.

A collision between the provincial government's commitment to putting bootleggers out of business and the city's embrace of austerity occurred after Ezra Carlow's arrival as the city's new police chief in July 1922.[119] The former detective sergeant and fingerprint expert from Victoria, with eleven years' experience on the beat and an additional eleven years in plainclothes, emerged as the city's "best police officer" ever.[120] While city newspapers did not consistently reproduce Carlow's monthly reports, those that did appear testified to his abilities.[121] Still, his efficiency proved to be his undoing, for, after a year of exemplary service, the property-owners' association in June 1923 pressed the police commission to cut the force in half. The commissioners refused, preferring to await the result of a joint meeting between council and the association. With Mayor Johnson dismissing the association's members as insufficiently "familiar with the services they were proposing to re-organize to make their findings of any value," council resisted the group's pressure.[122] The approaching civic election, in which the association actively backed R.W. Alward's mayoralty campaign against the incumbent Johnson, meant the issue was not settled. At the same time, the province launched a new approach to preventing municipal governments from dodging their financial

FIGURE 3.5   Constable Ezra Carlow, circa 1900, future
Prince George police chief. | S.J. Clarke Publishing Co.

obligations under the modern state. Beginning in January 1924, the share
of liquor profits returned to local government would be reduced to cover
municipalities' unpaid debts. As the *Citizen* observed, "it appears that the
government is using the finance department as a sort of clearing house,
and in the event of there being any unsettled claims owing to the government by any of the municipalities the amount of same is deducted
from the amount receivable from the liquor profits." In the case of Prince
George, the combination of costs associated with sending two local men
to the Old Men's Home at Kamloops and the government's expense in
bringing in spotters to secure convictions in two liquor cases had reduced
the share of liquor profits returned to the city by over $1,000.[123]

Repercussions were immediate. Having reviewed the previous year's
police budget, which included expenditures of $3,900 for two officers,
$1,100 for the magistrate, and $1,000 for the city solicitor, council dismissed solicitor P.E. Wilson while the police commission did the same to
Carlow and McMillan.[124] A single city policeman would be hired in their
place. In protest, Thomas Rush resigned from the police commission,
stating that, in Carlow, "Prince George had been fortunate in securing a
very desirable man, but so far as he could learn, this was not the view of
the majority of the commission."[125] Defending the decision, Alward, by
then the mayor, argued that declining fines gathered in police court justified a reduced police force. Rush rejected the argument, stating that, if
city finances were reliant on fines collected from citizens' illegal acts, it

was time to resign from the commission.[126] Carlow, who undoubtedly had gauged council's thinking, accepted the news without complaint and arranged to sell off his household furnishings before leaving the city.[127] Having received twenty-nine applications from men with experience in England, Ireland, Egypt, South Africa, and British Columbia, the commission again sided with the local man and rehired Neil McMillan.[128] A delay in announcing the appointment revealed that the city had been negotiating with the provincial government to have the BCPP assume responsibility for city policing. Talks faltered on the city's insistence that the local board of police commissioners continue to direct police policy. Understandably, the BCPP were uninterested in such an arrangement. McMillan was then offered the position but only, as later events revealed, on a day-to-day basis. He lasted barely six weeks.[129]

The factors undermining McMillan were evident from the outset. Alward's commitment to austerity and his unsuccessful negotiation with the BCPP indicated that the city force was on a short leash, even if an exit strategy remained undefined. Further, McMillan's probationary day-to-day appointment reflected the mayor's indifference to the city force. Even more telling – and embarrassing – was the city's tight-fisted mishandling of the Roy McKinley case, stemming from an incident a year earlier involving then chief Carlow and RCMP staff-sergeant R.W. MacLeod. Having joined forces to arrest McKinley on a charge of selling liquor to Indigenous people, the two policemen were wrong footed when, true to the lore of gun-toting toughs, the suspect pulled a pistol before making his escape on a freight train bound for the American west. Eventually arriving in Shelby, Montana, McKinley learned he was safe because of Prince George's unwillingness to foot the costs for extradition. He returned to Vancouver, where two city detectives, clutching the outstanding warrant, took him into custody. It was then that both the *Vancouver Sun* and the *Province* reported that Prince George was reluctant to prosecute, again because of the cost. Mayor Alward scrambled to attribute the report to "some person who had no power to give such instructions."[130] Bluster aside, it was left to the provincial attorney general's office to direct BCPP constable H.B. Martin of Prince Rupert to deliver McKinley to Prince George.[131] Bound over for trial before Mr. Justice Francis B. Gregory in late November 1924, McKinley was found guilty of assaulting Carlow and MacLeod, with the jury recommending mercy.[132] Acknowledging that McKinley "did not go to Sunday school very often," Gregory nonetheless felt that the accused "was not a very bad chap," and, despite the fact that McKinley had drunkenly pulled a pistol on Carlow and MacLeod, the judge concluded that he did not deserve the full sentence under the statute.[133]

As the McKinley case played out, Neil McMillan's service as city policeman ended. Pointing to complaints from the local Presbyterian church that the constable had failed to rid the town of prostitutes and pimps, Alward rationalized the dismissal. He also announced the rehiring of George Smith, who, it will be recalled, was fired after arresting councillors Alward and McKay, along with newspaper editor John Daniell, for driving motor vehicles without reflective lights.[134] Yet McMillan refused to go quietly. In a front-page open letter, the former constable claimed that he was unaware of why he had been dismissed. After admitting to commissioners that he lacked the means to corral local bootleggers, he concentrated on clearing the city of Black prostitutes. He had worked under the impression that the tenderloin in the Chinese district was off limits to the city police. "I do not know whether in the minds of the commission, I have been lax or overzealous."[135] Mayor Alward explained that McMillan's probationary appointment had been on a day-to-day basis and, while the constable had started out well in ridding the city of Black prostitutes and their consorts, his failure to follow a similar course along Quebec Street – the city's "Chinese" district – proved to be his undoing.[136] Nested within the long history of tolerating the sex trade in the Georges, the unapologetic racism of council's attack on Black residents in April 1921, and Alward's austerity policies, the mayor's version of events left a great deal unsaid.

Alward provided further elaboration three months later, defending his behaviour on the police board while casting his fellow commissioners in an unflattering light. Reminding voters that he had been elected to reduce police expenditures – along with a selective accounting of his austerity agenda targeting the city's budget writ large – Alward acknowledged that McMillan had not been "my choice" for city constable.[137] Nonetheless, the constable's dismissal had not been personal. Rather, McMillan had failed to perform as required. In truth, he had been saddled with contradictory instructions. While Alward wanted the city "cleaned up," the other two commissioners – R.J. Garvey and J.D. MacLeod – directed McMillan to leave well enough alone because local businessmen felt that the sex trade benefited the local economy. Further, a clamp down would simply disperse prostitutes into respectable neighborhoods.[138] McMillan followed the majority's instructions and, for his troubles, was dismissed by the mayor acting alone. Conscious of shielding his own reputation, and insisting that his fellow commissioners were responsible for the toleration of the sex trade, Alward concluded that "this is just how the matter of cleaning up the city stands at present."[139] And, despite having dismissed McMillan, the mayor claimed he did not fault the constable for taking the course he did. Had he been in the same position, he too would have followed the majority. Alward's further denial that conditions in the "Chinese" district were a product of police incompetence must have sent McMillan reeling.[140] Still insisting that an efficient man should be able to police the city, Alward allowed that, until such a man was found, it was reasonable to concede that two men were needed for the job. It was a bewildering performance, especially after Alward had led the charge to cut Carlow from the payroll, despite being acclaimed as the best policeman in the city's history.

The mayor's self-serving explanations guaranteed a response from his fellow commissioners.[141] At the police commission's monthly meeting in August, where the issue of vice was discussed, only a delegation representing the Presbyterian church was on hand, as local businessmen fled from any association that they, as individuals or as a group, had supported the red-light district's continued operation. Church spokesman Frank Clark asserted "that it was unsafe at the present time for a respectable woman to go into the vicinity of Quebec Street, without the fear of being accosted by partially drunken men." He continued: unless the commissioners acted, the delegation would "bring the matter to the attention of the attorney general of the province and ask him to police the city." Both Garvey and MacLeod remained steadfast: not only had the segregated district operated without complaints under Chief Carlow's watch, but, if it were closed, the sex workers would disperse throughout the city. To this, Clark countered that managing the red-light district was not the issue. Rather, were officials prepared to "get the women out of town altogether?" Having received the delegation, the commission resolved itself into committee and announced that deliberations would continue after the mayor returned to the city. Elsewhere in the same edition of the *Citizen*, it was noted that liquor board spotters were active in the city and that prosecutions were anticipated.[142]

When the police board convened for its third meeting in as many weeks, the results were predictable.[143] Holding to their preference for a well-regulated segregated district, Garvey and MacLeod accepted that the toleration policy had attracted organized opposition. Nonetheless, they insisted that a two-man police force could manage local affairs and proposed that Donald Stevenson be hired as chief, with George Smith as his second. Alward objected, countering that one experienced constable was more than sufficient, since local bootlegging was no longer a pressing menace – a claim belied by the fact that provincial liquor board spotters were active in Prince George. And while maintaining that the city ought to secure an "outside man" to take on the police work, the mayor did not explain how this individual would continue to be effective and able to perform undercover work once he became known to residents. Given the numerical balance on the board, the proposal to hire Stevenson and Smith was passed.

Despite the city's anxiety-inducing police history, the *Citizen* portrayed the latest developments in faintly comic tones. The writer suggested that this latest chapter, if not quite harmless fun, merely continued empty theatrics:

> Prince George is a staid little city once more ... It will not be necessary for Attorney General Manson to intervene in municipal police matters to make Prince George safe for democracy. In a word, the police commissioners decided on Thursday night to put a lid on the revels of the local tenderloin, to chase out the bootleggers and to darken the lights over the green tables. For a time, at least, Prince George is going to be as circumspect as a well-regulated Sunday school ... Already the janes who made the welkin ring, and who in the main were responsible for the moral upheaval, have gone. In an hour or two after the decision of the commissioners was known they were ready to flit, and those who were unable to catch a train stole away to rusticate on the shores of Bednesti Lake. With the ladies went their consorts. The gamblers have closed down, and a number of the ranking bootleggers have got on the other side of the provincial border and did not stand on the order of their going. It is quite a change to be wrought within a week.[144]

Had Prince George ever been a "staid little city"? Was this imagined past intended to scrub out the latest blot on the community's copybook? Was the clean-up campaign largely a gesture of reassurance for residents and artifice aimed at a broader audience? After all, given that some of the tenderloin's denizens had decamped to nearby Bednesti Lake, was it not merely a matter of time before they returned? Had the campaign to "clean-up" the city been fruitless? By one measure, the efforts had brought about the desired result. Read at the mid-September meeting of the police board, a letter from the provincial attorney general's office indicated satisfaction with the steps taken, with the result "that there is no necessity at the present time for the dispatch of government operators to the city."[145] At least that indignity had been avoided.

Concentrating on the exodus from the segregated district, the newspapers overlooked the beginnings of Chief Donald Stevenson's and Constable George Smith's terms as the city police force. Stevenson's career was short-lived. Just weeks after his appointment, the chief crashed his vehicle on night patrol. Discovered only the following morning, he was rushed to the hospital with a badly smashed leg. Fighting for his life and facing the prospect of amputation, Stevenson remained under close watch for over a month.[146] Smith was elevated to the role of chief until mid-October, when the police commission once again decided that a new man was needed.[147] Provincial policing priorities, however, had shifted, owing to Vancouver's scandal-ridden police force and the emerging consensus that "in many of the municipalities police administration has become a joke."[148] Consequently, Attorney General Manson began testing the waters concerning the centralization of municipal policing in Victoria and the creation of a metropolitan force covering Greater Vancouver. Movement on the municipal front came first. Passed by the end of 1924, the Police and Prisons Regulation Act created a mechanism for municipal governments to adopt the British Columbia Provincial Police as a city police force.[149] Addressing the troubles in Vancouver took longer: it was not until late 1928 that the Vancouver, Point Gray, and South Vancouver police forces were merged in search of greater efficiencies.[150] In the interim, Prince George again took up the search for a new chief. The position was filled by F.W. Shelton, who, following a stint with the federal government in the Hudson Bay district, had been police chief in Westaskiwin, Alberta.[151] A month later, the police commission unanimously voted to add a second officer to the city force, with the *Citizen* reporting that "a man will be brought in from the outside." F.S. Hodgson of Edmonton, with eight years of service with the RCMP, proved to be that man.[152] Hopes for a period of calm in local police matters lasted all of six days, following Hodgson's arrival, when, on 30 December, word arrived concerning the city's share of liquor revenues. Not only had the cost of the McKinley prosecution been deducted, but expenses for undercover operations in the city – investigations that had failed to yield any convictions – were also billed to the city. The completed tally revealed that the city's share of liquor profits and shared taxes, amounting to $3,784.71, had been trimmed by $2,429.19.[153] Council was livid.

The subsequent protest outlined three points of complaint: the province had not detailed the alleged expenses; the liquor board investigations had failed to produce any prosecutions, let alone convictions; and the entire process was irresponsible. The system invited abuse. It was quite possible for a hanger-on or henchman of the liquor control board to be put on the payroll and have his salary and expenses charged up to the city of Prince George; and so far as the city could know to the contrary the recipient of the salary might spend it in California or Monte Carlo, and never see Prince George. The viciousness and injustice of a system which permits of such a possibility is too apparent to need comment.[154]

Demanding full restitution of funds, council pressed for an inquiry as to whether other municipalities had experienced similar treatment. The *Vancouver Province* reported that similar deductions had occurred in both Cranbrook and Chilliwack, where the local share of liquor profits had been wiped out.[155] For its part, Vancouver City Council claimed that it was being "bled white" by the province. Defending the process, Attorney General Manson reiterated that the government remained committed to enforcing the liquor law. Further, he noted, most municipalities received a larger amount from liquor profits than expected and the deductions had covered the entire year. Some municipalities had invited liquor board investigations while several others continued to "glaringly" make no pretense at enforcement.[156] As to the intricate details of liquor board investigations, Manson was resolute. "Particulars of secret service work will not be given to the municipalities; that manifestly cannot be done. All I can hope is that the municipalities will render it unnecessary for provincial officers to intervene. They have the matter entirely in their own hands."[157] Municipal grumbling continued, but, from the province's perspective, the case was closed.

The following spring, news of Mayor Alward's departure for meetings in Victoria set tongues wagging.[158] While rumours imagined several possibilities, the *Citizen* reported that, like Duncan on Vancouver Island and Merritt in the southern Interior, Prince George was opening negotiations for the BCPP to assume responsibility for city policing. While the police commission had considered inviting the BCPP to police the city, there is no evidence that councillors had authorized the mayor to negotiate. When he returned with a draft agreement to bring in the provincial force, opinion on the commission and council was split. Although much of the subsequent debate centred on costs versus benefits, and whether the provincial government was likely to find another means of "raiding" the city's meagre coffers, the undeniable appeal of Alward's negotiated proposal was that council, with its limited revenues and little room to manoeuvre, would be spared the nuisance and frustration of dealing with policing while protecting the city's share of local liquor monies. As Alward explained,

Prince George would pay $4,750 for police services and another $2,000 for the local administration of justice and "would have something in the nature of a guarantee that the liquor board would not raid the treasury with any further charges for liquor act enforcement."[159]

While councillors worried over the details, wondered if the provincial government could be trusted, and questioned whether the city possessed the authority to enter into such an agreement, it was over the question of whether the matter ought to be subjected to a referendum that tempers flared. Four of the six councillors – H.B. Guest, A.M. Patterson, D.G. Fraser, and Edward Opie – favoured the proposal being brought before the public. Alward dismissed the suggestion as "a shirking of responsibility on the part of the aldermen if they refused to put his agreement into execution and passed the buck to the electors by taking a plebiscite."[160] This produced angry responses from both Opie and Guest, with Patterson chiding the mayor for attacking councillors, who had the right to voice an opinion. When the vote on the question of a plebiscite was called, Taylor, Opie, and Guest were in favour while Fraser, Patterson, and Lambert were opposed. Alward cast the deciding vote against. The votes followed the same line when the question was called on the agreement to have the BCPP replace the city police.

One week later, and with former mayor Hiram Carney as their spokesman, a delegation filed into council chambers, denouncing "the invasion of their liberties in the surrender of police control to the provincial authorities in the absence of any plebiscite upon the question."[161] The *Citizen*, choosing to forget the near perpetual scandal of Carney's term in office, heralded his leadership in pleading "a lost cause with all the fire of a people's champion of one hundred years ago, and the dangers which he pictured as the result of the breach made in the rampart of public liberty kept mounting until his auditors were almost persuaded that the family plate might even slip away with the loss of control of the municipal police." Full of righteous indignation, Carney pressed the point: "neither the board of police commissioners nor the city council had been given any mandate to surrender police control to the attorney-general." Alward denied that council had exceeded its powers, and asserted that, regardless of the merits of the petitioners' case, it was too late. Immediately following the council vote, the agreement had been finalized: "It was out of the question to reconsider the matter in any manner." Indeed, it would be "evidence of rank inconsistency and weakness on the part of council to reconsider the action taken." With the agreement stipulating that, on 15 June, the BCPP would assume responsibility for policing the city, Chief Shelton and

Constable Hodgson were given notice that, as of that date, their services would no longer be required.[162] The Prince George city police force and its ragged history had come to an end.

As the debate had played out, several councillors leaned into the non-sensical claim that, in the spring of 1924, conditions in the city were worse than ever. The suggestion was a pretense, allowing them to rationalize that their failures had been on account of the enormity of the task they had faced, rather than a product of their own indifference or incompetence. Councillor J.B. Lambert cut through the posturing by observing that, if the police board had coped with the situation in the city – that is, had commissioners been equal to the task – there would have been no reason to contract with the BCPP.[163] Tellingly, no one rose to defend their struggles against the blight of sporting women and illegal liquor. Moreover, and as the evidence demonstrates, Lambert's assessment applied at almost any point after the municipal election of 1919. Time and time again, municipal leaders had fallen short. And while the structure of municipal government, with its yearly elections, turnover, and penchant for opportunistic policy choices, and the province's evolving approach to liquor control had mapped out a difficult environment, it remains that the cadre of privileged white men controlling local power had been authors of their own misfortune. These realities, more than the local population's supposed inclinations toward liquor-fuelled excess – a characteristic shared with most communities in the province – hardened the community's dubious reputation acquired during the earlier townsite war.

Ultimately, for those who had come to the northern Interior to establish a well-ordered and law-abiding community, the spectacle of the post-1919 years left a worrisome legacy. While one could conveniently imagine that the persistence of local tumult had been the work of underworld schemers, local Indigenous people, non-preferred immigrants, Black interlopers, and Asian labourers, no one from those communities had occupied a place on council or the police commission when those august bodies had consistently failed to bring the city's affairs into order. While individuals from these unwelcomed communities were counted among those charged with various misdemeanors and with liquor and morals offences, none had been welcomed to seek the rights, responsibilities, and prerogatives of public office. None had been accused of attempting to operate an illegal liquor ring or been charged with perverting the administration of justice; none had rationalized the operation of a red-light district along Quebec Street as being good for local business; and none had championed an austerity regime that fatally undermined the city

police force. Those efforts had been the work of the city council and the
police commission. As historian Elizabeth Catte observed in another
context, here was "a pathetic guild of men complaining that the very
system they controlled was making their lives difficult."[164] And, in uttering
such a complaint, these privileged white men failed to acknowledge their
own roles in the city's lurching from crisis to crisis after 1919 and, thus,
in contributing another chapter to the Georges' notoriety. Although they
would not admit it, they shared responsibility for increasingly anxious
questions about Prince George and its place in the province's white settler
society. After all, if Prince George had become a byword – a ready example
of a community unable to govern itself, let alone impose order on "lesser"
peoples – how could these privileged white men expect to be counted
among British Columbia's natural leaders? It was indeed unsettling.

4

Holding Court in the Georges

A kin to the distinction of having a regional detachment of the provincial police, hosting regular court sittings – of Magistrate's Court, County Court, and, in time, Supreme Court assizes – offered further evidence of respectability and provided the opportunity for the district to see justice done. While Magistrate's Court may have been the "basement of justice," where foolish and sometimes unlucky people answered for petty misdeeds, it remained a crucial ingredient of the administration of justice.[1] Indeed, much of what transpired in Magistrate's Court in the Georges during the years straddling the Great War was an extension of what was imagined to be "real" policing. Often, its business was a dreary parade of alcoholic excess, casual violence, and short-sighted and regrettable behaviour. These summary hearings were perfunctory, sprinting from complaint to evidence to sentencing within minutes. When circumstances warranted, the proceedings might close with a homily delivered from the bench. Justice at this level was speedy, if not always fair. On other occasions, the court adopted a more measured pace, offering a preliminary glimpse of grave accusations en route to a full trial at either County Court sessions or Supreme Court assizes. These preliminaries were one-sided affairs, with the Crown presenting what it believed was compelling evidence warranting a full trial while the accused and their counsel mutely reserved their defence, awaiting a more fitting venue for a counter-narrative. At the same time, Magistrate's Court was also a setting for clashes of power and personality. In this, Charles B. Daniell, the

magistrate for almost a decade following the city's incorporation, failed
to prove himself a compliant and reliable member of Prince George's
privileged governing circle. In the friction within Magistrate's Court, we
see another conflict that, entwined with the post-1919 turmoil, threatened
to swamp city governance and, ultimately, contributed to the city's raucous
reputation.

The superior courts – first, the County Court, and, after the Great War,
the Supreme Court assize – offered more gravitas to the community. It
was easy to embrace the self-congratulatory idea that hosting County
Court sessions and, in time, the Supreme Court assize was a weighty duty
that the province would not have entrusted to a motley assortment of
rubes in a contrived settlement lacking prospects. Such responsibilities
were reserved for respectable communities on their way up, cities where
things were happening, cities that mattered. When combined with Prince
George's location at a transportation crossroads, becoming a judicial centre
hinted of new opportunities befitting a respectable city. It whispered that
the city would have "more." Indeed, being a court town with a resident
County Court judge and a coterie of lawyers drew people to Prince George
in pursuit of legal counsel and services, and this increased stream of visitors
generated a knock-on economic boost for hotels, restaurants, and local
provisioners. All this activity offered the comfort that the city and its out-
laying districts might be cushioned from unanticipated economic shocks.
Further, the fact that the city hosted these legal affairs provided ammuni-
tion for those arguing in favour of the refinement of local facilities.
Creating this infrastructure proved to be a drawn-out process. The eventual
construction in Prince George of a new provincial government building
and court facilities highlighted the need for improvement on the "temporary" offices built before the war on the former Hudson's Bay Company
(HBC) lands on the northern boundary of South Fort George. The possibilities were intoxicating. Surely the impress of these judicial functions
would banish memories of the townsite war, with its exaggerated depictions of a sordid collection of scarlet women, gin palaces, con artists, and
gambling dens. In this context, the community's ambition to become a
regional judicial centre was indisputably a good thing.

In practice, that prize proved to be less certain. While regular court
sessions contributed to local coffers, deepened the ranks of the community's legal profession, and contributed an air of stability, the addition
of a County Court and then the Supreme Court assize and their criminal
dockets, combined with preliminary hearings presided over by Magistrates Herne and Daniell, meant that the community was subjected to a

near-constant parade of alleged wrongdoers from across the northern Interior. While not every case was featured on the front page, at times it
must have felt as if the local newspapers were never free of crime reporting. After all, crime made good copy. Regardless of the story – whether
a racist account of Jael Quaw being arrested for public intoxication, a
summary of the first Supreme Court criminal assize, including an alleged
murder and a charge of breaking and entering from the Peace River
country and a wounding from Quesnel, or a supposed case of sorcery
among the "Siccannees" of the Liard River region of northern British Columbia – notions of the innate goodness of people drawn to the northern
Interior were exposed by the litany of charges.[2] As has been demonstrated
time and again, the notion that the settlement frontier would provide
new beginnings and a fresh start, free of the trials and tribulations experienced elsewhere, was revealed as fiction. Clinging to the idea that these
cases of human misery were not about the legitimate residents committed
to the region's long-term development invariably contributed to a sense
of anxiety about how the region and its residents were perceived by others.
Did opinion leaders, editors and other commentators, and public officials
elsewhere in the province take the time to understand whose behaviour
was responsible for the region's crowded criminal dockets, or was it easier
to believe that these cases confirmed that there was something amiss about
Prince George?

MAGISTRATE'S COURT

Originating in early fourteenth-century England, with the designation
"magistrate" taking hold in the early eighteenth century, justices of the
peace (JPs) or stipendiary magistrates (SMs) were recognizable figures
of British governance when they were introduced in both the Vancouver
Island and British Columbian colonies during the mid-nineteenth-century
gold rush.[3] As had been the case in the mother country five centuries
earlier, the advantage of having individuals dispersed throughout the
countryside with the authority to keep the peace was a prudent response
to the influx of 25,000 foreign miners on the Pacific slope. Governor James
Douglas hoped that the presence of several gold commissioners and
JPs, along with Chartres Brew and his colonial constabulary, would pre-
serve a modicum of order and bolster revenue from the Fraser River
diggings.[4] Magistrates emerged as a linchpin of colonial governance and,
according to one account, were the "forerunners of the post-Confederation

government agent," who administered every conceivable local service.[5] Consequently, by the time British Columbia entered Confederation in July 1871, the magistrate was already a fixture, combining law enforcement and governance. Beginning in the spring of 1883 and culminating before 1900, successive provincial governments introduced a series of acts establishing processes through which stipendiary magistrates – individuals who received a government stipend for services rendered – were to be appointed. Legislative considerations included their oath of office, their salaries (paid by local governments through funds generated from local fines, fees, and forfeitures), their obligation to submit quarterly returns to the provincial secretary, restrictions as to the specific county or electoral district for which they were appointed, the extension of their jurisdiction to include municipal acts and bylaws, and their protection from vexatious criminal complaints and civil suits.[6]

Conscious of the white settlement frontier creeping toward the confluence of the Fraser and Nechako Rivers, the provincial government appointed two local JPs in the spring and summer of 1907. The first was A.K. Bourchier, gazetted on 4 April 1907, followed three months later by James Cowie, the clerk in charge of the HBC post at Fort George.[7] Although the two were the only legal officials in the immediate district until the arrival of the first British Columbia Provincial Police (BCPP) constable in late November 1910 and a government agent in early April 1911, there is little evidence that either were hard pressed by their responsibilities. While the issuance of a liquor licence to A.G. Hamilton drew from Cowie the pregnant comment that there had "been no disturbance owing to liquor *as yet*," the HBC post journal did not suggest a surge of trouble, despite the field being left open to bootleggers following the withdrawal of Hamilton's licence.[8] New local and regional newspapers could have provided outlets for reports concerning liquor, legal and otherwise, but John Houston's *Fort George Tribune* tended to be of two minds about alcohol in the "New Cariboo." While supporting the local option and the sale of liquor only where food was served, he nonetheless bemoaned the possibility that Christmas 1909 might be dry. His relief was palpable in reporting the "unexpected arrival of two cases of liquor means that Fort George will have hot scotch, rum punch, tom-and-jerry, and eggnog on Christmas and headaches on the day following."[9] After the *Tribune* changed hands following Houston's death, the local preoccupation with the townsite war meant its approach to alcohol invariably played upon Fort George's supposed moral superiority in contrast to the imagined excesses in South Fort George, where, "almost any day can be witnessed the utter degradation of someone, invariably some worker who has perhaps come to this no license district to escape the temptations of the drink demon."[10] That the inebriated individual in this anecdote turned out to be Indigenous provided for a knowing comment on the advantages of "a ceaseless war on the 'blind-pig'" as well as the hope that the region's respectable citizens would be shielded from such undesirable scenes and people. A similar message, inherent in a report of two "Chinese" gamblers who were directed to leave the district after having been found guilty of operating a disorderly house, was testament to the racist provincial culture rather than local alarm about dice games and card playing.[11]

While the two JPs served the Georges' immediate needs, the rising population and the resulting push for local facilities and services meant that, while dithering over where the offices would be built, the provincial government was again compelled to act. Although it was announced that George J. Walker, the government agent, County Court registrar, assistant commissioner of lands for the Cariboo and Fort George Land Divisions of the Cariboo Recording District, and deputy mining recorder for the Cariboo Mining District of Barkerville, was to be relocated to Fort George in early April 1911, the appointment proved to be temporary. Diagnosed with failing vision shortly after the announcement, Walker was ill-suited to assume an office anticipating a rising tide of land preemption registrations, as well as additional legal and mining business. Consequently, Thomas W. Herne, who had already been appointed as magistrate for the Cariboo and was set to establish an agency office in Fort Fraser, was temporarily assigned to South Fort George in mid-May.[12] The appointment was made permanent a year later.[13] A son of empire, Herne had been born in India, where his father commanded the Bombay Fencibles (later amalgamated into the Royal Dublin Fusiliers).[14] The younger Herne was raised and educated in England and worked with a Liverpool-based cotton merchant before joining his brother in Argentina, where they operated a cattle ranch. He followed the gold rush to British Columbia, where he married Agnes Bouie, of the Bouie Brothers mining firm in Barkerville. Entering the provincial civil service in 1907, Herne was located in Nelson before being transferred first to Hazelton and then to South Fort George, where, on 6 July 1911, he supervised the official opening of the newly constructed government office.[15] The Hernes remained in South Fort George until 1923, when a transfer to Prince Rupert was requested in the hope that Agnes would find the coastal weather less taxing on her health. As it turned out, Thomas was felled by heart failure barely a year later. The *Citizen* eulogized him as a "broad-minded ... ideal administrator" who "unquestionably did

FIGURE 4.1   Provincial government buildings, South Fort George, circa 1917. |
Exploration Place, Prince George.

much to influence the frontier community in which he was placed during
the days of railway construction."[16]

Herne's tenure as the magistrate in the Georges fell into two unequal
portions divided by the incorporation of Fort George/Prince George in
the spring of 1915.[17] From the outset in May 1911, his authority extended
throughout the Cariboo district. Consequently, he handled cases from the
countryside as well as South Fort George, Fort George, and the tiny communities along the Grand Trunk Pacific, from Lucerne in the east to
Vanderhoof in the west. While this mandate remained undiluted following Charles B. Daniell's appointment as the city stipendiary magistrate
in July 1915, Herne dealt with misdemeanours and preliminary hearings
arising within Prince George's boundaries only if Daniell was absent or
faced a conflict of interest, or if a spate of cases obliged the two men to
share the load.[18] Further, as the distant communities acquired their own
JPs and SMs during and after the war, Herne's workload as magistrate nar-
rowed, while that as a government agent mirrored the broadening modern
state.[19] Given that his docket tracked BCPP policing, early on it reflected
the presence of Fort George Reserve No. 1, the emergence of the two competing white settler communities, and the uprooting of resident Indigenous
families to Reserve No. 2 at Shelly, before wartime dislocation, prohibition,
postwar recovery, and the introduction of government-controlled liquor

sales dominated the scene. Included in his purview were disputes over livestock, accusations of public drunkenness (on and off the reserve), charges of supplying liquor to Indigenous people, thieving from caches, stealing from railway boxcars, vagrancy, house breaking, carrying concealed weapons, using obscene language on a public street, and keeping gaming or disorderly houses.[20] The BCPP daily duty logs catalogued offences that went unreported in weekly newspapers, which were drawn to the unusual and the spectacular. Constables' notes traced the peaks of prewar policing, during which Herne's Magistrate's Court offered multiple sessions to clear the local cells of over-refreshed enthusiasts and petty criminals. By the same measure, his thinning court docket reflected the exodus of men volunteering and the rising importance of the city magistrate's court. Equally, the newspaper accounts of both magistrate's courts captured the expanding selection of infractions reflecting the modern state's slate of regulatory offences: showing moving pictures and holding sporting events on Sundays; burning brush without a permit; health, sanitary, and other inspection infractions; hoarding food stuffs; evading military service; truancy complaints against parents and absent students; and Game Act violations. In addition, the courts responded to the novelty of motor vehicle and highway complaints, prohibition violations, drug infractions, and accusations of aliens failing to report during and after the Great War.

While the impressionistic accounts of duty logs, constables' notes, and newspapers are compelling, quantitative measures are tricky, given the absence of consistent data over time. However, an assemblance of sources – annual reports for the Ministry of Mines along with dominion crime statistics, a celebratory news story from early 1915, a summary document prepared by Herne in late 1917, and a similar document provided by Charles Daniell in 1920 – provide some items for comparison. The first set of sources comes from the provincial Ministry of Mines and dominion crime statistics. Among the former are the Cariboo Mining District's receipts and revenue reports, which include the amounts collected as fines in the local JP/Magistrate's Courts, beginning in 1904 and continuing until 1913. The existence of these figures may owe something to the breadth of government agents' fields of activity, but no other district provided similar information. While this source is intriguing, one must acknowledge that, prior to 1911/12, only a tiny portion of these reported cases would have pertained to the population at the Nechako and Fraser Rivers. A comparison with the dominion criminal statistics raises still more questions.[21] As much as the figures suggest a relatively low number of summary convictions in the Cariboo during these years, the 1913 spike (repeated in

TABLE 4.1   Justice of the peace/Magistrate's Court fines and case numbers, 1905–14

Year	BC Ministry of Mines annual report: justice of the peace fines	Dominion criminal statistics: summary convictions
1904	$342.50	17
1905	$432.50	766 (Yale and Cariboo combined)
1906	$645.00	4
1907	$335.00	23
1908	$730.00	19
1909	$645.00	27
1910	$607.50	27
1911	$305.00	1
1912	$552.50	89
1913	$453.50	1,137

Source: BC Ministry of Mines Annual Reports, and Dominion Crime Statistics, *Sessional Papers*, 1904–14.

1914) testifies to the settlement rush into the region during that year. The dominion statistics trace a drop in case numbers during hostilities, compared to the two years immediately before the war (607 in 1915, 294 in 1916, 145 in 1917, and 145 in 1918). Essentially, while these two sources seemingly track the broad patterns in the whole district, the yearly totals for case numbers at the dominion level and fines collected at the provincial level are inconsistent. Acknowledging the rising white settlement at the Georges, the provincial Ministry of Mines report for 1914 separated out the "Fort George Section" of the district and indicated that "police court fines" totalled $5,521.25, an astonishing jump in comparison with earlier district-wide numbers.[22] Still, the figure broadly tallies with the dominion statistics for that year. The yearly totals from the Ministry of Mines were never again published.

Second and while failing to provide any figures to sustain its conclusions, a news story from the second week of January 1915 argued that, despite the murder charge laid against George Onooki for killing Harry Porters on Christmas Eve 1914, the end of railway construction in the spring of 1914 supposedly ushered in a new era that "has been singularly free of desperate crimes and criminals." While admitting that criminals remained in the immediate area, the editor of the *Fort George Herald*, John Daniell, urged readers to believe that the

fear of the law has been driven into the hearts of the most desperately in-
clined by the severe punishment meted out by Government Agent Herne
sitting as magistrate, and the prompt action of [BCPP] Chief W.R. Dunwoody in bringing to court and nipping in the bud all plots of these characters who visit the district with any intentions of tearing things up, as one
gang intended last year. This district, in consequence of the thoroughness
of the measures thus taken by these two Government officers, has been
singularly safe and free from crime to all our citizens. No frontier town has
ever had a clearer record than the Fort George District in this respect.[23]

This was hopeful nonsense. Still, while the summary offences from 1913
and 1914 and police court fines gathered in 1914 seemingly lend credence
to the Georges' rough-and-tumble identity, the police duty logs and
newspaper reporting during the war years indicate that these immediate
prewar years were exceptional. John Daniell's assertion that disorder and
crime were the work of villains and hard men coming from elsewhere
and "tearing things up" is equally noteworthy: in that portrait, the New
Cariboo's "genuine" residents were respectable people who stood behind
Herne and Dunwoody, the guardians of law and order. Trouble came from
outsiders who did not belong. A "stabbing affray" in mid-March 1915 that
disturbed the peace of the community distinguished the right kind of
resident from non-preferred immigrants. In that episode, at the "Balkan
House" rooming quarters, three Austrians brawled, and one, displaying
an "ungovernable temper," left another with a knife wound requiring
stitches, distinguishing the "right" kind of resident from ill-mannered non-
preferred immigrants.[24]

An inquiry in early 1918 sparked by Mayor Harry G. Perry's raising
the question of whether a Supreme Court assize might be scheduled for
Prince George is a third source that allows us a glimpse of crime in the
Georges. In considering the request, Deputy Attorney General A.M.
Johnson asked that government agent Herne provide a report with the
number of County and Supreme Court writs issued, the number of
County Court trials (speedy and otherwise), the local legal services revenue, and the number of SM cases.[25] While Perry's pressure failed to
secure an assize sitting, Herne's report provided a retrospective tally indicating that, for 1915 through 1916, the Magistrate's Court in Prince George
handled eighty-five cases, while there were sixty-six cases in South Fort
George. For the following year (1917), Prince George saw twenty-six cases
while South Fort George had fifty-eight.[26] Supposing that the years between 1904 and 1913 had been typical and that the totals between 1915

and 1917 reflected a wartime decline in patrolling and arrests, the volume of misdemeanours suggests that, despite their reputation, the Georges were not beset with petty crime such as public drunkenness, brawling, and minor theft. Once again, the 1914 figures increasingly appear as an echo of the settlement rush and construction boom that collapsed with the outbreak of the war.

Finally, C.B. Daniell's summary of his court's business for 1920 offers a fourth source on offences in the region. Prefacing his account with the observation "that there has been a considerable increase compared to previous years," he reported that he held 250 sessions, during which he presided over 204 cases, with 156 convictions, 48 dismissals, and 11 cases sent for trial in a higher court. This represented 53 more cases than had been heard during the peak twelve months after September 1915 (as indicated by Herne). Daniell also specified that fines, penalties, and costs during 1920 amounted to $8,793.25. The greatest proportion of cases (52) and the lion's share of fines collected concerned the unloved prohibition act.[27]

When the contextual influences of all these idiosyncratic figures are drawn together, it is arguable that, given the settlement rush between 1911 and 1914, the wartime retreat, and the extenuating influences boosting alcohol-related offences during prohibition and the new era of government sales, the Magistrate's Court in the Georges probably averaged fewer than a hundred cases per year between 1910 and 1925, and these, in turn, averaged significantly less than $5,000 in fines on an annual basis. While there is no question that spikes occurred in 1913 and 1914, it is equally clear that these were aberrations. Simply put, as far as summary offences were concerned, the Magistrate's Court evidence indicates that the community was not especially troubled by crime. This, however, did not mean that the Magistrate's Court failed to contribute to the vague notion that "something" about the Georges was amiss.

THE CITY MAGISTRATE
AND THE COURTING OF CONTROVERSY

Thomas Herne's multiple roles as government agent and magistrate accounted for his prominence before the Great War, but it was Charles B. Daniell, Prince George's first stipendiary magistrate, who dominated the police court scene from spring 1915 until his resignation in early November 1923. Born in Shropshire, England, Charles Bampfylde Daniell was educated at Bristol's Clifton College before taking up legal studies in Geneva,

Switzerland.[28] He returned to England and articled with the Parks firm on Bedford Road in London, where, after being admitted to practice, he established his own office in 1897. Arriving in Vancouver in 1904, he joined the Eberts and Taylor law firm. It is likely that Charles and his wife, Mary, moved to Prince George in 1914 to be close to their son John, founding editor of the *Cariboo Observer,* the *Fort George Herald,* the *Prince George Post,* and, upon his return from a German POW camp, the *Prince George Citizen.* Backed by local Conservative worthy A.G. Hamilton, the elder Daniell was appointed the city's first stipendiary magistrate in mid-June 1915.[29] A week later, he was named the small debts commissioner. He remained in the region until 1923, when he moved to Venice, California, where John had accepted an editorial post.[30]

The senior Daniell is an intriguing, if not necessarily likable figure, for several reasons. First, in comparison with Herne, who demonstrated an inclination to get on with his work as unobtrusively as possible, Daniell revealed a penchant for attracting attention, aided, in no small part, by his son's editorial efforts. John Daniell insisted that he took no side in his father's clashes with city officials, but there is no question that the younger Daniell authored supportive editorials and, when occasions warranted, provided newspaper space so that his father might fight his own corner. Second, although South Fort George's Magistrate's Court continued to handle its share of judicial work from the outlying districts, the senior Daniell's prominence reflected the fact that his court was increasingly the destination for urban summary trials. And as the city struggled with policing after 1919, in the wake of prohibition and then government-controlled liquor sales, the magistrate's role in maintaining law and order was increasingly subject to scrutiny, a result that was not always to his liking. Finally, because of his education and experience, Daniell was disinclined to concede a point, legal or otherwise, to anyone. On occasion, he acted as if no one else in the region possessed a comparable grasp of the law. The result was a tetchy and often mercurial figure, apt to provoke strong responses from those he treated as less able or, all too often, as simply wrong-headed.

His first clash with city council occurred in the aftermath of Mayor W.G. Gillett's re-election in January 1916, when hostilities erupted between Gillett and the Northern Telephone and Power Company. Facing financial collapse and with the city refusing to purchase the company's power plant, the company terminated service at the end of January. Days later, the mayor ordered that the company's wires should be cut, and he directed two city employees to undertake the work within city boundaries.

The company filed a criminal complaint, accusing the mayor of damaging its property. Daniell presided over the complaint and the subsequent preliminary hearing, which found that there was sufficient evidence to warrant a trial. Gillett was released on bail with two sureties of $250, with the trial initially set for County Court in Prince George before being rescheduled for the May assize at Clinton.[31] In the interim, Prince George City Council held a special meeting, on 4 May 1916, to discuss and then vote on Bylaw No. 31, which barred any company not under contract with the city from operating trucks or equipment on city streets without specific permission. Passed months after Gillett had ordered the wires to be cut, the bylaw was plainly a retroactive justification for the mayor's actions. At the same session in which the bylaw was passed, lickspittle councillors E.A. Eagel and G.A. James moved and seconded a motion stating that

> whereas Mr. C.B. Daniell the Police Magistrate of Prince George is in the opinion of this Council so biased & prejudiced in his opinions, and so absolutely incompetent to render a fair decision on any matter brought before him; And whereas on account of not being able to get our by-laws enforced it is impossible for the City Council or the City Officials to control or regulate the affairs of the City.
>
> And whereas instead of listening to the evidence on both sides, as a judge is duty bound to do, he takes the side of the prosecution or defense as the [case may] be, and argues the case from a Lawyer's point of view, and renders his judgment regardless of the evidence;
>
> And whereas in view of the above opinion, he is, in the opinion of this Council a menace to the well-being of the City.
>
> And be it further resolved that the Attorney-General be informed that this [council] refuses to pay any further salary to the said C.B. Daniell.[32]

Obviously, the mayor and his supporters on council expected the magistrate to toe the line. For his sins, Daniell was denied his salary and was compelled to find a new home for his court sessions, as he was no longer welcome at city hall.[33] The city clerk was directed to forward a copy of the resolution to the provincial attorney general. Following the vote, Councillor J.T. Armstrong, who opposed the resolution, threw the magistrate an anchor, argued that denying Daniell his wages was too harsh. After all, he was "an old man" and reliant on his salary for his living. Even this remark was too much for the mayor, whose bullying tendencies were already a matter of public record. No, Gillett insisted, Daniell had been incompetent from the outset and had to be schooled in connection to several of his decisions, especially those concerning drunkenness.[34]

Council's rough handling of the magistrate drew a comment from a *Prince George Citizen* reader, who admonished Gillett and encouraged him to "adopt a higher standard of activity." Specifically, the decision to refuse Daniell his salary, compelling the magistrate to sue the city for his pay and recompense for having to rent a room to hold court, was unseemly. In the writer's opinion, council's actions demonstrated the need for the province to oversee magistrates to protect them from local functionaries demanding blood in response to an unanticipated ruling. Moreover, for a city struggling to make ends meet, it was poor business to be courting legal troubles, which unerringly came with additional expense.[35] Yet Gillett proved unbending, and the Magistrate's Court returned to city hall only in mid-January 1917, with the election of a new mayor, Harry Perry.[36] Given Gillett's treatment of the magistrate, one imagines Daniell's satisfaction on learning of the mayor's withdrawal from municipal politics to run as an "independent Conservative" in the provincial election of September 1916.[37] Thrashed at the polls, Gillett lost his deposit before disappearing below the horizon.

Daniell, in turn, maintained a low profile throughout the war until Harry Perry's return to local politics in January 1920. Presented with the opportunity to determine whether provincially incorporated private clubs were businesses, and therefore obliged to purchase a business licence and pay mandated taxes, Daniell sided with Perry's reform agenda, which allowed greater local scrutiny over operations that were little more than common gambling houses reliant on their social function to "camouflage their more sinister purposes."[38] Club proponents argued that they were not "traders" within the city bylaw's meaning with respect to business licences, since profits generated through their services – the sale of cigars, tobacco, and "near beer" – were divided equally among members. Opponents of tighter regulation of these clubs argued that "the boys" would be disinclined to spend their paycheques in a city where they were unable to kick over the traces. How paying for a business licence prevented a good time being had was unexplained. Anticipating Daniell's decision, city council passed Bylaw No. 96, obliging local clubs to have a manager who was a British subject, was over twenty-one years of age, had been resident in the city for at least six months prior to his appointment, and was to remain a resident of the city while acting as manager. Further, all club licence applications were to be accompanied by a certificate of fitness issued by the police commission and required a $100 manager's licence, which was valid for six months.[39] In trying to dodge the business licence, which was a mere $5, the club operators had opened themselves to much greater expense and regulation. Infractions of the new "Club Manager's Bylaw" carried a $300 fine or three months' imprisonment. Daniell's finding that clubs were business and were obligated to secure local licences covering their activities, combined with the new bylaw, effectively shuttered any club that relied on illegal gambling revenue.[40] It was not until the third week of April that new club licences were issued to the Prince George Club and the Chinese Masonic Club.[41]

As discussed in Chapter 3, the summer of 1920 was an unsettling time for the mayor and council, the police commission, and Prince George's self-identified "respectable" citizens. T.M. Watson, former councillor and current police commissioner, faced a retrial on the charge of attempting to pervert the administration of justice and had been involved in a pistol drama with a gambler; city police chief Stewart had resigned; liquor board agents were making regular appearances in the city; the province was looking askance at city governance; and it seemed as if the mayor's reform platform of the previous January had unravelled, despite the success in regulating private clubs. With editor John Daniell railing against the "well-intentioned but misguided reform element," C.B. Daniell experienced two reversals on appeal, results that may have temporarily dulled the sheen of his own self-regard. The first concerned a case in which the new police chief, Alex Sinclair, had entered the Olympian Café to find the air liberally scented with whisky, papers and parcels soaked with a "jazzy" smelling liquid, several empty glasses in the sink, and an empty bottle.[42] Thinking quickly, Sinclair wrung out the papers into the empty bottle, arrested proprietor Teddy Pappas, and brought him before the city magistrate on a liquor charge. Under cross-examination, the chief acknowledged that the seized liquid had not been analyzed, but he was convinced it was whisky. Pappas denied everything, save for the fact he had been in the café.[43] Daniell held that the evidence failed to satisfy beyond a reasonable doubt and dismissed the case. Undaunted, Sinclair appealed the decision in County Court, where Mr. Justice H.E.A. Robertson reversed Daniell's verdict and sentenced Pappas to three months' imprisonment. On learning of the result, the *Citizen* offered the dubious opinion that appealing the magistrate's original decision signalled an abandonment of Perry's electoral promise that the city would pursue an "impartial enforcement of all laws."[44]

The second reversal involved the case of Jeanne Schlosser, arrested by Chief Sinclair while she was in possession of three cases of Watson's No.

10 Scotch Whisky in her Third Avenue house. She was charged with intent to sell. The complaint cited neither the Liquor Act nor the section that Schlosser had allegedly contravened. Nonetheless, Daniell reasoned that, since Schlosser's monthly income was $75, of which three-quarters was earmarked for rent and supporting her children, she did not possess the means to purchase the liquor. Given this rationale, he found her guilty of intent to sell and seized the liquor.[45] Her counsel appealed on the grounds that the verdict was contrary to law and that there was no evidence demonstrating that the liquor was being held for any purpose other than consumption in a dwelling house. The hearing was scheduled for 14 September in County Court, but, without notifying Magistrate Daniell of the change and without his notes being in evidence, it was heard on 23 August. Judge Robertson accepted the appeal and returned both the whisky and the $75 fine. With reason, the magistrate was dismayed, writing to Robertson that,

> in the interests of Justice, I would like to be advised as to whether your Honour takes cognizance of evidence given on the first hearing, and if so, whether the notes taken on that occasion should not be submitted for use in the hearing [of] such appeals ... I see little use in being served with notice of appeal in which the date of the hearing is fixed, if such date is altered without due notice being given to the parties served.[46]

While the evidence at hand suggests that Daniell's handling of the case had been problematic – his assessment of Schlosser's household budget was not direct evidence of her acting as a bootlegger – his annoyance at the shabby treatment by the County Court was justified.

Although Daniell's findings in these two cases did not suggest that he was either "hard" or "soft" on local crime, they were alike in that they were slapdash affairs. In the Pappas case, the liquid squeezed from the sodden papers had not been analyzed, and the police chief seemingly expected that his belief that it was whisky would be sufficient to secure a conviction. And, in the Schlosser case, not only had the complaint failed to properly cite the provincial statute that had been contravened, Daniell's paternalistic conclusion that the accused could not afford the seized liquor had no bearing on whether she had been bootlegging.

In late September, city police laid a raft of charges against local clubs for selling beer that was found to have more than the allowed 2.5 percent alcohol content, charges that were mirrored in a series of cases across the province. Following the rationale of his fellow magistrates, Daniell dismissed sixteen of the twenty-two charges brought before his court, holding that the clubs had purchased the "near beer" from the bottlers in good faith and therefore were not accountable if the alcohol content was greater than that allowed by law.[47] The younger Daniell described the magistrate's decision as a "well-considered and logical judgment" that was "supported by a very flagrant error in the manner of determining the strength of the liquor taken by the police."[48] Still, the two earlier reversals rankled, and, in his annual report covering 1920, the magistrate acknowledged that the province's prohibition act had been "a difficult one to administer." Nodding to the Pappas and Schlosser reversals, Daniell closed with swipes at Chief Sinclair and city solicitor P.E. Wilson: "The prosecution of cases brought before the Court is not quite what it should be, although somewhat improved, and if the coming year is to bring an increase of work, there should be a distinct improvement in this respect ... It is not fair or right that any Police Magistrate should be called upon to act as Public Prosecutor, or an advocate for the defense, which frequently arises here."[49]

A week later, and after new mayor Henry Wilson and council were sworn in, one of the first matters of council business was responding to P.E. Wilson's unanticipated resignation in the wake of Daniell's comments. Promising to investigate the matter, city council passed a motion requesting that Wilson withdraw his resignation "and that the city retain his services with the understanding that he at all times will protect the interests of the city."[50] Four days later, council convened a special meeting to discuss Daniell's report and, specifically, the comments directed at the city solicitor. Centred on placating Wilson and securing his continuation as city solicitor, the minutes are mute on the substance of Daniell's report. Newspaper coverage does not fill the void, as the *Citizen* edition for 28 January 1921 has not survived, and the *Leader* had not yet launched operations. However, events in early April provide a retrospective glimpse. That month saw council's attack on the city's Black neighbourhood, an outburst of finger pointing and insinuation on council and the police commission, and the eruption of a riot in Prince George's "Chinatown" – a combination of events unrivalled in the Georges' history. Meeting on the evening of 8 April 1921, council passed a motion moved by A.M. Patterson and seconded by Alex Wimbles directing city clerk D.G. Tate to inquire of the police commission whether the city police were receiving "the necessary assistance from the Police Magistrate" and recommending that commissioners might consider whether the police magistrate was lending sufficient support to the police.[51] Waiting ten days to respond to council's inquiry, the police commission laid the city's law and order ills at Daniell's feet:

> It seems to be almost an impossibility for the dominion, provincial or city police to bring in evidence which is sufficiently satisfactory to the present police magistrate to enable him to convict. The result of the continued dismissal of cases brought before the magistrate has been that this city has become the "dumping ground" for members of the underworld, and is putting up to the small police force of this city a heavy task to keep these undesirables in their place and protect the respectable citizens from annoyance ... We would recommend that the written opinion of the police magistrate be asked for, stating his view of wherein lies the cause of so many dismissals and that should this not prove satisfactory, a review of the evidence in a number of cases be taken by an independent solicitor, and should it be found in the opinion of the counsel that sufficient backing is not given by the police magistrate to the police force, the matter be taken up with the Lieut.-Governor in council with a view to a reorganization of the police magistrate's department.[52]

Asked for his opinion of the motion, city solicitor Wilson warned council that criticizing the magistrate's decisions was a serious matter, before hastening to add that the reversals in the spring of 1920 had marked "the fallacy of the bench's judgment on occasions."[53]

Undoubtedly aware that his father had drafted his own response to council's attack, John Daniell waded into what he characterized as a "dirty mess."[54] He opened with the claim that the "decent-living residents of the city" were unlikely to be convinced that the magistrate was responsible for local disorder. Rather, the editor thought a ventilation of the question would reveal that gambling and bootlegging worries belonged to the city administration, which had issued business licences to some dubious operators. For his part, the magistrate, who denied the police commission's right to demand any explanation for decisions made in the performance of his court duties, waited until 23 April to craft his response. The letter would not be discussed in council until 2 May; one day later, it was published in the *Citizen*.[55] Noting that the annual report from the previous January had revealed his concerns about Police Chief Sinclair's "very limited experience in police work" and knowledge of police court practice and procedure, Daniell characterized the chief as an improving "outside officer" who could not be expected "to understand what is necessary in obtaining evidence to convict," let alone handling a defence counsel's cross-examination.[56] Turning to the city solicitor, he noted that Wilson was burdened with challenging and difficult cases that in larger centres were taken on by "men of experience" in "combatting crime and criminal offences." Daniell's lukewarm endorsement spoke volumes. In addition, he pointed out that the city had yet to provide the magistrate's office with a complete set of the *Canadian Law Reports* or a court stenographer who would ensure that trial evidence was properly taken down. He finished with a flourish:

> I have now been engaged for over twenty-three years in magisterial work and should have some experience in what is called for in the duties I have to undertake ... I feel that the police commissioners could have, at any time, gathered information from me for the purpose of effectively carrying out their objects. I have never been invited to confer with the commissioners since my appointment, and I am naturally surprised to receive, and to read the statements made in public by so important a part of the city administration without one word of complaint have been made to me personally ... This is the first time I have raised the complaints referred to in this letter, as I have never wished to create trouble, but since it has been thrust upon me the time has come when I have to speak out plainly.[57]

The mayor was having none of Daniell's argument.[58]

Reading from prepared notes, Wilson resented any inference that the police chief was responsible for local troubles. Revealing the thinness of his own knowledge, including his lack of awareness that it was not the magistrate's duty to prepare the Crown's case, Wilson claimed that Daniell's refusal to accept evidence of the smell of liquor in the Pappas case and his failure to adjourn the case to have the liquid analyzed had been a denial of justice. In the near-beer cases, where Daniell had followed the lead of decisions rendered elsewhere in the province, Wilson insisted that convictions should have been rendered because "ignorance of the law was no defence."[59] Ultimately, council failed in its attempt to attach any blame on Daniell for the city's trouble with bootleggers, gamblers, and disorderly women. As the *Citizen* concluded, not only had the city's police commissioners been unable to make any substantive recommendations to the attorney general, let alone pin responsibility on the magistrate, but also, "in their zeal the commissioners may have been barking up the wrong tree." Indeed, they might do well to invite the attorney general's office to investigate "the whole sordid business."[60] But such an option carried its own risks in that this inquiry might conclude that responsibility, in fact, lay within the city's offices.

Battered and embarrassed by the failure of its attempt to saddle the magistrate with the responsibility for the city's policing problems, council retreated in the following years. At the same time, while Daniell continued to preside over his court and was occasionally featured in a newspaper headline, he largely withdrew into the background before submitting his resignation in mid-October 1923.[61] His fellow magistrate Herne had cited health reasons for seeking a transfer to Prince Rupert, and Daniell did likewise in explaining his own withdrawal from the bench. Two weeks later, he was given a celebratory lunch attended by the mayor, council, Police Chief Sinclair, city solicitor Wilson, the police commission, former mayors Hiram Carney and Henry Wilson, and a smattering of other municipal officials.[62] Mayor Johnson acknowledged that "any person holding the office of police magistrate in a city such as Prince George, which was more or less in the making, would come in for a certain amount of criticism, as no magistrate could please everyone." But while some had disagreed with Magistrate Daniell on occasion, no one had "ever impugned the honesty or disinterested nature" of those rulings. Following the mayor's comments, Wilson added that he and the magistrate had entered city service at about the same time but that he would leave it to others to say whether anyone had made a greater and more honest effort than the two of them at bettering the community. And, while there were instances in which they parted company, he knew that Daniell "believed his decisions had been framed strictly in accord with his conscience, and that they were strictly honest." To the extent that there had been hard feelings between the two men, these were successfully put aside as the magistrate exited the stage.

Like much of the Georges' early twentieth-century policing and crime history, the Magistrate's Court offers a more nuanced image than that of the imagined enormities of "a wild and immoral netherland."[63] For, while we do encounter labourers seeking momentary escape in glasses of beer or an opium pipe, aspiring hardmen and chancers, and wrong-footed residents unfamiliar with the strictures of the modernizing state, the evidence suggests the prosaic reality that this community was no better or worse than any other in British Columbia. Yet at the same time, the scene was also populated with self-important mayors and over-matched councillors whose short comings and flawed behaviour created unnecessary and unwelcomed turbulence. The combination sometimes produced lamentable results. Local newspapers worried about how non-preferred immigrants and illegal liquor threatened the peace and order prized by the "decent-living residents of the city," while the great and the good blotted their copybooks with bullying, juvenile conceit, and insistent point-scoring. Rather than furthering the hopes for a well-governed, law-abiding white settler community, the Magistrate's Court revealed that the line separating the self-appointed respectable people from the disorderly was very thin. The implications for how the broader provincial community viewed the region remained a concern.

County Court

Long before the white settlement frontier neared the Nechako and Fraser Rivers, the County Court of the Cariboo had established its place in British Columbia's history. Owing to the gold rush drawing prospectors and adventurers deep into the colony's Interior, a County Court was established in the Cariboo in the early summer of 1865.[64] Established amidst the diggings at Richfield and Barkerville, the court was initially presided over by lay magistrate William G. Cox from 1865 to September 1871. It was then handed over to Henry M. Ball, another lay magistrate, who continued in the role until 1883, when the province's county courts were re-christened under the Canadian Confederation's division of responsibility for the administration of justice, courts, and the judiciary.[65] Ball's replacement was the Cariboo County Court's first legally trained judge, Eli Harrison Jr., appointed on 25 April 1884; he was followed by Clement Francis Cornwall, a former BC senator and lieutenant governor, named to the county bench on 19 September 1889.[66] Cornwall held the post for just over fifteen years: he resigned on 8 January 1907, to be replaced eleven days later by Frederick Calder.[67] Resident at Ashcroft, Calder was the first County Court judge to preside over sessions at South Fort George. Initially scheduled for 12 June 1911, the inaugural sitting was cancelled owing to the difficulties of travel caused by "high water on the Fraser."[68] Although the sitting was rescheduled for 25 September 1911, there is no evidence that the court was convened. Therefore, the first confirmed County Court sitting at South Fort George occurred on 15 June 1912, with a docket of two small debt cases.[69] Consistent with the police duty logs and newspaper reports of Thomas Herne's activities as magistrate, the court was not initially rushed off its feet, but the pace quickened over the ensuing two years. By early May 1914, the *Fort George Herald* reported that the approaching County Court docket, containing forty cases from across the region, was the largest on record. At the same time, the court and its business had become a source of popular attention, with South Fort George's modest facilities crammed to the gunnels with spectators.[70] Although civil suits occupied most of the court's attention, a prosecution alleging the selling of liquor without a licence and multiple criminal charges levelled against a former BCPP constable, A.E. Thomas, attracted "much local interest." Arrested by Chief W.R. Dunwoody on 12 April 1914 and committed for trial, the ex-constable escaped custody on 6 May, only to be recaptured two days later by Constable W.J. Service.[71] Tried before Mr. Justice Calder and jury on four separate counts of false pretenses, theft, and breaking out of jail, Thomas was found guilty on all charges and sentenced to eleven years in the penitentiary.[72] By the time Calder had dealt with the crowded docket, the sitting had consumed three weeks, another Cariboo court record, according to the *Herald*.[73]

The heavy civil calendar dovetailed with developments elsewhere in the province. Specifically, in February 1915, the Provincial Redistribution Commission, chaired by Mr. Justice Aulay M. Morrison, with Mr. Justice James A. Macdonald as his fellow commissioner, recommended an expansion of the number of seats in the legislature, with Morrison pressing for five additional seats, for a total of forty-seven, while Macdonald believed that three new ridings represented a truer accounting of the public sentiment.[74] The two judges agreed that, given the post-1910 burst of settlement, the Cariboo electoral district ought to be divided into two ridings. Acceptance of this recommendation led, in turn, to the May 1915 appointment of Herbert E.A. Robertson as resident County Court judge based in Prince George.[75] One of three sons of former BC Supreme Court judge Mr. Justice A.R. Robertson, the new County Court judge had been educated at Osgoode Hall in Toronto and admitted to the Ontario bar before returning to British Columbia, where he established a lucrative Vancouver practice representing clients in both criminal and civil matters. Maintaining ties with the provincial Conservative Party, Robertson was named as a commissioner investigating disputes over Courtney's incorporation as a city in the summer of 1914.[76]

Characterized as a "long-wanted appointment," Robertson's elevation provided the Georges with a judge whose robust enthusiasm for life in the wilds endeared him to residents across the region. A year after settling into his new duties, he undertook a canoe-and-portage judicial circuit to the Peace River country in the autumn of 1916, which the *Kamloops*

FIGURE 4.2   County Court judge H.E.A. Robertson. |
Mackenzie Museum.

Standard Sentinel exaggerated as establishing a precedent "in way of the
administration of justice, with rivers and lakes as the highway of travel
and a paddle propelled canoe as the means of locomotion."[77] This Peace
country circuit, the homeward leg of which consisted of travel via the
Edmonton-Dunvegan Railway and the Grand Trunk Pacific (later the Canadian National Railway), continued as an annual rite well into the 1930s.[78]
Robertson remained on the bench until his early seventies, when he was
felled by a stroke in mid-March 1942. His official retirement was reported
on 16 April, three weeks before his passing on 3 May.[79] Recalled in Prince
George as an able jurist and a patient and considerate man, he was locally
known as "the judge" and, according to city solicitor P.E. Wilson, consistently demonstrated good "horse sense" and, in that, earned plaudits from
the legal profession and the public.[80]

Robertson's inaugural court session proved to be representative of his
first decade on the bench. After summarizing the judge's handling of

fifteen civil suits and framing the sole criminal case in knowing language as a drunken row between two Finns, a newspaper report congratulated Robertson for establishing a courtroom environment where "the best ideals of substantial justice, the quibbles and technical evasions of learned legal lights [were] being given no more consideration than the introduction of such influences demand."[81] Although not always as stark a contrast as this first sitting, subsequent criminal dockets proved to be relatively light during the years straddling the First World War. Based on numbers derived from the court registers, which provide a more reliable tally than those from the surviving archival case files, the mean was just over nineteen cases per year between 1913 and 1925. Essentially, the Cariboo County Court dealt with an average of fewer than two criminal prosecutions per month from 1913 to 1925 – hardly a deluge of disorder and criminality. Further, these prosecutions involved an assortment of charges similar to those found elsewhere in the nation: iterations of theft, assault, indecent assault, break and enter, and liquor-related offences. Again, and consistent with the duty logs and Magistrate's Court records, the County Court record does not suggest that disorder leading to crime was endemic in British Columbia's northern Interior.

TABLE 4.2   Cariboo County Court criminal case load, 1913–25

Year	Per County Court register	Per extant case files
1913	7	
1914	27	12
1915	21	24
1916	10	7
1917	11	6
1918	14	11
1919	12	9
1920	31	12
1921	31	12
1922	28	17
1923	9	14
1924		0
1925		1
Totals	201	125

Sources: British Columbia Archives, GR 0017, Cariboo County Court Registers (South Fort George and Prince George), 1913–23, and GR 2788, 1–4.

SUPREME COURT AND THE GRAND JURY

While its status as the County Court seat offered Prince George a cachet of respectability, securing the Supreme Court assize was a prize of a different order. For one, it symbolized how far the community had come. Barely a decade after the Georges had been a collection of shacks, storefronts, and oversized ambitions at the confluence of the Fraser and Nechako Rivers, Prince George was hoping to host both the County and Supreme Court sessions, enabling it to become the district's unrivalled judicial centre. And while the County Court's financial limits for civil suits had sufficed since 1915, a regular assize suggested that the scale and complexity of business being transacted in the region – and the disputes that sometimes followed – warranted Supreme Court sittings. A regular assize signalled, for some, that Prince George had come into its own.

Although the early war years reined in judicial ambitions, in 1917 city solicitor P.E. Wilson, on behalf of the board of trade, championed a request that the attorney general schedule an assize, with an eye to reducing the expense and nuisance of local litigants having to travel to Clinton to pursue legal redress.[82] While there was no immediate action from Victoria, the following November, Deputy Attorney General A.M. Johnson inquired of Thomas Herne as to the number of probable civil cases on the calendar as well as the court registry's business since January 1916.[83] Herne's reply outlined the probable civil suits along with an accounting of County Court, speedy trials, and magistrate's cases over the preceding two years. The numbers did not demonstrate that an assize was especially needed, leaving the proponents to forward another request in the early spring of 1919, when, once again, Johnson inquired as to the number of suits liable to be ready for trial.[84] Responding with another summary of likely actions, Herne voiced trepidation at the possibility of an assize, given that the courtroom at South Fort George "is hardly big enough for a Supreme Court sitting." He wondered if the Ritts-Kifer Hall (on the corner of George Street and Fifth Avenue) – one of the largest such buildings in the Georges – would suffice.[85] It was then that fate lent a hand. In the early hours of 23 March 1919, the thirty-six-year-old Clinton courthouse, located at the north end of the Fraser Canyon, burned to the ground. Two weeks later, W.B. Colvin, the chief clerk in the attorney general's office, confirmed that the assize would be held in Prince George's city hall.[86] Here was the opportunity for the city to put its best foot forward in demonstrating that it had the makings of a regional judicial centre. Events suggested otherwise when, in the third week of April, with the assize already scheduled, anti-foreigner rioters, dominated by returned veterans, destroyed the Arcade Café, Max Schenk's real-estate office, and Conrad Reinharz's land-location business, before attempting to run Joseph Tadin, Martin Zadelovich, Schenk, Reinharz, and former city police chief James Dolan out of town. Although the BCPP detachment at South Fort George was on tenterhooks for days following the riot, there were no further disturbances.[87] The first assize opened as scheduled on the morning of 11 June 1919.

A newspaper account from the summer of 1921 offers a glimpse at what the assize provided. With a "host of lawyers, witnesses, police and others called here to attend the assize," the city was humming.[88] Still, this acknowledgment of the city's rising status came at a price. While local Supreme Court sittings reduced bother and expense for those involved in civil suits, the criminal side of the docket could be worrying. Were there unanticipated costs associated with hosting an increased number of criminal trials – beyond those already handled in County Court – with their dispiriting display of violence, depravity, and greed? While the County Court sessions had dealt with an assortment of charges, serious felonies such as rape, manslaughter, and murder had invariably involved the Supreme Court. Now, with a regular assize in Prince George, these cases would fuel conversation and comment in the city. For instance, counted among that first assize in June 1919 was the Edward Auton murder case from Pouce Coupé in northeastern British Columbia; a break-and-enter and theft charge, also from the Peace region; and an especially unsettling Quesnel case, in which a former BCPP constable – Herbert V. Harris – a married man infatuated with a woman named Evelyn Moffat, was accused of attempting to murder her.[89] Months later, in the lead up to the winter assize in 1920, the *Citizen* was chagrined to remark that the dockets were "the heaviest in both civil and criminal cases of any assize outside of Vancouver." Indeed, owing to Prince George's case load the next assize, in Kamloops, had to be rescheduled.[90] While all these charges did not necessarily reflect on local conditions and residents, would the twice-yearly parade of violence and wrongdoing from across the region color anxieties about the city's reputation? Would those cases bleed into the imagined portrait of Prince George? Would they cause the good and the great to wonder whether their respectable community was as orderly as they hoped?

The docket for June 1921 proved no different, with a "very heavy" calendar listing two murders, two attempted murders, and five or six civil suits, including two divorces.[91] Presiding over the assize, Mr. Justice Francis

B. Gregory disapprovingly acknowledged the number and character of the cases, drawing an unflattering comparison with Vancouver.[92] The one saving grace, at least from the perspective of the *Leader*, was that, in the aftermath of the city's second riot – the mid-April "Chinese" affray on Quebec Street – those charged were, with the exception of a single white man, "Chinamen and Indians."[93] Surely, no fair-minded white commentator from the Lower Mainland would conclude that the behaviour of such people reflected, in any fashion, on Prince George's character – that, at least, was to be hoped. And when the autumn assize proved to be lighter, the *Citizen* rushed to add that the heavy docket of the preceding summer had been filled with cases "from points scattered all over the big district which is tributary to Prince George."[94] The message was clear: these cases did not reflect Prince George's legitimate and respectable residents. A year later, when both the civil and criminal side of the calendar was again sparse, the *Citizen* emphasized that, after Mr. Justice Gregory had formerly lamented the northern Interior's volume of business, "an air of virtuous indignation struggled against the record of cases, and the learned judge's remark sank in, and passed by." However, with the autumn assize approaching and both the civil and criminal docket empty,

> the people of the enormous Cariboo district, which stretches from Lillooet to the Liard River have been "wearing the white flower of a blameless life" according to the best of all records, those of the police. This is rather hard on the newspapers, and on the learned gentlemen of the legal profession, but it is gratifying to the puritanical and it is to be hoped that the criminally inclined will forego any violence, or predatory activities, until the trial date has passed by with a clean sheet before His Honor.[95]

The editor's wish was granted, and after attending to a couple of matters in chambers – including Jeanne Schlosser's latest brush with the criminal law in the Magistrate's Court – Mr. Justice Morrison returned to the coast.[96] Occasional "heavy" dockets still occurred, but defenders of the Georges' reputation could explain them away by the Cariboo judicial district's enormous size or by veiled inferences about the type of people who ran afoul of the criminal law.

While acting as the northern Interior's designated judicial centre remained a point of pride for the city, the location and quality of the provincial government buildings on the former HBC reserve north of South Fort George remained unfinished business. Specifically, the offices' location "between" South Fort George and Fort George continued to rankle, and the passage of years had left the short-term solution in increasingly ragged condition. The cells were unsafe fire traps; there were no facilities for female prisoners; the building smelled of nearby cesspools; the police office had insufficient accommodations for constables; the courtroom could barely house County Court sessions, let alone the larger retinue accompanying the Supreme Court; and the entire operation was physically inconvenient for all concerned. Complaints about the location and the facilities had begun almost as soon as they were constructed. Within months of convening the first Prince George City Council in the early summer of 1915, Mayor W.G. Gillett approached the provincial attorney general, requesting the construction of an appropriate courthouse. The request fell on deaf ears.[97] While the war years militated against an expenditure for government offices and a courthouse, a campaign emerged to secure a new building as the end of hostilities neared. According to a *Citizen* report, the

district has long been handicapped and made to suffer from the inadequacy of proper government representation ... The old temporary government offices erected on the Hudson's Bay reserve eight years ago are now altogether inadequate and inaccessible. Court sittings are a nightmare of crowded quarters and general inconvenience, and noon adjournments necessitates a two mile hike each way for lunch.[98]

The Supreme Court's arrival, in concert with the grand jury's statutory obligation to report on local conditions and felt necessities, provided a regular opportunity to press for new facilities.[99] Although the grand jury's mid-June 1919 plea was pushed from the newspaper by details of the attempted murder charge levelled against former BCPP constable Harris and by reports of the Winnipeg General Strike, Thomas Herne submitted an unvarnished report to J.H. King, the minister of public works:

While commending the officials at the Provincial jail for the satisfactory conditions existing under adverse circumstances, your jury unhesitatingly condemn as unfit for further use, and a reflection on a civilized community, the present provincial jail.

We found practically no sanitary arrangements in said jail, no bath accommodation for prisoners or civil servants. There are 26 cells in a closely confined space with little light and practically no ventilation. We found two cesspools adjoining the kitchen where food is cooked and stored. The effluvia from these cesspools permeates the entire building. The only provision for female prisoners is in a small room with two cells crowded in and no separate entrance or exit from the male ward. The exercise yard cannot be used as it is not considered safe and already one prisoner has escaped.

The courtroom is so small that it will hardly hold the court officials and juries. The general condition of the building is very bad, and your jury are convinced it would not be consistent with good business to make these most necessary improvements and therefore earnestly request your Lordship to suggest to the proper authorities to abandon said buildings and inaccessible location.[100]

Having heard nothing from the provincial government, the grand jury reminded Victoria in late October 1919 of the earlier damning report on local facilities.[101]

Convened for the spring 1920 assize, the grand jury noted the dubious state of the city's public-school buildings, the inadequate and unsanitary condition of the post office, the desirability of increasing the salaries of provincial constables, and the need for a local land-registry and assessment office in Prince George. Its report opened, however, with the terse description of the courthouse and jail at South Fort George as "totally inadequate for the requirements of the district." While council chambers at city hall had provided an alternative setting for Supreme Court sessions the jail lacked any facilities for female prisoners, and constables were obliged to sleep in the courtroom, owing to the limitations of quarters on site.[102] Although County Court and then Supreme Court sessions had been construed by some as evidence that Prince George was to be counted among the province's leading communities, the state of the city's infrastructure suggested that Victoria remained indifferent to the region's needs. The situation was such that, at the end of the 1920 autumn assize, Mr. Justice Murphy added his voice to the conversation, noting that, when the court took over city hall, the mayor was ejected from his office, city magistrate Daniell was compelled to give way so that his office might serve as a jury room, and police court sessions were held in the basement.[103]

The list of concerns continued to grow. Each cell in the original jail required a separate key rather than a master key. If a fire were to break out, the possibility of prisoners perishing was genuine.[104] When, in the following spring, on behalf of the court of which he was one official, Sheriff E.A. Peters inquired as to the availability of city hall for the assize, council highlighted the disruptions caused by the effort to accommodate the court. "The magistrate has to hold court in the basement, the mayor is thrown out of his office and the lawyers robe and shuffle their briefs in

the main office, while jurymen, witnesses, and onlookers ramble all over
the building." It was hoped that charging the attorney general's office $20
per day for as long as the assize was in session might encourage the provincial government to build a proper courthouse in Prince George.[105]
Captured by the *Citizen,* the realities of the assize were less impressive
than residents had hoped. For, rather than a sense of awe and reverence,
the newspaper offered

> the spectacle of Mr. Justice Gregory trying to hold a court of assize in the
> municipal building. One might say the humble sardine, as prepared for
> market, suffers no more from congestion than do the human cogs who
> make up the justice machine, at present trying to clean up the criminal
> calendar for the County of Cariboo. At the risk of irreverence, one is forced
> to say the sight of the court, perched on its little chair, with the swarm of
> lawyers, court officers, jurors and witnesses squeezed into the little council
> chamber, suggests nothing so strongly as a spelling-bee in a crossroads
> schoolhouse, or the seat of justice in the hick-town of the comic.[106]

The effect was neither magisterial nor intimidating.[107]

Local annoyance with the third-rate facilities and the provincial government's refusal to answer the city's pleas was exacerbated by the news that
Prince Rupert, represented by T.D. Pattullo, minister of lands and future
premier, was to be home to an estimated $400,000 to $500,000 "federal-
style" government building.[108] Venting its righteous indignation, the
Citizen pulled no punches for what it considered an example of a fairy-tale
account of a despot's favourite winning out over the spurned brother. It
pointed to Pattullo's influence in rewarding his riding, a conclusion align-
ing with biographer Robin Fisher's assessment of the building as "a tangible
testimonial" to the minister's political power.[109] Noting that local MLA
H.G. Perry had "assumed a rather brusque manner towards the provincial
government owing to its attitude towards the north," the *Citizen* touched
on the frosty relations between Perry and his colleagues, no doubt aggravated by the contrast in facilities between Prince Rupert and Prince
George.[110] For residents concerned that opinion leaders and decision-
makers in Vancouver and Victoria were interested in the northern Interior
only when it came to how many trees were felled or how things went in
the mines, the persistent irritation over the construction of suitable government buildings in the city likely confirmed suspicions about the indifference of those in the province's southwest corner. And while some might
be tempted to dismiss the complaints as little more than northern carping

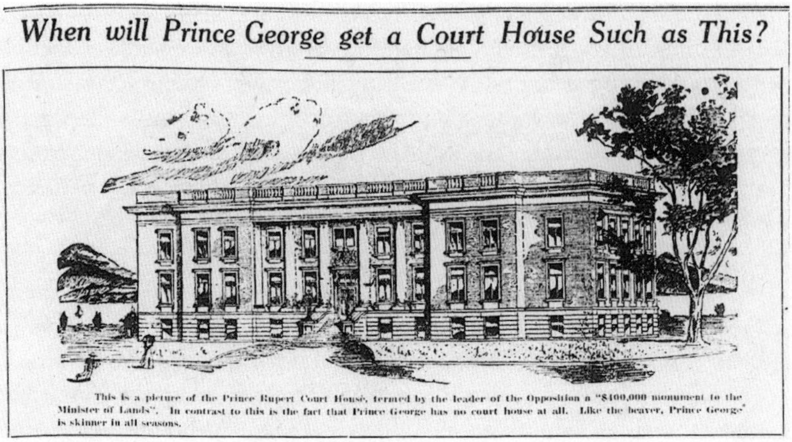

When will Prince George get a Court House Such as This?

This is a picture of the Prince Rupert Court House, termed by the leader of the Opposition a "$400,000 monument to the Minister of Lands". In contrast to this is the fact that Prince George has no court house at all. Like the beaver, Prince George is skinner in all seasons.

FIGURE 4.3   Prince Rupert's provincial government building, 1921. | *Prince George Citizen.*

about urban British Columbia's attitude toward the rest of the province, Mr. Justice McDonald sarcastically wondered during the autumn 1921 assize if the court had taken over the "whole" city hall when the juggling of juries, lawyers, and the magistrate meant that, if pressed, police court might convene in the basement's coal hole.[111]

As had been the case with the Clinton courthouse fire and its role in delivering the Supreme Court assize to Prince George, fortune again interceded on the town's behalf. Having been a presence in the Georges almost from the beginnings of South Fort George, and then as the purchaser of Nick Clark's Fort George Lumber and Navigation Company in early November 1910, the J.D. McArthur Company in the summer of 1922 acquired the HBC lands on which the original government offices rested.[112] Intending to build a sawmill on the site, rumours of a pulp mill project also caused a local stir. As the *Citizen* pointed out as soon as the purchase was made public, an incidental benefit was that after sustained foot-dragging, the provincial government would be compelled to relocate its facilities to better-situated and more appropriate surroundings. "Verily Mr. McArthur is doing a great work in buying the site on which the government buildings have been squatting for eleven years, and it is to be hoped that he will serve notice to quit, which would have the effect of driving the offices into a position convenient for the public in the City of Prince George."[113] While the acquisition did propel the provincial government to seek out a new home for its offices, talk of mills on the former HBC land lingered, even after McArthur's death on 10 January 1927, though they ultimately amounted to nothing.[114]

Finally, during the Christmas season of 1922, whispers made the rounds that Victoria had earmarked $100,000 for renovations to a city building so it could serve the "new" provincial governmental offices as well as a courtroom and headquarters for the local detachment of the provincial police. Although the rumoured amount was well short of what would have been required for a brick or stone building on the order of that in Prince Rupert, the *Citizen* remained hopeful that progress was finally to be made.[115] This rumour was paired with another suggesting that the long-lamented jail at South Fort George was to be closed, while the entire provincial force was to be reconfigured to align more closely with the RCMP.[116] The possible closure of the jail was especially worrisome for city officials, not because the facility functioned well, but because its absence would mean that the city would be on the hook for the cost of transporting prisoners either to Kamloops in the southern Interior or the Oakalla prison farm in the Lower Mainland. The expense would represent a new irritant for a city administration facing perennial budgetary challenges.[117] Indeed, as Magistrate Daniell pointed out, the logistical challenges created by closing the provincial jail could be resolved only by a shared-cost arrangement between the city and province.[118] After years of complaining about the conditions of the facilities at South Fort George, local officials were caught off balance when faced with the possibility that the province might simply close them and leave the community without a replacement. In early June 1923, the *Citizen* confirmed that, rather than constructing an impressive brick-and-stone building, the provincial government had secured J.H. Johnson's Alexandra Hotel on the corner of Third Avenue and Brunswick with the intent of refurbishing it in response to local needs. The former hotel had served as home for the RCMP since the force's arrival in 1919, and the notion of centralizing all legal business there was appealing, even if the city, as the Cariboo's judicial seat, would have preferred a bespoke building. Nonetheless, the *Citizen* attempted to portray the news in a positive light, in which the project answered the city's long-held concerns while demonstrating fiscal prudence. "It is estimated that in making use of the hotel property the government will be enabled to give Prince George much greater accommodation in the way of public offices than would have been possible in any other manner with the expenditure of a like sum of money."[119] The work on the building consumed three months, and by mid-December the various departments were populated with officials and staff. Following a tour of the building, the newspaper's reporter assured readers that, while the "lack of proper courtroom accommodation for a number of years has kept Prince George in the joke class in the administration of justice throughout the province," the new facilities would bestow the necessary dignity of the local administration of justice.[120] Counted among the government offices was the Land Settlement Board, the Forest Branch, the Public Works Department, and the district engineer and foreman, although, unfortunately, there was "no immediate prospect" of a land registry.

While the renovated provincial government building answered most grumbles about inadequate administrative facilities, the fate of the South Fort George provincial jail remained unsettled. Rumours circulated that the local complement of constables might be reduced to merely one man before BCPP commissioner J.H. McMullin's announcement in early February that the jail would simply be closed. McMullin further explained that since a new government building would not have facilities approved to hold inmates for over thirty days, prisoners would have to be sent to the Lower Mainland to serve their sentences.[121] The commissioner also acknowledged that the McArthur Company wished to begin constructing its proposed mill on the site, and, consequently, the province's occupation of the land where the jail stood could not be extended.[122] The following year, the plan to transport prisoners to the southern Interior or the coast was abandoned after word was received that a provincial Order in Council had designated the jail in the new government building a "common jail," which meant that prisoners could be detained there for up to six months.[123] Thus, the "temporary" offices on the Hudson's Bay parcel had finally run their course.

In exploring whether the presence of the superior courts in Prince George delivered the patina of respectability hoped for by an anxious community, we encounter a mixed verdict. The idea that becoming the region's judicial centre might paper over the rougher parts of the Georges' reputation proved to be too optimistic. While the County Court sessions and the twice-yearly Supreme Court assize provided occasions to display symbols of order and "justice," in one reading it is apparent that the criminal side of the calendar underlined the region's notoriety. Performed, first, in a rough-panelled and earthy-smelling courtroom and, later, in the make-do surroundings of Prince George's council chambers, these judicial displays struggled against the provincial audience's inability or unwillingness to suspend disbelief about the region's reputation. Empathizing with the complexities and hard edges of life lived beyond the Lower Mainland and Vancouver Island was too great a task for those convinced that Prince

George and the northern Interior were the very gates of hell.[124] In this, that half-forgotten "something" about the Georges remained more durable – and serviceable – than the locally preferred narrative of a well-ordered northern judicial centre populated by law-abiding, respectable people. Caricatures of the region as one of perpetual excess offered a ready rejoinder to outside commentators worried about the threats, real and imagined, of a quickening modern world: "we" may have troubles, but it could be worse – consider Prince George. That the community remained saddled with the tarnished reputation of an ill-mannered beggar at the feast was nowhere more evident than in news that Prince Rupert was to be home to a stately government building and courthouse. Here was a modern fairy story in which Prince George, forever cast in the role of the unloved sibling, was fated to bear witness to the prizes and heralds bestowed upon the tyrant's favoured child. Expected to be satisfied with "only the bare necessities of existence," the city was left to make do and mumble its gratitude when the provincial government was forced by circumstance to refurbish a former hotel so that it might perform the service of a "new" government building. The story had echoes of the struggle to attract a provincial constable as well as the drawn-out campaign to construct a government building so that, in the least, a policeman – along with other representatives of the provincial government – might occupy an office or a serviceable courtroom. The *Citizen* could only conclude that the "extravagant" sum spent on such a building in Prince Rupert was "little short of an insult to the city of Prince George."[125] Occurring at the same time that the province was extracting "huge revenues" from the Interior in timber royalties, taxes, and fees, the slight was evidence that policy-makers and opinion leaders in southern and urban British Columbia neither heard nor cared about concerns existing beyond their own communities. It was a belittling experience, and one that continued to resonate through the years.

The symbolic weight of being a regional judicial centre and, through that, a respectable and well-ordered community, could forward Prince George's cause only so far. The wider public believed whatever it chose to believe, regardless of evidence urging a different narrative. Once an identity had taken hold, it was difficult to loosen its grip. Changing people's minds was a daunting prospect, especially when, as the following chapter details, astonishing police investigations and trials populated with sensational characters from the northern Interior paraded across the province's front pages. Keen to exploit a story that had the potential to seize the public's imagination and sell newspapers, accounts from the northern Interior, often enough constructed as dispatches from a distant edge of civilization, made good copy. And whether readers were familiar with the region or knew relatively little, boldly drawn stories built around contrasts of good and evil were sure to capture and hold public attention.

5

Sensations, Front-Page Crime, and Community Identity

Anticipating the January 1926 assize, the *Prince George Citizen* remarked that, while the docket contained only one civil suit, it listed seven criminal prosecutions, including a homicide. The details of the latter were remarkable. Trapper Fred Cyr had mushed his dog sled for nine days from Chilco Lake to Hanceville to report his killing of Alexander Ducharme. Initial reports suggested that the fatal clash concerned a trapline.[1] As it turned out, Cyr's plan to prospect near Chilco Lake had antagonized Ducharme, who feared that prospectors would invade "the wild little kingdom which he had come to regard as his own." Simmering friction between the two grew until they faced each other in an armed stare-down that ended with Ducharme dead. Having outlined Cyr's version of events, the *Citizen* concluded that the account could spark "one of the most remarkable trials in the history of the province."[2]

The other six cases also hinted at intrigue. They included allegations of intimidation by a woman brandishing a .22 rifle in a dispute over sawn logs intended for a schoolhouse, an attempted murder, a charge of seduction, carnal knowledge of a ward, an assault, and a complaint of theft from the Hudson's Bay Company.[3] Nothing about the docket presented an encouraging image of the Cariboo, although Prince George residents may have offered a prayer of thanks that, save for the assault, which involved local resident Arthur Bellos, no one from the city was on trial. By the close of proceedings, the accused thief, the woman charged with intimidation, and Cyr had been acquitted. The charge of carnal knowledge of a ward brought a conviction, with the accused sentenced to one year in the penitentiary; the attempted murder trial ended with a declaration of temporary insanity; and Bellos, to whom we will return, was convicted of assault, and sentenced to eighteen months.

As the *Citizen* had predicted, the Cyr case became a sensation, with the *Vancouver Province* fanning the flames. Its 2 December 1925 edition reported that Cyr and an Indigenous man dubbed "Eagle Lake Henry" were guiding Constable Ian Macrae of Hanceville, coroner Hubert Campbell of Williams Lake, and an eight-man jury to Chilco Lake for an inquest. Carrying a month of provisions, the party hoped to wrap things up before Christmas.[4] Travelling by car, sleigh, horse, foot, and rowboat, they arrived on 10 December at their destination, where Ducharme was disinterred, allowing the jury to conclude that he had died owing to Cyr's gunshots.[5] Have whetted readers' appetites for the excesses of life and death in the northern Interior, the newspaper concluded with a full criminal case listing of the Prince George assize.[6] Finally, in summarizing the single day of testimony concerning Ducharme's death, two Vancouver dailies delivered bold front-page headlines, with the *Province* teasing "Cyr's Dramatic Tale" just beneath the masthead, while the *Sun* offered a "Drama of Wilds Is Bared: Prospector Shoots Trapper in Terrific Gun Battle."[7] Headlines such as these were precisely the kind of sensationalism that worried "respectable" Prince George residents.

While investigating Alexander Ducharme's violent death amounted to what most residents imagined was "real" police work, not every investigation – even those with an effusion of blood – became a sensation. Indeed, a garden-variety felony revealing little good sense and an excess of passion, masculinity, or liquor was unlikely to hold the public interest. Such instances were common enough across the province and beyond. Sensations required more. Headline-grabbing crimes needed sufficient time to seize and hold public attention. In this, the Georges faced challenges. Beyond brief experiments, local newspapers remained weekly affairs, and the most a local criminal trial could expect was coverage and commentary spanning two editions. Consequently, "trial by newspaper" was less likely in the Interior than in the Lower Mainland.[8] Still, as was the case with Ducharme and Cyr, a drawn-out police investigation allowed weeklies to pique public interest. Yet even in such an instance, northern Interior weekly newspapers invariably ran behind news broadcast by barstool prophets and street-corner conversations. Other than in rare instances when a news flash arrived just as the type was being set, most local newspaper accounts were outdated before they hit the streets. Moreover, in serious felonies, the accused could choose a jury trial, which meant that such cases, along with aggravated assaults, attempted homicides, and murder charges, migrated to a Supreme Court assize, which were not held in the Georges until 1919. So, while investigations and preliminary hearings captured a local audience, the trial, verdict, and sentencing occurred elsewhere. For instance, the Georges' biggest prewar sensation, John Daniell's October 1912 criminal libel trial for his attacks on George Hammond and the Natural Resources Security Company, culminated in Kamloops. There was, in effect, an alchemy in constituting a sensation, and, until after the Great War, there were few opportunities for a genuine headline-grabbing sensation to worry the northern Interior. But when a sensation did occur, anxious residents knew that, once the investigation and trial were past and the particulars faded in the rush of days, a recollection would linger on the edge of memory about Prince George, with its wild-eyed trappers, rifle-wielding women, sexual impropriety, and running gun battles. Little good came from "true-crime" sensations.

KNOWN TO AUTHORITIES

One form of sensation involved instances where those involved were "known to authorities" and had already featured in newspaper reports detailing a series of misdeeds, both great and small. Irene Jordan, who was a brothel keeper in South Fort George but had never faced a criminal complaint, was a case in point. The notoriety of Guangdong merchant Chow Lee and the Bellos brothers also offer compelling illustrations. Chow first attracted unwanted attention in the summer of 1918 following an arrest for possessing two suitcases full of liquor and opium. His customers were in lumber camps east of Prince George. The liquor offence earned him a $100 fine, while the opium charge netted an additional $50.[9] Almost two years to the day, he reappeared before Magistrate Herne, again charged with having liquor in his possession, on this occasion intended for labourers west of the city. This second offence brought a $300 fine.[10] Perhaps hoping to improve his reputation, Chow contributed $15 to the Great War Veterans Association and, on two occasions, $4 to the Red Cross Society.[11] This pursuit of respectability was temporary, and there followed a series of convictions for conducting a disorderly house, a charge of keeping opium in his store, an intriguing conviction shared with Arthur

Bellos for running the Fraser Club without a club-manager's licence, and yet another opium conviction in the spring of 1923. This final case concerned five pounds of opium found in ten canisters in a building that Chow owned but that two other "Chinese" men rented. Standing before Magistrate C.B. Daniell, Chow sought leniency owing to his being "well known in local business" and his residency in the province since 1896, along with his wife and their seven children, all of whom had been born in Prince George. His counsel, W.P. Ogilvie, sought the minimum sentence. Stressing Canada's sustained efforts to "stamp out" the illegal drug traffic, Daniell sentenced Chow to six months in prison in addition to a $750 fine. The conviction carried a near certainty of deportation.[12]

Chow completed his six-month term but, to extend his chance of avoiding deportation, he refused to pay the fine, which resulted in six more months in the local jail. An initial attempt to reverse the conviction failed.[13] The *Citizen* reported that Chow had not secured "naturalization when this proceeding was a matter of form." Despite the newspaper's sneer, the archival records of the Cariboo district's government agent demonstrate that the observation had merit: the naturalization of racialized Chinese men in the Cariboo began no later than August 1885 and continued through a flurry of applications in 1903.[14] More important to the newspaper was the possibility that, by sending Chow out of the country, his family might become "a charge upon the municipality." At this point, and for undisclosed reasons, Magistrate Daniell amended his original conviction order. Working through Ogilvie, Chow secured the services of renowned lawyer Stuart Henderson, who applied for a writ of habeas corpus, arguing that, since the original complaint and the subsequent conviction order no longer agreed, the conviction ought to be quashed.[15] Mr. Chief Justice Gordon Hunter agreed and freed Chow from further confinement, effectively ending the deportation threat.[16] Perhaps chastened by his legal troubles and the threat they represented to his family, Chow retreated from public view and the perils of being a sensation.

That Chow's troubles unearthed a connection with Arthur Bellos is intriguing. The second of three brothers – William the eldest, and Nicholas the youngest – Arthur was a magnet for trouble, although William also had his share of local infamy (Nicholas distanced himself from his older brothers). Beginning in 1916, William and Arthur dot police records as well as those of the Magistrate's, County, and Supreme Courts, with a case involving Arthur eventually rising to the Supreme Court of Canada. Arriving in the northern Interior in 1912 as a labourer on the Grand Trunk

FIGURE 5.1   Nicholas, Arthur, and William Bellos (seated). | Central BC Railway and Forestry Museum.

Pacific (GTP) Railway, William first appeared in the local press when he acquired the Queen's Hotel – renamed the Royal Hotel – on George Street in downtown Prince George in late 1916.[17] He was twenty-five years old.[18] A year later, Arthur, who had also worked with the GTP, enlisted with the Canadian Expeditionary Force, despite being a Greek national.[19] Back in the Georges a few months before the armistice, he was called up before Magistrate Daniell in August 1918 following an altercation with Conrad Reinharz, who had supposedly declared, in Arthur's presence, that he was glad to be German. Daniell acquitted Bellos, reasoning that the provocation had been "very great." Convicted months later on a charge of discouraging enlistment, Reinharz then had his land office destroyed by rioting veterans in the third week of April 1919.[20] Diagnosed as suffering from gonorrheal rheumatism in his right knee, Bellos returned to civilian life in November 1918.

Arthur's brush with the law was the first in a series of incidents bringing him and his brother William before local judges.[21] At one point in 1922,

William (along with newspaper editor John Daniell) tangled with aspirant labour leader H.P. Hansen, who had unsuccessfully led a strike of
local railroad tie makers and, as a result, "was breathing fire and impreca-
tions upon the people of the town for their lack of sympathy for the cause
of labor."[22] Aggressively ruminating in his cups, Hansen had attempted
to assault Bellos with a hotel telephone. The incident, which ended with
Judge Robertson fining Hansen and requiring the securing of a peace
bond, caught the eye of two Vancouver-based newspapers. It was the type
of notice that the city's "respectable" residents deplored.[23] There was more
to come.

With William striving to become respectable in the late 1920s, Arthur's
penchant for trouble continued. The final occasions when both brothers
were before a criminal court was in the summer of 1925. Arthur, along with
Sam Limeratos (aka I. Nimbaratos, aka Sam Nimbaratos), appeared before
Police Magistrate P.J. Moran, accused of battering Richard Brotherston
in the early hours of 28 June 1925. The attack, in which Bellos had allegedly
wielded a blackjack, occurred in the Quebec Street rooms of a woman by
the name of Grace Ryan. Days later, Bellos and Ryan were married, a
coupling that prevented her from testifying against her new husband.[24]
A week later, William also appeared before Moran, charged with allowing
after-hours drinking in the Royal's beer parlour. The guilty verdict triggered a suspension of the hotel's beer licence. An appeal in County Court
failed.[25] Arthur's pending assault trial returned to the news in mid-
September, when Grace, who failed to appear in Prince George on a liquor
charge, was arrested in Prince Rupert for her non-appearance.[26] That same
weekend, she filed a complaint against Arthur for assault while the police
charged her with bigamy.[27] As the *Province* quipped, by marrying Bellos
she ceased to be a compellable witness, "but the police assert Bellos made
one husband too many."[28]

Given the back story, Arthur's jury trial before Mr. Justice Denis
Murphy was sensational. As the *Citizen* recounted, Brotherston and two
other men had blown into Prince George from Giscome and spent two
days "absorbing" a considerable quantity of beer and whisky in the city's
watering holes before appearing at Ryan's rooms for an impromptu
party.[29] According to two Crown witnesses – John Mose Berman, known
as "Johnnie the Jew," and a man named Homewood – Brotherston bested
Bellos in a scuffle during the festivities. Picking himself up, Bellos spoke
of getting his "gat" (a pistol) and returning "to clean the house up." When
Bellos, Homewood, and Sam Limeratos – "Sam the Greek" – did arrive,
Brotherston received a thrashing. With the court's protection in exchange

for providing testimony, Limeratos admitted striking Brotherston in self-defence when the man menaced him with a broken bottle. Summarizing the evidence, Justice Murphy explained to the jury that, if Bellos and Limeratos had agreed to attack Brotherston – that is, had formed a common intention to prosecute an unlawful purpose – Bellos remained criminally responsible. Both the *Prince Rupert Daily News* and the *Victoria Times-Colonist* interpreted the instructions as Murphy guiding the jury to ignore the Limeratos "confession."[30] Deliberating for ninety minutes, the jury found Bellos guilty, and Murphy sentenced him to thirty months in the penitentiary. Bellos signalled his intent to appeal.[31]

Further complications surfaced. Before his appeal proceeded, Bellos alleged that his trial had been unfair.[32] Specifically, eight affidavits, including one from grand jury foreman Richard Corless, indicated that "several members" of the trial jury "had made up their minds to convict Bellos regardless of the evidence." Corless added that Bellos could not receive a fair trial "because public opinion in Prince George, which is a comparatively small town, was against the prisoner and in favor of Brotherston, who was well-liked and popular." And in explaining her absence from proceedings, Grace Bellos swore that "she had become frightened and ran away from Prince George on account of public sentiment against" her husband. Nonetheless, she insisted that Sam Limeratos had assaulted Brotherston. The *Citizen* scoffed at the contention that the city was brimming with so many "disorderly persons" that Grace Bellos had fled in fear.[33] In a separate column, the newspaper dismissed the affidavits alleging that the jury was prejudicial, noting that one of the deponents worked for William Bellos, another worked for Arthur, a third had once been convicted on a liquor offence, and a fourth was a "half-breed Indian."[34] While Chief Justice James Macdonald discounted Grace Bellos's testimony, he concluded that Arthur Bellos had been denied a fair trial. Leave to appeal was granted.

Still, the appeal did not centre on whether the jury had denied Bellos a fair trial, but on the question of whether British Columbia Provincial Police (BCPP) sergeant W.A. Walker, after warning the accused that anything he said could be used against him during the trial, had unfairly persisted in his questioning.[35] Walker's testimony at the original trial left the impression that Bellos's version of events concerning the Brotherston beating had been dishonest. On the question of whether Walker's actions represented an injustice, Mr. Justice Archer Martin, speaking for the Appeal Court of British Columbia, indicated that the sergeant had exceeded his duty. According to Martin, "it is the duty of a police officer when making an arrest to keep his mouth shut and his ears open."[36] Four days later, the provincial attorney general's office announced that it was appealing the decision to the Supreme Court of Canada.[37] Before this occurred, Arthur Bellos was again arrested, this time in Vancouver, on a charge of counselling the commission of an indictable offence, when, along with Joseph Pepo, he attempted to convince Ernest de Lui to break into a store on Hastings Street and on a second charge concerning Bellos's orchestration of a plan to rob the Pantages Theatre.[38] The Hastings Street charge was dismissed, and the Pantages Theatre complaint withdrawn. In time, the Supreme Court in Ottawa determined that Sergeant Walker's continued questioning of Bellos did not amount to an inducement or persuasion. Consequently, his incriminating answers remained admissible.[39] Bellos was returned to custody. While the specifics of Chow's and the Bellos brothers' legal tangles faded, they assuredly contributed to the idea that the northern Interior boasted a disproportionate number of "interesting characters" with criminal tendencies. That such things and notorious individuals existed elsewhere in the province – with examples filling mainland newspaper columns competing for readers – failed to counter an increasingly hard-packed narrative that there was "something" about the Georges. That these men and their cases were not representative did not matter. Indeed, that William Bellos became an inventor, an accomplished local contractor, and a man of business was irrelevant. The exploits confirmed the reflexive impression that, regardless of what occurred elsewhere or what had since happened, the Georges remained notorious.

RACE AND CRIME IN A WHITE MAN'S PROVINCE

Another tendency that contributed to notoriety and sensation, and one consistent with the era's prejudices, was the linking of "race" with an imagined penchant for crime and disorder. This association informed Chow Lee's experience and, in a different fashion, shaped events swirling around the Bellos brothers. The experiences of both Chow and the Greek-born Bellos brothers suggest the prevalence of the racist idea that specific people – often people of colour – were, because of their ethnicity, prone to disorderly and criminal behaviour. Such ideas were commonly expressed in the press. For example, when the *Leader* summarized Inspector T.W.S. Parsons's report on the local BCPP detachment's activities during 1921, it concluded its observations on the decline in the local opium traffic with the comment that "few whites are addicted to the habit."[40] The *Citizen's* longer version was more explicit: concern over illegal drugs had retreated because the "Chinese" had abandoned the region's larger towns and the exodus had reduced the drug traffic.[41] Simply put, race shaped the meaning of the criminal law, and notions about whiteness remained an assumed standard for interpreting all behaviour. Consequently, when County Court judge H.E.A. Robertson enjoyed an evening of poker in a local hotel while on the Peace country circuit, it was an example of masculine entertainment on the white settlement frontier. After all, when played "in a fair and legitimate manner," poker was a game of skill rather than chance.[42] But if a group of Guangdong men crowded around a game of fan-tan or pai gow or a punch board – games of chance – it was an occasion for a fine. Indeed, a fondness for gambling supposedly ran in Chinese blood.[43]

Such imagined distinctions were everywhere. White settlers were celebrated; Black farmers were an invading army. White labour was prized; Asian labour was degrading. White citizens understood and appreciated the wonders of technology; "half-breeds" were struck silent by the sight of an oil-burning locomotive, while Indigenous people thought of trains as houses on wheels.[44] Such commonplace racism was ingrained in everyday language throughout the northern Interior and beyond.[45] It was reinforced in countless ways. When Thomas Herne assumed the position of local government agent in 1911, one of his first acts was to "instruct ... the Chiefs of the Indian Reserve here that no Indian will be permitted off the Reserve after dark." The *Fort George Herald* thought it "an excellent rule."[46] While, in a moment of clarity, a local observer might admit that white men were much more prominent than any other group in accounts of police duty and summaries of both lower and superior courts, the *Herald* nonetheless congratulated Herne for "teaching the red man that their orgies are not only distasteful to the public but against the law" and that hard-labour sentences were a welcome curative.[47] The statement confirmed the unquestioned: British Columbia was a white man's province. To reverse sagging spirits as the Great War dragged on, residents were invited to a masquerade ball with the "Chink, Jap, Mongolian, Arab, Spaniard, Italian, Russian, Egyptian, Filipino, French, Swiss, Scotch, Irish, English, Canadian, American, Mexican and a whole lot of other countries and cities – all will be represented, besides the fun-producing characters every ready to dispel your feelings of dissatisfaction with life generally."[48] Offered up as racist caricatures to entertain, these representations reinforced, and were reinforced by, the imagined structures of everyday life. They shaped the constable's discretionary gaze, the magistrate's quick dispatch of alcohol-fuelled misdemeanours, the matter-of-fact preliminary hearing, the trial, verdict, and sentencing in one of the superior courts, and how, in the end, the accused, the guilty, and witnesses were displayed in local newspapers.

As was the case elsewhere in the nation, whiteness was a privileged contrivance equating skin colour, British heritage and morality, the idealization of English "fair play" and justice, and a contradictory collection of paternalistic obligations and responsibilities. For those subjected to this artifice, the expected response was to meekly accept their place in society while understanding that their enjoyment of the benefits of life in Canada was a matter of sufferance. Thus, for example, Mennonites, whose agricultural aptitude might have suggested that they were attractive settlers, were thought unsuitable for British Columbia's northern Interior, where wartime antipathies coloured them a "plague" of undesirables.[49] While, for some, circumstances might change after the war, others would never fit. As the *Prince George Herald* argued,

> The black man has never been assimilated in America. An octoroon, in the eyes of the white man, is still a negro, and the same will hold true in the case of the oriental. The Japanese and Chinese are so totally different in their ways and customs, as are also the Hindus, that the white race refuses to assimilate them. This is not so much a matter of choice, as it is the following of a natural law ... Centuries of progress and the cultivation of a taste for better things have raised the white man's standard of living away above that of the Oriental, and for that reason the white man demands more, and is entitled to more – in his own country at least – than the yellow man.[50]

Here was a perspective resting upon and creating its own anxieties. While the Georges' "decent-living" residents embraced the assumptions of white respectability – in their anxious pursuit of admission into the select company of the province's "natural" leaders – it was a performance that fostered unease among those whose presence was "tolerated." And, in this process, there were few tools more powerful and purposively unsettling than those of the law and legal redress. Being etched with the identity of a "drunken Indian," "a fiendish Chinaman," a Black "brute," or a "Jezebel" reduced a person to a category, a problem to be policed, or, ultimately, a cancer to be excised from the body politic.

There is no shortage of examples illustrating the assumed links between race, disorder, and crime in the northern Interior. These include early arrests for drunkenness among a small collection of Indigenous people before the erasure of Fort George Indian Reserve No. 1 and the relocation of the Lheidli T'enneh to Shelly; the reliance of "Chinaman" as a placeholder for names in BCPP duty logs; local newspapers' unapologetic racism in explaining trouble within local ethnic communities; and the normality of racist epithets directed at the handful of Black residents. All these practices are apparent in the archive of local reporting and advertising and in depositions, coroners' findings, and city council minutes. Consider, for example, the following account in a newspaper column on local events:

> [The] old story of the small boy, the 22-rifle, and the accidental shot cropped up here again this week. In this instance the shriek of the victim went forth from the peaceful home of Jimmy Bird, the well-known and respected half-breed who lives west of the Hudson Bay property. Frank Bird, age 14, was sitting at his father's table, when his little brother seized upon the loaded 22-rifle, which he discharged and landed a bullet in his brother's head. From all appearances the boy will recover. He is doing well, and is not in any danger unless complications set in. The bullet entered his temple and followed the edge of his skull.[51]

The same column informed readers that local justices of the peace were busy dealing with "drunk and disorderly Finns found on the Indian reservation with bottles of 'hooch' ... whilst a dago with a name like a sneeze paid a $20 fine for the same complaint. The dago ran amuck in the Gore & McGregor building and sought to exercise his bloodthirsty designs with a piece of Camorra cutlery of keen edge and graceful curve." A local man named Art Sheridan, boasting a boxing championship in the United States, "resented the black-hand idea by knocking sneeze down a flight of stairs, at the bottom of which he landed in a puddle of blood."[52] Reducing "outsiders" to a racist stereotype when they ran afoul of the criminal law, while celebrating the manly virtues of those who, in their own style, upheld law and order, made for good copy and reassured the reading public that the preferred "truths" prevailed in the Georges, even if opinion leaders elsewhere did not notice.

In such a setting, the barbed commentary in the local press after the arrival in the Georges of 500 "Chinese coolies," whose labour on ballasting gangs on the GTP was suspended in early January 1919 by cold weather, was no surprise.[53] Although most were former residents of Guangdong province and answered to the descriptor "Guangdong," they were invariably labelled "Chinese," an identity imbued with a raft of negative characteristics.[54] The *Citizen* reported that the "holidaying heathen[s]" were crowded into any available accommodation, where they amused themselves by playing yănqián (an ancient game of chance commonly known as fan-tan). With the alleged steady parade of these labourers to the city's water standpipe, Councillor Thomas Porter pressed the mayor to confirm whether the newcomers were paying the going water rate. Although Guangdong had been in the region as miners and trappers since the late nineteenth century, the arrival of such a large group in Prince George was unprecedented. Indeed, if the newspaper's estimate was sound, the numbers meant that, on a per capita basis, Prince George had become one of the province's largest Guangdong communities.[55] Admittedly, precise population figures are elusive. Local historian Lily Chow offers the unsubstantiated claim that, by a "conservative estimate," there were at least 600 racialized Chinese in Prince George by 1920. For its part, by mid-April 1921, the *Citizen* estimated that the Guangdong population was about 400, while the late May census of that year enumerated fewer than 130 "Chinese" in the community.[56] When queried on the subject, Police Chief Alexander Sinclair thought there were two main factions within the population – the Chee Kong Tong (CKT)/"Chinese Freemasons" and the Kuomintang (KMT)/Nationalists – that numbered about 100 and 75. Ultimately, what mattered was that, after years of subscribing to racially motivated fears of the threat that Asian immigration posed to the emergence of the New Cariboo, Prince George residents were, for the first time, presented with a significant Guangdong population. The response from the police commission and the city police force was predictable. Here was the group that could be blamed for the city's bad reputation.

By the end of January, acting on orders from the police commission, Police Chief Louis Vibbard and Police Commissioner George Fisher raided "alleged gambling dives," Chow Lee's store, and "Chinese" rented rooms.[57] Chow, of course, was already known to the police.[58] After his store was secured, one man fled the scene but succeeded only in leading the police to a nearby card game, where the participants were arrested. The accumulated evidence, including paraphernalia for opium smoking, was transferred to the city hall vault, where, coincidentally, it was discovered that seven cans of opium and fifty-two quarts of whisky seized by the BCPP in August had vanished.[59] That gambling among the Guangdong suddenly warranted the police gaze is striking, especially since concern about games of chance had been largely rhetorical prior to the war. Nonetheless, the *Citizen* offered a "cordial commendation" to the city police commission "for the firm stand they have taken in curbing the lawless conditions that were rapidly growing in Prince George. Heretofore the excuse has prevailed that while the authorities were cognizant of such disregard of the laws it was impossible to secure a conviction."[60] No doubt with great relief, the perennial concern with crime and disorder in the region could now be brought home to the growing "Chinese" population. Appearing before the stipendiary magistrate, Chow pled guilty to conducting a disorderly house and was fined $100 plus costs. Two men, Chow Kim and Yum Lee were found guilty of being frequenters of said house and were fined $20 each plus costs. A second raid tallied twenty-two additional arrests, along with gambling equipment, money, and a small amount of opium.[61] The flurry confirmed, for some, assumptions about the inherent unsuitability of the racialized Chinese. For their part, portions of the local Guangdong population rejected the dismissal.

Attempting to explain their traditions and cultural practices, in early February the Chinese Reading Room Association, initially referred to in the *Citizen* as a Young Chinese Men's Club, hosted a Chinese New Year celebration for invited guests and the newspaper.[62] Led by George Young, as secretary and master of ceremonies, the program delivered speeches and songs for the invited guests, followed by a six-course dinner.[63] The same edition of the newspaper describing the festivities added that Chow Lee, Mrs. Li Kow, and the Chinese YMCA had contributed to the city's Red Cross fundraising campaign. A similar note, thanking the Chinese Freemasons, appeared a week later alongside an intriguing clarification.[64] As it turned out, members of the Reading Room Association objected to the "young men's club" label because they did not want to be confused with other similarly described organizations.[65] The most likely explanation was rooted in community dynamics and revealed some of the forces at play among the province's "Chinese." Most Guangdong in British Columbia belonged to political organizations like the Kuomintang, the Chinese Freemasons, or benevolent cultural associations such as the Chee Duck Tong, which embraced the Chow (Zhou), Choy (Cai), Wu (Ng), Cho (Cao), and Young (Weng) families.[66] The clarification possibly sought to distance the Reading Room from overt "political" groups like the Freemasons and the KMT. Few local white residents would have been conscious of such divisions, and Vibbard's raids likely confirmed popular caricatures of the "Chinese" community as one populated only by transient men, criminals, gamblers, and opium users. No one suggested otherwise.

Eight months later, the North-West Mounted Police opened its Prince George detachment in order to pursue their responsibilities for exposing supposed Bolshevik revolutionaries and policing the amended Opium and Narcotic Drug Act (ONDA).[67] Evidence of the latter was displayed with the mid-December 1920 arrests and successful prosecution of Ah Joe, Wing Song, Wing Kee, and Yee Yock.[68] The *Citizen* offered the racist headline "Chinks Pay Heavily for 'Hitting Pipe'" before characterizing Yee as a "heathen Chinee" who had run afoul of the ONDA and its goal of stamping out illicit drugs.[69] The headline attracted immediate attention, forcing the *Citizen* to apologize for its "common error" of using "Chinks," a term that "a prominent member" of the Kuomintang explained was a "grave offence."[70] This would be the first of two occasions when the newspaper "apologized" for what it claimed to be an accidental slight.[71] Hoping to counter the demonization woven into such slights and defend their presence in the region, in early January 1921 the Kuomintang – the Nationalists – hosted a celebration at their Second Avenue headquarters marking the installation of their new officers. Pat Louis, owner of the Waymore Café and English-language secretary/interpreter for the society, organized the event along with the group's executive.[72]

Approvingly portrayed by the *Citizen* as "a very interesting meeting" of a "progressive oriental organization," the Chinese National League opened its Second Avenue headquarters to host an "impressive ceremony" ushering in the society's new leadership. Included among the new executives was Sun Hon, proprietor of the George Street Chop Suey Parlor, which boasted "delightful" Chinese dishes, as well as "real" Chinese noodles and tea.[73] After the New Year's Day investiture, the guests, who included Reverend William Graham and his wife Evelyn, were invited to address the gathering. Reverend Graham spoke of the Nationalists pursuing the "higher ideals amongst their own countrymen, improving the quality of and access to education, domestic political unity, language unity, and the assimilation of China's five races – Chinese, Manchurians, Mongolians, Turkistan, and Tibetans." The KMT sought out "the higher or more general ideals of true socialism." The celebrations also publicized Pat Louis's night classes in math and English as well as Evelyn Graham's lessons in Christianity for interested Guangdong locals. Although enrolment in the classes numbered only twelve, it was hoped that a larger collection of "boys" would take advantage of the classes.[74] The news reports following the gathering were instructive. As scholar Timothy Stanley has argued, similar events orchestrated by elite merchants in Vancouver and Victoria were conscious attempts to "ingratiate themselves into public activities" as one part of a broader project of creating a space for the Guangdong in the province.[75] At a time that the ONDA was criminalizing the entire "Chinese" community, the Nationalists' event can be understood as an effort by the Kuomintang and a handful of white residents to present a positive counterimage. There were limits, however. While white society was willing to entertain the notion that different beliefs and practices were not inherently threatening, let alone criminal, it would not admit the possibility of equality for the racialized Chinese. Specifically, that the handful of students attending night classes were infantilized as "boys" traced an important distinction. From the newspaper's perspective, and perhaps that of the Grahams and Pat Louis, the courses offered to the "boys" provided them an opportunity to demonstrate their fitness to one day be counted as men.[76] Armed with Christian faith, the English language, and western arithmetic, they sought a space in respectable society, but the racialized provincial discourse declared otherwise.[77] That such a space for the Guangdong did not exist took statutory form in the Chinese Immigration Act of 1923, which, for a generation, effectively denied the opportunity of admitting new arrivals, let alone citizenship.[78]

Inasmuch as the view from the present fastens onto this humiliation awaiting in 1923, local examples of violence and strong-arm tactics within the Guangdong community reflecting its internal politics confirmed for then contemporary commentators that the racialized Chinese were a poor fit for northern British Columbia and, indeed, the province. As news of famine and discord in Republican China animated storefront conversations among the Guangdong, the enforcement of the ONDA also aggravated tensions between the Kuomintang and the Chinese Freemasons.[79] An alleged assault of Arthur Gee at the hands of Woo Hon Sun (aka One Hop Sun), Chu Chow, and Chang Fong in the aftermath of the Nationalists' investiture of their association's new executive exposed the anxiety. The altercation was initially attributed to Gee's having patronized a Japanese merchant, which, owing to long-standing hostilities, clashed with KMT policy. When Gee refused to pay the prescribed fine, a beating followed.[80] By the time the assault was brought before Magistrate C.B. Daniell, the context had shifted to Gee's refusal to "to subscribe to a fund being raised to assist their own starving countrymen in China."[81] Regardless, both explanations revealed that the KMT was using violence, or the threat of violence, to impose its will on fellow Guangdong. That the accused were represented by L.W. Patmore, a Prince Rupert lawyer, suggested that, despite the case being tried in the Magistrate's Court, the circumstances amounted to something more serious than an ill-advised punch-up. In reporting the evolving story, the *Citizen* revealed more than it realized by commenting that the case was "of great importance to those involved."[82]

The initial court appearance for the accused in the Gee case coincided with other cases involving local Guangdong men. While Gee's alleged assailants were remanded in anticipation of a later hearing, the preliminary hearings for eleven charges of playing fan-tan were held over in anticipation of city solicitor P.E. Wilson returning from the coast. The third case was another preliminary hearing for Chow Lee, who had been accused of keeping opium in his store. He was released on bail. Chan Foi, who had been on the premises with Chow, was also charged.

The final case involved a summary hearing for Yee Yock, proprietor of the New York Laundry, charged and convicted for illegally selling liquor. Unable to pay the $325 fine, Yee was sentenced to four months in the local jail.[83] A week later, Chow Yen was charged and convicted with having cocaine and morphine in his possession. Rather than pay the $225 fine, he chose a three-month jail term. The fan-tan cases were again held over and a matter involving three allegations of contravening the ONDA was also heard, although Stipendiary Magistrate Daniell was awaiting defence counsel statements.[84] When finally heard, the gambling charges arising from the Chinese Freemasons' club were all dismissed, owing to the absence of evidence that the club was taking a share of the winnings. Without this "rake off," the club failed to meet the definition of a disorderly house.[85] Directly relevant was a news item on 2 April 1921 in the *Chinese Times*, a Vancouver paper, indicating that the Prince George Chinese Freemasons had "excommunicated" W.Y. Young and Yuanzhao Huang, who were accused of openly assisting another organization "and caused deep troubles within the Chee Kong Tong which led to the arrest of 11 other Chinese. Chee Kong Tong [sic] cannot tolerate such notorious behavior and decided to excommunicate them forever."[86] Although the other organization was unnamed, the tenor of local events suggests that the local Kuomintang had worked behind the scenes to trigger the raid on the Chinese Freemason's club.

Events took a decided turn on the morning of 8 April, when another assault case involving members of the Guangdong community came before the stipendiary magistrate. In this instance, it was alleged that Chew Chow and Yuen Hock had assaulted Chow Wing (aka Chew Wing Hon). Called before the magistrate, Chew denied any knowledge of the matter, and the two accused were discharged.[87] Reporting on the proceedings, the *Leader* noted that the courtroom was "crowded with the citizens from the flowery kingdom who were much interested in the case" before concluding that "it would seem that there is going to be further trouble with the various factions in Chinatown."[88] For its part, the *Citizen* added "that a member of the Nationalists is acting as interpreter in the court seems to be a sore point, according to the information secured from that party." It was alleged by some of the Guangdong that the interpreter favoured Nationalist perspectives, and that this behaviour, was a cause of indignation.[89] Seeking a comment from members of the Freemasons, the newspaper learned that not only were they aggrieved by the Nationalist interpreter but they were also offended by the posting of notices in Chinatown describing one of their members, who had been assaulted, as being a "mountain monkey" with a head like an orange and a mouth like white rice.[90] Similar posters targeting other Freemasons were circulating. Following the dismissal, a skirmish erupted between the two factions, with the *Leader* claiming that bricks "were flying fast and furious, doing considerable damage to members of the rival tongs."[91]

Four days later, the two groups once again met in police court, held at city hall. On this occasion, a charge had been laid by Kuomintang members alleging gambling offences against Li Kow. Owing to the absence of witnesses, the case was adjourned, and, as had occurred days before, the two groups milled about, exchanging allegations and insults. Scuffles erupted, and it was left to lawyers P.E. Wilson and W.P. Ogilvie to separate their respective clients. Celebrating heroic white masculinity, the *Citizen* reported that "Ogilvie, who is an old boxing man and stands six feet in his stockings, with about the same breadth as the back of a cab, threw Chinamen all over the lot and the fight broke up with the contestants flying down George Street to Chinatown for reinforcements."[92] Unlike the earlier fracas, which had dampened animosities, the brawl at city hall ignited additional trouble. Later that afternoon, hard words and blows were exchanged as combatants chased each other along Quebec Street and down adjoining laneways. In one instance, Mah Gong (aka Mah Gowo) twice discharged a revolver at Freemason Len Kee, who was spared fatal injury by a misfire and then by a bullet passing clean through his buttocks and out his left thigh. Mah was taken into custody, charged with attempted murder, and later found guilty of wounding with intent to do grievous bodily harm.[93]

As Mah pursued Len, the Freemasons and the Nationalists met for a set-piece battle in the empty lot between the IOOF Hall and the Prince George Bakery on Quebec Street.[94] Spectators from across the city ringed the lot. With approximately fifty or sixty Kuomintang arrayed in a line at one end of the lot and a like number of the Freemasons at the other, the two groups "advanced upon each other crying defiance and casting blots upon the escutcheons of illustrious ancestors" before unleashing a series of parries, thrusts, and "vicious wallops" with spruce clubs and bats.[95] Included among the onlookers was Police Chief Alexander Sinclair, who, on witnessing the exchange of furious blows, demanded that everyone "get busy and grab a Chinaman."[96] Ten of the combatants were wrestled to the ground by onlookers and forced into nearby vehicles, which then formed a parade toward the BCPP lock-up in South Fort George, where charges of participating in an "affray" were laid. Days later, the preliminary hearings were held. The *Citizen* named Chinese Freemasons Ken Nang (Neng), Wong Young, Chew Chong, Henry Fai, and Wong Duck as being involved in what it called a tong war. None of the Nationalists were named by the local press.[97] The preliminary hearings reportedly attracted observers from across western Canada and beyond, including a "white man who holds a high position in one of the Chinese orders, and who speaks the difficult language of the Chinese fluently ... He arrived from Edmonton to watch the proceedings."[98] This turned out to be Morris "Two Gun" Cohen, an adventurer who was born in the East End of London and who was about to establish himself as Sun Yat-sen's "bodyguard."[99] The anticlimactic trial two months later produced ten guilty pleas for participating in an affray, with all the men paying a $40 fine rather than spending three months in jail.[100] For its part, the *Chinese Times* remained resolute in defending the Freemasons, reporting that, after the verdict and fines, "the evil Kuomintang did not give up. They planned to assassinate some members of the Chee Kung Tong. Fortunately, their vicious plan was discovered and reported to the Court. The judge made the right decision to sentence the no. 1 villain to prison for two years and nine months."[101]

Despite the spectacle of men armed with clubs and bats and engaged in hand-to-hand combat contributing to the widely held view that the racialized Chinese were unsuitable for Canadian society, the response to the affray was muted. In comparison to the late April 1919 riot during which returned veterans and their supporters tried to run their quarry out of the city before destroying three businesses – an outburst that was indisputably the work of local whites – the battle on Quebec Street was an "all-Chinese" affair in which white officials had acted as the protectors of public order. This meant that the affray could be employed to reiterate the vast differences between the Guangdong and the local whites. In the least, it illustrated that the northern Interior, akin to the Lower Mainland, was burdened with the non-preferred and permanently alien "Chinese." While potentially another blot in the city's copybook, it was expected that commentators, and opinion leaders elsewhere in the province, would recognize the racial character of the latest outburst and embrace the common cause shared with Prince George. Ultimately, while both the *Citizen* and the *Leader* offered versions of the internal politics behind the events, the fracas was dismissed in broadly racist tones and with caricatures of the "inscrutable" and "childish Chinese." With the riot and its participants imagined to correspond with the image that local disorder and crime were the work of outsiders who did not fit into the northern Interior, the tumult of mid-April 1921 reinforced the felt necessity that the prosecutions linked to liquor infractions and the ONDA should continue. As to the friction between the Nationalists and the Chinese Freemasons, despite predictions that more violence was likely, the shooting and the pitched battle apparently consumed most of the pent-up antagonisms.[102]

The affray's retreat into the background owed something to council's ill-timed and breathtakingly racist attack on the city's small Black community. While single-term mayor Henry Wilson was on the coast, seeking financial support for the city's bonds, a special council meeting was convened on the evening of 8 April 1921, the day of the first fracas outside city hall, following Arthur Gee's adjourned assault case.[103] At the meeting, Councillor A.M. Patterson, seconded by Alex Wimbles, moved that

> the Clerk be instructed to forward to the Police Commissions a recommendation expressing strongly the Council's opinion that the Police Commission should take active and immediate steps to clean up the city in respect of Drunks; driving cars at an excessive rate of speed; driving cars while under the influence of liquor; driving cars by persons under-age; selling of liquor by "Bootleggers."
>
> They would also draw the Commissioners' attention to the state of "Nigger town" and recommend that all undesirables be ordered out of town.[104]

Rather than occupying themselves with defusing the tensions within the local Guangdong community, council took advantage of the mayor's absence to launch a program of "uplift" and level a racist assault on Black residents. The motion passed unanimously. Four days later, the so-called tong war erupted on Quebec Street.

Given the continuing unrest among the Guangdong community, the decision to single out Black residents was unexpected, but council's resolution represented merely a shift in target and not tone. For local whites, heaping scorn on the undesired other and non-preferred immigrants was a convenient reflex to explain away persistent disorder. Still, scapegoating the local Black population was not a random act. Beginning in 1911,

Canadians, and especially western Canadians, were inundated with racist reports of an "invasion" of Black settlers, triggering warnings of miscegenation and rising crime rates.[105] The death of Vancouver city police chief M.B. MacLennan at the hands of Robert Tate, described as "a drug-crazed negro," in March 1917 provided a face and a name for the supposed race-based threat feeding into that city's anti-drug campaign.[106] Edmonton police magistrate Emily Murphy's postwar anti-drug campaign, including pieces published in *Maclean's* magazine that anticipated her 1922 book, *The Black Candle,* added more fuel to the fire. Known in part for the racial animus in her writings, where the "Chinese" menace loomed large behind the threat of illegal drugs and the danger they posed to white Canadian society, Murphy depicted Black men as members of a conspiracy employing illegal drugs as a means to rule the world.[107] Although there is limited evidence suggesting a direct line between this context and attitudes in Prince George, the claim that "peddling of dope," presumably by racialized populations, was a police concern, suggests that the allegations were consistent with the province's postwar marketplace of ideas.

It was not until 6 May that the attack on local Black residents drew public comment. The author was Charles S. Sager, an American-born actor, singer, playwright, and barber, who, after achieving success as co-founder of the Pekin Theatre in Chicago and touring throughout the American northwest, launched an ingenious floating barbershop and bathhouse that served work camps along the Fraser River before the Great War.[108] By the autumn of 1914, he was directing performances in aid of the Methodist Ladies' auxiliary, and, in March 1915, opened the Metropolitan Baths in the centre of the city's business district on Third Avenue, just off the corner of George Street.[109] Called upon to direct local stage productions, Sager and his wife, Willa, were fondly remembered by Reverend H. Lloyd Morrison of the Methodist church, who described Sager as "a very intelligent man of fine character, ... [with] a wonderful bass voice. Unfortunately, color prejudice did not allow us to use his talents as much as we wished." Morrison then added that Willa Sager could easily have passed for a white woman.[110]

Published two weeks after the violence along Quebec Street, Sager's letter to the *Leader* concerning council's language opened with a reflection on the options presented to the local Black population. Black men had been confronted with "the forces of prejudice fighting to keep him in that bondage of prejudice because of race" and denied citizenship because of "caste or color." City council's attack had come at a "critical time" for Black residents.[111] He stressed that "race prejudice" was "not so much a matter of startling deeds as of petty insinuations" that branded the entirety of a community with the flaws of its worst members while denying them the honours of its best. This refusal to differentiate between the street thug and the successful entrepreneur presented "a direct challenge to every self-respecting Negro in Prince George – in Canada." Such an attitude presented "a vulgar appeal to insult and violence; it demoralizes, debases, and promotes hate and envy – the very ground root of race prejudice." Sager noted that the claim that "it is not the color aimed at, but the conduct" convinced no one in the Black community who was "forced to bear the full responsibility of the wicked and vicious members of our race, forced into the lowest menial occupations and then despised for doing so." Every Black person recognized the malice, and there was no mistaking the sneering in the council's call to action.

Sager's letter addressed head-on the province's aspiration, as well as that of the northern Interior, to be "a white man's country": "Set the example; teach the fine qualities of citizenship; let us see what you mean by law, order, and democracy. As one of the great trees of the forest, all nations will enjoy your refreshing shadow, and will praise you for the excellent quality of fruit you bear." Sager then articulated his community's principles: "We hold no brief for the criminal and disreputable characters of our group. We ask that the law be enforced impartially, remembering that a 'white fiend' is as dangerous to this community as a 'black brute.'" The effect of city council's motion, Sager argued, was to belittle and destroy

> the last vestige of hope, manhood, and self-respect left in him [i.e., the Black man], after two hundred years of the most cruel slavery on earth. We feel reasonably sure that under normal conditions, thinking men would not close the door of ambition and opportunity in the face of any man on account of his color; and yet it is the very thing done, and the principal cause of race antagonism today ... We ask a square deal; the equality of opportunity and of privilege from the powers that be, and the honest endeavor to cultivate interracial respect. Believing that we will find more to praise and less to complain in one of the best little cities in Canada.

Sager had called out council and, indeed, the city's self-respecting whites to stand behind their highest ideals rather than cowering behind a poisonous slur that demoralized and alienated. Still, and akin to the Quebec Street affray, Sager's commentary could be passed off as another example of why "these people" would never truly fit in British Columbia society. Silence answered Sager's pleas. After all, it was a white man's province.

Homicide and the Anxiety of Place

The Halden Family

Because of their rarity, as well as the presence of an accused who evoked empathy or revulsion, whose mystifying behaviour hinted at obscure motives, or whose actions ran counter to contemporary expectations, homicides provided the alchemy for sensational front-page crime. In the northern Interior, where some imagined that they might escape the ills of modern society, eruptions of homicidal violence, and what such cruelties said about place and identity, were especially apt to generate newspaper headlines. Thus, when the Halden family – father Arthur, mother Adah, and adopted son Stanley – vanished from their family farm outside Quesnel in late October 1920, it was little wonder that what soon became a province-wide sensation posed unsettling questions about the New Cariboo, while feeding into a literary tradition of police derring-do on the settlement frontier.[112]

The circumstances of the Halden family's disappearance were, from the outset, curious. The individual suspected in the disappearance, David Clark – variously described as a hired hand, Arthur Halden's partner, or a wealthy rancher in his own right – claimed that, after Arthur received a telegram carrying word of a brother's death in Spokane, Washington, he hired a car for the trip south and departed with his family on 29 October. Events then became muddled. Arthur, who was supposedly registered as the sole guest at a Kamloops hotel on 3 November, allegedly returned to the farm in search of the property deed and Adah's jewellery. There, according to Clark, the two men met, and Clark demanded repayment from Arthur of money he claimed to have lent him, along with wages he was owed. Clark stated that Arthur offered him the jewellery in exchange for extinguishing the debt. Outside of this alleged meeting with Clark, neither Arthur Halden nor the rest of the family were seen again. Whether Arthur had been a guest at the Kamloops hotel was never confirmed. Later, Clark approached Quesnel lawyer E.J. Avison, presenting him with a signed $1,250 promissory note as evidence that Arthur Halden owed him a considerable sum of money. Having examined the document, the lawyer advised that legal proceedings be initiated to secure the note's value, in addition to $762 in owed wages. Early in the new year, a notice appeared in the *Quesnel Cariboo Observer* inviting Arthur or Adah Halden to dispute the promissory note in Quesnel's County Court registry.[113] In the interim, Clark was seen in possession of Adah

Halden's jewellery, either having offered separate pieces as gifts to two women or claiming that a ring and a brooch were security for the promissory note and the wages.

Clark's behaviour and circulating rumours piqued BCPP constable G.H. Greenwood's attention and led him to investigate the alleged Spokane trip. There was no record of the supposed telegram, nor any indication of a telephone call or messages relayed to Arthur Halden. Nor was there any evidence of family connections, living or dead, in Washington State. Although Arthur's Vancouver solicitors could verify Adah and Arthur's purchase of the farm, the firm had been without any contact with the couple since early June 1920. The solicitors were, however, able to put Greenwood in touch with Adah Halden's sister Thurza Hughes, who explained that Adah's first husband had died in England and that she, along with Stanley, had moved to Vancouver in 1915, where she married Arthur in 1919 before moving to Quesnel. When shown the jewellery that had been in Clark's possession, Hughes produced a wedding photograph in which Adah was pictured wearing the broach. Greenwood filed a complaint for theft against Clark and arrested him on 17 April 1921. With Clark in custody, the Halden farm, buildings, and adjoining land were searched, and the nearby river dragged for evidence. News of partially burned debris, including dynamite pieces, portions of a skull found in a corner of the farm, and a partial dental plate discovered in a stove's ashes were reported across the nation.[114] A day after the finds, newspapers revealed that the "skull" and remains were those of a decomposed sheep.[115] Nothing more was reported of the false teeth.

With the original murder complaint withdrawn, Clark appeared before two justices of the peace in Quesnel on 6 May on three theft charges. Brought before Mr. Justice Frederick Calder four days later, Clark chose a jury trial and was committed to appear at the spring assize in Prince George.[116] There, after two hours of deliberations, the jury could not agree, and the case was traversed for a retrial at the next assize. Unable to raise $5,000 in bail, Clark was returned to Oakalla Prison.[117] The second trial on 18 November ended in a theft conviction and a two-year sentence.[118] Seven months later, the mystery remained unsolved, and an administrator was appointed to oversee Adah Halden's estate, including the 120-acre farm, estimated to be $10,000 in value.[119]

The Halden sensation's final chapter opened with Clark's arrest as soon as he completed his two-year penitentiary term. Newly promoted Chief Constable Greenwood was waiting at the penitentiary's gates with a warrant for Clark's arrest on a forgery charge related to Arthur Halden's alleged signature on the $1,250 promissory note. Arraigned in district court in New Westminster, Clark was returned to custody to await an appearance in district court before Mr. Justice Frederick W. Howay, where, once again, the accused elected a jury trial at the next assize.[120] There, he was found guilty before Mr. Justice Aulay M. Morrison and jury. Obliged to await sentencing until the assize was complete, Clark returned to the courtroom appearing the worse for wear: he had been on a hunger strike since hearing the jury's verdict. Requiring assistance to enter the prisoner's dock, he learned that his latest conviction came with a heavy price: he was sentenced to ten years in the penitentiary.[121] In mid-May 1928, Mr. Justice D.A. Macdonald declared the Halden family dead, so that the estate might finally be settled.[122] Rumours of three skeletons being found in late July 1934 reignited speculation in Quesnel, but the story proved to be groundless.[123] The Halden family's ultimate fate remains one of the province's more perplexing mysteries.

For some, the Halden/Clark case put a lie to the notion that the northern interior was a safe extension of the "civilized" lower mainland and southern tip of Vancouver Island. Rather, the region's identity as an enormous and thinly populated region occupied, in part, by a pool of transient men who seemingly posed a constant threat, persisted. Indeed, Clark symbolized a terrifying menace, capable of an unimaginable horror in orchestrating the disappearance of an entire family. The headlines revealed a horrid possibility, an entire family had been obliterated on an isolated farm too distant from neighbours to offer any hope of rescue.[124] True, these spaces may have been free of the urban landscape's threats, but clearly the trackless countryside had its own dangers with countless opportunities to secret evidence and hide bodies. How, one might wonder, could anyone expect to find a well-ordered white civilization in such a place? The prospect could drive a person to despair; perhaps, even, to murder.

Elizabeth Coward

What Elizabeth Coward and her common law husband, James, thought about the BC Interior is lost to time. Given their individual and shared backgrounds, it is likely they knew little when they turned their eyes northward in May 1915. Still, Elizabeth was familiar with challenges. By the time she arrived at a preemption outside of Fort St. James, 160 kilometres northwest of the new Prince George townsite, the thirty-two-year-old had already experienced a life of hard knocks.[125] Born Elizabeth

Schaffer to an Italian mother on New York's East Side, Elizabeth was first married in Colorado at age thirteen. In telling Elizabeth's story, the *Vancouver Province* described the first marriage as having been forced on the girl.[126] Six months after this marriage, her first husband, a man named Dellaquadra, perished in a mine explosion.[127] Elizabeth later married a man named Calibrise in Iowa. Together they had five children, one of whom died.[128] After being together for fifteen or sixteen years, they divorced around 1910. Her story then became muddled. According to former BCPP deputy commissioner Cecil Clark's embellished version of Elizabeth's life, it was in Iowa where she met James Coward, a thirty-year-old city marshal with a wife and children.[129] Taking up with Elizabeth, he abandoned his family, and the two fled to Oakland, California, where Elizabeth began running a boarding house. There, her meagre earnings did not meet expenses. Whether James obtained a divorce is unlikely, but, at some point, he produced a marriage licence to convince Elizabeth that they were married, despite the absence of a ceremony. Her second-eldest daughter, Rose, believed her mother married James in late May or early June 1914, and, throughout her ordeal, Elizabeth steadfastly referred to James as her husband.[130] He worked as a guard at the Panama-Pacific International Exposition grounds prior to its grand opening but was discharged in late December 1914 or early January 1915, because of poison pen letters to exposition management from Elizabeth.[131] Her motives for sending the letters remain clouded. Still, James continued to work on the exposition grounds until the spring of 1915, when the two agreed to sell the rooming house and set out for British Columbia's northern Interior.[132] With the decision made, they put the youngest child, Elsie, into care; son Ralph went to live with his father; and Rose moved in with her married sister, Margaret Youngberg. Once the couple was settled, the plan was to send for all the children, including Margaret and her husband.

Arriving at the Prince George townsite and carrying a letter of introduction, James and Elizabeth presented themselves to Chief Constable W.R. Dunwoody at the South Fort George police station, seeking counsel on securing a preemption. Dunwoody directed them next door to government agent Thomas Herne. The two new arrivals soon boarded the train to Vanderhoof, where fellow-settler John Roberts lent them the cabin of his brother, Griffiths, on a piece of land situated about a kilometre from the Cowards' preemption.[133] Left in the cabin was a .38 "Ivor Johnston" revolver. The Cowards' days were absorbed acclimatizing to their new surroundings and preparing their own cabin in anticipation of furniture arriving from California. Financed by borrowed money, Rose arrived in

Fort St. James on 9 July to allay her mother's loneliness. The spartan conditions in the cabin and, perhaps, tensions between Elizabeth and James, led to him sleeping outside in a bed fashioned in a sleigh's box covered by a canvas tent and mosquito netting.

Although statements contradict, the events of 6 September 1915 indicate that, during a visit with neighbour Lusetta McInnes and her guest Florence Whiteside, an unsettled Elizabeth spoke of advancing danger and of James having troubles with an Indigenous man. Returning to their cabin, Rose and Elizabeth prepared an evening meal, which they ate alone. James arrived from Fort St. James around 8 p.m., ate his dinner, and, an hour later, bade them goodnight before retiring to the sleigh. According to Rose and Elizabeth, as they were turning in, a shot was heard outside the cabin, and both women fled to the McInnes cabin, which was 250 metres in the opposite direction from the sleigh. Having steeled themselves, half an hour later and armed with a .22 rifle, Rose, Elizabeth, and Lusetta McInnes returned to the cabin (Whiteside remained at the McInnes home), although they were too frightened to go near the sleigh. Firing a shot into the air did not attract any help, and they returned to the McInnes cabin. Stirring around 5 a.m., all four women waited for light before going back to the cabin and examining the sleigh. Although Rose and Elizabeth peered under the canvas, they did not investigate but concluded that James was dead. John Roberts was summoned around 6:30 a.m., and, recording that Coward had been shot in the head, left for Fort St. James to report the incident. Word was relayed by magistrate and coroner J.E. Hooson to BCPP constable Rupert Raynor in Vanderhoof, who, once he arrived to examine the scene and the body on 8 September, telegraphed Chief Constable Dunwoody in South Fort George.[134] Dunwoody left on the 8 p.m. train for Fort St. James, arriving at noon and then assuming charge of the investigation.[135]

A search for the murder weapon took a decided turn after the inquest, during which Dr. William R. Stone examined the bullet extracted from James Coward's head. It was believed that he had been shot with a .32 revolver, owing to a shell casing having been found at the site. But after Stone produced the slug, discussions between Dunwoody, Raynor, livery-man David Hoye, and Hooson concluded that it was too light to be a .32 bullet – a .38 caliber was more likely. The search began anew.[136] Shortly thereafter, Hoye overturned a tin washtub beside the cabin and discovered the .38 revolver that Griffiths Roberts had left in the cabin. Following Dunwoody's directions, the revolver was left under the tub, which was returned to its original position. Knowing that Elizabeth Coward had

FIGURE 5.2   Chief Constable William R.
Dunwoody. | Gray's Publishing.

made numerous requests to return to the cabin in search of clean clothes, he authorized the visit, but directed Raynor to watch her behaviour from a hidden location. As Coward walked around the cabin, Raynor saw her make "a sharp glance at the tub," hesitate, and make a "pause over this tub as though she was looking for something. She not only looked at the one side but bent and looked over the other side and paused, I should judge, nearly a minute."[137] Coward, Rose, a Mrs. Murray, and teamster John J. Vachon then departed. Having learned from Raynor what had occurred, and sceptical of Elizabeth's flimsy and contradictory statements concerning the events of 6 September, Dunwoody placed both Elizabeth and Rose under arrest for murder. The preliminary hearing consumed two days, after which the women were taken first to South Fort George and then to the Kamloops jail to await trial at the early October assize in Clinton. Answering to orders from headquarters, Dunwoody reported to Victoria, briefed the commissioner and deputy attorney general, and was then sent to California to investigate Elizabeth's and James Coward's backgrounds.[138]

Throughout her trial, Elizabeth Coward held to the argument that there had been "trouble" between her late husband and an Indigenous man. This was why she insisted that an "Indian" had killed her husband. Jimmie Ahoul, the man in question, testified that, while there had been a dispute over who was to pay for hauling Rose's trunk from the GTP station to the cabin, the debt had long since been settled. He denied that there was any lingering animosity. Beyond that, Elizabeth's defence counsel offered little, save to emphasize that the evidence against her was circumstantial, while hinting of her fragile mental condition. Mr. Justice Denis Murphy's charge to the jury, filling twenty-two typed pages and taking over an hour to deliver, reviewed the meaning of homicide, the nature of culpable and non-culpable homicide, the distinction within culpable homicide between murder and manslaughter, Canadian law's reliance on a standard of reasonable care on the part of an accused person, the importance of reasonable doubt, and the Crown's obligation to prove its case rather than the defendant having to prove her innocence. The jury retired at 6:18 p.m. and returned barely forty minutes later with a guilty verdict. Having read the verdict, Murphy ordered that Coward was to be confined until 23 December 1915, when "you shall be hanged by your neck until you are dead. May God have mercy on your soul."[139] Coward swooned at hearing the sentence. In the space of one month – 6 October to 7 November 1915 – Elizabeth Coward had gone from being a lonely woman on a preemption outside of Fort St. James to a convicted murderer in a Kamloops cell, awaiting her fate at the end of a rope. She was the only woman sentenced to hang in the province's history.

None of the authors who have discussed the Coward case, Cecil Clark or F. Murray Greenwood, and Beverley Boissery, concentrated on the commutation campaign that followed the conviction. Yet here was a case, akin to that of Angelina Napolitano, convicted of killing her husband in northern Ontario, in which the effort to spare a woman from the noose pulled out all the stops.[140] Petitions counting tens of thousands of signatures poured into the Department of Justice offices in Ottawa. And, like the Napolitano case, the pursuit of a commutation demanded Coward's reconstruction into an appropriately sympathetic figure. The picture that emerged was of a dark-skinned and attractive woman of "foreign extraction," who, though poor and overwhelmed by the isolation and solitude of British Columbia's "wilds," remained "bright and courageous."[141] Literary licence was present in abundance, and, in this, the *Vancouver Daily World* was second to none.[142] "Plunged so early in childhood into the full responsibilities of womanhood, considerable sympathy has been expressed for her by those with whom she has come in contact since her trial. According to one thoroughly familiar with her experiences, she has drifted on and on and, being used to a life of adventure and accustomed to using firearms freely, she did not realize the enormity of her crime until it was all over."[143] Unsurprisingly, distant newspapers, such as those in Iowa, where James and Elizabeth first met, constructed details out of whole cloth, reporting that the crime occurred "way out on the bleak prairie of British Columbia," where the Mounted Police investigated who had cut James Coward's throat.[144] Fanciful images appeared in the hope of rendering the desired point:

> What mainly concerns us is the question of this woman's life. It is granted that she was living under such conditions as would have a tendency to derange a brain weakened by adversity and deprivations. It is the case of a woman who has been residing in the crowded slums of large American cities being suddenly transported to the silence and loneliness of a shack in the forests of northern British Columbia. It may be a case of *mania transitoria*.[145]

For good measure, this article wondered if Coward had been affected by epilepsy, paralysis, or any one of a number of nervous diseases. After all, "it will be admitted that many persons do become insane when removed from thickly populated centers to the loneliness of the North West Territories and such sparsely peopled localities."[146] Vancouver's *Daily News Advertiser*, Victoria's *Daily Times*, and Saskatoon's *Star Phoenix* followed suit in reflecting on how northern British Columbia's "wilds" had triggered Coward's fatal choice.[147] The *Vancouver Sun* suggested that the combination of moving "from the slums of a great American city to the lonely wilds of British Columbia" and "the privations she had undergone had affected her mind."[148] All this despite a medical examination by Dr. J.G. Mackay of New Westminster that did not identify any evidence of a mental affliction.[149]

While newspapers provided a running commentary on the likelihood of commutation, the decision remained squarely with the Department of Justice in Ottawa and its preparation of an advisory report for cabinet. The process has been thoroughly detailed by historian Carolyn Strange, and thus, there's no need to dwell on it here, save to note that, in 1915, Deputy Minister of Justice Pierre M. Coté oversaw the process of generating a memorandum for the minister in anticipation of cabinet's deliberation.[150] Included in the archival records pertaining to the case is the first of several letters from J. Edward Bird of Bird, Macdonald, and

Ross, Barristers and Solicitors, Vancouver, who forwarded an appeal from the American consul inquiring about the possibility of Coward being granted a new trial, in part because she had little money to finance her defence, her counsel had been young and inexperienced, and the matter had moved from investigation to preliminary hearing to trial with great speed. Revealing his unfamiliarity with Coward, Bird described her as appearing "to have been gently nurtured and cared for, and who in appearance has been accustomed to much better things than the life of a pioneer in the woods."[151] Nonetheless, and despite this initial misstep, it was evident that he had assumed the lead in the commutation campaign and, over the ensuing weeks, would forward several petitions – one of which carried 7,000 signatures – to the minister of justice.

These efforts to spare Coward placed her in the company of two other women. One was Mrs. Jennie Hawkes, an Albertan found guilty in the shooting death of Rosella Stolsie in Lewisville, amid suspicions that the deceased had been involved with Hawkes's husband.[152] In this case, the first mention of a petition seeking commutation of the death sentence appeared in the *Edmonton Journal* on 9 November 1915, two days after Coward's sentencing.[153] By early December, an estimated 30,000 women had signed the petition seeking mercy for Hawkes. Although the measure of such things was never simple, the prospect of two women answering for their crimes on the gallows, within days of Christmas, conjured up unsettling images. Further, commentators evidently thought that, of the two, Hawkes was more likely to have her capital sentence commuted, as she had shot Stolsie three times in what was portrayed as an emotional defence of her family. Thus, when word arrived in mid-December that Hawkes's death sentence had been commuted, Coward's backers feared that the cabinet would spare one and hang the other, despite the rumour in some quarters that Coward, too, would escape the gallows.[154]

The second woman playing a supporting role in Coward's fate was English nurse Edith Cavell, who was executed by a German firing-squad on 12 October 1915 for her part in aiding the escape of approximately 200 Allied soldiers in occupied Belgium. Writing to Minister of Justice C.J. Doherty on 23 November, Bird pressed the comparison, despite the possibility that it "rather shocks one's ideas of reasonableness":

> Mrs. Coward was convicted by properly constituted Canadian authorities
> of an offence that merited the death sentence. Miss Edith Cavell in Belgium
> was convicted by properly constituted legal authority of an offence that
> merited the death sentence. There is this in common between the two

cases, that they were both women, that they were both sentenced by legal constituted authorities for offences that merited the death sentence. The one in the case of Edith Cavell has raised a protest of indignation that is world-wide, and justly so. The sentiment of the community evidences that women shall not be treated in this manner, notwithstanding the laws to the contrary.[155]

In making the comparison, Bird's courage, sense of proportion, and professional mien allowed him to go only so far. What he would not commit to writing was the argument that, if Coward were executed, Canada would find itself facing similar international condemnation as that heaped on Germany for executing Cavell. Surely the threat of being lumped in with the detested Hun was reason enough to give pause. This parallel was also conveyed by W.J. Bowser, British Columbia's attorney general, who, while convinced of Coward's guilt, did "very much doubt under the circumstances, particularly taking into consideration the execution of Miss Cavell, if it would be in the interests of Justice to have the law take its course."[156]

In his memorandum on the case, Coté quoted Bowser's letter at length, adding that, because Coward was a woman, the deep sentiment, reflected in the volume of petitions, was that inflicting the death penalty would be unduly harsh. Opining that "the expediency of carrying out the extreme penalty of the law is questionable," Coté favoured commutation.[157] Cabinet agreed. On 20 December, notice that Coward had been spared was dispatched to Bird, Macdonald, and Ross; Margaret Youngberg, Coward's eldest daughter; defence counsel William Scott; the American consul in Vancouver; Attorney General Bowser; and, most importantly, to the Kamloops sheriff. Several newspapers insisted that the commutation was owing to Coward's state of mind at the time of the shooting, a factor that was mentioned only in passing by Coté and was, at most, a minor ingredient in the decision.[158]

Occurring after the outbreak of the First World War and the collapse of the white settlement rush to the northern Interior, the Coward case, with its assertion that life in the "wilds" of northern British Columbia could drive some to murder, was unwelcomed advertising for the region and its prospects. That a woman, whose presence was supposed to soften and "civilize" the settlement frontier, had killed her husband magnified the unease. For, while there was an element of resigned acceptance that men on the frontier too readily turned to violence, women supposedly possessed greater self-control.[159] That, at least, was the accepted wisdom of the day.

Edith Frye

Edith Frye's postwar horror, set in the region's eastern borderland, confirmed Elizabeth Coward's unsettling lesson. The parallels are intriguing. Like the Coward case, the Frye family had familial links to California; both looked to British Columbia's northern Interior as a place to start anew, yet found the experience exacted a horrendous toll; and, in the end, both attracted the support of organizations hoping to save the women from the fatal consequences of killing their husbands.

Following the surveyors and preceding the Grand Trunk Pacific Railway, the Frye family arrived in the Robson Valley in the autumn of 1910.[160] There they set up a farmstead about sixty-five kilometres south of Henningville (Mile Fortynine) on the anticipated rail corridor between Tête Jaune Cache and Kamloops. Long before they settled in the shadow of the Albreda Glacier, relations between Edith and Fred Frye were deeply etched by alcohol and violence. Fred was a powerful man with a murderous temper that worsened with liquor. He targeted anyone at hand, and Edith and the children were routinely subjected to his wrath. Supporting his family with lucrative supply contracts for the Canadian Northern Railway, Fred worked doggedly, but, in his spare hours, he had constructed a still in the scrub-brush beyond their rough-hewn cabin. His increasing consumption of moonshine reduced his family to hostages awaiting the next outburst. The only respite occurred when Fred took the family to Kamloops, where he performed as the doting father, or when he was absent or passed out from his latest drinking bout. In hindsight, deadly violence was only a matter of time.

As narrated in the published account of the family's troubles, the preamble to the events of 16 November 1922 was a blur of intimidation, moonshine, and thrashings meted out to Edith and the children Ella (fifteen) and Mike (twelve) while the youngest children huddled in the root cellar. Having been dispatched to go hunting, Charles (nineteen) and Francis (seventeen) returned without any game, only to be ordered by Fred to go back and not return empty handed. Suspecting that trouble was likely, they agreed that their mother could not be abandoned to deal with their father's latest spree. Returning to the cabin, the fatal events were already in motion. Armed with his knife, Fred had Edith by the neck while she struggled to kick herself free. Francis and Charles pulled Fred away from their mother, and Francis threw the knife into the wood stove's firebox. Begging Fred to calm down, they pinned him to the bed until he relented. An anxious silence descended. As the children were being fed,

FIGURE 5.3   Edith and Fred Frye family, 1920. | Hancock House Publishing.

Fred returned to his feet, brushed aside Charles and Francis, and sent Edith sprawling with his closed fist. He grabbed the shotgun, slotted the shells into their chambers and targeted Edith, declaring his intent to kill the entire family. Again, Francis and Charles seized and disarmed their father, as Edith returned the now loaded shotgun to beneath the bed. Shouting hellfire, Fred railed against his oppressors. Picking up Charles's .303 "Savage" lever-action rifle and snapping two cartridges into the breach, Edith ordered all the children out of the cabin as Fred roared. When he bent to retrieve the shotgun from beneath the bed, Edith squeezed the rifle trigger. The single bullet passed through Fred's neck and heart, ending his reign of terror.

Purposively returning the rifle to its pegs on the wall, Edith walked out into the yard and, to Francis's stunned disbelief, said "I've shot your father." She directed Charles to take the children to the Stewarts' home down the road, tell Peter Stewart what had occurred, and ask him to send word for the police. Stewart contacted telephone operator P.C. Arnold at the Canadian Northern Railway station, who relayed the message to BCPP constable Alex Sinclair (former chief of the Prince George city police), then stationed at Lucerne. He notified Deputy Inspector T.W.S. Parsons at South Fort George via telegraph. A day later, Sinclair accompanied Dr. Thomas O'Hagan to the Frye preemption, where, after

Sinclair officially charged Edith with murder, the doctor performed an autopsy.[161] Following the inquest, Edith was taken into custody and was delivered by train to McBride and placed in the lock-up to await a preliminary hearing on 21 November before Thomas Lloyd, JP.[162] Absent legal counsel, Edith said nothing and was committed to the Oakalla Prison to await her trial.

News of the shooting appeared in newspapers as early as 17 November 1922, with a column in the *Kamloops Standard Sentinel* reporting that the local Elks organization wanted a searching inquiry into Fred's death.[163] Within a day, coverage extended to Victoria, Regina, and Winnipeg.[164] As details circulated, the language of a tragedy, "extenuating circumstances," and a family kept in "a perfect hell" marked the shifting public sentiment.[165] Once again, the northern Interior was at the centre of a sensation. Yet unlike the Coward case, where the petitions appeared following the trial and death sentence, Edith Frye's backers urged the attorney general's office to release her from custody before the trial began. With the petitions claiming that the cruel abuse and the crude conditions at the Frye preemption ought not to exist in a civilized country, pressure mounted for the Crown to spare the surviving family members "the ignominy of a trial for murder."[166] Given the circumstances, the possibility of the attorney general simply releasing Edith Frye was remote. Nonetheless, and in portraying several contextual perspectives at play, the *Kamloops Telegram* tried to make sense of the case:

> Men who claim to know of the conditions obtaining at the Frye "home" declare that the conduct of Frye toward his family, particularly toward his two elder daughters, aged seventeen and fifteen, was atrocious, almost unthinkable. They declare that the published treatment of the girls was mild compared with the facts. While we cannot condone the conduct of Mrs. Frye in taking the law in her own hands, if the stories are true, it was hardly to be expected that she – a mother – would think of the law at all but would simply act. Her defense will be shooting in self-defense, and whether this be technically true, the best way out of it would appear to be the letting of the claim of self-defense rule without exacting direct proof.[167]

By early December, Prince George women had altered course. Rather than insisting that Frye be released outright, efforts turned toward having her released from custody, pending the spring assize. By the time the *Citizen* reported on the effort, 125 signatures had been gathered, and the plan was to circulate the petition to all women's organizations in the city and to have copies available for signing at two downtown businesses. According to the newspaper, "the case will also be drawn to the attention of the women's organizations at the coast, and there is every reason to believe, when the circumstances are fully understood by the attorney general, he will arrange to give Mrs. Frye her liberty."[168] A week later, a 222-name petition was dispatched to the attorney general. Allegedly, "few murder cases in British Columbia have created so much public interest as the tragedy which was enacted on the Frye homestead when the wife and mother, driven to desperation by the threats of the drink-crazed husband, sent a bullet through his heart." The *Citizen* confirmed its principles: "Isolated, as Mrs. Frye was, there was no one to help her. Her husband had loaded the shotgun for the express purpose of killing off the entire family. It was his life or the lives of all the children, and her own as well, and Mrs. Frye steeled herself to end it all, and did so."[169] Yet in claiming that the women's signatures were "representative of the entire community," the newspaper inadvertently raised the question whether the city could provide the Crown a fair hearing on one of the Criminal Code's most serious charges.

As it turned out, the petition seeking Frye's release pending her trial arrived on Attorney General Manson's desk before the preliminary hearing's transcript. By then, Frye was already free on her own recognizance, with a $5,000 bond assuring her attendance at the assize. Where these funds were secured was unexplained, since no sureties were listed and it was understood that the family was destitute.[170] Nonetheless, the attorney general assured the petitioners that their request would be considered and, further, Frye would not be undefended by professional counsel in a trial with fatal consequences.[171] In fact, the Crown was funding Frye's travel costs and ensuring that her children were not taken into care by the Children's Aid Society. Deputy Inspector Parsons also directed Constable Sinclair to cover any necessities for the family once Frye awaited her trial back at the farmstead.[172] Events interceded. When it was realized that neither Prince Rupert nor Prince George had any significant business for either the civil or criminal side of the docket in the spring of 1923, rather than organize a northern Interior sitting, the Frye case was traversed to Kamloops.[173] The news moved that city's women to approach A.D. McIntyre, with thirty years of local experience, to lead the defence. His fees would be defrayed by fundraising.[174] Held before Mr. Justice Denis Murphy and jury, just as Elizabeth Coward's trial had been, the Frye trial drew additional attention because it was one of the first capital cases in the province held after women became eligible jurors.[175] As it turned out, no women were drawn to determine Edith Frye's fate. Yet, having heard the evidence, the all-male jury took a mere fifteen minutes to deliver a not guilty verdict. Murphy quickly doused the gallery's roar of approval.[176] Edith Frye escaped the gallows and prison to live out her years back in the shadow of the Albreda Glacier, where, as the family history records, she kept herself busy while earning a reputation for helping newcomers adapt to life in the northern Interior. She died on 15 May 1956, at eighty-three years of age.

While local readers were satisfied with Edith Frye's acquittal, the case, and the attention it earned, once again cast the northern Interior in an unflattering light. While some may have taken comfort in the fact that local women had led a campaign seeking a higher form of justice for a woman defending her family, the distressing circumstances of the entire affair remained. Was the region one where women needed to protect themselves and their children against husbands rendered mad by bootleg liquor? Had things changed so little in the nearly two decades since the Georges' founding? While some might dismiss as exceptions cases like Frye's and Coward's, the disappearance of the Halden family, the Bellos brothers' exploits, and Chow Lee's career, they reflected an increasingly fixed regional identity. The northern Interior seemed destined to be a place where excess was the norm, where a sense of place always lurked and, often enough, supplied newspaper fodder across the province and beyond. And if these cases were understood to be morality plays or cautionary tales, what was the lesson? Was it the perils of liquor, the persistent threat of transient workers waiting to pounce, the peril of sharp-eyed confidence men? Was it the insistent danger of the white settlement frontier? The weight of isolation and the unordered wilderness? Or was the warning simply that, regardless of where a person lived, the modern state would find them. After all, neither Fred Cyr nor Edith Frye attempted to evade the consequences of their actions; rather, they had sought out the police, despite being on a distant edge of "civilization." It was a principle that, in the aftermath of the Frye trial, the *Kamloops Telegram* emphasized. While the acquittal had been "widely popular," Edith Frye would not set a precedent.[177] The rules mattered, *even* in the wilds of northern British Columbia. For readers in and around the Georges, the message probably resonated, but, for commentators and opinion leaders elsewhere in the province, was it easier – perhaps more convenient – to hold onto the imagined truth about the notorious Georges and the northern Interior?

Epilogue

That Prince George Business

The Georges' worry about their reputation persisted well beyond 1925. Having been branded as the gates of hell within years of their founding, the notoriety remains a century later. Indeed, a backwards glance lends the impression that the narrative of their tarnished reputation was revisited regularly enough to reinforce a collective memory, one that hardened into the opposite of a claim to fame. While others in British Columbia might claim the best scenery, skiing, wineries, or most-welcoming farmer's market, the Georges were shackled to an identity of alcoholic excess, disorder, and crime. And even when the context of the times shifted in the province and the nation – through the Great Depression, Second World War, the postwar economic and baby boom, labour upset, and the national shame of the Highway of Tears – the Georges' imagined identity persisted.

Akin to other Canadian communities, Prince George was hard hit by the Great Depression of the 1930s. Confronted with a ravaged economy, lives upset in countless ways, and elected representatives seemingly unable or unwilling to provide effective solutions, hardship and want became a national shared experience.[1] Prince George's efforts to provide relief to local families were crippled by a shrinking municipal tax-base tied to a collapsing regional economy. Intractable problems multiplied overnight. Aid from Victoria and Ottawa was unreliable and insufficient, as politicians and bureaucrats struggled with the advantages and failures of direct and indirect relief and the repercussions of "better" relief levels in one province in comparison to another. As the local pool of unemployed grew in Prince George – with 1,673 men registered for relief work between 1 October 1930 and 14 February 1931 in a total population of 2,479 – efforts faltered as empty coffers loomed and there were predictions of over 300 unmarried men being left to fend for themselves.[2] As it turned out, city resources lasted only until mid-April 1931.[3]

A protest two months later ended amicably, with the unemployed men satisfied that their concerns had been heard and addressed with promises of a highway construction relief project between Prince George and the Tête Jaune junction, 272 kilometres to the east. Reports that the long-delayed Pacific Great Eastern Railway might be restarted as a relief project buoyed hopeful speculation.[4] Nonetheless, the June protest proved to be the first of a series of walkouts, petitions, confrontations, and demonstrations through which the communist-linked National Unemployed Workers Association (NUWA) emerged at the forefront of the attempt to articulate workers' demands. Frustrations boiled over in a clash on 13 May 1935 between striking workers and British Columbia Provincial Police (BCPP) Inspector Thomas van Dyk, Sergeant C.K. McKenzie, Constables F. Cooke, W. Smith, and A.J. Pomeroy, and provincial game officers W. Forrester and Gordon Copeland. The latter two were badly beaten, leading the police to fire shots over the strikers to end the melee. Later that day, strikers Frederick Barker, Heitman Johnson, Jack Routlege, and Gus Edvall were brought before Stipendiary Magistrate George Milburn on charges of assaulting peace officers discharging their duties.[5] Reported in Vancouver and Victoria, the clash was portrayed as communist-led mob violence in Prince George.[6] While police reinforcements were dispatched from Vancouver, both city council and local residents signalled that enough was enough, seizing upon the idea of mounting a patriotically themed Empire/Victoria Day parade and festivities to underline the community's respect for law and order as well as its opposition to communist influence.[7]

Reflecting on this unusual burst of patriotism in a community that had rarely shown such enthusiasm, the *Prince George Citizen* pointed to the unemployed protesters and the supposed communist threat as motivators: "There can be little doubt that resentment against this condition of affairs, with its challenge to authority and law and order, was a factor in influencing the citizens of Prince George in their determination to put on a patriotic demonstration on Victoria Day."[8] For editor R.A. Renwick, the lesson was clear: local merchants and residents had lost patience with the "men who had been persistently fomenting trouble," and "the public generally appears to have made up its mind that the time has arrived to call the bluff of the few strike leaders who have undertaken to set at defiance the administration of law and order."[9] The paper failed to explore what proportion of this "public" was populated by parents and teenaged children seeking any form of paid employment to make ends meet.

Magistrate Milburn sentenced Heitman Johnson to eighteen months' imprisonment and meted out six-month terms to the other three strikers involved in the beating. Renwick reassured his readers that the whole affair had been the work of communist agitators who "engineered the trouble but kept out of the actual conflict so as not to jeopardize their personal liberty."[10] In his telling, the community had turned its back on violence and showed that "the people of Prince George have nothing in common with the Communists." The authentic residents, those who truly belonged, cherished a well-ordered and law-abiding community.[11] It was a familiar claim. And while readers may have embraced such sentiments, the fact that violence *had* erupted was a reminder that, patriotic demonstrations aside, disorder and tumult continued to characterize outsiders' impressions of life in the Georges.

While the Second World War brought about an end to the hardship and want of the 1930s, wartime realities produced new disruptions. As Mia Reimers has ably demonstrated, the war transformed Prince George in countless way, leading to a novel identity as a base community and home of the Pacific Northwest Defense Command, housing thousands of soldiers tasked with defending the province's north.[12] The city's population, stuck between 2,100 and 2,500 since the end of the Great War was swamped by over 6,000 military personnel.[13] Most were accommodated in barracks outside of the city proper, but civilian employees and military wives absorbed every conceivable space and overwhelmed local restaurants, hotels, and recreational facilities, while resurrecting distant memories of a city on the rise. The influx strained relations between residents and the newcomers, never more so than when it came to civilian animosity toward those National Resources Mobilization Act (NRMA) conscripts, derisively referred to as "zombies."[14] As the war dragged on, the NRMA men, posted to home-front duties in response to their refusal to volunteer for overseas service, were constantly pressured by the public and governmental officials to accept standard deployment.[15] Unhappy with the news that a change in federal policy meant they were to be sent overseas, the NRMA men staged several protests in late November 1944. In Prince George, they protested by refusing to stand for the national anthem at a hockey game; they then held an 800-man parade through the downtown business district on a Saturday afternoon, which corresponded with the alarming mutiny in Terrace to the west. Another smaller demonstration in Prince George followed two days later.[16] Although it was clear that the protesters were not permanent residents of the region, and, in fact, were voicing sentiments antagonistic to the unquestioning loyalty expressed by most locals, the spectacle aligned neatly with preconceived notions that the province's north, and Prince George specifically, had a penchant for trouble. Although the protests passed quickly enough, they were nonetheless an unwelcome reminder that there was always "something" about the Georges.

The postwar years and boom economy of the 1950s finally brought about the economic bounce that Prince George had long been expecting. Riding a wave created by a housing rush on the Prairies, the city's lumber industry took off. In the northern Interior, the industry was still largely a collection of small and medium-sized operations, but the scale of demand and the anticipation of better times brought the industry to the cusp of change. Unsurprisingly, not everyone agreed on what these changes would mean or, indeed, if novel ways of doing business were appealing. For a portion of industry workers, unionization emerged as a desirable option, which drew the International Woodworkers of America (IWA) into the Interior, seeking union recognition and wage parity with the coast. The union's efforts sparked discord, pitting independent mill owners against employees who had often been viewed as members of company families. Disagreements in such intimate quarters were bitter. A strike that began on 28 September 1953 ran for over a hundred days, until 6 January 1954, unleashing discord unlike anything ever seen in the region.[17] It was, according to a retrospective *Citizen* editorial thirty years after the fact, "one of the bitterest and most brutal strikes this city has ever known":[18]

> Goon squads went up against goon squads. If only two or three men were on the picket line, they would get beaten up, so a dozen had to go together. Mill management had to travel in packs. At times it wasn't safe to be the wife or child of a member of management. Homes were vandalized. Within a week after the strike was started, management had two "security groups" in town ... Union tactics were no better than management's. One millowner's wife and children were terrified by a phone call from a unionist. The next day the millowner saw the unionist on the street. According to five people interviewed, he felled the man with a single blow, then picked him up and kicked him, then picked him up and kicked him – for three blocks down Victoria [Street] in Prince George.[19]

Brawls, gunfire, assaults, housebreaking, vandalism, and threats of violence were the order of the day, and workers and mill owners alike worried about mortgages, bills, and how to put food on the table. Families fled the city, in search of work and away from the turmoil. By mid-November, newspaper readers in Vancouver were learning of goon squads and fisticuffs on Prince George's streets, with reminders a month later as Judge A.E. Lord attempted to resolve the strike amid allegations of union violence and intimidation.[20] According to journalist turned historian Ken Bernsohn, by two months into the strike, "almost a quarter of the town's population had departed, including those who had watched their retail businesses die because of lack of customers."[21] That the conflict on the ground involved residents invested in the community's long-term success made it difficult to blame the strike and the violence on outsiders. Nonetheless, the *Citizen* attributed the union's stubbornness to "communist sympathizers" on the union board, while a letter writer connected the local trouble to excessive liquor consumption in Prince George and "a few transient workers" whose actions threatened to "cripple and ruin our development and prosperity in the north."[22] Although the criticism directed at transient workers generated push back within days, the association between liquor, transient workers, and disorder was all too familiar.[23] Looking back from a distance of four years after the dispute was settled, journalist Vera Kelsey claimed that "Prince George was so intent on forgetting its checkered past to realize its glorious tomorrow that it viewed its present merely as an economic springboard."[24] To imply that, in a province with a thick history of labour violence as workers fought for living wages, the Georges were particularly saddled with a "checkered past" was, at minimum, a blinkered reading of the historical record.

The end of the strike did not usher the city out of the spotlight. Postwar worries about juvenile delinquency, a local variant of widespread moral panic about teenagers across much of the western world, signalled that, despite its sense of isolation, Prince George was caught up in broader trends. Although concern about youth problems had been voiced well before the end of the war, local trouble erupted in late April 1953 with a "rumble" at the former Second World War airstrip outside the city limits. Reports indicated that approximately forty witnesses and combatants had parked their vehicles in a circle to contain the melee.[25] The dust-up recalls the Quebec Street battle thirty-two years earlier, suggesting, among other things, that April could be a difficult month in the Georges. Worries about teenagers and juvenile delinquency persisted and then reignited in early

April 1957, when the *Citizen* offered a bold front-page headline declaring that "Gang Terror Flares up in City."[26] Reporting that "hoodlums" armed with knives and bicycle chains were roaming the streets and terrorizing the public suggested a return to the imagined bad old days. And, like the criticism heaped on Magistrate C.B. Daniell in April 1921, the threat of juvenile delinquents running wild in Prince George was reason to demand the dismissal of Magistrate P.J. Moran.[27]

Once again, the tumult captured newspaper attention in the Lower Mainland. The *Province,* with an all-capitals headline spanning the front page, announced "Prince George Asks Help – 'Hoodlums Running Wild.'" A day later, the *Vancouver Sun* was slightly less alarmist in publishing, on page 20, Prince George mayor John Morrison's demand that Moran be fired.[28] While a *Province* editorial offered that "we in Vancouver have a fellow feeling for the people of Prince George" and that "this is not the problem of Prince George alone. It is the problem of people and parents everywhere," the chosen title – "The Hoodlums in Prince George" – was true to the long-lived unease about the Interior community.[29] Confirming the link three days later, a separate report about an alleged juvenile extortion gang in Burnaby quoted a worried mother who characterized the trouble as "something like that Prince George business."[30] Indeed.

Unfortunately for Prince George, and despite Mayor Morrison's assertion that the *Province*'s news coverage had allegedly solved the hoodlum problem, Lorne Downey, Prince George's high school principal, had a rock pitched through his home's front window just a few days later.[31] The vandalism came less than a week after vice-principal Tony Embleton told the provincial teachers' convention in Vancouver that the Prince George toughs were "no worse than in other cities but we have got adverse publicity because we decided to do something about it and not hush up this trouble."[32] The glass littering Downey's front room argued that whatever was being done had failed to reap benefits. Over the course of the ensuing six weeks, three youths – aged eighteen, nineteen, and twenty – none of whom were high school students, appeared in County Court to answer several charges, including assault and break and enter. Two were fined before leaving town and the third was sentenced to ninety days in Oakalla Prison. Unconnected with the more serious charges, the two boys who smashed Downey's front window were found to be delinquent and ordered to pay restitution. By then, the latest sensation had run its course revealing that despite the overwrought headlines and declarations suggesting that Prince George was a "hoodlum trouble center," the entire episode was best understood as an iteration of a contrived moral panic repeated across

North America and beyond.[33] Nonetheless, the formula was proven. Confronted with news of disorder, conflict, or violence, residents assured themselves that dangerous ideas, newcomers, troublemakers, and people who did not belong were responsible, while outside commentators drew on the established narrative that Prince George had a well-earned reputation for trouble. Every story, every account, became a self-fulfilling prophecy.

When ninety unionized workers walked off the job at Prince George's Canadian Tire store on 5 December 1983, launching what was the first strike in that company's history, events – and reportage – over the following twenty-seven months adhered to expectations. Antagonisms, finger pointing, and anxiety were accompanied by a shooting incident, rumours of brake tampering targeting workers who crossed the picket lines, shotgun shells being left in strikers' burn barrels in the hope that they would detonate, a series of picket-line fights leading to unsuccessful criminal prosecutions, scuffles involving picketers and customers, and setting off "stink-bombs" inside the store.[34] It was ugly, and true to most labour disruptions, anxious contract negotiations, and fights for union recognition that played out through the 1960s, 1970s, and 1980s. While residents can be forgiven for believing that incidents close to home were more frightening than those occurring at General Motors, Abitibi Pulp and Paper, BC Telephone, and Eaton's, what played out in Prince George was part of larger struggles elsewhere.[35] Reacting to reports of employee Betty Johnson being shot at as she drove away from work – as well as what appeared to be a bullet hole in the vehicle's side panel – store owner Tom Steadman argued that, although there had been a "dramatic escalation of violence directed at store employees," he believed the incident was not "representative of Prince George or the labor movement in general."[36] His point was familiar: to explain away outbursts of disorder, white residents had long relied on the claim that authentic residents were law abiding and responsible. That sentiment was sorely tested in 1984, when, in addition to the Canadian Tire strike, the Canadian Paperworkers Union and the Pulp, Paper, and Woodworkers Union were locked out from 2 February to 29 March at the same time as a separate six-week strike of support staff at the College of New Caledonia.[37] When, in late October, a *Citizen* editorial reflected on the Canadian Tire strike's approaching anniversary and its legacy for the community, the worry that prolonging the dispute would leave permanent scars on Prince George echoed the historical concern over reputation. Culture, after all, comprises stories that we tell ourselves, about ourselves.[38]

The headlines in *Maclean's* magazine on 15 December 2011 spared no blushes. For the second time in as many years, the magazine labelled Prince George – British Columbia's self-proclaimed northern capital – "Canada's most dangerous city." Opening with a summary of the deaths of Loren Leslie, Jill Stuchenko, Cynthia Mass, and Natasha Montgomery at the hands of a serial killer, the magazine noted that Prince George's crime ranking was 114 percent above the national average and that the combination of gang wars and drug abuse was contributing to a disturbing local scene.[39] Responses in the city ranged from disbelieving outrage to the pained rejoinder that the community "always" received a "bad rap." Many, no doubt, found comfort in the assertion that their experiences told a markedly different story about life in the northern Interior. That the accused serial killer had been from the small lumber-industry community of Fort St. James did not dilute the magazine's insistence that there was something worrying, if not sinister, about Prince George. While the subject of a great deal of pearl-clutching, the *Maclean's* ranking and Prince George's uninterrupted run as number one for three years in a row was hardly the only source of concern. The 725-kilometre-long Highway of Tears, stretching from Prince Rupert on the Pacific coast to Prince George, traced a macabre half-century. Depending on which source is credited, the number of women killed along Highway 16 since 1970 ranges between the mid-teens and forty.[40] While the highway stretches for two-thirds of the province's width, and the disappearances occurred along its length, the presence of the city of Prince George at its one end fed into the established narrative and reinforced an association with violence directed at women in general, and Indigenous women in particular.

Reenforcing that impression was the horror story associated with the 2002 indictment of Judge David Ramsay, a former Provincial Court judge, resident in Prince George, who targeted and sexually assaulted a number of Indigenous girls who had appeared in his court.[41] Born in Nova Scotia, educated in Victoria, and articling in Prince George before working at a law firm in Whitehorse, Ramsay opened the city's first legal aid office before returning to private practice until he was appointed to the Provincial Court in 1991. Did his connections with the city somehow "explain" his behaviour? Had the city's alleged violent DNA entwined with his? For some, the subtext wrote the story. After all, it was Prince George. Yet, as the Canadian National Inquiry into Missing and Murdered Indigenous Women and Girls has powerfully demonstrated, these local tragedies are part of a nation-wide crisis for which all Canadians carry the burden of responsibility.[42] Believing that the evidence demonstrated that there is something bred in the bone in Prince George ignores and trivializes the complex reality of systemic violence against women, particularly Indigenous women, in Canada. *Maclean's* recognized as much in August 2014, noting that

> an Aboriginal girl born in Canada today will die up to ten years earlier than the national average. She is more likely to live in a crowded home without access to clean running water. She is more likely to be sexually or physically abused and stands a far greater chance of becoming addicted to tobacco, alcohol, and drugs. She is more prone to a host of life-threatening ailments like diabetes, heart disease and cancer. Worse yet, as a recent RCMP report showed, she is five times more likely than her non-Aboriginal counterpart to meet a violent end at the hands of another.[43]

Choosing to believe that violence against Indigenous women is yet another example of "that Prince George business" ignores what remains a national tragedy.

The legacy of these incidents of violence, vandalism, and conflict is complicated. For one, while other communities experienced their own sensations and moments of bad press, too often it appeared that the imprint was never as deep or as dark as when Prince George was the subject. It seems as if every untoward incident in the Georges served to confirm assumed truths. And even in those instances when the news was good or offered a reason to acknowledge and celebrate local or regional accomplishments, commentators, armed with a knowing attitude, implied that there was *always* a subtext. Nothing about Prince George was straightforward; nothing could be taken on its own merit. As was the case in the years straddling the First World War, some residents accepted that like every other community the Georges were not perfect; those same residents argued that the Georges had been treated unfairly. Further, they chose to minimize any examples of disorder and crime as products of an assortment of contextual factors, or explain that the perpetrators of such outrages were not "real" residents who had banked their futures on a long-term commitment to the community. And akin to newspaper editors and public officials among the community's first generation of white settlers, some of these voices point to trouble arising from newly arrived immigrants, Asian residents, the poor, the unhoused, the Indigenous or mixed-heritage community, and Black or Brown citizens – anyone except the respectable, privileged, white community. This, despite the historical evidence that the city's dubious reputation owed a great deal to the actions and words of white newspaper men, developers, promoters, and locally elected municipal politicians. Others push back more forcefully, dismissing the caricatures, advocating for a subtler, more searching impression, and seeking an image that celebrates the increasing diversification of what had been a white settler community that actively marginalized communities out of step with the preferred narrative, while recognizing that the city has always been buffeted by racism, class difference, paternalism, and privilege. And while these forces have too often exerted an oversized and negative influence on community life in Prince George, they are integral to the workings of modern British Columbia.

What, then, does the anxiety at the "gates of hell" tell us? Rendered through a crime history of community and identity informed by the historian's tools of empathy and imagination, the conversation moves beyond caricature toward a deeper and more nuanced image of the Georges. As much as the northern Interior had its share of tumult, disorder, and crime, the evidence demonstrates that the community was no different than any other in a province marked by an early twentieth-century alcohol-fuelled masculine culture. Policing in such an environment relied on a peacekeeping approach that made no pretense at altering what observers considered to be human nature. At its best, this police culture, with at least two or three notable exceptions, checked events from spiralling out of control. The BCPP proved more adept at such efforts than did the Prince George city police. Policing, akin to the tenor of community life across the province, relied on racism to direct the constable's discretionary gaze in a white man's province. Those targeted by these presumptions experienced their own brand of anxiety, which was distinct from that troubling the self-identified respectable residents. If residents anticipated achieving greater respectability when the Georges became the region's judicial centre, the reality was more ambiguous, as the regular parade of misdemeanours in the Magistrate's Court, and more serious felonies in the County Court and Supreme Court assize, provided a near-constant reminder that every community was home to individuals prone to making poor decisions. Some cases and suspects became front-page sensations and, in having their transgressions broadcast in the province's newspapers, reinforced the belief that there was "something" awry in the Georges, an echo of unease about the community and its residents.

This study reminds us of the value of historical mindedness as central to understanding the present. For, rather than being merely an expedition into a distant and almost foreign land, this exploration of identity provides a glimpse of the frustration and self-doubt at the root of contemporary small-town Canada's disenchantment and anger with its place in the nation. We see how the pursuit of respectability – indeed, of respect – echoes the worry that one's hopes, ideals, morals, and way of life have not only failed to secure a warm welcome in the councils of the good and the great, but have been found wanting. By turning their eyes northward and delivering what they imagined to be white civilization to the northern Interior, that first generation of white settlers felt as if they had lost something. They had become less. And as the years passed, that sense of loss hardened into a grievance of being overlooked, dismissed, and marginalized. In this we are reminded that what some may dismiss as small history – favouring the local rather than braving big themes spanning continents – speaks to bigger truths. Thus, engaging with a community's anxiety over reputation and respectability reveals that, in no uncertain terms, the local invariably colours the region and the nation.

Notes

INTRODUCTION: ANXIOUS AT THE VERY GATES OF HELL

1 The *Westminster Hall Magazine* was produced by Presbyterian seminarian students enrolled in the Westminster Hall theological college at the University of British Columbia. The magazine recalled "Mel" Wright's brief attendance at the hall (where he took one semester of his theological studies) before being assigned to Fort George. See "The Church's Outposts: Pioneer Work at Fort George," *Westminster Hall Magazine* 1, 10/11 (April 1912): 28–29; "Pioneering Outpost Work," *Westminster Hall Magazine* 2, 4 (October 1912): 40, 42; and "Should Men Bribe the Devil?" *Westminster Hall Magazine* 3, 6 (June 1913): 5–8.

2 Reverend C.M. Wright, "The Church's Task in Canada," in Presbyterian Church of Canada, *Pre-Assembly Congress of the Presbyterian Church in Canada* (Toronto: Board of Foreign Missions, Presbyterian Church of Canada, 1913), 95.

3 "Walked 350 Miles from the Very Gates of Hell," *TG*, 3 June 1913, 4; "Worth Struggle to Defeat Sin at the Gates of Hell," *TS*, 3 June 1913, 4. Wright's speech echoed Reverend John G. Shearer's condemnation of Winnipeg in 1910. See Marianna Valverde, *The Age of Light, Soap, and Water: Moral Reform in English Canada, 1885–1925* (Toronto: McClelland and Stewart, 1991), 57.

4 "Lurid Pictures of Northern Interior – Minister from Fort George Creates Sensation at Toronto Gathering – Tells of Weary Trek from the Very Gates of Hell – All Manner of Vice Exists in Smaller Towns, Declares Rev. C.M. Wright – An Appeal for Aid in Work of Church in Remote Districts," *VP*, 3 June 1913, 1; "Fled from the Suburbs of Hades," *FGH*, 14 June 1913, 3.

5 "Fled from the Suburbs of Hades," *FGH*, 14 June 1913, 3. Acknowledging that he had located South Fort George at the gates of hell, Wright attempted to distance himself from the comments by blaming the *Globe* reporter. See "Letter from Wright of Fort George," *Westminster Hall Magazine* 3, 6 (June 1913): 24.

6 "Fled from the Suburbs of Hades," *FGH,* 14 June 1913, 3. Wright exaggerated: the Hotel Northern possessed the only liquor licence in the region.

7 Copy of letter from Reverend Alfred T. Bell, Empress, Alberta, 4 January 1937; Dr. George A. Wilson to Reverend F.J. Runnalls, 6 April 1943 in Reverend F.J. Runnalls Papers, EPA, A986.5.4a.

8 *FGH,* 14 June 1913, 2. A *Vancouver Province* editorial added that, while Wright had been earnest in his comments, he had "unconsciously" libelled the "salt-of-the earth" people developing the northern Interior. See "The Gates of Hell," *VP,* 4 June 1916, 6. An edited version of the *Province* article was republished in Quesnel: "Gates of Hell," *CO,* 14 June 1913, 2.

9 *FGH,* 14 June 1913, 2.

10 F.E. Runnalls, *The History of the Knox United Church, Prince George, British Columbia* (Prince George: Prince George Printers, 1986), 21. The "Georges" is a reference to the original white settler communities of Fort George and South Fort George, and later included a third community, Prince George. Much to the chagrin of local settlers, nonresidents rarely differentiated between South Fort George and Fort George.

11 Unless otherwise cited, the following is based on "Has This Town Let Bars Down," *FGT,* 12 July 1913, 1.

12 Unless otherwise cited, the following is based upon "Daily Newspaper for Fort George," *VS,* 10 May 1912, 4. According to the *Sun,* managing editor W.E. Playfair intended to turn the *Tribune* into a daily newspaper on 1 June 1912; W.R. Gordon remained the content editor. The few surviving copies of the *Tribune* indicate that it never expanded operations beyond a weekly format.

13 "Has This Town Let Bars Down," *FGT,* 12 July 1913, 1.

14 The name Bessie Peters draws a second glance, given the fact that Sheriff E.S. Peters's wife was named Bessie. There is no evidence, however, that these two women were one and the same.

15 Unless otherwise cited, the following is based on "Segregated District in the Limelight," *FGH,* 19 July 1913, 1.

16 "Women Were Made Dupes Of," *FGH,* 16 August 1913, 3.

17 "Fort George Women Send to Vancouver for Help in Straits," *VS,* 19 July 1913, 1–2. The petition did not attract any local news commentary until 9 August 1913. "New Police Chief Acts," *FGT,* 9 August 1913, 1–2.

18 Generally, see Veronica Strong-Boag, *Liberal-Labour Lady: The Life and Times of Mary Ellen Spear Smith* (Vancouver: UBC Press, 2021).

19 Superintendent Colin S. Campbell, Victoria, to Attorney General W.J. Bowser, Victoria, 29 July 1913, (commenting on the relayed content of Johnson's letter), BCA, GR 64, reel B07395, vol. 7, 14.

20 *FGH,* 9 August 1913, 6. Also see "New Police Chief Acts," *FGT,* 9 August 1913, 1–2.

21 Nancy Christie and Michael Gauvreau, *A Full-Orbed Christianity: The Protestant Churches and Social Welfare in Canada, 1900–1940* (Montreal and Kingston: McGill-Queen's University Press, 1996), 22–23, 42, and 53.

22 Unless otherwise cited, the following is based on "Series of Lectures on Social Evil," *FGT,* 13 September 1913, 5. Reflecting on his years spent ministering in the Fort George district, Reverend A.C. Justice recalled to amateur historian F.E. Runnalls an incident in which one woman in the segregated sex-trade district committed suicide by drinking carbolic

acid after learning of her sister's death. In another instance, during one of the typhoid outbreaks in South Fort George, a sex worker ended up in the local "hospital." From there, thanks to a subscription from her fellow workers and concerned citizens, she was delivered "to friends in the US." Rev. A.C. Justice to Rev. F.E. Runnalls, 9 February 1943, EPA, A986.5.4a.

23 "Wonderful Appeal by Social Worker," *WFP,* 5 March 1914, 1–2. See also Marie Christine Ratté, "Rescue Work for Girls," in *Social Service Congress, Ottawa, 1914: Report of Addresses and Proceedings* (Toronto: Social Service Council of Canada, 1914), 222–25.

24 Clifford Geertz, "Notes on the Balinese Cockfight," in *The Interpretation of Cultures* (New York: Basic Books, 1973), 448.

25 Alan Artibise, "Boosterism and the Development of Prairie Cities, 1871–1913," in *The Prairie West: Historical Readings,* ed. R. Douglas Francis and Howard Palmer (Edmonton: Pica Pica Press, 1992), 515–43. While Max Foran's exploration follows Artibise's outward projection of the booster mindset and method, Foran concentrates on individuals rather than institutional sources; see Max Foran, "The Boosters in Boosterism: Some Calgary Examples," *Urban History Review* 8, 2 (October 1979): 77–82. Also see Paul Voisey, *Vulcan: The Making of a Prairie Community* (Toronto: University of Toronto Press, 1988) and Max Foran, *High River and the Times: An Albertan Community and Its Weekly Newspaper, 1905–1966* (Edmonton: University of Alberta Press, 2004).

26 Ranajit Guha, "Not at Home in Empire," *Critical Inquiry* 23, 3 (Spring 1997): 486–87; Joanna Bourke, "Feature: Fear, Ambivalence and Admiration," *History Workshop Journal* 55 (2003): 126.

27 Karen Dubinsky, *Improper Advances: Rape and Heterosexual Conflict in Ontario, 1880–1929* (Chicago: University of Chicago Press, 1993), 147–48, 152, and 155.

28 Dubinsky, *Improper Advances,* 145.

29 Ken Bernsohn, *Slabs, Scabs and Skidders: A History of the IWA in the Central Interior* (Prince George: IWA Local I-424, 1981), 30.

30 Michael Dawson, *The Mountie from Dime Novel to Disney* (Toronto: Between the Lines, 1998), xii.

31 Leonard Cohen, "Anthem," *Live in London* (2009).

32 Lisa Helps, "Bodies Public, City Spaces: Becoming Modern Victoria, British Columbia, 1871–1901" (master's thesis, University of Victoria, 2002), 13–16.

33 Helps, "Bodies Public," 44.

34 Nicholas Blomley, "Law, Property, and the Geography of Violence: The Frontier, the Survey, and the Grid," *Annals of the Association of American Geographers* 93, 1 (March 2003): 131–33.

35 Robert M. Cover, "Violence and the Word," *Yale Law Journal* 95, 8 (July 1986): 1601–2.

36 Allan Silver, "The Demand for Order in Civil Society: A Review of Some Themes in the History of Urban Crime, Police, and Riot," in *The Police: Six Sociological Essays,* ed. David J. Bordua (New York: John Wiley and Sons, 1967), 1–24. Also see Kristian Williams, "The Demand for Order and the Birth of Modern Policing," *Monthly Review* 55, 7 (December 2003), https://monthlyreview.org/2003/12/01/the-demand-for-order-and-the-birth-of-modern-policing/.

37 See David Vogt and David Alexander Gamble, "'You Don't Suppose the Dominion Government Wants to Cheat the Indians?' The Grand Trunk Pacific Railway and the Fort George Reserve, 1908–12," *BC Studies* 166 (Summer 2010): 55–72.

38 Kenton Storey, *Settler Anxiety at the Outposts of Empire: Colonial Relations, Humanitarian Discourses, and the Imperial Press* (Vancouver: UBC Press, 2016); Robert Hogg, *Men and Manliness on the Frontier: Queensland and British Columbia in the Mid-Nineteenth Century* (Basingstoke, UK: Palgrave Macmillan, 2012).

39 Although there are considerable differences between the context of the Georges and those at play in the Okanagan, the legacy of whiteness has also been identified by Daniel Keyes and Luis Aguiar. See "Introduction," in their *White Space: Race, Privilege, and Cultural Economies of the Okanagan Valley* (Vancouver: UBC Press, 2021), 7. Beyond generalities, how far one can legitimately compare two such disparate regions remains an open question.

40 Dubinsky, *Improper Advances*, 143–62. In a similar vein, see Karen Dubinsky and Franca Iacovetta, "Murder, Womanly Virtue, and Motherhood: The Case of Angelina Napolitano, 1911–1922," *Canadian Historical Review* 72, 4 (1991): 505–31.

41 Dubinsky, *Improper Advances*, 145 and 147. See also Jonathan Swainger, "Breaking the Peace: Fictions of the Law-Abiding Peace River Country, 1930–50," *BC Studies* 119 (Autumn 1998): 5–25.

42 Dubinsky, *Improper Advances*, 152 and 160.

43 Lynne Marks, *Infidels and the Damn Churches: Irreligion and Religion in Settler British Columbia* (Vancouver: UBC Press, 2017), 215.

44 Robin Winks, *The Blacks in Canada: A History,* 2nd ed. (Montreal and Kingston: McGill-Queen's University Press, 1997); Barrington Walker, ed., *The African Canadian Legal Odyssey: Historical Essays* (Toronto: Osgoode Society for Canadian Legal History, 2012); Sarah-Jane Mathieu, *North of the Color Line: Migration and Black Resistance in Canada, 1870–1955* (Chapel Hill: University of North Carolina Press, 2010).

45 Mathieu, *North of the Color Line*, 24.

46 Walker, "Introduction," 29.

47 Patricia Roy, *A White Man's Province: British Columbia Politicians and Chinese and Japanese Immigrants* (Vancouver: UBC Press, 1989); W. Peter Ward, *White Canada Forever: Popular Attitudes and Public Policy towards Orientals in British Columbia* (Montreal and Kingston: McGill-Queen's University Press, 1978); Kay Anderson, *Vancouver's Chinatown: Racial Discourse in Canada, 1875–1980* (Montreal and Kingston: McGill-Queen's University Press, 1991); Timothy Stanley, *Contesting White Supremacy: School Segregation, Anti-Racism, and the Making of Chinese Canadians* (Vancouver: UBC Press, 2011); Lily Chow, *Sojourners in the North* (Prince George: Caitlin Press, 1996).

48 Stanley, *Contesting White Supremacy,* 17–18.

49 Margaret Whitehead, *They Call Me Father: Memoirs of Father Nicolas Coccola* (Vancouver: UBC Press, 1988); Brenda Ireland, "'Working a Great Hardship on Us': First Nations People, the State and Fur Conservation in British Columbia before 1935" (master's thesis, University of Calgary, 1995); Ireland, "'Working a Great Hardship on Us': First Nations People, the State and Fur Conservation in British Columbia Prior to 1935," *Native Studies Review* 11, 1 (1996): 65–90; Robert Diaz, "Reshaping the Land: An Environmental History of Prince George, British Columbia" (master's thesis, University of Northern British Columbia, 1996); Vogt and Gamble, "'You Don't Suppose.'"

50 Joseph Arthur Lower, "The Grand Trunk Pacific Railway and British Columbia" (master's thesis, University of British Columbia, 1939), 62.

51 See Frank Leonard, "Grand Trunk Pacific and the Establishment of the City of Prince George," *BC Studies* 63 (Autumn 1984): 29–54, and Leonard, "'In the Hollow of the

Corporation's Hand': Prince George," in *A Thousand Blunders: The Grand Trunk Pacific Railway and Northern British Columbia* (Vancouver: UBC Press, 1996), 186–217.

52 Acting Chief Constable John Bourne, duty log, BCA, GR 445, box 16, file 6, 22–25 and 27 November 1918, and box 48, file 16, 1–2 December 1918; Constable Carl Johnson, duty log, BCA, GR 445, box 46, file 16, 22–23 and 25–29 November 1918, and box 48, file 16, 1–2 December 1918. Also see "Local and Personal," *PGC,* 3 December 1918, 1.

53 "Things We Need," *PGC,* 27 September 1921, 2. See also "When Will Prince George Get a Court House Such as This," *PGC,* 11 November 1921, 3. On Duff Pattullo's backing of new governmental offices in Prince Rupert, see Robin Fisher, *Duff Pattullo of British Columbia* (Toronto: University of Toronto Press, 1991), 161.

54 See Dubinsky, *Improper Advances,* 143–62.

55 Prince George City Council Minutes, 8 April 1921, City Clerk's Office, Prince George City Hall; "Council Plans a Clean-Up on Coloured Undesirables," *PGC,* 19 April 1921, 1; "Bootleggers Must Go Is Decision of City Council," *TL,* 22 April 1921, 1.

56 Chief Constable W.R. Dunwoody evicted the International Workers of the World from the Central Fort George townsite in the third week of April 1913, and, beginning in late April 1919, Acting Chief Constable John Bourne made several visits to Prince George after having learned of a planned sympathy walk-out by GTP shop and station men in support of the Winnipeg General Strike. See W.R. Dunwoody, duty log, 22 April 1913, BCA, GR 445, box 8, file 7, and John Bourne, duty log, 30 April 1919 and 28 and 29 May 1919, BCA, GR 445, box 56, file 6. Similar inquiries were made by Constable Dave Long on 9 May and 29–31 May, BCA, GR 445, box 56, file 6. "Shop Men and Station Men from Edmonton to Rupert Join Sympathetic Strike," *PGC,* 28 May 1919, 1. On the BCPP and labour, see Lynne Stonier-Newman, *Policing a Pioneer Province: The BC Provincial Police, 1858–1950* (Madeira Park, BC: Harbour Publishing, 1991), 115–33.

CHAPTER ONE: ESTABLISHING THE GEORGES AND THE BIRTH OF A BAD REPUTATION

1 Unless otherwise cited, the following is drawn from Frank Leonard, *A Thousand Blunders: The Grand Trunk Pacific Railway and Northern British Columbia* (Vancouver: UBC Press, 1996), 20–25. Also see Leonard's "'A Closed Book': The Canadian Pacific Railway Survey and North-Central British Columbia," *Western Geography* 12 (2002): 163–84.

2 Leonard, *A Thousand Blunders,* 25–26. McBride's Conservatives secured twenty-two of the forty-two seats in the October 1903 election. See Patricia Roy, *Boundless Optimism: Richard McBride's British Columbia* (Vancouver: UBC Press, 2012), 82.

3 Roy, *Boundless Optimism,* 95.

4 Allotted by Peter O'Reilly, British Columbian Indian Reserve Commission, and surveyor Francis A. Devereux in early October 1892, the reserves were surveyed two years later, and then confirmed on 21 September 1895. *Fort George Journal* (New Caledonia), HBCA, B.280/a/3, 3–4 October 1892, B.280/a/4, 24–25 September and 8–9 October 1894. See Hudson's Bay Company Canada, "Schedule of Indian Reserves in the Dominion: Babine Agency" in "Annual Report of the Department of Indian Affairs for the Year Ended June 30 1900," *Sessional Papers* 27, Part 2 (Ottawa: Printed by S.E. Dawson, Printer to the Queen's Most Excellent Majesty, 1901), 66. For O'Reilly's notes confirming Fort George Reserves 1 to 4, see Canada, "Fort George Indians," in *Federal and Provincial Collections of Minutes of Decision, Correspondence, and Sketches: Material Provided by*

the Joint Indian Reserve Commission and Indian Reserve Commission, 1876–1910, Binder
11, Documents 780/93, 5 October 1892. Also see David Ricardo Williams, "O'Reilly,
Peter," *Dictionary of Canadian Biography,* http://www.biographi.ca/en/bio/o_reilly_
peter_13E.html.

5 Spellings of "Tapage" vary: see "The Story of Thapage," *FGH,* 23 March 1912, 2; "Tales
of the Pioneers: Joe Merrienne Sousa Thapage," *PGC,* 30 January 1920, 3; and "Sousa
Thappage Dead," *PGC,* 15 July 1921, 8. Dr. Ted Binnema brought these articles to my
attention. Hamilton's advertisement in the 13 November 1909 edition of the *Fort George
Tribune* declared that he was sole owner of the South Fort George townsite. See "A.G.
Hamilton," *FGT,* 13 November 1909, 3, and "People Inquiring about Fort George," *FGT,*
27 November 1909, 3.

6 Superintendent F.S. Hussey, BCPP, Victoria, to Alexander G. Hamilton, Kaslo, 28 January
1897, and Hussey to Hamilton, 9 March 1897, BCA, GR 61, reel B02571, vol. 8, 667 and
915. Hamilton was officially appointed 11 March 1897 at the rate of $68 per month. See
*Annual Report of the Superintendent of Police Representing the Police and Prisons of British
Columbia for the Year Ending 31st October* (Victoria: Richard Wolfenden, 1897), 921.

7 On Hamilton's career as a BCPP constable, see "Court of Investigation held in regard to
certain charges made against A.G. Hamilton, Provincial Constable, embodied in three
declarations," 16 August 1897, BCA, GR 99, box 2, file 7. Superintendent Hussey mentions
the dismissal without naming Hamilton in the annual report: *Annual Report of the
Superintendent of Police Representing the Police and Prisons of British Columbia for the Year
Ending 31st October* (Victoria: Richard Wolfenden, Printer to the Queen's Most Excellent
Majesty, 1898), 669.

8 "Around the City," *PGP,* 19 December 1914, 6; "A.G. Hamilton, Pioneer Trader, Choice
of the Local Conservatives," *PGP,* 27 March 1915, 1. Hamilton's name is not included
among NWMP personnel from 1873 to 1904: "North West Mounted Police (NWMP)
– Personnel Records, 1873–1904," LAC, https://www.bac-lac.gc.ca/eng/discover/nwmp
-personnel-records/Pages/search.aspx. Thanks to Dr. R.C. Macleod for bringing the LAC
website to my attention.

9 "Nominated at Prince George," *TPV,* 26 March 1915, 11; "Conservative Convention:
A.G. Hamilton of South Fort George Received Nomination on Fifth Ballot," *FGH,* 26
March 1915, 1; "A.G. Hamilton, Pioneer Trader, Choice of the Local Conservatives," *PGP,*
27 March 1915, 1; A.G. Hamilton Nominated," *VDT,* 27 March 1915, 2; "The Conservative
Candidate Returns from the Coast," *PGP,* 19 June 1915, 4; "Pro-Hamilton," *PGH,* 16 July
1915, 2.

10 John Calam, ed., *Alex Lord's British Columbia: Recollections of a Rural School Inspector*
(Vancouver: UBC Press, 1991), 58–59; "Hosmer Notes," *FDL,* 1 March 1913, 5; "Hosmer
Notes," *FDL,* 14 February 1914, 4; "Conservatives Celebrate with a Big Smoker," *FDL,* 26
December 1914, 1; "Other Fernie Items," *FDL,* 10 April 1915.

11 "Supreme Court Suit," *VDC,* 11 June 1915, 5; "Conservatives Will Chose Candidate on
24th Inst.," *PGC,* 14 June 1916, 1; "Leave for North," *VDC,* 15 June 1916, 7; "Reserves
Judgment," *VDC,* 15 June 1916, 6.

12 "A Pioneer Visits," *PGC,* 8 July 1921, 2.

13 Incorporation of "The Fort George Lumber and Navigation Company, Limited," 31 March
1909, *British Columbia Gazette* 44, 14 (8 April 1909): 1329. See Willis J. West, "The 'BX'
and the Rush to Fort George," *British Columbia Historical Quarterly* 13, 3/4 (July–October
1949), for an encyclopedic treatment of riverboats on the Fraser River.

14 Stockholders in the Northern Development Company eventually included G.E. McLaughlin and Dr. J.K. McLennan of the J.D. McArthur Company; the latter acquired a controlling share of Clark's Fort George Lumber and Navigation Company. See "Looking over Townsite with View to Improvements," *FGH*, 27 May 1911, 1; "Another Townsite for Fort George," *CO*, 29 January 1910, 1; and "Local and District," *FGH*, 20 August 1910, 4. The Northern Development Company ran a half-page advertisement on the same page.

15 Adding to the confusion is the small paid feature on the Northern Development Company in *BC Saturday Sunset*, asserting that, as of 9 July 1910, the company had "only been established this year." See "Northern Development Co.," *BC Saturday Sunset*, 9 July 1910, 18. Also see "The 'Sunset' Lies in the Limelight: Facts Regarding 'Bruce's' Libelous Articles," *FGH*, 17 December 1910, 1, and "Second Birth of Fort George: History of Pioneer Lumber Firm," *FGH*, 18 February 1914, 1. Advertisements for the Northern Development Company's holdings in (South) Fort George first appeared in *VP*, on 19 February 1910: "Fort George to the Public," 13. Incorporation of the "Northern Development Company, Limited," *British Columbia Gazette* 50, 51 (December 1910): 14915–916.

16 "Provincial News," *VP*, 30 April 1910, 28.

17 "Financiers Take Hold," *FGH*, 5 November 1910, 1; "Order to Wind Up Company's Affairs," *VDW*, 4 January 1911, 17; "Timber Company in Difficulties," *VDW*, 16 March 1911, 17; "Winnipeg Capital Invested in BC," *VDW*, 4 April 1911, 19; "Second Birth of Fort George: History of Pioneer Lumber Firm," *FGH*, 18 February 1914, 1.

18 "Nick Clarke [sic] Passed through Town Tuesday," *PGC*, 3 June 1921, 7.

19 "George J. Hammond," in *Who's Who and Why: A Biographical Dictionary of Notable Men and Women of Western Canada*, ed. C.W. Parker (Vancouver: Canadian Press, 1912), 2: 223; E.O.S. Scholefield, ed., *British Columbia from Earliest Times to the Present* (Vancouver: S.J. Clarke Publishing Co., 1914), 3: 22 and 25.

20 John Hill Jr., *Gold Bricks of Speculation: A Study of Speculation and Its Counterfeits, and an Exposé of the Methods of Bucketshop and "Get-Rich-Quick" Swindles* (Chicago: Lincoln Book Concern, 1904), 34.

21 David Hochfelder, "'Where the Common People Could Speculate': The Ticker, Bucket Shops, and the Origins of Popular Participation in Financial Markets, 1880–1920," *Journal of American History* 93, 2 (September 2006): 338. The Combination Investment Company was incorporated with $50,000 in capital stock in the summer of 1899: see "New Corporations," *CT*, 22 June 1899, 10; "'Inside Tip' Concern Closed – Customers of Combination Investment Company Find Doors Shut – A Receiver Takes Charge," *CT*, 5 December 1899, 1; "Finds $50,000 for Creditors," *CIO*, 6 December 1899, 5; "Indicted after Three Years: President of Chicago Investment Concerns Charged with Appropriating $40,000," *NYT*, 27 February 1903, 1; "Indicted for Swindling," *IJ*, 27 February 1903, 5; "G.J. Hammond Arrested," *CT*, 28 February 1903, 16; "Cash Bond of $21,000 Is Up: George Hammond Deposits Amount in Criminal Court," *CIO*, 4 March 1903, 12; "Witness Tampered With: Open Charge Made in Court by Assistant State's Attorney Barnes," *CIO*, 7 August 1903, 9; "Chicago Board Brings Suit Here," *MJ*, 22 March 1902, 1; "Chicago Board Had Detectives Here," *ST*, 26 March 1902, 7; "Bucket Shop War: Case against Coe Commission Co. Comes Up June 14," *MJ*, 2 June 1901, 6; "Beat Bucket Shops," *SPG*, 8 October 1902, 3; "Hammond Is Amused," *ST*, 11 October 1902, 6; "Hammond under Fire," *MJ*, 27 October 1902, 5; "Waives Extradition," *ST*, 29 October 1902, 7; "Bucket Shops Defeated," *SPG*, 30 October 1902, 7; "Show Down Due: If Hammond Is Indicted, His Trial Will Shed Light on Bucket Shop Methods," *MJ*, 15 November 1902, 7; "G.J.

Hammond Arraigned: Indicted Commission Man Pleads Not Guilty and Deposits Cash Bail," *SPG*, 25 November 1902, 4; "Warrant for a Bucket-Shop Man," *MJ*, 8 December 1902, 1; "Bucket-Shop War's Latest," *MJ*, 19 January 1903, 1; "Chamber Holds Warm Meeting," *SPG*, 21 January 1903, 3; "He Had Worn Prison Garb," *MJ*, 27 January 1903, 1; "Bucket Shops Knocked Out," *BT*, 22 February 1905, 1; "Wins Suit on Gambling Loss," *CT*, 23 February 1905, 13; "Grain Markets Are Closed," *CIO*, 23 February 1905, 9; "Commission Co. Charges Reports to Enemies," *MJ*, 27 February 1905, 5; "A Receiver for Coe Commission," *MJ*, 7 March 1905, 1; "Receiver for a Big Concern," *BDP*, 7 March 1905, 1; "Coe Commission Co. Is Declared Insolvent," *MT*, 8 March 1905, 3; "Receiver in Charge of Bucket Shop," *SPG*, 8 March 1905; "Claims against Coe Co. Pour In," *MJ*, 8 March 1905, 1; "Immense Task of Straightening out Affairs of Insolvent Coe Commission Company," *ST*, 9 March 1905, 3; and "Coe Company Is Bankrupt," *MJ*, 11 March 1905, 1.

22 "George J. Hammond Has Operation for Appendicitis," *ST*, 21 July 1905, 7; "Lightning Strikes Room Where George J. Hammond Was Recovering from Operation," *ST*, 4 August 1905, 7.

23 "Got Electric Shock," *MJ*, 4 August 1905, 4; "New Sensation Is Sprung in Sherman Smith Case," *ST*, 21 January 1908, 1; "Only $22.00 More Needed," *NDC*, 16 April 1908, 1; "Develop Natural Resources," *TP*, 23 October 1909, 3; "Central Fort George Registered Town," *TP*, 22 July 1910, 24; Scholefield, *British Columbia from Earliest Times*, 3: 22; "Early History of the Three Georges," *PGC*, 26 May 1938, 15.

24 Certificate of Incorporation for the "Natural Resources Security Company Limited," *British Columbia Gazette* 49, 31 (August 1909): 3489; "Central Fort George Registered Town," *TP*, 22 July 1910, 24; "British Columbia," *TP*, 10 September 1909, 11.

25 Unless otherwise cited, the following is based on "No. 1: Introduction," *VDW*, 20 October 1909, 18, and *TPV*, 20 October 1909, 13.

26 This was an exaggeration. Advertisements appeared in several Lower Mainland and Vancouver Island newspapers in October 1909 before spreading through western Canada. Similar advertisements appeared in Washington State in the spring of 1910 and in the American Midwest that summer, before arriving in Pennsylvania by late August and Kansas, Missouri, Minnesota, Illinois, New York, and the District of Columbia in September. Similar advertisements pre-dating the 20 October 1909 launch appeared in the *Winnipeg Free Press*, with newspapers in southern Alberta later following suit.

27 "No 4: Still More Proof," *VDW*, 23 October 1909, 29; *TP*, 23 October 1909, 40.

28 "No. 5: Ft. George," *VDW*, 26 October 1909, 14.

29 "The Station Site," *FGH*, 21 November 1914, 1.

30 "Of Fort George, Its Site and Future," *TP*, 19 December 1910, 24; "G.J. Hammond Tells Status," *VDW*, 19 December 1910, 2. West claimed that Hammond spent over $500,000 on advertising his townsite: see West, "The 'BX,'" 178.

31 For both the $100,000 and $171,000 figures, see Leonard, *A Thousand Blunders*, 187.

32 "British Columbia," *WT*, 10 September 1910, 17; *TP*, 10 September 1910, 11; *WT*, 10 September 1910, 17; *VDT*, 17 September 1910, 8; *CH*, 17 September 1910, 18; *EJ*, 17 September 1910; *LP*, 24 September 1910, 35; *NP*, 1 October 1910, 15; *SSP*, 8 October 1910, 11; "No. 1: Introduction," *VDW*, 20 October 1909, 18; "Fort George," *VDT*, 26 October 1909, 13; "How Those Western Canadian Cities Do Grow," *SFE*, 6 November 1910, 39; "Fort George," *TP*, 1 December 1909, 8; "Up to Date Facts about Fort George," *FGT*, 3 December 1910, 4. For the list of nationalities of people who purchased lots in Central Fort George, see Neil Bradford Holmes, "The Promotion of Early Growth in the Western

Canadian City: A Case Study of Prince George, B.C., 1909–1915" (honours thesis, University of British Columbia, 1974), 4.

33 Anna Bumby, "The Sales Campaign of George J. Hammond and the Natural Resources Security Company" (undergraduate essay, College of New Caledonia, 1981), 9.

34 "Of Fort George, Its Site and Future," *TP,* 19 December 1910, 24.

35 "Winnipeg Men Handle $300,000 Deal in BC," *WT,* 28 May 1910, 13.

36 See "Record Deal by Winnipeg Men," *WT,* 14 July 1911, 1; "Quarter Million Realty Deal," *WT,* 28 July 1911, 5; and "Sues for $249,837 in Winnipeg Court," *WT,* 29 September 1921, 20.

37 "Titanic Victims' Memory Honored," *WT,* 18 November 1912, 8; "Titanic Victims' Heroism Is Told for Future Ages," *WT,* 18 December 1912, 1; Bumby, "The Sales Campaign," 8. On the Fort George Townsite Company, see *Saturday Night,* 14 May 1910, 5.

38 In "Fort George: The Hub of British Columbia's Railways and Waterways," *TP,* 13 May 1910, 22, Hammond stated that his company owned half of the Fort George townsite. Also see "Double Victory: Fort George Wins," *VDT,* 28 May 1913, 13.

39 "Fort George: The True Situation," *VDC,* 25 October 1911, 17.

40 "Court Proceedings in Criminal Libel Suit," *FGH,* 1 June 1912, 4.

41 "Gold and Dross," *Saturday Night,* 12 March 1910, 5, and 26 March 1910, 6. According to *Saturday Night*'s editor, "the president of the Natural Resources Security Company, owners of what they are pleased to call the "townsite" of Fort George, becomes peevish over *Saturday Night*'s criticism of their proposition," *Saturday Night,* 18 June 1910, 23.

42 "Not Entitled to Injunction: Motion of Fort George Townsite Promoters Refused," *TDME,* 17 September 1910, 5; "At Osgoode Hall: Plaintiffs Fail to Secure Injunction," *TG,* 17 September 1910, 7; "Judge Middleton's Decision Affecting a Western Real Estate Promotion," *OJ,* 28 September 1910, 8. On Middleton, see John D. Arnup, *Middleton: The Beloved Judge* (Toronto: Osgoode Society for Canadian Legal History, 1988).

43 "A Plain Statement of Facts Regarding South Fort George and Central British Columbia by the South Fort George Board of Trade," *Saturday Night,* 24 September 1910, 21. On Cooke, see "Captain W.F. Cook," *PGS,* 23 March 1917, 5.

44 Clifford Geertz, "Notes on the Balinese Cockfight," in *The Interpretation of Cultures* (New York: Basic Books, 1973), 448. The booster mentalité is explored in Alan Artibise, "Boosterism and the Development of Prairie Cities, 1871–1913," in *The Prairie West: Historical Readings,* ed. R. Douglas Francis and Howard Palmer (Edmonton: Pica Pica Press, 1992), 515–43.

45 Ranajit Guha, "Not at Home in Empire," *Critical Inquiry* 23, 3 (Spring 1997): 486–87; Joanna Bourke, "Feature: Fear, Ambivalence and Admiration," *History Workshop Journal* 55 (2003): 126.

46 Tiffin and Alexander, Barristers and Solicitors, Vancouver, to D'Arcy Tate, Solicitor, Grand Trunk Railway Company, Winnipeg, 20 March 1912, LAC, RG 30, vol. 3339, file 1392, FC 3849.P7 A57 1911, c. 2, found in the College of New Caledonia Library, Prince George, BC.

47 "An Absurd Move," *FGH,* 20 January 1912, 1 and 4.

48 "Big Fire Wipes Out Central Avenue Block," *FGT,* 14 November 1914, 1; "Fire Sweeps Whole Block in Business Section of Fort George," *FGH,* 14 November 1912, 1.

49 "Early History of the Three Georges," *PGC,* 26 May 1938, 15.

50 "Put Hammond at Bar of Legislature Demanded by Member," *VS,* 21 March 1916, 1; "Denies That He Was Ever Indicted as Wiretapper," *TP,* 24 March 1916, 15; "Hammond's

Record Is Discussed in Legislature," *TP,* 21 March 1916, 11; "Mr. Hammond on Trip through Okanagan," *TP,* 3 May 1916, 2; "All against Compensation," *VDW,* 8 May 1916, 2. On Robert Hammond's death, see "Former City Man Killed in Crash," *TP,* 16 March 1943, 21.

51 Thanks to Susan Smith-Josephy for locating the date of Hammond's passing.

52 "Fort George Wins Station and Name from the GTP," *OH,* 16 May 1913, 3; West, "The 'BX,'" 175; Frank Leonard, "Grand Trunk Pacific and the Establishment of the City of Prince George, 1911–1915," *BC Studies* 63 (Autumn 1984): 31.

53 David Vogt and David Alexander Gamble, "'You Don't Suppose the Dominion Government Wants to Cheat the Indians?' The Grand Trunk Pacific Railway and the Fort George Reserve, 1908–12," *BC Studies* 166 (Summer 2010): 60.

54 Leonard, *A Thousand Blunders,* 167.

55 Vogt and Gamble, "'You Don't Suppose'"; Leonard, *A Thousand Blunders,* 166–77.

56 Leonard, *A Thousand Blunders,* 205–6. The *FGH* approved of the company's "Indian"-themed station names: "GTP Adopts Sensible Names for Stations East of Rupert," *FGH,* 11 February 1911, 1; "Head of the BC Express Co. in the District," *FGH,* 29 June 1912, 1; "Decide to Retain Name of South Fort George," *FGH,* 11 January 1913, 1.

57 "Grand Trunk Townsite Named 'Prince George,'" *FGH,* 11 January 1913, 1.

58 See Leonard, *A Thousand Blunders,* 207–11. Other accounts include Runnalls, *A History of Prince George* (Vancouver: Wrigley Printing Co., 1946), 135–36; Holmes, "The Promotion of Early Growth," 55–75; Bev Christensen, *Prince George: Rivers, Railways, and Timber* (Burlington, Ontario: Windsor Publications, 1989), 41, 42–44; and Rhys Pugh, "The Newspaper Wars in Prince George, BC, 1909–1918" (master's thesis, University of Northern British Columbia, 2004), 42–59.

59 Hugh H. Hansard to Pooley, Luxton, and Pooley, 10 December 1913, in Grand Trunk Pacific Railway, *Correspondence Relating to Prince George Incorporation, 1913–1920,* vol. 1 (Prince George: College of New Caledonia, n.d.). This bound copy of original documents from LAC, RG 30, vol. 3437, is available at the College of New Caledonia library in Prince George.

60 R.J. Bradley, chairman, Prince George Incorporation Committee, to H.H. Hansard, solicitor, Grand Trunk Pacific Railway, Winnipeg, 15 January 1915, in GTP, *Correspondence,* and Leonard, *A Thousand Blunders,* 210.

61 An Act to Incorporate the City of Fort George, SBC 1915, c. 29.7, s. 12; "W.C. Gillett Is Elected First Mayor of Prince George," *PGH,* 21 May 1915, 1; "Prince George Elects W.G. Gillett Mayor with 100 Majority," *FGT,* 22 May 1915, 1.

62 "Real Estate," *BC Saturday Sunset,* 30 March 1912, 15.

63 See Patrick Wolfe, "Tramp Printer Extraordinary: British Columbia's John 'Truth' Houston," *BC Studies* 40 (Winter 1978–79): 5–31, and Lynne Marks, *Infidels and the Damn Churches: Irreligion and Religion in Settler British Columbia* (Vancouver: UBC Press, 2017), 74–77.

64 Unless otherwise cited, the following is based on the editorial, *FGT,* 27 November 1909, 2. Based in Quesnel, John Daniell took offence at Houston's articulation of the "New" versus the "Old" Cariboo: see untitled article in editorial in *CO,* 11 December 1909, 1 and 2, and editorial, *CO,* 15 January 1910, 1.

65 *FGT,* 18 December 1909, 2.

66 *CO,* 8 January 1910, 1; "It Pays to Advertise," *CO,* 15 January 1910, 1; editorial, *CO,* 15 January 1910, 2.

67   "Old John's New Party," *CO*, 12 February 1910, 1; "In the Sunset Glow," *BC Saturday Sunset*, 19 February 1910, 1. The *Vancouver Daily World* wondered if Houston was to be "the Joshua who will lead Liberals out of the wilderness into the Promised Land": "A New Party," *VDW*, 2 February 1910, 6.

68   "In the Sunset Glow," *BC Saturday Sunset*, 19 February 1910, 1.

69   "A New Party," *VDW*, 2 February 1910, 6; "The Fort George Liberal Platform," *BC Saturday Sunset*, 19 February 1910, 3. The *Cariboo Observer* report overlooked the second provision concerning stock ownership of provincially supported railroad companies: "Old John's New Party," *CO*, 12 February 1910, 1.

70   Houston was taken first to the HBC post: Fort George HBC post journal, 27 January 1910, HBCA, B.280/1/9. "Death of John Houston," *CO*, 12 March 1910, 1; *VDC*, 13 March 1910, Sunday Supplement, 11; "His Last Tramp," *SS*, 16 March 1910, 1. Rumours of Houston's death had appeared days before in the provincial press: "John Houston Is Still Alive," *VDW*, 4 March 1910, 1; "We Beg to Differ," *CO*, 5 March 1910, 1. Also see "Career of John Houston," *NDN*, 5 March 1910, 2, and "John Houston," *CO*, 13 March 1910, 2. Also see "A History of John Houston," Kootenay History, http://www.kootenayhistory.com/john-houston/.

71   Fort George HBC post journal, 2 August 1908, HBCA B.280/1/9.

72   "Criminal Libel Charge Proved," *KS*, 18 October 1912, 1; "Farewell to the Public" and "The Last Post – For a While," *FGH*, 15 November 1913, 1 and 2; "The Newspapers of Cariboo," *PGC*, 13 March 1923, 2.

73   "Suspends Publication," *PGP*, 9 October 1915, 1; "The Newspapers of Cariboo," *PGC*, 13 March 1923, 2; Leonard, *A Thousand Blunders*, 52.

74   *PGP*, 28 August 1915, 4; "Accepted as Candidate for Naval Air Service," *PGP*, 11 September 1915, 1.

75   "Sub-Lieutenant Daniell Now in the Old Country," *PGC*, 31 May 1916, 1; "Jack Daniell Now Doing His Share to Assist the Empire," *PGS*, 12 January 1917, 4

76   Re John Bampfylde Daniell, National Archives (UK) Kew, Air Officer's service record, AIR 76/121/154 (book no. 57, part 2) and Register of Officers' Services, ADM 273/9/74; "Sidelights on Life in a German Prison Camp," *PGC*, 15 October 1919, 1 and 5.

77   "'Jack' Daniell Is Reported Missing," *PGS*, 15 May 1917, 1; "Editor-Flier Named in List of Missing," *VW*, 21 May 1917, 10; "Former Victorian Reported Missing," *VDT*, 23 May 1917, 13; "Is Prisoner of War," *VDT*, 20 June 1917, 19; "Edits Paper in Germany," *VDT*, 11 March 1918, 7; "Prisoner of War Editing a Paper," *VS*, 8 August 1918, 4. Also see J.B. Daniell, "Some Experiences of an Embryo Flier," *The Barb Magazine*, October 1918, 19–25, link available on the Vickers Machine Gun website, https://vickersmg.blog/about/remembrance/pte-frederick-john-hinton/.

78   "Change of Ownership," *PGC*, 9 January 1920, 2; *CO*, 24 January 1920, 1; "The Newspapers of Cariboo," *PGC*, 13 March 1923, 2.

79   "Local Happenings," *PGC*, 5 April 1923, 8; *CO*, 14 April 1923, 1; "John Daniell, Early Publisher, Sends Greetings," *PGC*, 13 September 1945, 4.

80   "John Bampfylde Daniell," deceased 31 December 1964, Los Angeles County, Local Registrar of Births and Deaths.

81   "J.P. McConnell Dies at Toronto," *OC*, 9 July 1926, 7; "J.P. McConnell, Eminent News and Ad. Man Dead," *WT*, 9 July 1926, 5; "John P. McConnell," *VS*, 9 July 1926, 8.

82   For the comparisons, see "Bouquets and Bricks: What Others Think of Us," *BC Saturday Sunset*, 6 July 1907, 13.

83 "Vancouver Now Has an Exclusion League," *VDC*, 15 August 1907, 5; Patricia E. Roy, *A White Man's Province: British Columbian Politicians and Chinese and Japanese Immigrants, 1858–1914* (Vancouver: UBC Press, 1989), 190–91.

84 "The Morning Sun," *VS*, 12 February 1912, 6.

85 "Important Changes in Advertising Agency," *LH*, 22 January 1921, 15; John Mackie, "Our Liberal Beginnings," *VS*, 11 February 2012, I5.

86 "Hammond: Has Opportunity to Explain Where Coe Commission Company Money Went," *ST*, 6 June 1907, 7; *FGH*, 1 October 1910, 1. Dollenmayer is also rendered as Dollenmeyer. See "Juggling with Facts: 'Bruce' of *Saturday Sunset* Bases His Arguments Anent [sic] Fort George on Trivial Technicalities," *FGH*, 8 October 1910, 1–2.

87 "Local and Provincial," *FGH*, 24 June 1911, 1.

88 *Saturday Night*, 14 May 1910, 5; "Gold and Dross," *Saturday Night*, 18 June 1910, 23; "Gold and Dross," *Saturday Night*, 9 July 1910, 18; "The Front Page," *Saturday Night*, 23 July 1910, 1; "Shacks and Forest at Fort George," *Saturday Night*, 30 July 1910, 21.

89 "Shacks and Forest at Fort George," *Saturday Night*, 30 July 1910, 21.

90 "In the Sunset Glow," *BC Saturday Sunset*, 30 July 1910, 1. McConnell knew W.H. Hammond, a potato-growing entrepreneur and brother of George Hammond, owner of the Basque Ranch at Ashcroft.

91 On the origins of "Bruce," see "In the Sunset Glow," *BC Saturday Sunset*, 15 June 1907, 1. On the voyage into the Interior, see "In the Sunset Glow," *BC Saturday Sunset*, 6 August 1910, 1.

92 "In the Sunset Glow," *BC Saturday Sunset*, 13 August 1910, 1–2; "Fort George as It Is Today: Its Agricultural Resources," 3.

93 "*Saturday Night;* or the Morning After," *FGH*, 20 August 1910, 1.

94 "*Saturday Night;* or the Morning After," *FGH*, 20 August 1910, 1.

95 "The Front Page," *Saturday Night*, 27 August 1910, 1.

96 "In the Sunset Glow," *BC Saturday Sunset*, 10 September 1910, 1.

97 The *Fort George Herald* claimed that Hammond had attempted to purchase *Saturday Night* prior to seeking the injunction. See "Juggling with Facts," *FGH*, 8 October 1910, 1–2.

98 "Not Entitled to Injunction: Motion of Fort George Townsite Promoters Refused," *TDME*, 17 September 1910, 5.

99 Editorial, *FGH*, 4 October 1910, 2; "Juggling with Facts," *FGH*, 8 October 1910, 2.

100 A "tinhorn" was an uninitiated or naïve would-be gambler; a "frisker" obtained money under false pretenses; a "four-flusher" was a bluffer who threw away a losing hand without revealing its contents; a "piker" was a petty and overly cautious gambler or investor; and a "bootlegger" peddled illicit whisky to "Indians." Set in the post–Second World War era, Christopher Dummit's *The Manly Modern: Masculinity in Post-War Canada* (Vancouver: UBC Press, 2007) provides a glimpse of the constructed manly identity.

101 "In the Sunset Glow," *BC Saturday Sunset*, 19 November 1910, 1. The firm included founder Joseph Ambrose Russell, younger brother Finlay Robert McDonald Russell, and Robert W. Hannington. See "The Russells of Russell and Russell," in *Russell & DuMoulin: The First Century, 1889–1989*, ed. Christine Mullins and Arthur E. Harvey (Vancouver: Russell & DuMoulin, Barristers and Solicitors, 1989), 10–23.

102 "LIES, LIES, LIES: *Saturday Sunset* Eclipses all Its Previous Brilliant Advertisements for the Natural Resources Co.," *FGH*, 19 November 1910, 1.

103 "Juggling with Facts," *FGH*, 8 October 1910, 1–2; *FGH*, 3 December 1910, 2; "The 'Sunset' Lies in the Limelight," *FGH*, 17 December 1910, 1; "Natural Resources Maverick Branded with the Letter L," *FGH*, 31 December 1910, 1.

104 "Correspondence," *CO*, 24 April 1909, 1.
105 "The 'Sunset' Lies in the Limelight," *FGH*, 17 December 1910, 1.
106 "In the Sunset Glow," *BC Saturday Sunset*, 19 November 1910, 1.
107 "In the Sunset Glow," *BC Saturday Sunset*, 26 November 1910, 1; "In the Sunset Glow,"
       BC Saturday Sunset, 10 December 1910, 1
108 "In the Sunset Glow," *BC Saturday Sunset*, 24 December 1910, 1–2; "Financiers Take Hold,"
       FGH, 5 November 1910, 1; "Order to Wind Up Company's Affairs," *VDW*, 4 January 1911,
       17; "Assets of Fort George Lumber & Navigation Co. Bought by Winnipeg Capitalists,"
       FGH, 11 March 1911, 1; "Timber Company in Difficulties," *VDW*, 16 March 1911, 17;
       "Winnipegers Invest," *CO*, 18 March 1911, 1; "Winnipeg Capital Invested in BC," *VDW*,
       4 April 1911, 19; "Arrange Plans for Season," *CO*, 29 April 1911, 5; "Second Birth of Fort
       George: History of Pioneer Lumber Firm," *FGH*, 18 February 1914, 1.
109 "Heaviest Calendar in City's History," *VW*, 1 May 1911, 4; "No Bill Returned," *VDC*, 11
       May 1911, 1; "Finds No Bill in *Sunset* Libel Suit," *VDW*, 11 May 1911, 12; editorial, *BC
       Saturday Sunset*, 13 May 1911, 2; "The Worm," *FGH*, 13 May 1911, 1.
110 "In the Sunset Glow," *BC Saturday Sunset*, 24 December 1910, 1–2.
111 The reference is to American physician Dr. Frederick A. Cook, who fraudulently claimed
       to have reached the North Pole in April 1908. See John Edward Weems, "The 'Humble'
       Fraud Who Claimed the North Pole," *Maclean's*, 13 February 1960, 24–25, 46–50.
112 The meagre case file for the trial is *Rex v. John B. Daniell*, BCA, GR 2486, box 83-0932-
       0045. See also "G.J. Hammond Involves the Law: Townsite Promoter Suing for Libel,"
       FGH, 2 December 1911, 1; "Court Appoints Commission to Investigate Hammond's
       Career," *FGH*, 4 May 1912, 1; *FGH*, 2 December 1911, 2; *FGH*, 17 February 1911, 2; "Daniell
       Up against a Criminal Libel Charge," *CO*, 24 February 1912, 1; "Daniell Sent for Trial,"
       CO, 2 March 1912, 4; "Criminal Libel Action Dismissed," *CO*, 4 May 1912, 1; "The Daniell
       Case Not Dismissed," *CO*, 25 May 1912, 1; "Court Proceedings in Criminal Libel Suit,"
       FGH, 1 June 1912, 1, 3, 4, and 5; "Judge Allows *Herald* Editor to Apologize," *VDW*, 18
       October 1912, 14; "Criminal Libel Charge Proved," *KS*, 18 October 1912, 1; and "Daniell
       Found Guilty," *CO*, 19 October 1912, 1. Also see Pugh, "The Newspaper Wars in Prince
       George," 19.
113 Unless otherwise cited, the following is based on the verbatim account of the Clinton
       trial proceedings published as "Court Proceedings in Criminal Libel Suit," *FGH*, 1 June
       1912, 1, 3, 4, and 5.
114 The indictment ran just over eight pages in length. See *Rex v. John B. Daniell*, BCA, GR
       2486, box 83-0932-0045.
115 Historian David Williams described Stuart Henderson as "the foremost criminal lawyer
       of the day [and] perhaps the most effective criminal lawyer British Columbia has known."
       See David Ricardo Williams, *Trapline Outlaw* (Victoria: Sono Nis Press, 1982), 13.
116 The only source on the collapse of Daniell's defence is "Daniell's Statement Regarding
       the Recent Libel Suit: John Hill, Jr., of the Chicago Board of Trade, Reviews the Situa-
       tion," *FGH*, 14 December 1912, 2.
117 See "Taylor, Sidney Stockton," in Parker, *Who's Who and Why*, 752.
118 *Rex v. John B. Daniell*, BCA, GR 2486, box 83-0932-0045; "Geo. Hammond Objects to
       Cariboo Jury," *FGH*, 5 October 1912, 1.
119 "Daniell's Statement Regarding the Recent Libel Suit," *FGH*, 14 December 1912, 2.
120 "Power of the Press on Side of Justice; Must Not Be Abused," *VS*, 18 October 1912, 3;
       "Criminal Libel Charge Proved," *KS*, 18 October 1912, 1.

121 "Judge Allows *Herald* Editor to Apologize," *VDW,* 18 October 1912, 14; "Daniell's Statement Regarding Recent Libel Suit," *FGH,* 14 December 1912, 1–2.

122 "Daniell's Statement Regarding Recent Libel Suit," *FGH,* 14 December 1912, 1–2.

123 "The Newspapers of Cariboo," *PGC,* 13 March 1923, 2. A contemporary account indicated that W.E. Playfair of the *Fort George Tribune* headed the group that bought out Daniell: *CO,* 29 November 1913, 1. On Walker, see Russell R. Walker, *Bacon, Beans 'n' Brave Hearts* (Lillooet: Lillooet Publishers, 1972), and "Returns to City," *PGP,* 18 September 1915, 1.

124 See Adele Perry, *On the Edge of Empire: Gender, Race, and the Making of British Columbia, 1849–1871* (Vancouver: UBC Press, 2001), and Marks, *Infidels and the Damn Churches.*

CHAPTER TWO: THE BRITISH COLUMBIA PROVINCIAL POLICE,
REGULATORY POLICING, AND KEEPING THE PEACE

1 "Provincial Police Regulations," s. 6, *Annual Report of the Superintendent of Police Representing the Police and Prisons of British Columbia* (Victoria: Richard Wolfenden, Printer to the Queen's Most Excellent Majesty, 1896), 882.

2 Robert Hogg, *Men and Manliness on the Frontier: Queensland and British Columbia in the Mid-Nineteenth Century* (Basingstoke, UK: Palgrave Macmillan, 2012), 122.

3 Hogg, *Men and Manliness,* 124.

4 On McMynn, see Lynne Stonier-Newman, *Policing a Pioneer Province: The BC Provincial Police, 1858–1950* (Madeira Park, BC: Harbour Publishing, 1991), 117.

5 Unless otherwise cited, the following is based on Acting Chief Constable John Bourne, BCPP, South Fort George to Superintendent William G. McMynn, BCPP, Victoria, 21 September 1918, BCA, RG 0057, box 25, file 2.

6 The *Citizen* reported that the acting chief constable had been particularly zealous in his pursuit of enemy aliens possessing firearms: see "Aliens with Firearms Brought into Court," *PGC,* 17 September 1918, 1.

7 Minty turned down a transfer to South Fort George in 1913 but accepted the post after W.R. Dunwoody was relocated to Nanaimo in late 1916. Superintendent Colin S. Campbell, BCPP, Victoria, to Chief Constable A.C. Minty, Fernie, 25 March 1913, BCA, GR 0061, vol. 41, reel B02590; Superintendent Colin S. Campbell, BCPP, Victoria, to Chief Constable W.R. Dunwoody, 29 September 1916, BCA, GR 0061, vol. 67, reel B02605; Superintendent Colin S. Campbell, BCPP, Victoria, to Chief Constable A.C. Minty, Hazelton, 7 October 1916, BCA GR 0061, vol. 67, reel B02605; "Chief Provincial Police Gets Well-Earned Promotion – Goes to Nanaimo," *PGS,* 20 October 1916; Acting Chief Constable John Bourne, duty log, August 1918, BCA, GR 445, box 48, file 16.

8 Acting Chief Constable John Bourne, duty log, November 1919, BCA, GR 445, box 56, file 6.

9 Constable H.H. Mansell recorded that, during December 1919, he chauffeured Bourne during the day: Constable H.H. Mansell, duty log, December 1919, BCA, GR 445, box 56, file 6.

10 Constable A. McNeill, duty log, March 1920, BCA, GR 445, box 62, file 3.

11 Dr. E.J. Lyon, South Fort George, to T.W. Herne, government agent, South Fort George, 2 March 1920, BCA, GR 2880, container 914268-0080, file 5269 re John Bourne.

12 Stonier-Newman, *Policing a Pioneer Province,* 117–18.

13	"Statement to be forwarded to the Medical Superintendent when Application is made for the Reception of a Patient," 3 March 1920, and Dr. Carl Ewert, "Medical Certificate," 3 March 1920, BCA, GR 2880, container 914268-0080, file 5269 re John Bourne.

14	Constable H.H. Mansell, duty log, March 1920, BCA, GR 445, box 62, file 3.

15	"Laboratory Record" re John Bourne, 9 and 12 March 1920, BCA, GR 2880, container 914268-0080, file 5269 re John Bourne.

16	Constable H.H. Mansell, duty log, March 1920, BCA GR 445, box 62, file 3.

17	Mr. McPherson, Attorney General's Office, Victoria, to Colonel Doherty, medical superintendent mental hospital, Essondale, 15 March 1920, BCA, GR 2880, container 914268-0080, file 5269 re John Bourne.

18	Medical Superintendent Dr. E.E. Doherty, Essondale, to Mr. McPherson, Attorney General's Office, Victoria, 19 March 1920, BCA, GR 2880, container 914268-0080, file 5269 re John Bourne.

19	Assistant Medical Superintendent Dr. A.L. Crease to Mrs. J. Bourne, Ashcroft, 26 May 1920, BCA, GR 2880, container 91426-0080, file 5269 re John Bourne.

20	Assistant Medical Superintendent Dr. A.L. Crease to Mrs. J. Bourne, Ashcroft, 12 August 1920, BCA, GR 2880, container 914268-0080, file 5269 re John Bourne.

21	Mrs. J. Bourne, Ashcroft, to Dr. A.L. Crease, assistant medical superintendent, Essondale, 25 November 1920.

22	Assistant Medical Superintendent Dr. A.L. Crease to Mrs. J. Bourne, Ashcroft, 24 January 1921, BCA, GR 2880, container 914268-0080, file 5269 re John Bourne.

23	"Ward Notes" re John Bourne, 5 February 1921, BCA, GR 2880, container 914268-0080, file 5269 re John Bourne.

24	"Training School," *Annual Report of the Superintendent of Provincial Police, 1930* (Victoria: Charles F. Banfield, Printer to the King's Most Excellent Majesty, 1931), 12–13.

25	"Provincial Police Regulations," s. 31, *Annual Report of the Superintendent of Police Representing the Police and Prisons of British Columbia 1896*, 884.

26	Greg Marquis, *Policing Canada's Century: A History of the Canadian Association of Chiefs of Police* (Toronto: Osgoode Society for Canadian Legal History and University of Toronto Press, 1993), 123–24.

27	*British Columbia Provincial Police Regulations* (Victoria: Charles F. Banfield, Printer to the King's Most Excellent Majesty, 1924).

28	See An Act Respecting the Provincial Police Force and Provincial Gaols, SBC 1924, c. 57, s. 16. See also Stonier-Newman, *Policing a Pioneer Province*, 154–55, and Marquis, *Policing Canada's Century*, 55–56, 77–79. Centred on police chiefs, Marquis's study demonstrates that the language of professionalism was felt throughout the nation's police forces.

29	See, generally, Renisa Mawani, *Colonial Proximities: Crossracial Encounters and Juridical Truths in British Columbia, 1871–1921* (Vancouver: UBC Press, 2009), especially chapter 4.

30	"Bad Indians under Arrest," *VDC*, 20 June 1901, 8.

31	See Father A.G. Morice, William's Lake Mission, to the Honorable Attorney General David MacEwen Eberts, Victoria, 3 June 1902, BCA, GR 429, reel B09321, file 1, folio 1994/02, and "Murders Chinaman," *VDC*, 5 November 1901, 5.

32	"Fort George Bad Indians," *Ashcroft Journal*, 28 June 1902, n.p., BCA, GR 429, reel B09321, box 9, file 1, folio 2280/02.

33	*Re Rex v. Louis Tsan* (murder), 3 October 1902, BCA GR 429, reel B09321, box 9, file 3, folio 3180/02.

34 See *Fort George Journal*, 8 September 1907, HBCA, B.280/a/9, 21, and F.S. Hussey, super-intendent Provincial Police (Victoria) to W.J. Bowser, attorney general (Victoria), 5 June 1909, BCA, GR 64, reel B07393.

35 See *Fort George Journal*, 8 September 1907, HBCA, B.280/a/9, 21. The BCPP were aware of the allegations concerning Hamilton: Attorney General W.J. Bowser (Victoria) to Superintendent F.S. Hussey (Victoria), 14 October 1909, BCA, GR 0063, box 5, file 3; . Hussey to W.J. Bowser, attorney general (Victoria), 23 October 1909, BCA, GR 0064, reel B07393, vol. 3. Also see "Illegal Sale of 'Booze' at Fort George," *FGT*, 13 November 1909, 4.

36 "Illegal Sale of 'Booze' at Fort George," *FGT*, 13 November 1909, 4.

37 One of the men who swore out an affidavit against Hamilton was David S. Wallbridge, who was represented by W.J. Bowser, of the law firm Boswer, Godfrey and Christie. "A Mere Stringer," *Sandon Paystreak*, 14 August 1897, 1.

38 F.A. Talbot, *The New Garden of Canada: By Packhorse and Canoe through Undeveloped New British Columbia* (London: Cassell and Co., 1912). Also see "The Right Stuff about Rupert," *PRO*, 25 March 1911, 6.

39 Talbot, *The New Garden of Canada*, 168.

40 F.E. Runnalls, *A History of Prince George* (Vancouver: Wrigley Printing Co., 1946), 127. DTs are delirium tremens: alcohol withdrawal symptoms following a sustained period of overindulgence.

41 "'Blind-Pigs' Beware: Illicit Booze Venders Are Supplying Indians," *FGH*, 2 September 1911, 1; "The Ball Game," *FGH*, 24 August 1912, 1; "City Police Court," *PGC*, 12 January 1917, 1; "Mah Moon's Christmas Party Declared Off," *PGC*, 17 December 1919, 1; "Open Season for Gamblers and Bootleggers," *PGC*, 31 December 1919. Also see Renisa Mawani, "In Between and Out of Place: Mixed-Race Identity, Liquor, and the Law in British Columbia, 1850–1913," in *Race, Space, and the Law: Unmapping a White Settler Society*, ed. Sherene H. Razack (Toronto: Between the Lines, 2002), 57 and 59.

42 In the murder trial alleging that George Onooki killed Harry Porters, defense counsel James Murphy suggested to Chief Constable W.R. Dunwoody that the sight of a man "besmeared with blood" would not have been out of the ordinary in South Fort George. The chief constable rebuffed the suggestion, stating that the community was free of "any assaults, any serious assaults or anything of that nature." When pressed that the community would be unfazed by "a certain amount of fights," Dunwoody conceded that he did not think any more so "than another place like that." See sworn testimony of Chief Constable W.R. Dunwoody, *Re George Onooki* (1914), LAC, RG 13, vol. 1466, file 513A.

43 "Indian Reserve Sold: Consideration $100,000," *FGH*, 2 September 1911, 1.

44 Unless otherwise cited, the following is based on "'Blind-Pigs' Beware: Illicit Booze Venders Are Supplying Indians," *FGH*, 2 September 1911, 1.

45 Mawani, "In Between and Out of Place," 57 and 59. Also see Mawani, *Colonial Proximities*.

46 "Local and District," *FGH*, 24 May 1913, 8. The newspaper date is incorrect, as it clashes with both Jackson's duty log and the date on Daunt's report. The electronic copy of the newspaper for 24 May has nine pages, including two pages numbered eight, while the newspaper for 31 May had seven pages. Given the clash of dates and the errant pagination, the page carrying the report on Kirkpatrick (despite the date on the news sheet) belongs in the 31 May 1913 edition. For confirmation of when the fracas occurred, see Constable Joseph Jackson, duty log, 30 May 1913, BCA, GR 445, box 8, file 7.

47 Chief Constable A. O'Neill Daunt, South Fort George, to Colin Campbell, superintendent Provincial Police, Victoria, 30 May 1913, BAC, GR 0091, box 8, file T–Z, re Charles Henry Thomas's application as special constable.
48 Mawani, *Colonial Proximities,* 161.
49 Douglas Hamilton, *Sobering Dilemma: A History of Prohibition in British Columbia* (Vancouver: Ronsdale Press, 2004), 66.
50 Lynne Marks, *Infidels and the Damn Churches: Irreligion and Religion in Settler British Columbia* (Vancouver: UBC Press, 2017), 73–74.
51 John Belshaw, *Colonization and Community: The Vancouver Island Coalfield and the Making of the British Columbia Working Class* (Montreal and Kingston: McGill-Queen's University Press, 2002), 180.
52 Craig Herron, *Booze: A Distilled History* (Toronto: Between the Lines, 2003), 383. For a similar sentiment, see Robert Campbell, *Demon Rum or Easy Money: Government Control of Liquor in British Columbia from Prohibition to Privatization* (Ottawa: Carleton University Press, 1991), 16.
53 "Applicant for position as Constable, re Frederick Gosby," BCA, GR 0056, vol. 2, E–H, 30 November 1907.
54 "BCPP paylist," EPA, 1026.14, citing BCPP personnel records for 15 September 1910, BCA, GR 0091, vol. 18; "Leaves of Absence" re Constable Gosby, Fort George, 3 November 1910, BCA, GR 0056; *FGH,* 3 December 1910, 1.
55 *FGH,* 3 December 1912, 1; "Constable with No Official Residence," *FGH,* 31 December 1910, 1; "A Community without a Jail," *FGH,* 24 June 1911, 1.
56 "Fort George Buildings," *TP,* 23 July 1910, 14; "Fort George Is Growing," *CO,* 23 July 1910, 1; "Controversy over Site of Building," *CO,* 30 July 1910, 1; "Government Buildings for Fort George," *VDW,* 3 August 1910, 10. For a slightly fuller version of the decision, see "Another Estimate of 'Bruce,'" *FGH,* 19 November 1910, 1. On the ferry development, see "Government Supervisor Chooses Ferry Location," *FGT,* 31 December 1910, 1.
57 Walker stated that locating the office in Fort George made little sense when "the business was being done" in South Fort George. See "Another Estimate of 'Bruce,'" *FGH,* 19 November 1911, 1.
58 "Controversy over Site of Building," *CO,* 30 July 1910, 1.
59 "That Board of Trade (?) Public Meeting," *FGT,* 6 August 1910, 1.
60 "South Fort George Is Chosen Site," *CO,* 6 August 1910, 1; "That Board of Trade (?) Public Meeting," *FGT,* 6 August 1910, 1; *FGH,* 20 August 1910, 1.
61 "Premier M'Bride on His Way North," *VDC,* 25 August 1910, 1; "By the Back Door Route," *PRO,* 26 August 1910, 4; "Our Distinguished Visitors," *FGH,* 27 August 1910, 2; "Well Received in Old Cariboo," *VCD,* 31 August 1910, 1. Also see Patricia Roy, *Boundless Optimism: Richard McBride's British Columbia* (Vancouver: UBC Press, 2012), 182.
62 "The Cobwebs Gather: Government Building Site Still an Undecided Problem – Matter Ends in a Fiasco?" *FGH,* 29 October 1910, 1; *FGH,* 12 November 1910, 1.
63 Constable D.H. Anderson of Quesnel had been instructed that construction of facilities at the Georges would not begin until the following spring and was directed to take the necessary steps to ensure that the building material already dispatched was stored safely. Superintendent F.S. Hussey, BCPP, Victoria, to Constable D.H. Anderson, BCPP, Quesnel, 16 September 1910, BCC, GR 0061, reel B02585, vol. 31, 974. "Offices Not Built though Equipment Is Here," *FGH,* 3 December 1910, 1, and "The Time Has Come the Walrus Said," *FGH,* 18 March 1911, 2.

64 "Government Offices to be Erected Immediately: Will be Located on the Hudson's Bay
    Company's Property," *FGH,* 1 April 1911, 1; "Government Office at Fort George," *CO,* 1
    April 1911, 1; "Site Selected for Government Offices," *FGH,* 20 May 1911, 1; "A Community
    without a Jail," *FGH,* 24 June 1911, 1.
65 *FGH,* 1 April 1911, 2.
66 *FGH,* 27 May 1911, 1; "Fort George News Items," *CO,* 22 July 1911, 1.
67 "A Community without a Jail," *FGH,* 24 June 1911, 1.
68 *FGH,* 7 October 1911, 1.
69 Constable F. Gosby BCPP, South Fort George, to Superintendent F.S. Hussey, BCPP,
    Victoria, 12 April 1911, BCA, GR 0056, box 10, file 16. Gosby's pay at South Fort George
    aligns with that earned by constables elsewhere in the province; see Newman, *Policing a
    Pioneer Province,* 84. On the pay in the Chilcotin District, see *Annual Report of the
    Superintendent of Police Representing the Police and Prisons of British Columbia 1897,* 670.
70 Telegram from F. Gosby, South Fort George, to F.S. Hussey, Victoria, 20 April 1911, BCA,
    GR 0056, box 10, file 16; *FGH,* 29 April 1911, 1; A.E. Forrest, South Fort George, to F.S.
    Hussey, Victoria, 3 May 1911, and J. MacAulay, South Fort George, to F.S. Hussey, Victoria,
    9 May 1911, BCA, GR 0056, box 10, file 16. In mid-July, Constable MacAulay inquired
    about the pay owing to Andrew Forrest for his work as a special constable. See Constable
    J. MacAulay, provincial constable, South Fort George, to F.S. Hussey, superintendent
    Provincial Police, Victoria, 14 July 1911, BCA, GR 0056, box 10, file 16. Andrew Forrest
    later became foreman at the Penny camp for unemployed men during the 1930s. His
    behaviour there almost sparked an outbreak of violence. See Gordon Hak, "The Com-
    munists and the Unemployed in the Prince George District, 1930–1935," *BC Studies* 68
    (Winter 1985–86): 52–53.
71 "Anti-Prohibition Literature," *FGH,* 6 May 1911, 1.
72 Constable F. Gosby, BCPP, South Fort George, to Superintendent F.S. Hussey, BCPP,
    Victoria, 23 December 1910, and Gosby to Hussey, 16 January 1911, BCA, GR 0056, box
    10, file 16.
73 "District News," *FGH,* 24 December 1910, 1; "Constable with No Official Residence,"
    FGH, 12 December 1910, 1. On the battle over the location of the provincial government
    buildings, including the police station, see Jonathan Swainger, "Anxiety at the Gates of
    Hell: Community Reputation in the Georges, 1908–15," *BC Studies* 205 (Spring 2020):
    57–78.
74 Constable F. Gosby, BCPP, South Fort George, to Superintendent F.S. Hussey, BCPP,
    Victoria, 2 March 1911, and Gosby to Hussey, 24 April 1911, BCA, GR 0056, box 10, file
    16; "Fatal Accident," *FGH,* 22 April 1911, 1.
75 Special Constable A.E. Forrest, BCPP, South Fort George, to Superintendent F.S. Hussey,
    BCPP, Victoria, 3 May 1911, BCA, GR 0056, box 10, file 16.
76 Constable John MacAulay, BCPP, South Fort George, to Superintendent F.S. Hussey,
    BCPP, Victoria, 13 May 1911, BCA, GR 0056, box 10, file 16.
77 Constable J. MacAulay, BCPP, South Fort George, to Superintendent F.S Hussey, BCPP,
    Victoria, 18 May 1911, BCA, GR 0056, box 10, file 16.
78 For constables granting liquor licences, see An Act respecting Liquor Licences and the
    Traffic in Intoxicating Liquors (the Liquor Act), SBC 1910, c. 30, part 1, ss. 7–11. F.E.
    Runnalls, *The History of the Knox United Church, Prince George, British Columbia* (Prince
    George: Prince George Printers, 1945, 1986), 15; "First Hotel in North," *FGH,* 22 October
    1910, 1; "Hotel Granted License," *FGH,* 3 December 1910, 1. Rumours of a licence being

granted triggered opposition from the Indigenous community and segments of the settler population; see Hussey to W.J. Bowser, 12 February 1910, BCA, GR 0064, reel B07393. The first hotel was named the Hotel Northern, while their second was called the Northern Hotel.

79 Charles Orme, "The Wine and the Gallows," in National Temperance Society and Publication House, *Temperance Tracts*, tract no. 91 (New York: National Temperance Society and Publication House, 1881), 1. Reverend Dr. Daniel Spencer, a Baptist minister from Victoria, was superintendent of British Columbia's Local Option League. See Albert John Hiebert, "Prohibition in British Columbia" (master's thesis, Simon Fraser University, 1969), 49, and "Local Option Convention," *VDW*, 21 November 1908, 10. Thanks to Dr. Jamie Morton of the Alberni Valley Museum for clarifying Spencer's identity.

80 See Marks, *Infidels and the Damn Churches*, 100–33.

81 Campbell, *Demon Rum or Easy Money*, 19.

82 Constable J. MacAulay, BCPP, South Fort George, to Superintendent F.S. Hussey, BCPP, Victoria, 26 May 1911, BCA, GR 0056, box 10, file 16.

83 "A Community without a Jail," *FGH*, 24 June 1911, 1. The failure to construct government offices and a jail in South Fort George triggered that community's first attempt at incorporation.

84 "Local and Provincial," *FGH*, 29 July 1911, 1. The *Herald* is inconsistent as to when the cells arrived. In one account, the newspaper indicated that it was August 1910, whereas another alleged the date to have been November 1910. For the former date, see *FGH*, 7 October 1911, 1.

85 "First Hotel in North," *FGH*, 22 October 1910, 1; "Saturday Morning's Dismal Fire," *FGH*, 8 July 1911, 1.

86 "Saturday Morning's Dismal Fire," *FGH*, 8 July 1911, 1.

87 Constable J. MacAulay, BCPP, South Fort George, to Superintendent F.S. Hussey, BCPP, Victoria, 3 July 1911, BCA, GR 0056, box 10, file 16; F.S. Hussey, BCPP, Victoria, to Constable J. MacAulay, BCPP, South Fort George, 8 July 1911, BCA, GR 0061, reel B02586.

88 "Natural Resources Wants a License for Central," *FGH*, 22 July 1911, 1.

89 "Natural Resources Wants a License for Central," *FGH*, 22 July 1911, 1. The Hotel Fort George, built by J.A. Shearer, opened in the summer of 1910 but was owned by the Natural Resources Security Company and George Hammond. See Runnalls, *A History of Prince George*, 111, and "George J. Hammond: A Prohibition Leader," *PGP*, 18 September 1915, 2.

90 Constable D.G. Cox, BCPP, Victoria, to J.P. Macleod, deputy attorney general, Victoria, Confidential, 25 July 1911, BCA, GR 0064, reel B07394. The original 1910 application for a liquor licence had been denied in January 1911. See "Central's License Given a Bump," *FGH*, 7 January 1911, 1.

91 Constable John MacAulay, BCPP, South Fort George, to Superintendent F.S. Hussey, BCPP, Victoria, 19 July 1911, BCA, GR 0056, box 10, file 16.

92 Constable J. MacAulay, South Fort George, to F.S. Hussey, superintendent, Provincial Police, Victoria, 19 July 1911 and 4 August 1911, BCA, GR 56, box 10, file 16.

93 Acting Superintendent Colin Campbell, BCPP, Victoria, to Constable J. MacAulay, BCPP, South Fort George, and Campbell to MacAulay, 25 August 1911, BCA, GR 56, box 10, file 16. The Liquor Act, SBC 1910, c. 30, part 1, ss. 7–11.

94 Thomas W. Herne, stipendiary magistrate and acting government agent, South Fort George, to Superintendent Colin S. Campbell, BCPP, Victoria, 2 March 1912, BCA, GR

0056, box 10, file 8. Herne became the permanent government agent in early May: see "Govt Agent Herne Will Remain Here," *FGH,* 11 May 1912, 1.

95 Superintendent Colin S. Campbell, BCPP, Victoria, to Constable Thomas MacAulay, 29 June 1912, and MacAulay to Colin S. Campbell, 6 July 1912, BCA, GR 0056, box 10, file 16; Thomas Higginbottom, Files of the Canadian Expeditionary Force, LAC, RG 150, regimental no. 13453; Alfred Grundy, Application to be filled in by Applicant for position as Constable, BCA, GR 91, box 5 (February–August 1911 D-G); "Shuffle in Cops," *FGH,* 13 July 1912, 4.

96 Stipendiary magistrate and acting government agent Thomas Herne sketched the proposed building. See Thomas W. Herne, acting government agent, South Fort George, to Superintendent Colin Campbell, BCPP, Victoria, 2 March 1912, BCA, GR 56, box 10, file 8. The drawing can be found in BCA, GR 56, box 10, file 16. The reference to the railway workers is in Constable Alfred Grundy, BCPP, South Fort George, to Superintendent Colin S. Campbell, BCPP, Victoria, 19 July 1912, BCA, GR 56, box 10, file 16; the detention sheds are noted in *FGH,* 27 July 1912, 2.

97 Stonier-Newman, *Policing a Pioneer Province,* 93.

98 On Irene Jordan being told to permanently close her brothel, see Constable Charles F. Evan, BCPP duty log, 22 February 1917, BCA, GR 445, box 42, file 2.

99 "Pioneer Park Ranger Has First Auto Ride: Mr. Henry Avison Visits City and Renews Host of Old Acquaintances," *VDW,* 17 March 1913, 15; "Funeral of Henry Avison Largely Attended by Residents Last Sunday," *PGC,* 10 April 1921, 1; "Stanley Park's Beauty Was Irishman's Dream," *TP,* 4 May 1940, 50; Henry Avison, sanitary inspector, Prince Rupert, to Frank DeGrey, chief sanitary inspector, Victoria, December 1913, *Sixteenth Annual Report of the Provincial Board of Health for the Fiscal Year Ended March 31st 1913* (Victoria: Printed by William H. Cullin, Printer to the King's Most Excellent Majesty, 1914), F11–F14; *British Columbia Public Accounts, for the Fiscal Year Ended 31st March 1916: Period from 1st April 1915 to 31st March 1916* (Victoria: William H. Cullin, Printer to the King's Most Excellent Majesty, 1917), C119; "Administration of Justice other than Salaries," Vote no. 73, Special Constables, *British Columbia Public Accounts for the Fiscal Year Ended 31st March, 1918* (Victoria: Printer to the King's Most Excellency Majesty, 1919), B103; *British Columbia Public Accounts for the Fiscal Year Ended 31st March 1917: Period from 1st April 1916 to 31st March 1917* (Victoria: William H. Cullin, Printer to the King's Most Excellent Majesty, 1918), C279.

100 Fort George continued to be patrolled out of the South Fort George office. Constable E.A. Hawkins was the last BCPP constable stationed at Fort George, although he was often required at the local detachment: see Constable E.A. Hawkins, duty log, December 1915, BCA, GR 445, box 34, file 11.

101 Chief Constable W.R. Dunwoody, South Fort George, duty log, 9 and 10 July 1915, BCA, GR 445, box 26, file 7; Chief Constable W.R. Dunwoody, South Fort George, duty log, 5 January 1916, BCA, GR 445, box 34, file 13; Constable V. Lewis, South Fort George, duty log, 9 March 1916, BCA, GR 445, box 34, file 12; Inspector T.W.S. Parsons, South Fort George, duty log, 24 January 1919, BCA, GR 445, box 56, file 6; Inspector T.W.S. Parsons, South Fort George, duty log, 5, 7, and 10 July 1920, BCA, GR 445, box 62, file 3.

102 Stonier-Newman, *Policing a Pioneer Province,* 94.

103 Acting Chief Constable John Bourne, duty log, "Remarks," June 1919, and Constable David Long, duty log, June 1919, BCA, GR 445, box 56, file 6.

104 See Jonathan Swainger, "Police Culture in British Columbia and 'Ordinary Duty,'" in *People and Place: Historical Influences on Legal Culture*, ed. Jonathan Swainger and Constance Backhouse (Vancouver: UBC Press, 2003), 198–223.

105 On the province's experiment with prohibition, see Albert John Hiebert, "Prohibition in British Columbia" (master's thesis, Simon Fraser University, 1969); Mimi Ajzenstadt, "The Medical-Moral Economy of Regulations: Alcohol Legislation in BC, 1871–1925" (PhD diss., Simon Fraser University, 1992); and Hamilton, *Sobering Dilemma*.

106 Constable W.R. Henley, BCPP, Vanderhoof, duty logs, 5 March 1921, BCA, GR 445, box 67, file 12.

107 A version of the negotiation is narrated in "Indians Confess to Murder," *Shoulder Strap* 1 (October 1938): 98.

108 "Indians Brought in for a Killing Committed in 1914," *PGC*, 5 April 1921, 1.

109 "Example to Indians," *PGC*, 17 May 1921, 7.

110 "Committed for Trial," *PGC*, 23 May 1921, 1; "Inspector Parsons Has Large Sized Job On," *PGC*, 3 June 1921, 1.

111 Unless otherwise cited, the following is based on "Assize Court Disposes of Criminal Cases Rapidly," *PGC*, 17 July 1921, 5. This newspaper edition is part of a printing error in the *Citizen*'s production. Save for the front page on 17 June, the entire content of that edition is included and dated as 24 June 1921. The 24 June edition counts fifteen pages, with duplicate pages numbered 2 through 8. Internal evidence has been used to reconstruct the 17 June coverage.

112 "Assize Court Disposes of Criminal Cases Rapidly," *PGC*, 17 July 1921, 5.

113 "Arm of Law Reaches into Far North to Grab Indians Wanted for Murder in 1914," *IN*, 13 April 1921, 8.

114 See "Report of Police Division Carries an Optimistic Tone," *PGC*, 2 February 1923, 1 and 3; "Police Head Makes Report," *TL*, 1 February 1923, 3.

115 "Report of Police Division Carries an Optimistic Tone," *PGC*, 2 February 1923, 1.

116 "Police Head Makes Report," *TL*, 1 February 1923, 3.

117 "Report of Police Division Carries an Optimistic Tone," *PGC*, 2 February 1923, 3.

118 "Report of Police Division Carries an Optimistic Tone," *PGC*, 2 February 1923, 3.

119 "Police Head Makes Report," *TL*, 1 February 1923, 3.

120 See "Report of Police Division Carries an Optimistic Tone," *PGC*, 2 February 1923, 1 and 3.

121 "Report of Police Division Carries an Optimistic Tone," *PGC*, 2 February 1923, 3.

122 For the broad context of the state's involvement in wildlife management, see Tina Loo, *States of Nature: Conserving Canada's Wildlife in the Twentieth Century* (Vancouver: UBC Press, 2006), 11–38. Also see "Report," in *First Annual Report of the Provincial Game Warden of the Province of British Columbia, 1905* (Victoria: Printed by Richard Wolfenden, Printer to the King's Most Excellent Majesty, 1906), D6.

123 On Williams's career, see Georgiana Genevieve Ball, "A History of Wildlife Management in British Columbia to 1918" (master's thesis, University of Victoria, 1981), 57–90.

124 Ball, "A History of Wildlife Management," 59.

125 An Act to Amend the "Game Protection Act," SBC 1913, c. 27, ss. 8 and 20. The categories were as follows: 1) Ordinary Gun Licences, which permitted the holder to hunt birds and deer, subject to provincial regulations; 2) General Licences, which permitted the holder to hunt birds, subject to provincial regulations; 3) Special Licences, which permitted the holder to hunt birds and animals and to trap fur-bearing animals, subject to provincial

regulations; and 4) a Farmer's Firearm Licence, which allowed the holder to hunt on the lands where they were resident.

126 R. Blake Brown, *Arming and Disarming: A History of Gun Control in Canada* (Toronto: Osgoode Society for Canadian Legal History, 2012), 82. Also see Tina Loo, "Of Moose and Men: Hunting for Masculinities in British Columbia, 1880–1930," *Western Historical Quarterly* 32, 3 (2011): 296–319.

127 Brenda Ireland, "'Working a Great Hardships on Us': First Nations People, the State, and Fur-Bearer Conservation in British Columbia Prior to 1930," *Native Studies Review* 11, 1 (1996): 70–71.

128 *First Annual Report of the Provincial Game Warden of the Province of British Columbia, 1905*, D14.

129 *First Annual Report of the Provincial Game Warden of the Province of British Columbia, 1905*, D15.

130 *First Annual Report of the Provincial Game Warden of the Province of British Columbia, 1905*, D15–16.

131 *Second Annual Report of the Provincial Game Warden of the Province of British Columbia, 1906*, F11.

132 An Act to amend the "Game Act," SBC 1918, c. 30, ss. 18 and 19–20. Also see *Annual Report of the Provincial Game Warden of the Province of British Columbia, 1918*, S 5–7.

133 Ball, "A History of Wildlife Management," 87–88.

134 See BCA, GR 445 re South Fort George duty reports, 1918–1921.

135 Constable W.R. Henley, duty log, February 1919, BCA, GR 445, box 49, file 11.

136 Constable Reginald Jobson, duty log, October–December 1919, BCA, GR 445, box 50, file 15. See Reginald Jobson, Files of the Canadian Expeditionary Force LAC, RG 150, regimental no. 102501, accession 1992-93/166, box 4839A-68.

137 *Annual Report of the Provincial Game Warden of the Province of British Columbia, 1918*, S18. For a broader context see Ireland, "'Working a Great Hardship on Us,'" 73.

138 "Shooting Season to Open Next October," *TPV*, 23 July 1921, 24; "New Rules for Hunters of Game," *VP*, 28 July 1921, 17; "Many Changes in Game Laws," *VDW*, 29 July 1921, 9; "Many Changes in 1921 Game Rules," *VS*, 29 July 1921, 12.

139 "Chairman Game Conservation Board Discusses Purchase of Beaver Pelts," *PGC*, 29 July 1921, 1.

140 "Official Fur Bootlegging," *IN*, 20 July 1921, 2. Also see "The White Man's Law," *PGC*, 28 October 1921, 5.

141 "Chairman Game Conservation Will Be Here Next Week to Discuss Beaver Skin Purchases," *TL*, 22 July 1921, 1; "Policy of Watchful Waiting in the Illicit Beaver Trade," *PGC*, 26 July 1921, 1.

142 "Regulation of Beaver Traffic Will Be Aired," *PGC*, 21 October 1921, 1 and 4.

143 "Beaver Investigation Begins to Grow Exceedingly Warm," *TL*, 9 December 1921, 1.

144 *Royal Commission re Albert Richard Baker, Chairman of Game Conservation Board* (Victoria: William H. Cullin, Printer to the King's Most Excellent Majesty, 1922), 20. "Doctor Baker Is Guiltless Rules Commissioner Shaw," *PGC*, 21 February 1922, 1.

145 "Dr. Baker Quits Post for Good," *VS*, 23 February 1922, 10; "Re-Instated; Quits Post," *VDW*, 23 February 1922, 10; "Dr. Baker's Resignation Has Been Accepted," *PGC*, 24 February 1922, 1.

146 "Spanish Influenza" and "Strong German System of Trenches Taken by Allies," *PGC*, 27 September 1918, 1; "Spanish Influenza Spreads in the East" and "Local and Personal,"

PGC, 11 October 1918, 1 and 8. Unless otherwise cited, the details of Parsons's actions are from his duty log; see Deputy Inspector T.W.S. Parson, duty log, October 1918, BCA, GR 445, box 48, file 16.

147 "The Influenza," *PGC,* 15 October 1918, 2.

148 The newspaper reported that Manson had dealt with three Indigenous people from west of Prince George, but Parsons's duty log indicated four. "Assemblies Forbidden in City; Twenty-Two Cases of Influenza," "How to Keep from Getting Influenza," and "What to Do if You Have Influenza," *PGC,* 18 October 1919, 1. For the consequences of the pandemic on Indigenous peoples in the province, see Mary-Ellen Kelm, *Colonizing Bodies: Aboriginal Health and Healing in British Columbia, 1900–50* (Vancouver: UBC Press, 1998); Kelm, "British Columbia First Nations and the Influenza Pandemic of 1918–19," *BC Studies* 122 (Summer 1999): 23–47; and Kelm, "Flu Stories: Engaging with Disease, Death, and Modernity in British Columbia, 1918–19," in *Epidemic Encounters: Influenza, Society, and Culture in Canada, 1918–20,* ed. Magda Fahrni and Esyllt Jones (Vancouver: UBC Press 2012), 167–92.

149 For the notice, see *PGC,* 18 October 1918, 4, and 1 November 1918, 2.

150 Acting Chief Constable John Bourne, duty log, October 1918, BCA, GR 445, box 48, file 16. An unnamed person dying from pneumonia is recorded in the Corless Funeral Ledger for 22 October 1918; see Richard Corless Funeral Ledger, 2007.23.1.1, NBCA, https://search.nbca.unbc.ca/index.php/richard-corless-funeral-ledger. Richard Corless came to South Fort George in 1913 and, in time, established a funeral parlour at the corner of Quebec Street and Fourth Avenue in Prince George.

151 Constable H.R. Henley, duty log, Vanderhoof, 17–31 October 1918, BCA, GR 445, box 46, file 6.

152 "Little Improvement Shown in Local Influenza Situation," *PGC,* 1 November 1918, 1.

153 "Influenza Epidemic Rapidly Subsiding," *PGC,* 5 November 1918, 1.

154 "Believe Influenza Epidemic Is Now on the Decline," *PGC,* 29 October 1918, 1; "Spanish Influenza Worse than War," *PGC,* 12 November 1918, 1; "Plague More Deadly than World War," *PGC,* 24 December 1918, 7.

155 "Many Indians Die of Spanish Influenza," *PGC,* 15 November 1918, 3.

156 *PGC,* 10 December 1918, 6.

157 See *PGC,* 17 December 1918, 1, and "Nearly One-Tenth of Local Indians Influenza Victims," *PGC,* 24 December 1918, 1.

158 "Epidemic Is Now on Decline," *PGC,* 12 November 1918, 1. On Dr. David B. Lazier, see Files of the Canadian Expeditionary Force, LAC, RG 150, 1992-93/166, box 5479-31.

159 "Provincial Police Have Lifted Ban," *PGC,* 15 November 1918, 1.

160 "Eighteen Hundred Cases of Influenza in Northern BC," *PGC,* 14 January 1919, 5.

161 Deputy Inspector T.W.S. Parsons, duty log, December 1918, BCA GR 445, box 48, file 18. See "General Remarks."

162 Magda Fahrni and Esyllt Jones, "Introduction," in *Epidemic Encounters,* 7.

163 R.C. Macleod, *The North-West Mounted Police and Law Enforcement 1873–1905* (Toronto: University of Toronto Press, 1976); Carl Betke, "Pioneers and Police on the Canadian Prairies, 1885–1914," *Historical Papers/Communications historiques* 15, 1 (1980): 9–32; William Morrison, *Showing the Flag: The Mounted Police and Canadian Sovereignty in the North, 1894–1925* (Vancouver: UBC Press, 1985).

164 Wilbur R. Miller, *Cops and Bobbies: Police Authority in New York and London, 1830–1870* (Chicago: University of Chicago Press, 1973), 1.

165 Lawrence M. Friedman and Robert V. Percival, *The Roots of Justice: Crime and Punishment in Alameda County, California* (Chapel Hill: University of North Carolina Press, 1981), 313.

166 The following is based on the joint publication of the police regulations and manual, in *British Columbia Provincial Police, Police Regulations and Constables' Manual* (Victoria: The King's Printer, 1924).

167 *Annual Report of the Superintendent of Provincial Police for the Year Ended December 31st, 1924* (Victoria: The King's Printer), X6.

168 On the rise of detectives, see Clive Emsley and Haia Shpayer-Makov, eds., *Police Detectives in History, 1750–1950* (Aldershot, UK: Ashgate Publishing, 2006), and Haia Shpayer-Makov, *The Ascent of the Detective: Police Sleuths in Victorian and Edwardian England* (Oxford: Oxford University Press, 2011).

CHAPTER THREE:
CITY GOVERNANCE AND THE PRINCE GEORGE CITY POLICE

1 An Act to Incorporate the City of Fort George, SBC 1915, c. 29. Section 12(1) provided that the community would be named Fort George, while section 12(2) provided for a vote to be held in conjunction with the first municipal election to determine whether the city name would be Fort George or Prince George. The name Prince George was declared official on 17 June 1915: see "The City of Prince George," *FGH,* 26 June 1915, 1. During the mayoralty campaign in May 1915, Gillett, the former Nelson mayor (acting 1905; 1906–7) and described as "a contractor, builder, and a principal in the Prince George Amusement Company," was portrayed by the *Herald* (which, along with the *Prince George Post,* supported mayoralty candidate Neil Gething) as representing George Hammond's interests and thus favouring a western GTP station on Oak Street, which was in the vicinity of contemporary Prince George's Fort Street. Gillett later altered course in favour of the GTP station being placed at the end of Victoria Street. See "W.G. Gillett Is a Candidate for Mayor," *PGP,* 1 May 1915, 1; "Who Shall Be First Mayor?" *FGH,* 7 May 1915, 2; "Our Position on the Mayoralty," *FGH,* 14 May 1915, 2; and "To Aid the Election of Neil Gething," *PGP,* 15 May 1915, 2.

2 Prince George City Council Minutes, 22 May 1915, City Clerk's Office, Prince George City Hall. Given the community's prospective name-change, all references will be to "Prince George City Council Minutes."

3 Prince George City Water, Light and Power Committee minutes, 22 May 1915, City Clerk's Office, Prince George City Hall.

4 Prince George City Council Minutes, 22 May 1915, City Clerk's Office, Prince George City Hall.

5 Chief Constable W.R. Dunwoody, duty log, 29 May 1915, BCA, GR 445, box 26, file 6. Writing in the third week of May to government agent T.W. Herne, Mr. Justice Fred Calder recalled speaking to Dunwoody in Prince Rupert, where, at the hotel, Dunwoody "met an old and very unruly friend and I was saying to him it was a darn shame for him to spend so much money going all the way to Ireland for a wife when he could be so well suited right there." Mr. Justice Calder to T.W. Herne, 27 February 1915, BCA, GR 2792, box 1, file 1914/1-6. On Dunwoody's arrival with an Irish bride, see "Chief Dunwoody Brings Home Bride," *PGP,* 22 June 1915, 1.

6 The Municipal Clauses Act, SBC 1896, c. 37; An Act to Consolidate and Amend the Law Relating to Electors and Elections in Municipalities, SBC 1896, c. 38; An Act to Consolidate

and Amend the Law Relating to the Incorporation of Municipalities, SBC 1896, c. 39. Thanks to Leslie Kellett, legislative coordinator of the Legislative Service Division, Prince George City Hall, for lending a hand with the terms in office for local mayors and councillors and for locating items from the council minutes.

7 The Municipal Clauses Act, SBC 1896, c. 37, ss. 199–213 and 214–31.

8 Philip C. Stenning, *Police Commissions and Boards in Canada* (Toronto: University of Toronto Centre of Criminology, 1981), 140.

9 An Act to Amend the "Municipal Act," SBC 1917, c. 45, s. 61.

10 The Municipal Elections Act, SBC 1896, c. 38, s. 3.

11 The Municipal Elections Act, SBC 1896, c. 38, s. 3–5. In practice, the postwar question of whether women were "persons" may have barred women from the municipal franchise in Prince George, although, by mid-December 1922, British Columbian women who were property holders had acquired both the local franchise and the right to sit on juries. See "Women to Sit on BC Juries," *VDP,* 15 December 1922, 4; "Women Eligible for Jury Duty," *VDW,* 15 December 1922, 16; and, more broadly, Robert Sharpe and Patricia McMahon, *The Persons Case: The Origins and Legacy of the Fight for Legal Personhood* (Toronto: Osgoode Society for Canadian Legal History, 2007).

12 The city's first female councillor, Carrie Jane Gray, was elected in 1952 and later served as mayor for two terms, in 1958–59. See Rebecca Shorten, "The Shapeliest Legs under the Table: Defining the Feminist Influence on Women in British Columbia Municipal Politics, 1950–1980" (master's thesis, University of Northern British Columbia, 2008).

13 For Daniell's appointment see "Appointments," 17 June 1915, *British Columbia Gazette* 2 (2 July 1915): 1795; City of Prince George Council minutes, 24 June 1915, Prince George City Hall; and "Magistrates and Commissioners Are Appointed," *PGH,* 25 June 1915, 1.

14 "No Police Chief Yet," *PGP,* 3 July 1915, 1.

15 Chief Constable W.R. Dunwoody, duty log, 9 July 1915, BCA, GR 445, box 26, file 7.

16 "Former Disorderly House to Be Temporary City Hall," *PGH,* 9 July 1915, 1. Item 13 in Gillett's mayoralty platform was the promise of "a clean and orderly city." See "Mayor Gillett's Platform," *PGH,* 21 May 1915, 1.

17 Prince George City Council Minutes, 8 July 1915, City Clerk's Office, Prince George City Hall.

18 On Gillett financing the city and his threat to resign, see "Mayor Gillett Withdraws Threat of Resignation," *PGH,* 4 June 1915, 1.

19 "Former Disorderly House to Be Temporary City Hall," *PGH,* 9 July 1915, 1.

20 "House of Ill Fame Chosen for Temporary City Hall," *PGP,* 10 July 1915, 1. The dismissal of renting from Jordan was made in "Good Prospects for Temporary City Hall," *PGP,* 26 June 1915, 1. The *Post* was openly antagonistic toward Gillett. The interior of the building was destroyed by fire on 19 March 1917 but was rebuilt using insurance funds: see "City Hall Interior Mass Ruins; Firemen Do Quick Work," *PGS,* 20 March 1917, 1.

21 The evidence indicates that, at the time, three newspapers vied for subscribers in the community: the *Prince George Herald,* which had been located in South Fort George and was owned by Norman Wesley and managed/edited by J.C. Quinn; the *Prince George Post,* which was owned by a conglomerate that relied on financing from the GTP Railway and which was edited by J.B. Daniell; and the *Daily News.* The last was mentioned by Daniell, but evidence of its operations has not survived: see "Distorted Vision," *PGP,* 17 July 1915, 2. The *Daily News* was launched in the spring of 1915 with the backing of George Hartford of the *Chicago Inter-Ocean* along with Tom McQuire, a pitcher for the Newark

Peppers of the Federal Baseball League in the United States. The newspaper was discontinued within the year. See "The Newspapers of Cariboo," *PGC*, 13 March 1923, 2.

22 On the designation of Duchess Park as a temporary athletic ground, see "Temporary Athletic Ground," 12 June 1915, *PGP*, 1.

23 "No Police Chief Yet," *PGP*, 3 July 1915, 1; "Chief of Police Was Appointed Yesterday," *PGP*, 10 July 1915, 1.

24 On Bosworth's career in England, see "Today's Police News," *DDT*, 1 May 1902, 3; "Today's Police News," *DDT*, 4 February 1903, 3; and "Today's Police News," *DDT*, 29 June 1903, 3.

25 "Two Police Sergeants Are Fired," *LP*, 11 March 1914, 1 and 4; "Police Commission Sets Aside Chief's Recommendation and Reinstates Constable Cook," *LP*, 13 January 1914, 16.

26 "Turf Club Nominates Discharged Policemen as Special Constables; Asks Commission to Swear Men In," *LP*, 16 June 1914, 9. On Regina's police chief Theodore Zeats's resignation, see "Resignation of Chief Zeats Was Accepted," *LP*, 5 March 1914, 4.

27 "Constables All Go to War," *PGP*, 10 July 1915, 3; "Another Batch of Recruits Left Here on Tuesday for the Big Camp at Vernon," *PGP*, 17 July 1915, 1.

28 Chief Constable W.R. Dunwoody, duty log, 10 July and 14 July 1915, BCA, GR 445, box 26, file 7.

29 On London's appointment, see Prince George City Council Minutes, 29 May 1915, City Clerk's Office, Prince George City Hall. On Bosworth, see "Police Court News," *PGP*, 24 July 1915, 2; "Chief Bosworth's Wife and Children Rescued from Liner," *PGP*, 11; and "Splendid Showing of Agricultural Exhibits at Fourth Annual Fair," *PGP*, 18 September 1912, 1.

30 "Bylaw 4 – A Bylaw for Regulating the Streets and Sidewalks, and the Traffic Thereon, and Relating to Boulevards and Shade Trees in the City of Prince George," 17 June 1915, s. 30, City of Prince George, City Clerk's Office.

31 "Local and District," *PGH*, 24 September 1915, 4.

32 "Around the City," *PGP*, 25 September 1915, 4.

33 Of the five local newspapers, the *Fort George Tribune*'s spotty issues ceased in May 1915, John Daniell's *Post* terminated operations following the New Year's season of 1915, the *Prince George Herald* ends with the 29 January 1916 edition, extant copies of the *Prince George Citizen* begin with its twenty-seventh issue, on 17 May 1916, and those of the *Prince George Star* start with its forty-ninth issue, on 6 October 1916. No copies of the *Prince George Daily News* have survived.

34 The *Prince George Star*, which provides the only surviving newspaper coverage of the 1917 municipal election, was squarely behind the Perry campaign. It characterized Perry's opponent, Hiram Carney, as a "Tammany Hall" politician who employed machine politics in lining up city employees in his favour. For the broad coverage, see *PGS*, 2–9 January 1917; for the allegation targeting Carney, see "Carney Meeting Poorly Attended," *PGS*, 5 January 1917, 6, and "Candidate Carney Gets Very Frosty Reception," *PGS*, 9 January 1917, 1.

35 *PGS*, 26 January 1917, 1.

36 "City News of Interest," *PGS*, 9 March 1917, 8.

37 "First Meeting Board Police Commissioners," *PGS*, 9 March 1917, 4. Irene Jordan, who operated a brothel in South Fort George, has been instructed by the BCPP to end operations that same month.

38 "Slot Machines Will Pay $20 per Year," *PGS*, 27 February 1917, 1. On the discomfort with slot machines and gambling in general, see Suzanne Morton, *At Odds: Gambling and Canadians, 1919–1969* (Toronto: University of Toronto Press, 2003).

39 "First Meeting Board Police Commissioners," *PGS,* 9 March 1917, 4.
40 "First Meeting Board Police Commissioners," *PGS,* 9 March 1917, 4. The extant city hall minutes do not include the police commission's deliberations.
41 "License Commissioners Hold Special Meeting," *PGS,* 9 March 1917, 7.
42 British Columbia's statutory path to prohibition in 1917 began with An Act for Referring to the Electors the Questions of the Expediency of Suppressing the Liquor Traffic in British Columbia by Prohibiting Transactions in Liquor, and of the Extension of the Electoral Franchise to Women, SBC 1916, c. 50, which provided for the referendum. This was followed by An Act intituled [sic] the "British Columbia Prohibition Act," SBC 1916, c. 49, and then An Act to Bring into Force the "British Columbia Prohibition Act," SBC 1917, c. 49. On the provincial police's enforcement challenges, see Lynne Stonier-Newman, *Policing a Pioneer Province: The BC Provincial Police, 1858–1950* (Madeira Park, BC: Harbour Publishing, 1991), 115–19.
43 An Act intituled [sic] the "British Columbia Prohibition Act," SBC 1916, c. 49, s. 7.
44 An Act intituled [sic] the "British Columbia Prohibition Act," SBC 1916, c. 49, s. 29(1).
45 "'Beerless' Is Now on Sale," *VDP,* 15; "Sell Soft Drinks in Victoria Bars," *VS,* 1 October 1917, 1. Also see Albert John Hiebert, "Prohibition in British Columbia" (master's thesis, Simon Fraser University, 1969), 100–1, and Douglas Hamilton, *Sobering Dilemma: A History of Prohibition in British Columbia* (Vancouver: Ronsdale Press, 2004), 147.
46 Hamilton, *Sobering Dilemma,* 124–39; Hiebert, "Prohibition in British Columbia," 105–15.
47 "Council Proceedings," *PGS,* 13 April 1917, 5. See Theodore Pappas, Files of the Canadian Expeditionary Force, LAC RG 150, regimental number 2140149.
48 "City Police Court," *PGC,* 11 June 1919, 1.
49 Only fourteen months of the *Prince George Citizen* have been preserved, and the *Prince George Star* run ended in May 1917 (at some point it merged with the *Citizen*). The gap in surviving copies renders it impossible to determine when the *Citizen* and the *Star* merged. However, the *Prince George Citizen* of 23 July 1918 (the first surviving edition for that year) notes, on the second page, that the two newspapers were amalgamated. The notice was absent from the 1 June 1917 edition of the *Citizen,* which is the last surviving edition until July 1918.
50 Constable James Mead, duty log, general remarks, August 1918, BCA, GR 445, box 48, file 16.
51 Constable James Mead, duty log, 12–16 August 1918, BCA, GR 445, box 48, file 16; Acting Chief Constable John Bourne, duty log, 14–16 August 1917, BCA, GR 445, box 48, file 16.
52 Constable James Mead, duty log, 19 August 1918, BCA, GR 445, box 48, file 16.
53 Deputy Inspector T.W.S. Parsons, duty log, 17, 21, 22, and 23 August 1917, BCA, GR 445, box 48, file 18.
54 Deputy Inspector T.W.S. Parsons, duty log, 5 September 1917, BCA, GR 445, box 48, file 18.
55 For example, see "Military Police Are Active in District," *PGC,* 6 September 1918, 1; "Military Delinquents Being Brought In," *PGC,* 13 September 1918, 1; and "Military Police Doings," *PGC,* 11 October 1918, 1.
56 Hamilton, *Sobering Dilemma,* 148.
57 "Probe of Whiskey Importation Follows Arrest of W.C. Findlay BC Prohibition Commissioner," *VP,* 12 December 1918, 1; "Prohibition Commissioner under Charges," *VDW,*

12 December 1918, 1; "Prohibition Commissioner Findlay Arrested Last Night – Charged with Illegally Importing Liquor into the Province – Car of Rye Whiskey Missing," *VDS*, 12 December 1918, 1; and "Whiskey Scandal British Columbia," *PGC*, 13 December 1918, 1; "This Province May Have Political Crisis," *PGC*, 14 January 1914, 3; "Findlay Acted Alone in Liquor Import," *PGC*, 14 January 1914, 7; "The New Crisis," *PGC*, 17 January 1919, 2; "Findlay Again Refuses to Give Testimony," *PGC*, 17 January 1919, 4; "Charge against Findlay Dismissed," *PGC*, 21 January 1919, 1; "Verdict of Guilty for W.C. Findlay," *PPC*, 28 May 1919, 6.

58 *PGC*, 17 December 1918, 2.

59 "Several Hundred Chinese Laborers Domiciled Here," *PGC*, 3 January 1919, 6.

60 *PGC*, 28 January 1919, 2.

61 "Mystery at City Hall," *PGC*, 31 January 1919, 6. The opium and liquor had been seized by Acting Chief Constable John Bourne and Constable James Mead of the BCPP on 15 August 1918 and stored at city hall for safe keeping. BCA, GR 445, box 48, file 16.

62 "Police Chief Appointed," *PGC*, 12 February 1919, 10; "Local and Personal," *PGC*, 28 January 1919, 1.

63 The following is based on "Communications," *PGC*, 16 April 1919, 1.

64 Prince George City Council Minutes, 17 April 1919, City Clerk's Office, Prince George City Hall.

65 See "Sedition Charged," *PGC*, 20 September 1918, and "Charge Dismissed," *PGC*, 24 September 1918, 1.

66 Unless otherwise cited, the following is based on "Considerable Property Damaged in Thursday Night's Demonstration," *PGC*, 30 April 1919, 1. The story was republished in Alberta's Peace River country: "Prince George Veterans and Citizens Drive Out German," *PRR*, 9 May 1919, 1.

67 The *Province* erroneously described Tadin as a foreigner who had made seditious comments. "Enemy Aliens Are Warned to Get Out," *VP*, 26 April 1919, 1.

68 Editorial, *PGC*, 30 April 1919, 2.

69 Editorial, *PGC*, 30 April 1919, 2.

70 *PGC*, 30 April 1919, 2.

71 "Police Court," *PGC*, 27 August 1919, 1.

72 "Bootleggers," *PGC*, 27 August 1919, 2.

73 "Strengths and Distribution," E Division, "Report of the Royal Northwest Mounted Police for the Year Ended September 30, 1919," Canada, *Sessional Papers* (1920), no. 28, 22. Throughout the 1920s, the detachment ranged between two and four men. It remained at Prince George until it was relocated to Vanderhoof in 1929 to better oversee the Indigenous community at Stoney Creek. See "Report of the Royal Canadian Mounted Police for the Year Ended September 30, 1929," in *Annual Departmental Reports, 1928–29*, vol. 3 (Ottawa: Printer to the King's Most Excellent Majesty, 1920), 34.

74 "Mounted Police Now Stationed in This City," *PGC*, 3 September 1919, 1. On the reorganization of the RNWMP, see Stonier-Newman, *Policing a Pioneer Province*, 126–34; Steven Hewitt, *Riding to the Rescue: The Transformation of the RCMP in Alberta and Saskatchewan, 1914–1939* (Toronto: University of Toronto Press, 2006), 13–14; and "RNWMP May Be Withdrawn from the Province," *PGC*, 24 March 1922, 3. Stonier-Newman's contention that "almost all the RCMP were withdrawn from British Columbia" by 1924 leaves a false impression, even though their ranks had thinned. The RCMP annual reports indicated that, in 1925, the province had seventy-nine officers and men in the ranks, compared with

238 in 1921. Prince George remained one of six detachments, along with Victoria, Esquimalt, Penticton, Prince Rupert, and Telkwa. "Report of the Royal Canadian Mounted Police for the Year Ended September 30, 1925," in *Annual Departmental Reports, 1924–25,* vol. 5 (Ottawa: Printer to the King's Most Excellent Majesty, 1927), 24. See also Stonier-Newman, *Policing a Pioneer Province,* 152.

75 "Up to the People," *PCG,* 26 November 1919, 2.
76 "H.G. Perry Elected Mayor by Majority of Thirty," *PGC,* 23 January 1920, 1.
77 "New City Council Enters on Duties," *PGC,* 23 January 1920, 1.
78 "New City Council Enters on Duties," *PGC,* 23 January 1920, 1; testimony of H.A. Stewart in *R. v. T.M. Watson* before Chief Justice Hunter and jury, 14 June 1920, BCA, GR 2239, file 19/20, 5.
79 Alexander Sinclair was also a returned veteran. See Alexander Floyd Sinclair, Files of the Canadian Expeditionary Force, LAC, RG 150, regimental no. 790182.
80 "Sensational Arrest of Two Ex-City Officials," *PGC,* 9 April 1920, 1. See Information and Complaint, 3 April 1920 in *Rex v. G.R. Fisher,* BCA, GR 2239, file 21/1920.
81 On Mr. Chief Justice Hunter's career, see David R. Verchere, *A Progression of Judges: A History of the Supreme Court of British Columbia* (Vancouver: UBC Press, 1988), 126–40 and 142–44, and Christopher Moore, *The British Columbia Court of Appeal: The First Hundred Years* (Vancouver: UBC Press for the Osgoode Society for Canadian Legal History, 2010), 16–18. Calendar, Supreme Court of British Columbia, Court of Oyer and Terminer and General Gaol Delivery, 8–16 June 1920, BCA, GR 47, Spring Court Calendar, 1920. See "Rex vs. Fisher Case Still Proceeding" and "Fisher Not Guilty," *PGC,* 11 June 1920, 1.
82 "Fisher Is Fined $125 and Costs," *PGC,* 25 June 1920, 1.
83 W.P. Ogilvie, in *Rex v. T.M. Watson,* before Chief Justice Hunter and jury, 14 June 1920, BCA, GR 2239, file 19/20, 53.
84 Jury foreman, in *Rex v. T.M. Watson,* before Chief Justice Hunter and jury, 14 June 1920, BCA, GR 2239, file 19/20, 121.
85 "Jury Disagree in Watson Case; Traversed to Fall Assize," *PGC,* 18 June 1920, 1.
86 On Mr. Justice Murphy, see Verchere, *A Progression of Judges,* 144–45.
87 Mr. Justice Murphy, charge to the jury, in *Rex v. T.M. Watson,* before Mr. Justice Murphy and jury, 23 October 1920, BCA, GR 2239, file 19/20, 3–4. Also see "Days of Unrest," *PGC,* 26 October 1920, 2.
88 See Mimi Ajzenstadt, "The Medical-Moral Economy of Regulations: Alcohol Legislation in B.C., 1871–1925 (PhD diss., Simon Fraser University, 1992), 118–60, and Hamilton, *Sobering Dilemma,* 173–74. "Huge Majority in Plebiscite Favors Government Control," *PGC,* 22 October 1920, 1; "No Prohibition Majorities in Fort George District," *PGC,* 22 October 1920, 1; "The Amazing Plebiscite," *PGC,* 22 October 1920, 2.
89 Mr. Justice Murphy, charge to the jury, in *Rex v. T.M. Watson,* before Mr. Justice Murphy and jury, 23 October 1920, BCA, GR 2239, file 19/20, 4 and 7.
90 "T.M. Watson Found Not Guilty of Bribery Charge," *PGC,* 26 October 1920, 1.
91 "Sensational Arrest of Two Ex-City Officials," *PGC,* 9 April 1920, 1; "A Strange Isolation," *PGC,* 16 April 1920, 2.
92 "A Strange Isolation," *PGC,* 16 April 1920, 2.
93 "The Bootleggers' Day," *PGC,* 18 April 1920, 2; Mr. Justice Murphy, charge to the jury, in *Rex v. T.M. Watson,* before Mr. Justice Murphy and jury, 23 October 1920, BCA, GR 2239, file 19/20, 4.

94 The following is based on "Tough Gent with Gun Causes Excitement," *PGC*, 16 July 1920, 1, and "Wild West Stuff," *PGC*, 16 July 1920, 2.

95 The club seems to have been licensed to sell legal low-alcohol beer.

96 "Wild West Stuff," *PGC*, 16 July 1920, 2.

97 "Police Chief Resigns," *PGC*, 16 July 1920, 1.

98 "Alex H. Sinclair Is New Chief of Police," *PGC*, 20 August 1920, 1.

99 "Magistrate Daniell Replies to Police Commissioners," *PGC*, 3 May 1921, 5.

100 "Bootleggers Must Go Is Decision of City Council," *TL*, 22 April 1921, 1.

101 "A Day of Reckoning," *PGC*, 10 December 1919, 2; *PGC*, 31 December 1919, 2.

102 Prince George City Council Minutes, 4 August 1921, City Clerk's Office, Prince George City Hall; "City Council," *PGC*, 5 August 1921, 1; "City Council," *TL*, 5 August 1921, 1; Henry Wilson and A.M. Patterson to His Worship the Mayor and Council, Prince George, British Columbia, Prince George City Council Minutes, 13 August 1921, City Clerk's Office, Prince George City Hall; "All Salaries Reduced by City Council," *TL*, 19 August 1921, 1.

103 "A Detective Story," *PGC*, 12 August 1921, 2.

104 "Mayor Wilson Fires Whole Police Force," *PGC*, 3 January 1922, 1; "Mayor Exceeded Powers: Police are Reinstated," *PGC*, 6 January 1922, 1 and 6; "Action of Mayor Was Not Endorsed," *TL*, 6 January 1922, 1.

105 "Janitor Reinstated," *PGC*, 10 January 1922, 5.

106 "Chief of Police Has Resigned," *PGC*, 20 January 1922, 1; "New Council Sworn In," *TL*, 20 January 1922, 1.

107 When testifying against police commissioner T.M. Watson, Sinclair indicated that he had been hired on 23 December 1919. See *Rex v. T.M. Watson*, Depositions before Police Magistrate C.B. Daniell, 22 April 1920, BCA, GR 2239, file 19/20, 4.

108 See "New Chief Wanted for Local Police," *PGC*, 30 May 1922, 1; "Chief of Police," *TL*, 2 June 1922, 3.

109 "Bootleggers Are Raided by an Effective Police Team," *PGC*, 2 June 1922, 1; "Morris and Innis Fined $100 Each for Selling Beer," *PGC*, 9 June 1922, 1. The newspaper identified the special constables as "T.B. Todd" and "James Todd."

110 "City Council Decides to Pay the Bonus for Liquor Conviction," *PGC*, 6 October 1922, 3.

111 See "Administration of Justice" and "Communications," *TL*, 2 June 1922, 2, and "Reflective Car Lighting Is Costly for Owners," *PGC*, 26 May 1922, 1.

112 Special Constable Smith may have later worked with the BCPP: see "Party Has Left to Rescue Stricken Man," *PGC*, 16 June 1922, 1.

113 "Administration of Justice," *TL*, 2 June 1922, 2.

114 For one of many clashes on council, see "Alderman Makes an Attempt to Hobble Energetic Mayor," *PGC*, 4 August 1922, 1 and 5. Narissa Chadwick argued that, although the Town Planning Act was passed in 1925, it was only in 1948 that amendments extended to establishing regional planning boards. See her "Regional Planning in British Columbia: 50 Years of Vision, Process and Practice" (master's thesis, University of British Columbia, 2002), 5. Also see John Bottomley, "Ideology, Planning and the Landscape: The Business Community, Urban Reform, and the Establishment of Town Planning in Vancouver, British Columbia, 1900–1940" (PhD diss., University of British Columbia, 1977). Prince George had early planning discussions: "Town Planning Suggestions Considered by the Council," *PGC*, 8 September 1922, 1.

115 See "An Announcement," *TL*, 21 December 1922, 1; "Candidates Will Be Pledged by the Association," *PGC*, 8 November 1923, 3; and "R.W. Alward to Make Another Race for Mayor," *PGC*, 13 December 1923, 1.

116 "Liquor Act Is Not Easy to Enforce," *TP*, 4 November 1922, 3; "Warning Note to Moderationists," 9 November 1922, 5. The notion of assuming responsibility for municipal policing was not new. Premier John Oliver and Attorney General John Wallace de Beque Farris indicated prior to the 1920 provincial election that, if the prohibition law remained unchanged, the "radical measure" of having the provincial police assume responsibility for the entire province would be considered: see "October 20 Is Date Selected for Vote," *TP*, 10 September 1920, 1.

117 "The Ordeal by Bottle," *PGC*, 30 January 1923, 2.

118 "Editorial Comment," *TL*, 21 December 1922, 2.

119 "Named Head of Police Force," *VDC*, 12 July 1922, 3; "Is Finger Print Expert," *PGC*, 14 July 1922, 1; "New Chief Arrives," *PGC*, 25 July 1922, 8. Carlow was involved in prosecuting alleged Sikh revolutionary Harnam Singh, who was later hanged in Rangoon, Burma. See Hugh Johnston, "The Surveillance of Indian Nationalists in North America, 1908–1918," *BC Studies* 78 (Summer 1988): 25.

120 "Chief Carlow Will Not Make Application for Position of Policeman," *PGC*, 31 January 1924, 1.

121 See, for example, "Police Commissioners Want Some Action," *TL*, 9 November 1922, 1; "Police Report for November," *TL*, 7 December 1922, 1; "Police Report for Month of November," *TL*, 8 December 1922, 4; and "Police Report for December," *TL*, 4 January 1923, 4.

122 "Police Commission Defers Action on Request for Reduction in Force," *PGC*, 7 June 1923, 5; "Road to Economy Will Be Rough Going for Citizens," *PGC*, 14 June 1923, 1 and 6; "Road to Economy Is Not Easy," *PGC*, 14 June 1923, 2.

123 "Liquor Profits Are Used to Adjust Debts," *PGC*, 10 January 1924, 1. See also Megan Davies, "Old Age in British Columbia: The Case of the 'Lonesome Prospector,'" *BC Studies* 11 (Summer 1998): 41–66, and Davies, *Into the House of Old: A History of Residential Care in British Columbia* (Montreal and Kingston: McGill-Queen's University Press, 2004).

124 "City Council Made Good during 1923," *PGC*, 17 January 1924, 3.

125 "Thos. R. Rush Resigns from Police Board," *PGC*, 7 February 1924, 5.

126 "Police Officers Dismissed on February 29" and "Civic Officials to Lose Their Heads Feb 29," *PGC*, 31 January 1924, 1.

127 "Chief Carlow Will Not Make Application for Position of Policeman," *PGC*, 31 January 1924, 1.

128 "Commissioners Delay Filling Police Vacancy," *PGC*, 28 February 1924, 4.

129 *PGC*, 6 March 1924, 4.

130 "Fugitive Is Not Wanted," *VS*, 21 March 1924, 1; "Financial Stringency at Prince George Is Lucky for Prisoner," *TP*, 21 March 1924, 27; *TP*, 27 March 1924, 26; "Roy McKinley Held by Police of Vancouver," *PGC*, 27 March 1924, 6.

131 "Provincial Police Will Bring Roy McKinley Back to the City This Evening," *PGC*, 10 April 1924, 1; "Local and District," *PGC*, 14 April 1924, 4.

132 "McKinley Has Hearing on Assault Today," *PGC*, 17 April 1924, 1. On Mr. Justice Gregory, see Verchere, *A Progression of Judges*, 145.

133 "McKinley Gets Off Lightly for Gun-Play," *PGC*, 4 November 1924, 6.

134 "Neil McMillan No Longer Head of Local Police," *PGC*, 17 April 1924, 1. That a delegation from the Presbyterian church had appeared before the police commission on 7 April
was noted in mid-August. See "Police Board May Be Forced into Action," *PGC*, 14 August
1924, 5.

135 "Social Evil and Bootlegging Are Deeply Rooted," *PGC*, 24 April 1924, 1.

136 "Mayor Alward Defines Position on Civic Issues," *PGC*, 8 May 1924, 3.

137 "Police Board Splits on Issue of Tenderloin," *PGC*, 7 August 1924, 3.

138 This was a concern elsewhere. See Gregory Marquis, "Vancouver Vice: The Police and the
Negotiation of Morality, 1904–35," in *Essays in the History of Canadian Law: BC and Yukon*,
ed. Hamar Foster and John McLaren (Toronto: Osgoode Society for Canadian Legal
History, 1995), 255 and 257; Charleen P. Smith, "Boomtown Brothels in the Kootenays,
1895–1905," in *People and Place: Historical Influences on Legal Culture*, ed. Jonathan Swainger
and Constance Backhouse (Vancouver: UBC Press, 2003), 131; and Lesley Erickson,
Westward Bound: Sex, Violence, the Law, and the Making of Settler Society (Vancouver: UBC
Press, 2011), 97.

139 "Police Board Splits on Issue of Tenderloin," *PGC*, 7 August 1924, 3.

140 Neil McMillan and family moved to Vancouver in the hope that he might secure employment with the police in that city. See "Local Happenings," *PGC*, 8 May 1924, 8.

141 Unless otherwise cited, the following is based on "Police Board May Be Forced into
Action," *PGC*, 14 August 1924, 5.

142 *PGC*, 14 August 1924, 8.

143 Unless otherwise cited, the following is based on "Wine and Women Fall under the Ban
of Police," *PGC*, 21 August 1924, 3.

144 "Wine and Women Fall under the Ban of Police," *PGC*, 21 August 1924, 3.

145 "Police Commissioners Consider Board Able to Police the City," *PGC*, 11 September
1924, 5.

146 "Chief Stevenson Has Auto Smash on the Loop," *PGC*, 4 September 1924, 1; "Local Happenings," *PGC*, 11 September 1924, 8; "Local Happenings," *PGC*, 23 October 1924, 8.

147 "Police Commissioners Decide to Seek to Decide fo [sic] New Chief for Force," *PGC*, 16
October 1924, 1.

148 "Manson Plans Police Reform," *PGC*, 25 September 1924, 2. Also see "Attorney-General
Considering Plans for Single Force," *TP*, 17 September 1924, 2; "Manson Preparing Data
about Police," *VP*, 3 October 1924, 12; "Police Heads to Discuss Merging," *VP*, 4 October
1924, 1; "Police System Is under Fire," *PGC*, 9 October 1924, 2; and "Grand Jurors Condemn
Police of Vancouver," *PGC*, 30 October 1924, 1.

149 An Act to amend the "Police and Prisons Regulation Act," SBC 1924, c. 40; *Annual Report
of the Superintendent of Provincial Police for the Year Ended December 31st, 1924* (Victoria:
King's Printer, 1925), X8.

150 See "Long to Merge Three Police Forces," *VP*, 7 December 1928, 1. The first individual
sworn in was none other than Chief Constable Alfred Grundy, who briefly served with
the BCPP in South Fort George. See "Chief Grundy Sworn In," *VP*, 2 January 1929, 30.

151 "New Chief of City Police Arrived in City Saturday Evening," *PGC*, 6 November 1924,
1. The same article appeared in the *Wetaskiwin Times* on 27 November.

152 "Commission Gives Police Chief the Assistance He Considers Necessary," *PGC*, 11
December 1924, 1; "Local Happenings," *PGC*, 24 December 1924, 8.

153 "Prince George Debited out of Liquor Profits," *PGC*, 31 December 1924, 1.

154 "Strong Protest against Liquor Board's Action," *PGC*, 8 January 1925, 3.

155 "Denied Share in Liquor Profits, BC Towns up in Arms," *VP*, 8 January 1925, 1; "Chilliwack Passes Complaint on Liquor Profits on to Union," *VP*, 27 January 1925, 2.

156 "'Interference Must Stop' Ultimatum to Government," *VP*, 9 January 1925, 1; "Mayor Taylor Says Vancouver Bled White," *PGC*, 15 January 1925, 6.

157 "Attorney-General Replies to Charge," *VP*, 9 January 1925, 12.

158 "Hotelmen Have Responsibilities Not Privileges," *PGC*, 29 January 1925, 7; "Civic Clean-Up Now under Way by the Police," *PGC*, 23 April 1925, 3; "Mayor Alward's Hurried Trip Starts Guessing," *PGC*, 16 April 1925, 1.

159 "Aldermen View with Suspicion New Police Plan" and "Majority Favor Change on the Police Board," *PGC*, 30 April 1925, 1.

160 "Police Transfer Gets Approval of City Council," *PGC*, 7 May 1925, 1.

161 Unless otherwise stated, the following is based on "Mayor Alward Stands Pat on Police Issue," *PGC*, 14 May 1925, 1 and "Point of Order Punctures the Police Protest," *PGC*, 21 May 1925, 3.

162 "Police Officers Receive Notice of Dismissal," *PGC*, 21 May 1925, 1.

163 "Police Transfer Gets Approval of City Council," *PGC*, 7 May 1925, 5.

164 Catte, *Pure America: Eugenics and the Making of Modern Virginia* (Cleveland: Belt Publishing, 2021), 60.

CHAPTER FOUR: HOLDING COURT IN THE GEORGES

1 Martin N. Friedman and Robert Percival, *The Roots of Justice: Crime and Punishment in Alameda County, California, 1870–1910* (Chapel Hill: University of North Carolina Press, 1981), 67. A similar description applied in Toronto, Calgary, Peterborough, Hamilton, and Halifax. See Gene Homel, "Denison's Law: Criminal Justice and the Police Court in Toronto," *Ontario History* 73 (September 1981): 170–86; Tom Thorner and Neil Watson, "Patterns of Prairie Crime: Calgary, 1875–1939," in *Crime and Criminal Justice in Europe and Canada*, ed. Louis A. Knafla (Waterloo: Wilfrid Laurier University Press, 1985), 219–55; Joan Sangster, "'Pardon Tales' from Magistrate's Court: Women, Crime, and the Court in Peterborough County, 1920–50," *Canadian Historical Review* 74 (June 1993): 161–97; John C. Weaver, *Crimes, Constables, and Courts: Order and Transgression in a Canadian City, 1816–1970* (Montreal and Kingston: McGill-Queen's University Press, 1995), 71–79; and Michael Boudreau, *City of Order: Crime and Society in Halifax, 1918–35* (Vancouver: UBC Press, 2012), 54–59.

2 "Jael Fails to Dodge Jail; Nailed by Law," *PGP*, 20 February 1915, 1; "First Assizes Held in Prince George Open This Morning," *PGC*, 11 June 1919, 1; "Sorcerer Meets Death at Hands of Siccannees," *PGC*, 2 October 1924, 4.

3 *The Independence of Justices of the Peace and Magistrates: Report No. 75* (Winnipeg: Manitoba Law Reform Commission, 1991), 5. On British Columbia's early law-enforcement history, see David M.L. Farr, "The Organization of the Judicial System of the Colonies of Vancouver Island and British Columbia, 1849–1871," *UBC Law Review* 3, 1 (March 1967): 1–35, and Hamar Foster, "Law Enforcement in Nineteenth-Century British Columbia," *BC Studies* 63 (August 1984): 3–28.

4 Colonial British Columbia's early police history is examined in Frederick John Hatch, "The British Columbia Police, 1858–1871" (master's thesis, University of British Columbia,

1955). On Brew, see Hatch, "The British Columbia Police," 19–29, and Lynne Stonier-Newman, *Policing a Pioneer Province: The BC Provincial Police, 1858–1950* (Madeira Park, BC: Harbour Publishing, 1991), 9–27.

5 Hatch, "The British Columbia Police," 30. Dennis Munroe Anholt, "Friends of the Government: An Administrative History of the British Columbia Government Agents" (PhD diss., University of Victoria, 1991), 33 and 38.

6 An Act Relating to the Appointment of Stipendiary Magistrates, SBC 1883, c. 30; An Act to Amend "An Act Relating to the Appointment of Stipendiary Magistrates," SBC 1885, c. 27; An Act to Amend the "Magistrates Act," SBC 1892, c. 29; An Act Respecting Justices of the Peace and other Magistrates, SBC 1897, c. 127. Additional changes affecting magistrates were introduced under iterations of the Municipal Act as well as the Incorporation Act for Vancouver, New Westminster, and Victoria.

7 For Bourchier, see *British Columbia Gazette* 47, 23 (6 June 1907), 3153; for Cowie, see *British Columbia Gazette* 47, 2 (8 August 1907): 4941. Bourchier unsuccessfully applied to become resident constable: see Alan K. Bouchier, South Fort George, to F.S. Hussey, Superintendent, BCPP, 7 September 1910, BCA, GR 91, vol. 4, file A-C. His resignation as justice of the peace was accepted on 9 April 1913; see *British Columbia Gazette* 53, 17 (24 April 1913): 3586.

8 "Illegal Sale of 'Booze' at Fort George," *FGT*, 13 November 1909, 4; *Fort George Journal*, 3 August 1906–18 November 1911, HBCA, B.280/a/9, 8 September 1907.

9 Compare *FGT*, 27 November 1909, 2, and *FGT*, 11 December 1909, 4.

10 Unless otherwise cited, the following is based on "Illegal Liquor-Selling," *FGT*, 6 August 1910, 2.

11 See *Fort George Journal*, 3 August 1906–18 November 1911, HBCA, B.280/a/9, 7 and 10 August 1907 and 29 August 1910. See Suzanne Morton, *At Odds: Gambling and Canadians, 1919–1969* (Toronto: University of Toronto Press, 2003), 108–36. A similar order to leave was issued to two bootleggers: see "The Fort George of the Future," *FGH*, 27 August 1910, 1.

12 Herne's biographical details are found in "Funeral of Late Thomas W. Herne Took Place at Victoria on Monday," *PGC*, 17 April 1924, 4. On the range of Herne's work as government agent, see "Office of the Man of Numerous Titles," *PGC*, 13 September 1921, 21.

13 "Govt Agent Herne Will Remain Here," *FGH*, 11 May 1912, 1.

14 The following is based on "Funeral of Late Thomas W. Herne Took Place at Victoria on Monday," *PGC*, 17 April 1924, 4.

15 *British Columbia Gazette* 51, 27 (6 July 1911): 9402.

16 "Thomas W. Herne Died of Heart Failure at Prince Rupert Last Night," *PGC*, 10 April 1924, 1

17 Incorporated as Fort George, the community officially changed its name to Prince George on 17 June 1915. See An Act to Incorporate the City of Fort George, SBC 1915, c. 29.

18 "Appointments," re Charles B. Daniell, *British Columbia Gazette* 55, 26 (2 July 1915): 1795; "Magistrate and Commissioners Are Appointed," *FGH*, 25 June 1915, 1.

19 Herne's experiences in the northern Interior were slightly out of step with the Lower Mainland. Throughout the war years and the immediate aftermath, he remained at the sharp end of things in overseeing the state's growth, while, in the Lower Mainland, specialist governmental functionaries emerged to carry the load. See Anholt, "Friends of the Government," Table 5, 107.

20 Re South Fort George and Fort George, 1913–21, BCA, GR 445.

21 See the reports for the Cariboo Mining District from 1904 to 1913 included in the "Annual Report of the Minister of Mines," published in the province's *Sessional Papers.* The dominion criminal statistics have been compiled from the *Sessional Papers.*

22 *Annual Report of the Minister of Mines, 31st December 1914* (Victoria: Richard Wolfenden, Printer to the King's Most Excellent Majesty, 1915), K55.

23 "Crime in the Fort George District," *FGH,* 16 January 1915, 2.

24 "Around the City," *FGH,* 13 March 1915, 6.

25 A.M. Johnson, deputy attorney general, Victoria, to Thomas Herne, government agent, South Fort George, 2 November 1917, BCA, GR 2792, box 1, file 1917/31-40.

26 Thomas Herne to A.M. Johnson, 13 November 1917, BCA, GR 2792, box 1, file 1917/31-40.

27 "Police Magistrate's Report for 1920," *PGC,* 14 January 1921, 7.

28 "Former Resident Dies in South," *VDC,* 23 September 1927, 5.

29 "Appointments," re Charles B. Daniell, *British Columbia Gazette* 55, 26 (2 July 1915): 1795; "Magistrate and Commissioners Are Appointed," *PGP,* 19 June 1915, 1.

30 "Local Happenings," *PGC,* 18 October 1923, 8; "City Officials Say Farewell to C.B. Daniell," *PGC,* 1 November 1923, 1 and 5.

31 The details of the case are in *R. v. Gillett,* BCA, GR 2787, file 11/1916. Also see "Prince George Mayor Cuts Lighting Wires," *PRDN,* 26 February 1916, 1.

32 Special Meeting of the Prince George City Council, 4 May 1916, City Clerk's Office, Prince George City Hall.

33 The courtesy of holding police court in council chambers had been extended to Daniell shortly after his appointment. A news item in 1915 indicated that "petty sessions" in the city were held at the police station but would be moved to council chambers if the situation required. See "Two More Bylaws Introduced to City," *PGP,* 26 June 1915, 1, and "In the Police Court," *PGP,* 21 August 1915, 4.

34 Special Meeting of the Prince George City Council, 4 May 1916, City Clerk's Office, Prince George City Hall.

35 "Communications," *PGC,* 14 June 1916, 1.

36 *PGS,* 19 January 1917, 6.

37 "Fort George Looks Worse than Fernie for Hon. Mr. Ross," *VS,* 10 August 1916, 1; "M'Innes Looks Like a Sure Winner over Mr. Ross – Outcast," *VS,* 12 August 1916, 7; "Election Result in Ft. George in Doubt at Present," *VS,* 16 September 1916, 2.

38 "Harry G. Perry Opens Mayoralty Campaign with Strong Policy of Reform," *PGC,* 9 January 1920, 1.

39 Bylaw No. 3 (14 June 1915) provided for the business licence regulation, while Bylaw No. 96 (30 January 1920) introduced the manager licensing stipulation. The city bylaws are housed in the City Clerk's Office, Prince George City Hall.

40 "Clubbing the Clubs," *PGC,* 30 January 1920, 4.

41 "Club Are Licensed," *PGC,* 23 April 1920, 1.

42 "A Long Wait for the Taxi Man," and "Enforcing the Law," *PGC,* 27 August 1920, 1 and 2.

43 The notes for the Pappas police court hearing are found in *Rex v. Jeanne Schlosser,* BCA, GR 2791, County Court appeals, file 1920/20.

44 "Enforcing the Law," *PGC,* 27 August 1920, 2.

45 "'Twas Three Cases of Too Much Watson," *PGC,* 20 August 1920, 1. Jeanne Schlosser is identified in the 1921 Census as a twenty-four-year-old Roman Catholic woman of Belgian

origin who arrived in Canada in 1907 and was naturalized in 1910. Canada, Census, 1921, District 14, sub-district 58, 8, available through Ancestry.ca.

46 Charles B. Daniell, police magistrate, Prince George, to His Honour Judge Robertson, South Fort George, *Rex v. Jeanne Schlosser*, BCA, GR 2791, file 1920/20, 24 August 1920.

47 "Sixteen Prohibition Cases Are Dismissed," *PGC*, 24 September 1920, 1.

48 "The Near-Beer Cases," *PGC*, 24 September 1980, 2.

49 "Police Magistrate's Report for 1920," *PGC*, 14 January 1921, 7.

50 Prince George City Council Minutes, 20 January 1921, City Clerk's Office, Prince George City Hall; "First Business Meeting of New Council Last Night," *PGC*, 21 January 1921, 1.

51 Prince George City Council Minutes, 8 April 1921, City Clerk's Office, Prince George City Hall.

52 "Shake-Up Threatened in the City Government," *PGC*, 22 April 1921, 1; "Bootleggers Must Go Is Decision of City Council," *TL*, 22 April 1921, 1.

53 "Shake-Up Threatened in the City Government," *PGC*, 22 April 1921, 1.

54 "Municipal House-Cleaning," *PGC*, 26 April 1921, 2.

55 See "Magistrate Daniell Replies to Police Commissioners," *PGC*, 3 May 1921, 1, 4 and 5. Daniell's letter is printed in full beginning on page 4.

56 The following is based on "Magistrate Daniell Replies to Police Commissioners," *PGC*, 3 May 1921, 4–5.

57 "Magistrate Daniell Replies to Police Commissioners," *PGC*, 3 May 1921, 1.

58 "Local Conditions Aired at Special Meeting of Police Commissioners; Magistrate's Letter Reviewed," *TL*, 6 May 1921, 1; "The Controversy," *TL*, 6 May 1921, 2.

59 "Local Conditions Aired at Special Meeting of Police Commissioners; Magistrate's Letter Reviewed," *TL*, 6 May 1921, 1.

60 "That Police Probe," *PGC*, 6 May 1921, 2.

61 Prince George City Council Minutes, 18 October 1923, City Clerk's Office, Prince George City Hall. The Daniell house, which stood on former Hudson's Bay Company property, was offered for sale as "an admirable investment" on lands believed to be of interest for the construction of either a lumber or pulp mill. See "Pleasant Home and Three Lots for Only $2500," *PGC*, 4 August 1927, 8.

62 The following is based on "Officials Say Farewell to C.B. Daniell," *PGC*, 1 November 1923, 1.

63 Karen Dubinsky, *Improper Advances: Rape and Heterosexual Conflict in Ontario* (Chicago: University of Chicago Press, 1993), 145.

64 "Cariboo County Court," *CO*, 12 June 1865, 5; David M.L. Farr, "The Organization of the Judicial System of the Colonies of Vancouver Island and British Columbia, 1849–1871" (bachelor's thesis, University of British Columbia, 1944), 75.

65 On Cox (referred to as George W. Cox), see Farr, "The Organization of the Judicial System" (1944), 81. Also see G.R. Newell, "Cox, William George," *Dictionary of Canadian Biography*, vol. 10, http://www.biographi.ca/en/bio/cox_william_george_10E.html, and An Act Relating to County Courts, SBC 1883, c. 5, s. 4. On Ball's continuance as a County Court judge after Confederation, see N. Omer Coté, *Political Appointments, Parliaments, and the Judicial Bench in the Dominion of Canada, 1867 to 1895* (Ottawa: Thoburn and Co., 1896), 384, and Alfred Watts, "County Court of British Columbia," *Advocate* 27 (1969): 76–77.

66 Appointment of Eli Harrison as judge of the County Court of Cariboo, 25 April 1884, LAC, RG 2, vol. 447, reel C-3394, https://recherche-collection-search.bac-lac.gc.ca/eng/

home/record?app=ordincou&IdNumber=27419&new=-8585555199919835553; Coté, *Political Appointments,* 386.

67 "Appointments," re Fred Calder, *Canada Gazette* 15, 29 (10 January 1907): 1643; "Bench and Bar," *Canada Law Journal* 43, 1/2 (1907): 80.

68 "Notice," *CO,* 15 April 1911, B4; "County Court Sittings," *CO,* 10 June 1911, A1; "Local and Provincial," *FGH,* 10 June 1911, 1.

69 "County Court," *FGH,* 15 June 1912, 1.

70 "Court Session," *FGH,* 9 May 1914, 1.

71 Constable W.R. Dunwoody, duty log, 12 April 1914 and 7 May 1914, BCA, GR 445, box 17. Service was later killed while on duty on 4 July 1938. See "Obituary," *Shoulder Strap* 1, 1 (October 1938): 70.

72 "Court Session," *FGH,* 9 May 1914, 1; *R. v. Alric E. Thomas,* BCA, GR 2788, file 139/14.

73 "Court Session Closed," *FGH,* 23 May 1914, 1.

74 "One Adds Five and the Other Three," *TP,* 8 February 1915, 1; "Reports of Judges on Redistribution Submitted to House," *VS,* 9 February 1915, 3; "Vancouver to Have One Additional Seat," *VDNA,* 9 February 1915, 3; "Forty-Seven to Be Total Membership," *VS,* 5 March 1915, 1.

75 "Is Appointed as a County Court Judge," *TP,* 22 April 1915, 5; "New Judge of County Court," *VDC,* 23 April 1915, 1; "County Court Judge for Prince George," *PGP,* 1 May 1915, 1.

76 "Heard Dispute in Courtney Valley," *TP,* 13 June 1914, 30; "More Candidates Chosen," *VDNA,* 23 March 1915, 7; "Farewell Banquet for New Cariboo Judge," *FGT,* 15 May 1915, 1. Robertson was also a charter member of the Vancouver Stock Exchange: "City Stock Exchange: Its Proud Record, Bright Future," *VDP,* 26 January 1910, 22.

77 "Of Provincial and General Interest," *KSS,* 6 October 1916, 3. On Robertson's place in northern British Columbia's sense of self, see Jonathan Swainger, "'Not in Keeping with the Tradition of the Cariboo Courts': Courts and Community Identity in Northeastern British Columbia, 1920–50," in *The Grand Experiment: Law and Legal Culture in British Settler Societies,* ed. Hamar Foster, Benjamin L. Berger, and A.R. Buck (Vancouver: UBC Press for the Osgoode Society for Canadian Legal History, 2008), 176–92.

78 "Judge Robertson Travels 600 Miles by Canoe," *PGC,* 15 October 1920, 2; "Judge Struggled in River's Icy Waters When Boat Capsized," *PRR,* 30 October 1926, 1; Monica Storrs diary, North Peace Museum, Fort St. John, entry for September 1936, 6; "Local and Personal," *PRBN,* 25 September 1936, 4.

79 "Judge Robertson Ill," *TP,* 11 March 1942, 6; "Judge Robertson Retires from Cariboo County Bench," *PRBN,* 16 April 1942, 1; "Death Claims Pioneer Jurist," *TP,* 4 May 1942, 6; "Judge H.E.A. Robertson Dies in Victoria," *VS,* 4 May 1942, 3; "County Court Jurist Passes," *VDC,* 5 May 1942, 5.

80 "Final Rites Observed for Judge Robertson, Veteran Cariboo Jurist," *PGC,* 7 May 1942, 1.

81 "County Court Session Commences Tuesday," *PGP,* 12 June 1915, 1; "County Court Sits Most of the Week," *PGP,* 18 June 1915, 4; "Assault Case Dismissed," *PGP,* 26 June 1915, 4.

82 "Board of Trade Deal with Many Questions Local Interest," *PGS,* 9 February 1917, 1.

83 A.M. Johnson, deputy attorney general, Victoria, to Thomas Herne, government agent, South Fort George, 2 November 1917, BCA, GR 2792, box 1, file 31-40.

84 A.M. Johnson to Thomas Herne, 12 March 1919, BCA, GR 2792, box 1, file 1919/11-20.

85 Located on the corner of George Street and Fifth Avenue, the Ritts-Kifer Hall was opened on 4 July 1914 and was destroyed by fire on 23 January 1957. *FGH,* 4 July 1914, 1; "$75,000

Fire Guts Building: Firemen Brave 40-Below Zero to Save Downtown City Block," *PGC,* 24 January 1957, 1 and 7.

86 W.B. Colvin, chief clerk, attorney general's office, Victoria, to Thomas Herne, government agent, South Fort George, 7 April 1919, BCA, GR 2792, box 1, file 1919/11-20.

87 City council discussed the advisability of issuing a liquor licence to Reinharz and Schenk in the third week of February 1918. Councillor Thomas Porter argued against the application since "these men were enemies to our country." Prince George City Council meeting minutes, 21 February 1918, City Clerk's Office, Prince George City Hall. See the BCPP duty logs for South Fort George beginning on 25 April 1919, BCA, GR 445, box 56, file.6.

88 "Heavy Assize Opens Today Involving Large Influx," *PGC,* 14 June 1921, 1.

89 "Important Cases to Be Tried by Supreme Court," *PGC,* 28 May 1919, 1. On the Auton case, see Jonathan Swainger, "Police Culture in British Columbia and 'Ordinary Duty' in the Peace River Country, 1910–1939," in *People and Place: Historical Influences on Legal Culture,* ed. Jonathan Swainger and Constance Backhouse (Vancouver: UBC Press, 2003), 198–224. On the Harris case, see "Attempted Murder," *CO,* 17 May 1919, 1; "BC Constable Attempts Killing of Quesnel Lady," *PGC,* 21 May 1919, 1; "Shot Because She Wanted to Dance," *PGC,* 28 May 1919, 2; "Found Guilty on Charge of Attempt to Murder," *PGC,* 18 June 1919, 1; and "Harris Sentenced to Three Years," *CO,* 21 June 1919, 1.

90 "Assize Court Opens Here with Very Heavy Docket," *PGC,* 22 October 1920, 1.

91 "Heavy Docket for Supreme Court Sittings," *TL,* 10 June 1921, 1.

92 "Heavy Assize Opens Today Involving Large Influx," *PGC,* 14 June 1921, 1.

93 "Criminal Cases Being Rapidly Disposed Of," *TL,* 17 June 1921, 1.

94 "Criminal Docket Is Not Very Heavy," *PGC,* 28 October 1921, 5.

95 "The Blameless Life," *PGC,* 10 March 1922, 2.

96 "Cariboo Has Stainless Record for Assize" and "Nice Legal Point Argued This Morning," *PGC,* 5 May 1922, 4; "No Criminal or Civil Cases to Be Heard," *TL,* 5 May 1922, 1; "Conviction of Jean Schlosser Upheld by Mr. Justice Morrison," *PGC,* 29 September 1922, 4.

97 Prince George City Council meeting minutes, 8 July 1915, City Clerk's Office, Prince George City Hall.

98 "Unjust to District," *PGC,* 31 January 1919, 2.

99 The grand jury's obligation to report to the Crown concerning the needs, conditions, and potential threats in the countryside extends back to twelfth-century England. By the late nineteenth century in Canada, several provincial jurisdictions had eliminated the grand jury. Several provinces never introduced the practice. For the abolition in British Columbia, see An Act to Amend the "Jury Act," SBC 1932, c. 22; "Spring Assizes Grand Jury May Be Last In BC," *VS,* 12 March 1932, 22; "Grand Juries," *VP,* 22 March 1932, 6; and "Lawyers OK Abolition of Grand Jury," *VS,* 26 March 1932, 12.

100 Thomas Herne, Supreme Court registrar, South Fort George, to the Honorable J.H. King, minister of public works, Victoria, 14 June 1919, BCA, GR 2792, file 1919/31-40.

101 "Jury Presentation Deplores Gambling Evil in the City," *PGC,* 29 October 1919, 1.

102 "Excellent Presentment by the Grand Jury," *PGC,* 11 June 1920, 9. On the absence of cells for women prisoners, see "South Town Jail Has No Female Accommodation," *PGC,* 16 August 1921, 8. The article is unapologetically racist.

103 "Grand Jury Criticizes Govt Buildings Again," *PGC,* 22 October 1920, 5.

104 *PGC,* 11 March 1922,

105 "Ald. Wimbles after Inspection Fee Return," *PGC*, 20 May 1921, 5.

106 *PGC*, 24 [sic] June 1921, 2. As noted in Chapter 4, this newspaper edition is part of a printing error in the *Citizen's* production. See the discussion attached to the Eugene Bull and David Joseph murder charge.

107 Douglas Hay, "Property, Authority and the Criminal Law," *Albion's Fatal Tree: Crime and Society in Eighteenth Century England*, ed. Douglas Hay, Peter Linebaugh, John Rule, E.P Thompson, and Cal Winslow (Harmondsworth, UK: Penguin Books, 1977), 17–63.

108 "The New Court House," *PGC*, 24 March 1921, 2.

109 Robin Fisher, *Duff Pattullo of British Columbia* (Toronto: University of Toronto Press, 1991), 161.

110 Fisher, *Duff Pattullo*, 162–63.

111 "'Some' Court House," *PGC*, 18 November 1921, 2.

112 "Financiers Take Hold," *FGH*, 5 November 1910, 1; "Northern Development Company," *FGH*, 26 November 1910, 1; "Will Build Large Sawmill Near City," *PGC*, 12 December 1921, 1; "J.D. McArthur Has Bought Site for Big Sawmill on Hudson's Bay Land" and "City Council Will Deal with Sawmill Project Tuesday," *PGC*, 7 July 1922, 1 and 6. Also see "Stimulating News," *PGC*, 7 July 1922, 2.

113 "An Incidental Result," *PGC*, 7 July 1922, 2. McArthur became the registered owner of the Hudson's Bay subdivision in late March or early April 1923. See "J.D. McArthur Completes Title to the Mill Site on Hudson's Bay Land," *PGC*, 5 April 1923, 1, and "Prospect Bright for Big Sawmill at Prince George," *PGC*, 3 December 1925, 1 and 4.

114 "Veteran Railroad Builder Dying at Battle Creek," *PGC*, 13 January 1927, 2; "J.D. McArthur Died in Winnipeg on Monday," *PGC*, 13 January 1927, 3; "McArthur Estate Is Removing Plant from Mill Site," *PGC*, 31 March 1927, 1.

115 "Prince George May Get New Public Buildings Soon," *PGC*, 22 December 1922, 1.

116 "BC Police to Be Khaki Force," *TP*, 10 November 1923, 1.

117 "Government May Close the Jail at South Fort George," *PGC*, 31 May 1923, 1.

118 "The Government Jail," *PGC*, 7 June 1923, 2.

119 "Alexandra Hotel Property Purchased by Government," *PGC*, 7 June 1923, 1. On the hotel's place in local history, see "Famous Hotel Rounds Out Its Eventful Career," *PGC*, 5 July 1923, 4.

120 "New Buildings Now Occupied [by] Local Officials," *PGC*, 13 December 1923, 4.

121 "Superintendent of Police to Visit City," *PGC*, 24 January 1924, 5; "Jail at South Will Be Closed at Early Date," *PGC*, 7 February 1924, 1.

122 The anticipated pulp mills did not arrive in Prince George until 1964.

123 The small notice indicated that, while ten cells had already been installed, there was sufficient room for an additional fourteen. See "Local and District," *PGC*, 13 March 1924, 4, and "Local Happenings," *PGC*, 3 December 1925, 8.

124 "When Will Prince George Get a Court House Such as This?" *PGC*, 11 November 1921, 3.

125 "When Will Prince George Get a Court House Such as This?" *PGC*, 11 November 1921, 3.

CHAPTER FIVE:
SENSATIONS, FRONT-PAGE CRIME, AND COMMUNITY IDENTITY

1 "Murder Case May Be Added to the Assize List Here," *PGC*, 3 December 1925, 1. Chilco Lake, 190 kilometres southwest of Williams Lake in the South Cariboo, is in one mountain range away from the Pacific coast.

2 "His Fear of Gold Rush Led to Death of Trapper," *VP,* 3 December 1925, 1; "Fred Cyr Tells Story of Duel to Death in Woods," *PGC,* 17 December 1925, 3.

3 "Seven Cases on Criminal List for Assize Court Opening January 13," *PGC,* 31 December 1925, 1.

4 "Coroner Takes Month's Supplies on Cariboo Inquest," *VP,* 2 December 1925, 1.

5 "Kicked Trapper's Gun Away and Then Killed Him," *VP,* 17 December 1925, 1; "How Inquest Was Held in the Wilds," *VP,* 27 December 1925, 13.

6 "Assize Court at Prince George," *VP,* 10 January 1926, 12.

7 "Cyr's Dramatic Tale: Story of How Fred Cyr Killed Ducharme Told to Assize at Prince George," *VP,* 21 January 1926, 1; "Drama of Wilds Is Bared," *VS,* 21 January 1926, 1.

8 Judith Flanders, *The Invention of Murder: How Victorians Revelled in Death and Detection and Created Modern Crime* (London: Harper Press, 2011), 20–98.

9 "Chow Lee, Joy Dispenser," *PGC,* 16 August 1918, 1; "Local and Personal," *PGC,* 20 August 1918, 6.

10 Constable A. McNeill, duty log, 2–3 August 1920, BCA, GR 445, box 62, file 3.

11 "GWVA," *PGC,* 11 October 1918, 4; "Red Cross Society," *PGC,* 3 December 1918, 6; "Red Cross Society," *PGC,* 5 February 1919, 6.

12 "Opium Found in Vegetable Box: Oriental Is Arrested," *VP,* 22 March 1923, 1; "Heavy Sentence Imposed in Chow Lee Opium Case," *PGC,* 29 March 1923, 5. According to the 1921 census, Chow Lee was forty-five years old, his wife (whose name was also recorded as Chow Lee) was thirty-two, and their family consisted of three daughters (five, four, and three years old) and two sons (eight and seven years old): Canada, *Sixth Census of Canada* (121) District 14, Sub-District 58, Prince George City and South Fort George, 18. Except for the eldest son, "George," the names are indecipherable.

13 Unless otherwise cited, the following is based on "Chinese Failed in Appeal from Drug Conviction," *PGC,* 29 November 1923, 1.

14 Cariboo government agency records, Finding Aid, BCA, GR 0216, 12–13.

15 "Habeas Corpus Case," *VDC,* 13 October 1923, 5.

16 "Chinese Given Their Freedom," *VDC,* 14 March 1924, 12; "Chow Lee Will Escape Deportation as a Result of Court's Decision," *PGC,* 1 May 1924, 1.

17 "Queen's Hotel Has Changed Management," *PGS,* 7 November 1916, 5.

18 William Apostolos Bellos, death certificate, 26 July 1989, Province of British Columbia, DTH 1989013564, https://www.ancestry.ca/genealogy/records/william-apostolos-bellos-24 -17hgxr4.

19 See Arthur Bellos, Files of the Canadian Expeditionary Force, LAC, RG 150, regimental no. 2023897.

20 "Assault Charge Dismissed," *PGC,* 16 August 1918, 1; "Local and Personal," *PGC,* 26 November 1918, 6. See Chapter 3 for the veterans' riot.

21 See *R. v. William Bellos,* assault, BCA, GR 2788, file 99/1920; *R. v. William Bellos,* possession of stolen goods, BCA, 2788, file 175/1920; *R. v. Levi Graham and Arthur Bellos,* violation of club manager bylaw, BCA, GR 2791, file 22/1920; *R. v. William Bellos,* theft, BCA, GR 2788, file 388/1922; *R. v. William Bellos,* assault, BCA, GR 2788, file 14/1923; and *R. v. Arthur Bellos,* assault causing grievous bodily harm, BCA, GR 2788, file 19/1923. "Midnight Fracas Results in Serious Assault Charge," *PGC,* 14 June 1923, 1; "Bellos Secures Acquittal on a Charge of Assault," *PGC,* 21 June 1923, 7; "Arthur Bellos on Trial Today for Assault," *PGC,* 19 July 1923, 1.

22 "Assault Charge Laid Against *Citizen* Editor," *PGC*, 21 March 1921, 5; "Labor Berserker in Jail after Frenzied Frolic," *VP*, 22 March 1922, 16; "Hansen Is Fined for Damaging Property," *PGC*, 24 March 1922, 5; "Cost the Editor $5.00 and Costs to Hit Hansen," *PGC*, 4 April 1921, 4; "*Citizen* Editor Was Guilty of Assault," *TL*, 7 April 1921, 5.

23 "Labor Berserker in Jail after Frenzied Frolic," *VP*, 22 March 1922, 16; "Tie-Makers at Mud River Camp Return to Work," *VDW*, 22 March 1922, 21.

24 "Assault Charges Follow Disturbance in Local Tenderloin on Sunday," *PGC*, 2 July 1925, 3; "Bellos Committed on Assault Charge by Magistrate," *PGC*, 9 July 1925, 1; "Seven Cases Make Criminal List at the Assize," *PGC*, 14 January 1926, 4.

25 "Conviction Secured against W. Bellos under Liquor Act," *PGC*, 16 July 1925, 1; "Local Happenings," *PGC*, 16 July 1925, 8; "William Bellos Loses Appeal from Conviction by Magistrate Moran," *PGC*, 6 August 1925, 2.

26 "Prince George Woman Is Arrested In City," *PRDN*, 16 September 1925, 1.

27 "Woman Arrested Here Is Fined in Interior," *PRDN*, 21 September 1925, 1; "Prince George Man in Assault Charge," *PRDN*, 26 September 1925, 1; "Local Happenings," *PGC*, 1 October 1925, 8.

28 "Prince George Woman Charged with Bigamy," *VP*, 27 September 1925, 20.

29 "Arthur Bellos Is Guilty of Assault on Brotherston," *PGC*, 21 January 1926, 6.

30 "Unique Case at Assizes," *PRDN*, 19 January 1926, 1; "Man's Confession Rejected by Jury," *VTC*, 19 January 1926, 14.

31 See *Annual Report of the Superintendent of Provincial Police for the Year Ended December 31st, 1925* (Victoria: Charles F. Banfield, Printer to the King's Most Excellent Majesty, 1927), Y16.

32 Unless otherwise cited, the following is based on "Brings Charge against Jury," *VP*, 14 April 1926, 1 and 3; "Prince George Appeal Case," *PRDN*, 15 April 1926, 1; "Jury Prejudiced Plea for Greek in Penitentiary," *VTC*, 24 June 1926, 9; "Bellos Case in Limelight," *PRDN*, 25 June 1926, 1.

33 "Mrs. Grace Ryan Bellos too Fearful to Appear in Court," *PGC*, 22 April 1926, 9.

34 "Court of Appeal Orders New Trial in Bellos Case," *PGC*, 25 November 1926, 1.

35 "Orders New Trial in Northern Case," *VP*, 18 November 1926, 30; "Quashes Sentence, Orders New Trial," *VS*, 18 November 1926, 14; "Prince George Case Quashed," *PRDN*, 19 November 1926, 1; "Court of Appeal Orders New Trial in Bellos Case," *PGC*, 25 November 1926, 1.

36 "Court of Appeal Orders New Trial in Bellos Case," *PGC*, 25 November 1926, 1.

37 "Will Appeal Case Involving Police Practices in BC," *VDT*, 29 November 1926; "New Case Menaces Police System in Use in Province," *VDT*, 31 December 1926, 9; "Decision in Bellos Case Appealed by Attorney-General," *PGC*, 6 January 1927, 1.

38 "Arthur Bellos Arrested in Vancouver on Charge of Planning Hold-Up," *PGC*, 3 February 1927, 1; "Decision Is Reserved in Bellos-Pepo Charge," *VP*, 4 March 1927, 26; "Bellos and Pepo Dismissed," *TP*, 7 March 1927, 17; "Court Dismisses Counselling Case," *VS*, 7 March 1927, 16.

39 *The King v. Bellos*, [1927] SCR, 258–61; "Court Upholds Police Method," *VS*, 25 February 1927, 18; "Police Right to Query Prisoners Upheld by Court," *NDN*, 26 February 1927, 1; "Right to Question Prisoners Upheld," *TP*, 26 February 1927, 20; "Supreme Court Decision Returns Bellos to Prison," *PGC*, 3 March 1927, 5.

40 "Provincial Police Report to Department," *TL*, 13 January 1922, 1.

41 "District Police Report Flattering to Force," *PGC*, 13 January 1922, 3.

42 On Robertson, see "George Hart" in *Lure of the South Peace: Tales of the Early Pioneers to 1945,* ed. Lillian York (Dawson Creek, BC: Peace River Block News, 1981), 177, and "Tin Horns and Glass Bottles," *PGC,* 5 March 1920, 1. For gambling and Canadian society, see Suzanne Morton, *At Odds: Gambling and Canadians, 1919–1969* (Toronto: University of Toronto Press, 2003).

43 Morton, *At Odds,* 112–13.

44 "Negroes Invading Alberta," *FGH,* 11 February 1911, 8; "Roads to Settlements Should Be Built," *FGT,* 20 November 1909, 4; "Billy Boucher Saw His First Train," *PGP,* 31 July 1925, 1; "Indians Brought in for a Killing Committed in 1914," *PGC,* 5 April 1921, 1.

45 The concept of race, as it was used in the late nineteenth and early twentieth centuries, has been dismissed as an illegitimate analytical device. Nonetheless, engaging with the years straddling the Great War obliges one to employ the term as it was then understood. See Matthew Frye Jacobson, *Whiteness of a Different Color: European Immigrants and the Alchemy of Race* (Cambridge, MA: Harvard University Press, 1998) and Robert Wald Sussman, *The Myth of Race: The Troubling Persistence of an Unscientific Idea* (Cambridge, MA: Harvard University Press, 2014).

46 "Local and Provincial," *FGH,* 3 June 1911, 1.

47 "City and District," *FGH,* 9 December 1911, 1.

48 "Masquerade Promises Plenty of Amusement," *PGS,* 2 February 1917, 1.

49 "Undesirable Settlers," *PGC,* 10 September 1918, 2. See a similar comment castigating railway and steamship companies for transporting "Hunnish hordes" rather than "the bull-dog breed" to Canada. See "Hand Picked Emigrants," *PGC,* 20 August 1918, 2.

50 "The Orient vs. Occident," *PGH,* 16 October 1915, 1.

51 "Local and District," *FHG,* 19 April 1913, 8.

52 "Local and District," *FHG,* 19 April 1913, 8.

53 "Several Hundred Chinese Laborers Domiciled Here," *PGC,* 3 January 1919, 6.

54 Despite the language employed by whites, there was no single "Chinese" identity or culture. Rather, the label "Chinese" was an accumulated image reliant on racist characterizations. See Chapters 2 and 3 in Timothy J. Stanley, *Contesting White Supremacy: School Segregation, Anti-Racism, and the Making of Chinese Canadians* (Vancouver: UBC Press, 2011), 47–95.

55 Prince George had a recorded population of 2,053 in 1921. Canada, *Sixth Census of Canada, 1921,* vol. 1, *Population,* Table 8, "Population by districts and sub-districts according to the Redistribution Act of 1914 and the amending act of 1915," 214.

56 Lily Chow, *Sojourners to the North* (Prince George: Caitlin Press, 1996), 120; Canada, *Sixth Census of Canada,* District 14, Sub-District 58, Prince George City and South Fort George, 17–19; "Census Commissioner Will Arrive Here Next Monday," *PGC,* 20 May 1921, 6; "Census Commissioner Meets Enumerators Here," *PGC,* 27 May 1921, 6.

57 Vibbard, a returned veteran, was a "land and timber cruiser." See L. Vibbard, *PGC,* 28 January 1919, 4, and Leonard Vibbard, Files of the Canadian Expeditionary Force, LAC, RG 150, regimental number 258483.

58 "Chow Lee, Joy Dispenser," *PGC,* 16 August 1918, 1; "Local and Personal," *PGC,* 20 August 1918, 6.

59 "Mystery at City Hall," *PGC,* 31 January 1919, 6. This discovery may shed light on Police Chief James J. Dolan's dismissal from office. See "Police Squad Raid Disorderly Premises," *PGC,* 28 January 1919, 1; *PGC,* 28 January 1919, 2.

60 "Police Squad Raid Disorderly Premises," *PGC,* 28 January 1919, 1.

61 *PGC,* 5 February 1919, 8.

62 "Chinese Young Men Celebrate Opening of Club," *PGC,* 5 February 1919, 1. The news-paper's confused report and the claim that the association was marking its second anni-versary led to other errors. Local historian Lily Chow concluded that the organization was, in fact, the Chee Duck Tong cultural association, founded in 1918. The later clarifica-tion of the Reading Room Association's name and the fact that the Chee Duck Tong was one year old in 1919 suggest that Chow is incorrect. She corrected this error in Lily Chow, *Challenging Racism: Past and Present in the Prince George Chinese Canadian Community* (Prince George: Exploration Place, 2003), 3.

63 The census of 1921 does not list a George Young as a resident of Prince George, and a newspaper search has failed to produce additional details.

64 "Chinese Young Men Celebrate Opening of Club," *PGC,* 5 February 1919, 1; "Red Cross Society," *PGC,* 5 February 1919, 6; "Local and Personal," *PGC,* 12 February 1919, 10. The alternative spelling is based on Lily Chow's historical research on the local Chinese Canadian community, which indicates that Li Kow's two sons attended Fort George Elementary School. See Chow, *Challenging Racism,* 2.

65 "Local and Personal," *PGC,* 12 February 1919, 10.

66 Lisa Rose Mar, *Brokering Belonging: Chinese in Canada's Exclusion Era, 1885–1945* (Toronto: Oxford University Press, 2010), 57. The Chee Duck Tong was established in Prince George on 29 August 1918 in concert with a celebration of Five Ancestor Remembrance Day. See "Chee Duck Tong in Prince George Was Officially Opened," *CTimes,* 19 September 1918, 3, and Chow, *Challenging Racism,* 3.

67 "Mounted Police Now Stationed in This City," *PGC,* 3 September 1919, 1; Steven Hewitt, *Riding to the Rescue: The Transformation of the RCMP in Alberta and Saskatchewan, 1914–1939* (Toronto: University of Toronto Press, 2006).

68 Rendered in local newspapers and, often enough, police reports, racialized Chinese names such as "Ah Joe" are difficult, given that a literal translation means "some guy named Joe." While repeating the racialized depiction, one is obliged to be true to the source.

69 "Chinks Pay Heavily for 'Hitting Pipe,'" *PGC,* 10 December 1920, 7. In the aftermath of the anti-Asiatic Riot in Vancouver, Canada's drug laws went through a series of revisions beginning with An Act to Prohibit the Importation, Manufacture and Sale of Opium for other than Medicinal Purposes, SC 1908, c. 50; An Act to Prohibit the Improper Use of Opium and other Drugs, SC 1911, c. 17; An Act to Amend The Opium and Drug Act, SC 1919, c. 25; An Act to Amend The Opium and Narcotic Drug Act, SC 1920, c. 31; and An Act to Prohibit Improper Use of Opium and other Drugs, SC 1923, c. 22.

70 "Local Happenings," *PGC,* 14 December 1920, 8.

71 "Local Happenings," *PGC,* 22 December 1922, 4.

72 The following is based on "Chinese Nationalist League Entertains – Progressive Oriental Organization Invites Many to Inauguration Ceremony," *PGC,* 7 January 1921, 5.

73 See "Chop Suey Made by Chinese Experts," *PGC,* 7 January 1921, 4.

74 *PGC,* 11 January 1921, 8. The Kuomintang were not alone in marking local accomplish-ments. Owing to a fundraising campaign extending back to September 1918, the Chee Duck Tong cultural organization opened its new building and unveiled a new executive. See "Chee Duck Tong in Prince George Thanks All Guests for Attending Its Opening Ceremony," *CTimes,* 27 January 1921, 3; Chow, *Sojourners in the North,* 161; and "A List of Executive Members of Chee Duck Tong in Prince George," *CTimes,* 1 February 1921, 3.

75 Stanley, *Contesting White Supremacy*, 176. Included among the gifts offered to the hospital staff and patients were cake, nuts, and "Chinese" lilies. "Hospital Acknowledges Many Christmas Gifts," *PGC*, 11 January 1921, 5.

76 A newspaper item beneath the installation report revealed that this diminutive status applied to women and men. Winnie Lee, a "Chinese" aviator from Edmonton taught by Lieutenant George Gorman and Captain Wop May, had visited the city. After completing her studies, "this ambitious lady" was returning "to China where she will be engaged in teaching 'China Girls' to fly." "Chinese Aviatrix Is Visiting City," *PGC*, 7 January 1921, 5.

77 For the tenor of postwar anti-Asiatic sentiment in British Columbia, see Patricia Roy, *The Oriental Question: Consolidating a White Man's Province, 1914–41* (Vancouver: UBC Press, 2003), 55–89.

78 An Act Respecting Chinese Immigration, SC 1923, c. 38.

79 Both the Kuomintang and the Chinese Freemasons (Chee Kong Tong) scheduled events in early January: the former with the installation of their new executive and the latter with the opening of their new building on 8 January 1921. See "Chee Kung Tong in Prince George Announced Its Opening Date," *CTimes*, 21 December 1920, 3.

80 Chow, *Sojourners in the North*, 184. The *Citizen* and the *Leader* provide different spellings for the accused. See "Chinaman Is Victim of Serious Assault," *PGC*, 8 February 1921, 1, and "Police Court News," *TL*, 8 April 1921, 1.

81 "Lawyers from Coast on Chinese Case: Assault Alleged to Have Arisen over Chinese Famine Fund," *PGC*, 15 February 1921, 1.

82 "Chinese in Court," *PGC*, 25 February 1921, 1.

83 "Chinaman Is Victim of Serious Assault," *PGC*, 8 February 1921, 1.

84 "Police Court Busy with Chinese Cases," *PGC*, 18 February 1921, 1.

85 "Decisions Rendered in Club Prosecutions Today – Cases Dismissed in Police Court This Morning – Police Magistrate's Ruling," *PGC*, 4 March 1921, 1.

86 "Excommunicate Yuanzhao Huang," *CTimes*, 2 April 1921, 3.

87 The spellings of the names of the complainant and accused vary between the newspaper accounts: see "Police Court Notes," *TL*, 8 April 1921, 1, and "Local Happenings" *PGC*, 8 April 1921, 8.

88 "Police Court Notes," *TL*, 8 April 1921, 1.

89 "What's All the Trouble in Chinatown Here?" *PGC*, 15 April 1921, 1.

90 "What's All the Trouble in Chinatown Here?" *PGC*, 15 April 1921, 1.

91 "Battle of Third Avenue Was Lively Affair," *TL*, 15 April 1921, 1.

92 "Tong War Breaks Out on Main Streets of the City," *PGC*, 12 April 1921, 4. The *Leader* reported that the fight at city hall had been sparked when "one Chink passed some remark." See "Battle of Third Avenue Was Lively Affair," *TL*, 15 April 1921, 1.

93 *R. v. Mah Gong* (aka Mah Gowo) before Mr. Justice Gregory and jury, 18 June 1921, BCA, GR 2239, box 1, file 10/1921.

94 "Battle of Third Avenue Was Lively Affair," *TL*, 15 April 1921, 1.

95 Testimony of Frank Delong, at trial before Mr. Justice Gregory and jury, 18 June 1921, *Rex v. Mah Gong*, BCA, GR 2239, file 10/1921, 37; "Battle of Third Avenue Was Lively Affair," *TL*, 15 April 1921, 1; "Tong War Breaks Out on Main Streets of the City," *PGC*, 12 April 1921, 4. The number of participants in the affray varies; BCPP constable Henry Avison, who apprehended one of the men, estimated that between thirty and forty men were fighting. See *R. v. Long Quon*, BCA, GR 2239, box 1, file 27/21, 4.

96 See deposition of Henry Stanley Avison, BCA, GR 2239, file 27/1921, *Rex v. Long Quon*, 2; deposition of Chief Constable A.F. Sinclair, BCA, GR 2239, file 25/1921, *Rex v. Wong Young*, 2; testimony of Chief Constable Alexander Sinclair, at trial before Justice Gregory and jury in the Supreme Court of British Columbia, 18 June 1921, *Rex v. Mah Gong*, BCA, GR 2239, file 10/1921, 47.

97 "Chinese Cases Congest City Police Court," *PGC*, 15 April 1921, 1.

98 "Chinese Cases Congest City Police Court," *PGC*, 15 April 1921, 1.

99 "Chinese Cases Congest City Police Court," *PGC*, 15 April 1921, 1. Cohen, a colourful confidence man, insinuated himself into the "Chinese" community in western Canada before travelling to China in 1922, where he became linked with Sun Yat-sen; see Daniel Levy, *Two-Gun Cohen: A Biography* (New York: St. Martin's Press, 1997). Also see "Morris A. Cohen Continues to Hold High Place in Chinese Politics," *PGC*, 28 June 1923, 2, and "Morris A. Cohen Brings Word That Sun Yat Sen Is Now on the Mend," *PGC*, 12 March 1925, 4.

100 "Supreme Court Assizes Have Been Concluded," *TL*, 24 June 1921, 1.

101 "Justice Fulfilled," *CTimes*, 21 June 1921, 3.

102 "Tong War Breaks Out on Main Streets of the City," *PGC*, 12 April 1921, 4.

103 See "Prince George Bonds to Be Sold in City," *VDW*, 26 March 1921, 17.

104 Council minutes, 8 April 1921, Prince George City Hall, 2; "Council Plans a Clean-Up on Coloured Undesirables," *PGC*, 19 April 1921, 1. Also see "Shake-up Threatened in the City Government," *PGC*, 22 April 1921, 1, and "Bootleggers Must Go Is Decision of City Council," *TL*, 22 April 1921, 1. The same language referring to "undesirables" was used by Vancouver mayor C.E. Tisdall in October 1922. See "Must Be Freed of Riff-Raff: All Undesirables to Be Driven from Town," *VDW*, 11 October 1922, 1. Thanks to Lani Russwurm for passing on this item.

105 Robin W. Winks, *The Blacks in Canada: A History*, 2nd ed. (Montreal and Kingston: McGill-Queen's University Press, 1997), 300–13 and 320–25; Sarah-Jane Mathieu, *North of the Color Line: Migration and Black Resistance in Canada, 1870–1955* (Chapel Hill: University of North Carolina Press, 2010), 22–27; "Negroes Invading Alberta," *FGH*, 11 February 1911, 8. Broadly, see Barrington Walker, *Race on Trial: Black Defendants in Ontario's Criminal Courts, 1858–1958* (Toronto: Osgoode Society for Canadian Legal History, 2010) and Walker, ed., *The African Canadian Legal Odyssey: Historical Essays* (Toronto: Osgoode Society for Canadian Legal History, 2012).

106 "Chief of Police M.B. MacLennan Killed Last Night While Leading an Attack against Desperate Negro," *TP*, 21 March 1917, 12. On Malcolm Bruce MacLennan, see Greg Marquis, in *Dictionary of Canadian Biography*, vol. 14, http://www.biographi.ca/en/bio/maclennan _malcolm_bruce_14E.html. On the MacLennan case, see Lani Russwurm, "What Frankie Said," 29 December 2008, *Past Tense: Vancouver Histories*, https://pasttensevancouver. wordpress.com/2008/12/29/what-frankie-said/. Angus McLaren noted that both MacLennan in 1917 and patrolman Robert G. MacBeath in 1922 were killed by Black men. See Angus McLaren, *The Trials of Masculinity: Policing Sexual Boundaries, 1870–1930* (Chicago: University of Chicago Press, 1997): 120.

107 See Emily Murphy, "The Grave Drug Menace," *Maclean's* 33, 3 (15 February 1920): 5, in which she rhetorically asks why an educated gentlewoman might consort "with the lowest classes of yellow and black men." Also see "The Underground System: Some Secrets of the Sale and Distribution of Drugs," *Maclean's* 33, 5 (15 March 1920): 13, where she refers

to the role of railway porters in smuggling drugs and "a certain blackamoor" whom she tried in Edmonton. Her later reference to "the faithful boys" who worked as porters was laden with racism. Also see Emily Murphy, *The Black Candle* (Toronto: Thomas Allen, 1922), 188–89. On a broader context, see Catherine Carstairs, *Jailed for Possession: Illegal Drug Use, Regulation, and Power in Canada, 1920–1961* (Toronto: University of Toronto Press, 2010), 21–27.

108 According to the 1921 Census, Charles Stuart Sager arrived in Canada in 1906 and was naturalized in 1909. While he and his parents were born in the United States, he claimed English origins, despite telling the *Fort George Herald* that he had been born "on the corner of Taylor and Jackson Street" in San Francisco. Sager gained prominence in March 1898, when the *Colored American* magazine of Washington, DC, reported that Sager, identified as from St. Paul, Minnesota, had produced a play entitled *The South in Slavery*. A year later, he produced a pageant entitled "The Negro" that opened in the Park Theatre, in Hannibal, Missouri, marking Emancipation Day celebrations. Appointed theatre manager, Sager toured the production through the American Midwest and West, including Great Falls, Montana, in 1895. For the latter, see "Comedy and Cake Walk," *GFDT* 26 November 1895, 1. Around 1900, he relocated to Chicago, where, in 1906, he became stage manager at the Black-owned Pekin Theater. See Errol G. Hill and James V. Hatch, eds., *A History of African American Theater* (New York: Cambridge University Press, 2003), 140; Thomas Bauman, *The Pekin: The Rise and Fall of Chicago's First Black-Owned Theater* (Champaign: University of Illinois Press, 2014), 36–37; Anthony D. Hill and Douglas Q. Barnett, *Historical Dictionary of African American Theatre* (Plymouth, UK: Scarecrow Press, 2009), 391; Bernard L. Petersen Jr., *A Century of Musicals in Black and White: An Encyclopedia of Musical Stage Works by, about, or Involving African Americans* (Westport, CT: Greenwood Press, 1993), 228; and Kate Van Orden, ed., *Music and the Cultures of Print* (New York: Routledge, 2000), 210. He was forty-seven years old at the time of his interview with the *Herald* in 1913. See "Canyon Cache Items," *FGH*, 20 September 1913, 5. The census of 1921 does not indicate that he was a Black man. See Canada, *Census*, 1921, District 14, Sub-district 58 (Prince George), 1. His wife, Willa Doulia Sager, died on 20 November 1926 at age fifty-four and was interred in Prince George: see Richard Coreless Funeral Ledger, NBCA, 2007.23, (part 4), 131.

109 *FGH*, 31 October 1914, 4; "Metropolitan Baths on Third Avenue," *FGH*, 26 March 1915, 4; "The Metropolitan Baths," *PGP*, 10 April 1915, 4.

110 Reverend H. Lloyd Morrison, Tweed, ON, to Reverend F.E. Runnalls, Prince George, 19 January 1943, Reverend F.J. Runnalls Papers, EPA, A 986.5.4a.

111 Unless otherwise cited, the following is based on "An Open Letter to the Honorable the Mayor and Members of Council, City of Prince George," *TL*, 6 May 1921, 4.

112 A popular account of the Halden family's disappearance was written by former BCPP deputy commissioner Cecil Clark. See his "Disappearance of the Halden Family," in *Tales of the British Columbia Provincial Police* (Sidney, BC: Gray's Publishing, 1971), 135–42, and "What Ever Happened to the Halden Family?" *BC Provincial Police Stories* (Surrey: Heritage House Publishing Company, 1986), 1: 84–89.

113 "Notice," *CO*, 8 January 1921, A1.

114 "Evidence of Foul Play Brought Out," *SP*, 27 April 1921, 1; "Report Discovery of Human Remains in West Mystery," *LP*, 27 April 1921, 1; "Quesnel Murder Mystery," *WFP*, 27 April 1921, 1; "Mysterious Case May Be Solved by Clues," *Bassano (AB) Mail*, 28 April 1921, 1;

"Quesnel Farm Mystery," *MG*, 28 April 1921, 9; "BC Family Was Obliterated: A Very Weird Case," *SDS*, 28 April 1921, 9; "Mystery of a Family," *WBW*, 28 April 1921, 8.

115 "No Solution as yet to Vanished Family Mystery," *PGC*, 29 April 1921, 1; "Only a Sheep, They Find," *SP*, 29 April 1921, 2; "Were Remains of Sheep," *MG*, 29 April 1921, 8.

116 "Committed for Trial," *CO*, 14 May 1921, A4; "Mystery Case Echoed in Theft Charge," *PGC*, 17 May 1921, 3; "Quesnel Man Is Committed for Trial," *TL*, 20 May 1921, 3.

117 "Supreme Court Assizes Have Been Concluded," *TL*, 24 June 1921, 1; *CO*, 25 June 1921, A1; "Clark in Okalla," *PGC*, 30 June 1921, 2.

118 "Clark Found Guilty," *PGC*, 18 November 1921, 1; "Guilty of Stealing the Halden Jewels," *TP*, 19 November 1921, 27; "Assize Cases at Prince George," *VDT*, 19 November 1921, 2; "David Clark Is Given Two Years," *TP*, 21 November 1921, 1; "Interesting Story of the Vanished Family Mystery," *PGC*, 22 November 1921, 1 and 5.

119 "Quesnel Trio Have Vanished," *TP*, 9 June 1922, 25; "Halden Case Still Is Deep Mystery," *VDW*, 10 June 1922, 23; "Estate of Vanished Woman Now with Administrator," *TL*, 16 June 1922, 3; "Mystery Not Solved Yet," *TP*, 19 July 1922, 3; "Whole Family Lost to Sight," *WT*, 4 August 1922, 15.

120 "Clark Is Arrested on Forgery Charge," *TP*, 18 August 1923, 21; "Family Missing, Forgery Charge Is the Sequel," *VDW*, 18 August 1923, 13; "Clark Re-Arrested on Forgery Charge," *CO*, 25 August 1923, A1; "Faces Trial on Forgery Charge," *TP*, 20 September 1923, 11.

121 "Drug Addict Is Sent to Prison for Five Years," *VS*, 13 December 1923, 2; "Clark Draws Stiff Sentences for Forgery," *PGC*, 20 December 1923, 3; "Clark Draws Stiff Sentence," *CO*, 29 December 1923, A1.

122 "Court Presumes Halden Dead," *TP*, 18 May 1928, 30.

123 "Discovery of Three Skeletons May Solve Tragic Cariboo Mystery," *TP*, 28 July 1934, 1; "Finding of Skulls and Car Not True," *CO*, 4 August 1924, A1.

124 "BC Family Was Obliterated: A Very Weird Case," *SDS*, 28 April 1921, 9.

125 The details of Elizabeth Coward's life are taken from Pierre M. Coté, deputy minister of justice, "Memorandum for the Honorable the Minister of Justice re The King vs Elizabeth Coward," 9 December 1915, *R. v. Elizabeth Coward*, LAC, RG 13, vol. 1486, file 56.

126 "To Seek Reprieve for Mrs. Coward," *TP*, 13 November 1915, 16.

127 Elizabeth Coward, testimony, *R. v. Elizabeth Coward*, LAC, RG 13, vol. 1486, file 56, 202. The page numbers refer to a repaginated version of the trial transcript, beginning with the first page of the trial evidence contained in the second *Coward* case file housed with LAC. This pagination corresponds with the original pagination on the transcript, which, unfortunately, is not consistently recorded on each page. "To Seek Reprieve for Mrs. Coward," *TP*, 13 November 1915, 16.

128 Elizabeth Coward, testimony, *R. v. Elizabeth Coward*, LAC, RG 13, vol. 1486, file 56, 207. There was a question about whether Margaret was born of Elizabeth's first marriage. The *Province* stated that, when her first husband was killed, Elizabeth was pregnant. "To Seek Reprieve for Mrs. Coward," *TP*, 13 November 1915, 16.

129 "Woman to Be Hanged," *ETR*, 15 November 1915, 2; "Woman to Hang for Iowa Man's Murder," *QCT*, 17 November 1915, 2.

130 Rose Dell, testimony, *R. v. Elizabeth Coward*, LAC, RG 13, vol. 1486, file 56, 192.

131 The letters were employed as evidence demonstrating Elizabeth's vindictiveness. William Hart, Pinkerton Detective Agency, testimony, *R. v. Elizabeth Coward*, LAC, RG 13, vol. 1486, file 56, 100.

132 William Hart, Pinkerton Detective Agency, testimony, *R. v. Elizabeth Coward*, LAC, RG 13, vol. 1486, file 56, 104. Elizabeth Coward, testimony, *R. v. Elizabeth Coward*, LAC, RG 13, vol. 1486, file 56, 219.

133 Elizabeth Coward, testimony, *R. v. Elizabeth Coward*, LAC, RG 13, vol. 1486, file 56, 194. It was Griffiths Roberts's cabin. See Griffiths Roberts testimony, *R. v. Elizabeth Coward*, LAC, RG 13, vol. 1486, file 56, 117.

134 Wright's *Northern British Columbia Index and Guide* for 1916 records that "J.E. Houson" was the local government agent in Fort St. James. The *Prince George Post* spelled the name "Hooson," the *Inland Sentinel* of Kamloops and the *Victoria Daily Times* offered "Hosson," while the trial transcript used "Houston." All versions undoubtedly referred to the Vanderhoof coroner and stipendiary magistrate. See F.S. Wright, *Northern British Columbia Index and Guide: General Information of the District* (Prince Rupert: F.S. Wright, 1916), 48; "Mother and Daughter of Stewart Lake Settler Charged with Murder," *PGP,* 18 September 1915, 1; "Held for Murder," *VDT,* 25 September 1915, 16; and "Murder Trial at Assize Involves Two Women," *IS,* 29 September 1915, 3.

135 Chief Constable William R. Dunwoody, duty log, 9–14 September 1915, BCA, GR 445, box 26, file 7. In their two accounts of the *Coward* case, Beverley Boissery and Murray Greenwood were openly antagonistic toward Dunwoody, arguing that he tilted the evidence to bring about Elizabeth's conviction. The claim, which may have been rooted in a reaction to Cecil Clark's gung-ho heroic depiction of the chief constable, is unsupported by evidence. See F. Murray Greenwood and Beverley Boissery, *Uncertain Justice: Canadian Women and Capital Punishment, 1754–1953* (Toronto: Osgoode Society for Canadian Legal History and Dundurn Press, 2000), 112–18, and Boissery and Greenwood, "The Trial of Elizabeth Coward: A British Columbia Woman Escapes the Noose," *The Beaver* 81, 3 (2001): 20–25.

136 David Henry Hoye (liveryman), testimony, *R. v. Elizabeth Coward*, LAC, RG 13, vol. 1486, file 56, 120.

137 Constable Rupert Raynor, testimony, *R. v. Elizabeth Coward*, LAC, RG 13, vol. 1486, file 56, 135. Cecil Clark claimed that Coward lifted the tub and looked beneath it, as if to confirm that the revolver was there. The trial testimonies do not support his contention. See Cecil Clark, "The Woman in the Plot," in *Tales of the British Columbia Provincial Police* (Sidney, BC: Gray's Publishing, 1971), 114.

138 Chief Constable William R. Dunwoody, duty log, 19–30 September 1915, BCA, GR 445, box 26, file 7.

139 Mr. Justice Denis Murphy, charge to the jury, *R. v. Elizabeth Coward*, LAC, RG 13, vol. 1486, file 56, 244.

140 Karen Dubinsky and Franca Iacovetta, "Murder, Womanly Virtue, and Motherhood: The Case of Angelina Napolitano, 1911–1922," *Canadian Historical Review* 72, 4 (1991): 505–31. Also useful is Kimberley White, *Negotiating Responsibility: Law, Murder, and States of Mind* (Vancouver: UBC Press, 2008). At a number of points, particularly concerning the roles played by psychiatrists, White's book intersects with Carolyn Strange, *The Death Penalty and Sex Murder in Canadian History* (Toronto: Osgoode Society for Canadian Legal History and University of Toronto Press, 2020).

141 On the reconstruction and portrayal of an accused woman's life, see White, *Negotiating Responsibility,* 120–21.

142 See "Mother and Daughter of Stewart Lake Settler Charged with Murder," *PGP,* 15 September 1915, 1; "Mother and Daughter Are Arrested on Charge of Killing Farmer," *EJ,*

20 September 1915, 1; "Woman Is Given Death Penalty," *TP*, 8 October 1915, 1; "Mrs. Coward Will Hang for Murder," *VS*, 8 October 1915, 1; "Guilty of Killing Husband," *EDB*, 8 October 1915, 1; "Shot Her Husband with a Revolver," *EJ*, 8 October 1915, 15; "BC Woman Found Guilty of Murder; to Hang Dec. 6," *LP*, 8 October 1915, 2; "Sentenced BC Woman to Die," *MG*, 8 October 1915, 19.

143 "New Trial Sought by Mrs. Dell's Daughter," *VDW*, 25 October 1915, 2.

144 "Woman to Be Hanged," *ETR*, 2; "Woman to Hang for Iowa Man's Murder," *Quad City Times* (Davenport, IA), 2.

145 *Mania transitoria* is temporary insanity.

146 Frank Richards, justice of the peace, "Must She Die?" *CH*, 29 November 1915, 6.

147 "Two Women to Die on Scaffold in Canada," *VDNA*, 2 December 1915, 1; "Two Women under Sentence of Death," *VDT*, 2 December 1915, 2; "Two Women Due to Be Hanged During Month," *SP*, 3 December 1915, 1; "Two Women May Hang in Christmas Week," *BNR*, 4 December 1915, 3.

148 "Wilds of Province Affected Her Mind," *VS*, 21 December 1915, 4.

149 "Mrs. Coward's Case," *IS*, 21 December 1915, 7.

150 Carolyn Strange, "The Lottery of Death: Capital Punishment, 1867–1976," *Manitoba Law Journal* 23, 3 (January 1996): 594–619; Strange, "Determining the Punishment of Sex Criminals in Confederation-Era Canada: A Matter of National Policy," *Canadian Historical Review* 99, 4 (December 2018): 541–62; and Strange, *The Death Penalty*.

151 J. Edward Bird, Bird, Macdonald, and Ross, Barristers and Solicitors, Vancouver, to the Honorable [Charles Doherty], minister of justice, Ottawa, 23 October 1915, 2, *R. v. Elizabeth Coward*, LAC, RG 13, vol. 1486, file 56, vol. 2.

152 "Murder Cases Will Be Tried at Wetaskiwin," 4 October 1915, *CH*, 9; "Wetaskiwin Murder Case Is Being Tried," *CH*, 6 October 1915, 8; "Murder Charge against Woman at Wetaskiwin," *EJ*, 6 October 1915, 2; "Son-in-Law in Granary was Star Witness," *CH*, 7 October 1915, 5; "To Be Hung in McLeod," *FMS*, 7 October 1915, 1; "Two Western Women Are Condemned to Death by Hanging for Murders," *CH*, 8 October 1915, 14; "Full Text of the Decision of Appeal Court Which Would Send Jennie Hawkes to the Gallows," *EMB*, 9 November 1915, 5.

153 "More Time for Petition," *EJ*, 9 November 1915, 2; "Mrs. Jennie Hawkes Meeting on Friday," *EMB*, 11 November 1915, 11; "Appeal for Jennie Hawkes Not Made Because She Is a Woman," *EJ*, 13 November 1915, 2; "Strong Appeals Are Made for Clemency to Mrs. Jennie Hawkes," *EMB*, 13 November 1915, 1.

154 "Huge Petition to Save Woman from Gallows," *WS*, 8 December 1915, 1; "Mrs. Coward Too," *CH*, 15 December 1915, 1; "Commuted Sentence," *OC*, 15 December 1915, 11; "How Good News Came to Jennie Hawkes," *EJ*, 18 December 1915, 9.

155 J. Edward Bird, Bird, Macdonald, and Ross, Barristers and Solicitors, Vancouver, to the Honorable [Charles Doherty], minister of justice, Ottawa, 23 November 1915, 2, *R. v. Elizabeth Coward*, LAC, RG 13, vol. 1486, file 56, vol. 2.

156 W.J. Bowser, attorney general, Victoria, to the Honorable C.J. Doherty, minister of justice, Ottawa, 30 November 1915, *R. v. Elizabeth Coward*, LAC, RG 13, vol. 1486, file 56, vol. 2.

157 Pierre M. Coté, "Memorandum for the Honorable [Charles Doherty] the Minister of Justice, *The King vs. Elizabeth Coward*," 9 December 1915, *R. v. Elizabeth Coward*, LAC, RG 13, vol. 1486, file 56, vol. 2, 28–29.

158 See "Governor-General Approves of Clemency," *SP*, 21 December 1915, 6, and "Wilds of Province Affected Her Mind," *VS*, 21 December 1915, 4.

159 Angus McLaren, "Males, Migrants, and Murder in British Columbia, 1900–1923," in *On the Case: Explorations in Social History,* ed. Franca Iacovetta and Wendy Mitchinson (Toronto: University of Toronto Press, 1998), 159–80.

160 The details of the family's trek from North Dakota to Moose Jaw and onward to Red Deer, Edson, and Jasper House (Fittshugh) are narrated in Ed Sager and Mike Frye, *The Bootlegger's Lady* (Surrey, BC: Hancock House Publishers, 1993).

161 See "Dr. Thomas O'Hagan – Obituary," *Alberta Medical Bulletin* 21, 2 (May 1957): 64.

162 "Warrant Remanding a Prisoner," *R. v. Edith Frye,* BCA, GR 2486, file 45/1922.

163 "Mrs. Fred Frye Kills Husband," *KSS,* 17 November 1922, 1.

164 "Murdered Husband," *VDC,* 18 November 1922, 1; "Coast Woman Held for Death of Her Husband," *LP,* 18 November 1922, 29; "Woman Is Charged with Murdering Her Husband," *WFPEB,* 18 November 1922, 45.

165 "Woman Kills in Tete Jaune Tragedy," *VDC,* 19 November 1922, 1; "Mrs. Frye Is Committed," *TL,* 23 November 1922, 1; "This Woman Fought for the Lives of Her Children," *PGC,* 24 November 1922, 1; "Self-Defense Is Plea of BC Woman Slayer," *LP,* 25 November 1922, 9; "Husband-Killer Sent for Trial," *MS,* 25 November 1922, 37; "Charged with Murder," *MG,* 25 November 1922, 11.

166 "Asking Attorney-General to Release Mrs. Frye," *TL,* 30 November 1922, 1.

167 *KT,* 2 December 1922, 2.

168 "Prince George Women Take up the Case of Mrs. Frye," *PGC,* 5 December 1922, 1. An invitation to sign the petition appeared on the issue's fourth page. The petitions were available at the Prince George Drug Store, Steacy's Pharmacy, and merchants Peck and Gillis, and Hughes and Drake.

169 "Women Send Petition for Release of Mrs. Frye," *PGC,* 13 December 1922, 1.

170 "Recognizance of Bail," 22 December 1922, *R. v. Edith Frye,* BCA, GR 2486, file 45/1922.

171 "Petition in the Case of Mrs. Frye Is Favorably Received," *PGC,* 29 December 1922, 1.

172 See J.L. White, deputy provincial secretary, 21 December 1922, and Deputy Inspector Parsons, South Fort George, to Constable A.F. Sinclair, Lucerne, 27 December 1922, *R. v. Edith Frye,* BCA, GR 2486, file 45/1922.

173 "Mr. Justice Morrison to Preside at Assize: But So Far There Are No Assizes to Be Presided at in Northern District," *PGC,* 14 April 1923, 8; "Change of Venue Granted," *VDT,* 16 April 1923, 9; "Trial of Mrs. Frye for Murder of Husband to Take Place in Kamloops," *KT,* 24 April 1923, 1; "Murder Trial Venue Changed," *VS,* 29 April 1923, 1.

174 "Women Interested in Murder Trial," *TP,* 19 May 1923, 22; "Woman to Face Murder Charge," *CH,* 21 May 1923, 1; "Woman to Be Tried in Kamloops, BC, Murder Charge," *EMB,* 21 May 1923, 3; "Women Raise Fund for Murder Defence," *NDN,* 21 May 1923, 1.

175 The topic of women jurors had provoked animated conversations in British Columbia since early 1921. "Women as Jurors," *VDW,* 27 January 1921, 4; "The Woman in the Jury Box," *VDW,* 29 January 1921, 4; "Women Jurors," *TP,* 8 March 1921, 6; "Women in Juries," *VDW,* 9 March 1921, 4; "Women Not to Be Picked for Jury Service," *VDW,* 14 March 1922, 15; "Women Now Required to Do Jury Duty," *PGC,* 15 December 1922, 1; "Women to Sit on BC Juries," *TP,* 15 December 1922, 4; "Women Eligible for Jury Duty," *VDW,* 15 December 1922, 16; "Women Jurors," *TP,* 16 December 1922, 6.

176 "Great Interest Manifested in Court," *KSS,* 29 May 1923, 1; "Mrs. Frye's Trial Opens," *PRDN,* 30 May 1923, 1; "Killed Husband in Self-Defence," *CH,* 31 May 1923, 1; "Mrs. Frye Found Not Guilty of Murdering Her Husband," *KT,* 31 May 1923, 1; "Woman Freed on

Murder Charge," *VS*, 31 May 1923, 13; "Mrs. Frye Found Not Guilty," *KSS*, 1 June 1923, 1 and 6; "Mrs. Frye Acquitted on Murder Charge," *PGC*, 7 June 1923, 7.

177   *KT*, 31 May 1923, 2.

Epilogue: That Prince George Business

1   Gordon Hak, "The Communists and the Unemployed in the Prince George District, 1930–1935," *BC Studies* 68 (Winter 1985–86): 45–61. A broader treatment focused on Vancouver during these years is Michael Ekers, "'The Dirty Scruff': Relief and the Production of the Unemployed in Depression Era British Columbia," *Antipode* 44, 4 (2012): 1119–42. Todd MacCallum's evocative "The Great Depression's First History? The Vancouver Archives of Major J.S. Matthews and the Writing of Hobo History," *Canadian Historical Review* 87, 1 (March 2006): 79–107, offers intriguing insights concentrated on Vancouver.

2   "Men Receiving Direct Relief to Be Put to Work," *PGC*, 19 February 1931, 1; "Sixteen Hundred Men Given Relief Work by Government," *PGC*, 19 February 1931, 2; "Relief Vote Will Be Exhausted by End of Month," *PGC*, 12 March 1931, 1. According to the 1931 Census, Prince George's population in 1931 was 2,479. See Dominion Bureau of Statistics, *Seventh Census of Canada, 1931*, vol. 2, *Population*, Table 12, "Population of Canada by Provinces, counties or census divisions and subdivisions, 1871–1931: Division no., 8 British Columbia" (Ottawa: J.O. Patenaude, Printer to His Most Excellent Majesty the King, 1933).

3   "City Relief Will Be Discontinued in Two Weeks," *PGC*, 26 March 1931, 1.

4   "Unemployed Men Demand Relief from Government," *PGC*, 18 June 1931, 1; "Tolmie Says Early Start to Be Made on Highway Extension," *PGC*, 25 June 1931, 1; and Hak, "The Communists and the Unemployed," 48.

5   "Relief Strikers in Clash with the Provincial Police," *PGC*, 16 May 1935, 1.

6   "Rifles Fired in BC Riot: Police Forced to Shoot over Heads of Attacking Mob at Pr. George," *TP*, 13 May 1935, 1 and 2; "Police, Strikers, CLASH," *VS*, 13 May 1935, 1; "Police Fire Pistols to Halt Clash," *VDC*, 14 May 1935, 1 and 3.

7   "Prince George Will Have Patriotic Parade Tomorrow," *PGC*, 23 May 1935, 1; "Prince George Staged Big Demonstration Empire Day," *PGC*, 30 May 1935, 1.

8   "Prince George Staged Big Demonstration Empire Day," *PGC*, 30 May 1935, 1.

9   "Friday's Parade Should Carry Its Lesson," *PGC*, 30 May 1935, 2.

10   "Sentences Imposed on Rioters Commendable," *PGC*, 13 June 1935, 2 and "Men Engaged in Rioting Received Sentence Tuesday," *PGC*, 13 June 1935.

11   "Sentences Imposed on Rioters Commendable," *PGC*, 13 June 1935, 2.

12   Mia Reimers, "The Glamour and the Horror: A Social History of Wartime in Northwest British Columbia, 1939–1945" (master's thesis, University of Northern British Columbia, 1999).

13   Tom Makowsky, "Prince George at War," in *Sa ts'e: Historical Perspectives on Northern British Columbia*, ed. Thomas Thorner (Prince George: College of New Caledonia Press, 1989), 444.

14   See Mercedes DuBois, "'Physically We Are a Mighty Nation, Nationally We Are Children': Conscription and Identity in Canada, 1940–1945" (master's thesis, University of Northern British Columbia, 2016), 48–49.

15 See, generally, Daniel Byers, "Mobilizing Canada: The National Resources Mobilization Act, the Department of National Defence, and Compulsory Military Service in Canada, 1940–1945" (PhD diss., McGill University, 2000); Byers, *Zombie Army: The Canadian Army and Conscription in the Second World War* (Vancouver: UBC Press, 2016); Reimers, "The Glamour and the Horror," 34–36; and DuBois, "'Physically We Are a Mighty Nation,'" 11–12.

16 "'Grievances' Parade by Zombies," *PGC*, 30 November 1944, 1 and 4; "Found Wanting," *PGC*, 30 November 1944, 2; Makowsky, "Prince George at War," 444–45; Reimers, "The Glamour and the Horror," 35–36.

17 "IWA Strike Orders Idles Thousands," *PGC*, 28 September 1953, 1; "IWA Men on Strike in North," *TP*, 28 September 1953, 1; "Workers Trek Back to Jobs as IWA, Employers Agree," *PGC*, 7 January 1954, 1. Also see Ken Bernsohn, *Cutting Up the North: The History of the Forest Industry in the Northern Interior* (Vancouver: Hancock House, 1981), 66–75; Andrew Neufeld and Andrew Parnaby, *The IWA in Canada: The Life and Times of an Industrial Union* (Vancouver: New Star Books, 2000), 125–31; and Gordon Hak, *Capital and Labour in the British Columbia Forestry Industry, 1934–74* (Vancouver: UBC Press, 2007), 91–92.

18 "Hurtful Strike," *PGC*, 29 October 1984, 4. The editorial misdates the IWA strike as 1952 rather than 1953.

19 Bernsohn, *Cutting Up the North*, 70–71.

20 "New Union Gov't Parley Set in BC Woods Strike: Violence Flares at Prince George," *VS*, 13 November 1953, 1; "IWA Protests Use of 'Goons,'" *TP*, 20 November 1953, 29; "Violence and Intimidation Charged in Lumber Strike," *VS*, 17 December 1953, 19.

21 Bernsohn, *Cutting Up the North*, 72–73. See also editorial, *PGC*, 26 November 1953, 4.

22 "The Lights Are Going Out," *PGC*, 8 October 1953, 2. See also "Operator's Opinion," *PGC*, 13 October 1953, 3.

23 See George F. Sullivan, "Defends Workers," *PGC*, 15 October 1953, 5. Sullivan, in turn, drew an angry rebuke from "Veteran," who described the strikers as being opposed to Canadian values: Veteran, "Anti-Canadian," *PGC*, 22 October 1953, 2.

24 Vera Kelsey, *British Columbia Rides a Star* (Toronto: J.M. Dent and Sons, 1958), 58.

25 "Strides Touch Off Bloody Gang War," *PGC*, 27 April 1953, 1. See also Jonathan Swainger, "Teen Trouble and Community Identity in Post–Second World War Northern British Columbia," *Journal of Canadian Studies* 47, 2 (Spring 2013): 150–79.

26 "Gang Terror Flares up in City," *PGC*, 8 April 1957, 1.

27 "Group Demands New Police Court Magistrate," *PGC*, 8 April 1957, 1.

28 "Prince George Asks Help – Hoodlums Running Wild – Magistrate under Fire," *TP*, 17 April 1957, 1 and 3; "Irate Mayor Wants Magistrate Fired," *VS*, 18 April 1957, 20.

29 "The Hoodlums in Prince George," *TP*, 20 April 1975, 6.

30 "Burnaby Police Probing Juvenile Protection Gang," *VNH*, 23 April 1957, 1.

31 *Province* Publicity Commended," *TP*, 27 April 1957, 48; "Hoodlums Hit at Principal," *PGC*, 29 April 1957, 1; "Police Quiz Students after Window-Smashing," *TP*, 30 April 1957, 3; "Prince George Rowdies Hit Principal's Home," *VS*, 30 April 1957, 3; "Rock Answers Teacher Stand," *VNH*, 1 May 1957, 1.

32 "Vice Principal Defends City High School Students," *PGC*, 23 April 1957, 3.

33 "Whipping of Thugs Sought," *TP*, 30 April 1957, 1.

34 "Mischief Penalty: Probation," *PGC*, 24 July 1985, 3.

35   See Carmela Patrias and Larry Savage, *Union Power: Solidarity and Struggle in Niagara* (Edmonton: Athabasca University Press, 2012) and Rod Mickleburgh, *On the Line: A History of the British Columbia Labour Movement* (Madeira Park, BC: Harbour Publishing, 2018).

36   "Police Probe Shooting," *PGC*, 11 January 1984, 1. Also see "Two Different Worlds: A Look at the Canadian Tire Dispute," *PGC*, 7 December 1985, 5, and Diane Bailey, "Marathon CanTire Strike Ending," *PGC*, 22 March 1986, 1.

37   John Spilker, "Pulp Mills Grind to Halt," *PGC*, 2 February 1984, 1; John Spilker, "Picket-Line Fighting Sparks Police Action," *PGC*, 29 February 1984, 1; "On the Picket Line," *PGC*, 8 March 1984, 4; "Lockout Ends, but Mills Still Idle," *PGC*, 2 April 1984, 1; John Spilker and Dave Paulson, "Pulp Unions Back on Job Today," *PGC*, 10 April 1984, 1; John Spilker, "College Support Staff on Strike," *PGC*, 29 August 1984, 1; John Spilker, "CNC Dispute Finally Ends," *PGC*, 16 October 1984, 1.

38   Clifford Geertz, "Notes on the Balinese Cockfight," in *The Interpretation of Culture* (New York: Basic Books, 1973), 448.

39   Ken McQueen and Patricia Treble, "Canada's Most Dangerous City: Prince George," *Maclean's*, 15 December 2011, https://www.macleans.ca/news/canada/crime-most-dangerous-cities.

40   Human Rights Watch, *Those Who Take Us Away: Abusive Policing and Failures in Protection of Indigenous Women and Girls in Northern British Columbia* (Washington, DC: Human Rights Watch, 2012).

41   "Former BC Judge Admits to Beating, Sexually Abusing Teens," CBC News, 3 May 2004, https://www.cbc.ca/news/canada/former-b-c-judge-admits-to-beating-sexually-abusing-teens-1.484272; Frank Peebles, "Hard Time: When Your Attacker Is the Judge," *PGC*, 1 March 2008, 13.

42   *Reclaiming Power and Place: The Final Report of the National Inquiry into Missing and Murdered Indigenous Women and Girls* (n.d.), https://www.mmiwg-ffada.ca/final-report/.

43   "Why the PM Should Call an Inquiry into Missing Aboriginal Women," *Maclean's*, 26 August 2014, https://www.macleans.ca/politics/ottawa/national-inquiry-into-missing-and-murdered-aboriginal-women/.

Bibliography

Unpublished Primary Documents

British Columbia Archives (BCA)

British Columbia. British Columbia attorney general. Correspondence (1872–1937), GR 0429.

–. British Columbia Provincial Police. Correspondence inward (1891–1910), GR 0055.

–. British Columbia Provincial Police. Correspondence inward (1910–12), GR 0056.

–. British Columbia Provincial Police. Correspondence outward (1864–1918), GR 0061.

–. British Columbia Provincial Police. Correspondence outward to attorney general (1898–1918), GR 0064.

–. British Columbia Provincial Police. Headquarters' personnel records (1896–1950), GR 0091.

–. British Columbia Provincial Police. (South Fort George) daily reports, GR 0445.

–. British Columbia Provincial Police. Superintendent, correspondence inward, GR 0066.

–. British Columbia Provincial Police. Superintendent, correspondence inward (1912–22), GR 0057.

–. British Columbia Provincial Police. Superintendent, correspondence inward from attorney general (1898–1912), GR 0063.

–. British Columbia Provincial Police. Superintendent, correspondence outward, GR 0067.

–. British Columbia Provincial Police. Superintendent, Prohibition files, GR 1425.

–. County Court (Fort George/Prince George), plaint and procedure book, GR 0017.

–. County Court (Prince George), appeals, GR 2791.

–. County Court (Prince George), criminal case files, GR 2788.

–. Kamloops Supreme Court criminal case files, GR 2486.

–. Mental Health Patient Records, GR 2880.

–. Supreme Court (Kamloops), record of assize, GR 2486.

–. Supreme Court (Prince George), cause book, GR 0016.

–. Supreme Court (Prince George), criminal case files, GR 2785.
–. Supreme Court (Prince George), jury lists, GR 0021.
–. Supreme Court (Prince George), record of assize, GR 0047.
Thomas William Stanner Parson Papers, MS 1134.

Library and Archives Canada (LAC)

Personnel Records of the First World War, Files of the Canadian Expeditionary Force, RG 150. https://www.bac-lac.gc.ca/eng/discover/military-heritage/first-world-war/personnel-records/Pages/personnel-records.aspx.
R. v. Albert Lester Clinger, RG 13, vol. 1469, file 554A.
R. v. Elizabeth Coward, RG 13, vol. 1485, files 1 and 2.
R. v. George Onooki, RG 13, vol. 1466, file 513A.

Other

Fort George Journal (New Caledonia), Hudson's Bay Company Archives, B.280/a/3.
Prince George City Bylaws, Prince George City Hall.
Prince George City Council Minutes, Prince George City Hall.
Reverend F.J. Runnalls Papers, Exploration Place Archives (Prince George), A 986.5.4a.
Richard Corless Funeral Ledger, Northern British Columbia Archives, 2007.23.1.1, https://search.nbca.unbc.ca/index.php/richard-corless-funeral-ledger.

PUBLISHED PRIMARY DOCUMENTS

British Columbia. *Annual Report of the Minister of Mines.*
–. *Annual Report of the Provincial Board of Health.*
–. *Annual Report of the Provincial Game Warden of the Province of British Columbia.*
–. *Annual Report of the Superintendent of Police Representing the Police and Prisons of British Columbia.*
–. *Annual Report of the Superintendent of Provincial Police.*
–. *British Columbia Provincial Police Regulations.*
–. *British Columbia Public Accounts.*
–. *Royal Commission re Albert Richard Baker, chairman of Game Conservation Board.* Victoria: William H. Cullin, Printer to the King's Most Excellent Majesty, 1922.
British Columbia Gazette.
Canada. "Annual Report of the Department of Indian Affairs." *Sessional Papers.*
–. "Annual Report of the North-West Mounted Police." *Sessional Papers.*
–. "Annual Report of the Royal Canadian Mounted Police." *Sessional Papers.*
–. "Fort George Indians." In *Federal and Provincial Collections of Minutes of Decision, Correspondence, and Sketches: Material Provided by the Joint Indian Reserve Commission and Indian Reserve Commission, 1876–1910,* 2010.
Grand Trunk Pacific Railway. *Correspondence Relating to Prince George Incorporation, 1913–1920.* Vol. 1. Prince George: College of New Caledonia, n.d.
Presbyterian Church of Canada. *Pre-Assembly Congress of the Presbyterian Church in Canada.* Toronto: Board of Foreign Missions, Presbyterian Church of Canada, 1913.
Social Service Congress, Ottawa – 1914: Report of Addresses and Proceedings. Toronto: Social Service Council of Canada, 1914.

Wright, F.S. *Northern British Columbia Index and Guide: General Information of the District.* Prince Rupert: F.S. Wright, 1916.

NEWSPAPERS/MAGAZINES

BC Saturday Sunset
Berlin News Record (Berlin; now Kitchener, ON)
Bismarck (ND) Tribune
British Columbia Magazine
British Columbia News (Kaslo)
Butte (MT) Daily Post
Calgary Herald
Cariboo Observer (Quesnel, BC)
Chicago Inter-Ocean
Chicago Tribune
Chinese Times (Vancouver)
Derby Daily Telegraph (UK)
Edmonton Daily Bulletin
Edmonton Journal
Edmonton Morning Bulletin
Evening Times Republican (Marshalltown, IA)
Fernie District Ledger
Fort George Herald
Fort George Tribune
Fort George Weekly Tribune
Great Falls Daily Tribune (Great Falls, MT)
Indianapolis Journal
Inland Sentinel (Kamloops, BC)
Interior News (Smithers, BC)
Kamloops Standard
Kamloops Standard Sentinel
Kamloops Telegram
Lethbridge Herald
Macleod Spectator (Fort Macleod, AB)
Minneapolis Journal
Minneapolis Star-Tribune
Montreal Gazette
Montreal Star
Nanaimo Daily News
National Post
Nelson (BC) Daily Canadian
New Denver (BC) Ledge
New York Times
Omineca Herald (New Hazelton, BC)
Ottawa Citizen
Ottawa Journal
Peace River Block News

Peace River Record
Prince George Citizen
Prince George Herald
Prince George Leader
Prince George Post
Prince George Star
Prince Rupert Daily News
Prince Rupert Journal
Prince Rupert Optimist
Quad City Times (Davenport, IA)
Regina Leader-Post
Saint Paul (MN) Globe
San Francisco Examiner
Sandon (BC) Paystreak
Saskatoon Star Phoenix
Saturday Night Magazine
Sault Daily Star (Sault St. Marie, ON)
Shoulder Strap
Similkameen Star (Similkameen, BC)
Spokane (WA) Chronicle
Toronto Globe
Toronto Mail and Empire
Toronto Star
Vancouver Daily News Advertiser
Vancouver Daily Province
Vancouver Daily World
Vancouver News Herald
Vancouver Province
Vancouver Sun
Vancouver World
Victoria Daily Colonist
Victoria Daily Times
Victoria Times Colonist
Weekly British Whig (Kingston, ON)
Westminster Hall Magazine (Vancouver, BC)
Windsor (ON) Star
Winnipeg Free Press
Winnipeg Free Press Evening Bulletin
Winnipeg Saturday Post
Winnipeg Tribune

Secondary Literature

Ajzenstadt, Mimi. "The Medical-Moral Economy of Regulations: Alcohol Legislation in BC, 1871–1925." PhD diss., Simon Fraser University, 1992.

Anderson, Kay. *Vancouver's Chinatown: Racial Discourse in Canada, 1875–1980.* Montreal and Kingston: McGill-Queen's University Press, 1991.

Anholt, Dennis Munroe. "Friends of the Government: An Administrative History of the British Columbia Government Agents." PhD diss., University of Victoria, 1991.

Arnup, John D. *Middleton: The Beloved Judge.* Toronto: Osgoode Society for Canadian Legal History, 1988.

Artibise, Alan. "Boosterism and the Development of Prairie Cities, 1871–1913." In *The Prairie West: Historical Readings,* edited by R. Douglas Francis and Howard Palmer, 515–43. Edmonton: Pica Pica Press, 1992.

Ball, Georgiana Genevieve. "A History of Wildlife Management in British Columbia to 1918." Master's thesis, University of Victoria, 1981.

Bauman, Thomas. *The Pekin: The Rise and Fall of Chicago's First Black-Owned Theater.* Champaign: University of Illinois Press, 2014.

Belshaw, John. *Colonization and Community: The Vancouver Island Coalfield and the Making of the British Columbia Working Class.* Montreal and Kingston: McGill-Queen's University Press, 2002.

Bernshon, Ken. *Cutting Up the North: The History of the Forest Industry in the Northern Interior.* Vancouver: Hancock House, 1981.

–. *Slabs, Scabs and Skidders: A History of the IWA in the Central Interior.* Prince George: IWA Local I-424, 1981.

Betke, Carl. "Pioneers and Police on the Canadian Prairies, 1885–1914." *Historical Papers/ Communications historiques* 15, 1 (1980): 9–32.

Blomley, Nicholas. "Law, Property, and the Geography of Violence: The Frontier, the Survey, and the Grid." *Annals of the Association of American Geographers* 93, 1 (March 2003): 121–41.

Boissery, Beverley, and F. Murray Greenwood. "The Trial of Elizabeth Coward: A British Columbia Woman Escapes the Noose." *The Beaver* 81, 3 (2001): 20–25.

Bottomley, John. "Ideology, Planning, and the Landscape: The Business Community, Urban Reform, and the Establishment of Town Planning in Vancouver, British Columbia, 1900–1940." PhD diss., University of British Columbia, 1977.

Boudreau, Michael. *City of Order: Crime and Society in Halifax, 1918–35.* Vancouver: UBC Press, 2012.

Bourke, Joanna. "Feature: Fear, Ambivalence and Admiration." *History Workshop Journal* 55 (2003): 111–33.

Brown, R. Blake. *Arming and Disarming: A History of Gun Control in Canada.* Toronto: Osgoode Society for Canadian Legal History, 2012.

Bumby, Anna. "The Sales Campaign of George J. Hammond and the Natural Resources Security Company." Undergraduate essay, College of New Caledonia, 1981.

Byers, Daniel. "Mobilizing Canada: The National Resources Mobilization Act, the Department of National Defence, and Compulsory Military Service in Canada, 1940–1945." PhD diss., McGill University, 2000.

–. *Zombie Army: The Canadian Army and Conscription in the Second World War.* Vancouver: UBC Press, 2016.

Calam, John, ed. *Alex Lord's British Columbia: Recollections of a Rural School Inspector.* Vancouver: UBC Press, 1991.

Campbell, Robert. *Demon Rum or Easy Money: Government Control of Liquor in British Columbia from Prohibition to Privatization.* Ottawa: Carleton University Press, 1991.

Carstairs, Catherine. *Jailed for Possession: Illegal Drug Use, Regulation, and Power in Canada, 1920–1961.* Toronto: University of Toronto Press, 2010.

Cassel, Jay. *The Secret Plague: Venereal Disease in Canada, 1838–1939.* Toronto: University of Toronto Press, 1987.

Catte, Elizabeth. *Pure America: Eugenics and the Making of Modern Virginia.* Cleveland: Belt Publishing, 2021.

Chadwick, Narissa. "Regional Planning in British Columbia: 50 Years of Vision, Process and Practice." Master's thesis, University of British Columbia, 2002.

Chow, Lily. *Challenging Racism: Past and Present in the Prince George Chinese Canadian Community.* Prince George: Exploration Place, 2003.

–. *Sojourners to the North.* Prince George: Caitlin Press, 1996.

Christensen, Bev. *Prince George: Rivers, Railways, and Timber.* Burlington, ON: Windsor Publications, 1989.

Christie, Nancy, and Michael Gauvreau. *A Full-Orbed Christianity: The Protestant Churches and Social Welfare in Canada, 1900–1940.* Montreal and Kingston: McGill-Queen's University Press, 1996.

Clark, Cecil. "Disappearance of the Halden Family." In *Tales of the British Columbia Provincial Police,* 135–42. Sidney, BC: Gray's Publishing, 1971.

–. "What Ever Happened to the Halden Family?" *BC Provincial Police Stories* 1: 84–89. Surrey: Heritage House Publishing Co., 1986.

–. "The Woman in the Plot." In *Tales of the British Columbia Provincial Police,* 109–16. Sidney, BC: Gray's Publishing, 1971.

Con, Harry, Reginald J. Con, Graham Johnson, Edgar Wickberg, and William E. Willmott. *From China to Canada: A History of the Chinese Communities in Canada.* Toronto: McClelland and Stewart, 1988.

Coté, N. Omer. *Political Appointments, Parliaments, and the Judicial Bench in the Dominion of Canada, 1867 to 1895.* Ottawa: Thoburn and Co., 1896.

Cover, Robert M. "Violence and the Word." *Yale Law Journal* 95, 8 (July 1986): 1601–2.

Davies, Megan. *Into the House of Old: A History of Residential Care in British Columbia.* Montreal and Kingston: McGill-Queen's University Press, 2004.

–. "Old Age in British Columbia: The Case of the 'Lonesome Prospector.'" *BC Studies* 11 (Summer 1998): 41–66.

Dawson, Michael. *The Mountie from Dime Novel to Disney.* Toronto: Between the Lines, 1998.

Diaz, Robert. "Reshaping the Land: An Environmental History of Prince George, British Columbia." Master's thesis, University of Northern British Columbia, 1996.

Dubinsky, Karen. *Improper Advances: Rape and Heterosexual Conflict in Ontario, 1880–1929.* Chicago: University of Chicago Press, 1993.

Dubinsky, Karen, and Franca Iacovetta. "Murder, Womanly Virtue, and Motherhood: The Case of Angelina Napolitano, 1911–1922." *Canadian Historical Review* 72, 4 (1991): 505–31.

DuBois, Mercedes. "'Physically We Are a Mighty Nation, Nationally We Are Children': Conscription and Identity in Canada, 1940–1945." Master's thesis, University of Northern British Columbia, 2016.

Ekers, Michael. "'The Dirty Scruff': Relief and the Production of the Unemployed in Depression Era British Columbia." *Antipode* 44, 4 (2012): 1119–42.

Emsley, Clive, and Haia Shpayer-Makov, eds. *Police Detectives in History, 1750–1950.* Aldershot, UK: Ashgate Publishing, 2006.

Erickson, Lesley. *Westward Bound: Sex, Violence, the Law, and the Making of Settler Society.* Vancouver: UBC Press, 2011.

Fahrni, Magda, and Esyllt Jones. "Introduction." In *Epidemic Encounters: Influenza, Society, and Culture in Canada, 1918–20,* edited by Magda Fahrni and Esyllt Jones, 1–18. Vancouver: UBC Press, 2012.

Farr, David M.L. "The Organization of the Judicial System of the Colonies of Vancouver Island and British Columbia, 1849–1871." Bachelor's thesis, University of British Columbia, 1944.

–. "The Organization of the Judicial System of the Colonies of Vancouver Island and British Columbia, 1849–1871." *UBC Law Review* 3, 1 (March 1967): 1–35.

Fisher, Robin. *Duff Pattullo of British Columbia.* Toronto: University of Toronto Press, 1991.

Flanders, Judith. *The Invention of Murder: How Victorians Revelled in Death and Detection and Created Modern Crime.* London: Harper Press, 2011.

Foran, Max. "The Boosters in Boosterism: Some Calgary Examples." *Urban History* (October 1979): 77–82.

–. *High River and the Times: An Albertan Community and Its Weekly Newspaper, 1905–1966.* Edmonton: University of Alberta Press, 2004.

Foster, Hamar. "Law Enforcement in Nineteenth-Century British Columbia." *BC Studies* 63 (August 1984): 3–28.

Friedman, Lawrence M., and Robert V. Percival. *The Roots of Justice: Crime and Punishment in Alameda County, California, 1870–1910.* Chapel Hill: University of North Carolina Press, 1981.

Geertz, Clifford. "Common Sense as a Cultural System." In *Local Knowledge: Further Essays in Interpretative Anthropology,* 3rd ed., 79–93. New York: Basic Books, 2000.

–. "Notes on the Balinese Cockfight." In *The Interpretation of Cultures,* 412–53. New York: Basic Books, 1973.

Greenwood, F. Murray, and Beverley Boissery. *Uncertain Justice: Canadian Women and Capital Punishment, 1754–1953.* Toronto: Osgoode Society for Canadian Legal History and Dundurn Press, 2000.

Guha, Ranajit. "Not at Home in Empire." *Critical Inquiry* 23, 3 (Spring 1997): 482–93.

Hak, Gordon. *Capital and Labour in the British Columbia Forestry Industry, 1934–74.* Vancouver: UBC Press, 2007.

–. "The Communists and the Unemployed in the Prince George District, 1930–1935." *BC Studies* 68 (Winter 1985–86): 45–61.

Hamilton, Douglas. *Sobering Dilemma: A History of Prohibition in British Columbia.* Vancouver: Ronsdale Press, 2004.

Hatch, Frederick John. "The British Columbia Police, 1858–1871." Master's thesis, University of British Columbia, 1955.

Hay, Douglas. "Property, Authority and the Criminal Law." In *Albion's Fatal Tree: Crime and Society in Eighteenth Century England,* edited by Douglas Hay, Peter Linebaugh, John Rule, E.P. Thompson, and Cal Winslow, 17–63. Harmondsworth, UK: Penguin Books, 1977.

Helps, Lisa. "Bodies Public, City Spaces: Becoming Modern Victoria, British Columbia, 1871–1901." Master's thesis, University of Victoria, 2002.

Herron, Craig. *Booze: A Distilled History.* Toronto: Between the Lines, 2003.

Hewitt, Steven. *Riding to the Rescue: The Transformation of the RCMP in Alberta and Saskatchewan, 1914–1939.* Toronto: University of Toronto Press, 2006.

Hiebert, Albert John. "Prohibition in British Columbia." Master's thesis, Simon Fraser University, 1969.

Hill, Anthony D., and Douglas Q. Barnett. *Historical Dictionary of African American Theatre.* Plymouth, UK: Scarecrow Press, 2009.

Hill, Errol G., and James V. Hatch, eds. *A History of African American Theater.* New York: Cambridge University Press, 2003.

Hill, John, Jr. *Gold Bricks of Speculation: A Study of Speculation and Its Counterfeits, and an Exposé of the Methods of Bucketshop and "Get-Rich-Quick" Swindles.* Chicago: Lincoln Book Concern, 1904.

Hochfelder, David. "'Where the Common People Could Speculate': The Ticker, Bucket Shops, and the Origins of Popular Participation in Financial Markets, 1880–1920." *Journal of American History* 93, 2 (September 2006): 335–58.

Hogg, Robert. *Men and Manliness on the Frontier: Queensland and British Columbia in the Mid-Nineteenth Century.* Basingstoke, UK: Palgrave Macmillan, 2012.

Holmes, Neil Bradford. "The Promotion of Early Growth in the Western Canadian City: A Case Study of Prince George, B.C., 1909–1915." Honours thesis, University of British Columbia, 1974.

Homel, Gene. "Denison's Law: Criminal Justice and the Police Court in Toronto." *Ontario History* 73 (September 1981): 170–86.

Human Rights Watch. *Those Who Take Us Away: Abusive Policing and Failures in Protection of Indigenous Women and Girls in Northern British Columbia.* Washington, DC: Human Rights Watch, 2012.

Ireland, Brenda. "'Working a Great Hardship on Us': First Nations People, the State and Fur Conservation in British Columbia before 1935." Master's thesis, University of Calgary, 1995.

–. "'Working a Great Hardships on Us': First Nations People, the State, and Fur-Bearer Conservation in British Columbia Prior to 1930." *Native Studies Review* 11, 1 (1996): 65–90.

Jacobson, Matthew Frye. *Whiteness of a Different Color: European Immigrants and the Alchemy of Race.* Cambridge, MA: Harvard University Press, 1998.

Johnston, Hugh. "The Surveillance of Indian Nationalists in North America, 1908–1918." *BC Studies* 78 (Summer 1988): 3–27.

Kelm, Mary-Ellen. "British Columbia First Nations and the Influenza Pandemic of 1918–19." *BC Studies* 122 (Summer 1999): 23–47.

–. *Colonizing Bodies: Aboriginal Health and Healing in British Columbia, 1900–50.* Vancouver: UBC Press, 1998.

–. "Flu Stories: Engaging with Disease, Death, and Modernity in British Columbia, 1918–19." In *Epidemic Encounters: Influenza, Society, and Culture in Canada, 1918–20,* edited by Magda Fahrni and Esyllt Jones, 167–92. Vancouver: UBC Press, 2012.

Kelsey, Vera. *British Columbia Rides a Star.* Toronto: J.M. Dent and Sons, 1958.

Keyes, Daniel, and Luis Aguiar. *White Space: Race, Privilege, and Cultural Economies of the Okanagan Valley.* Vancouver: UBC Press, 2021.

Leonard, Frank. "'A Closed Book': The Canadian Pacific Railway Survey and North-Central British Columbia." *Western Geography* 12 (2002): 163–84.

—. "Grand Trunk Pacific and the Establishment of the City of Prince George, 1911–1915." *BC Studies* 63 (Autumn 1984): 29–54.

—. *A Thousand Blunders: The Grand Trunk Pacific Railway and Northern British Columbia.* Vancouver: UBC Press, 1996.

Levy, Daniel. *Two-Gun Cohen: A Biography.* New York: St. Martin's Press, 1997.

Loo, Tina. "Of Moose and Men: Hunting for Masculinities in British Columbia, 1880–1930." *Western Historical Quarterly* 32, 3 (2011): 296–319.

—. *States of Nature: Conserving Canada's Wildlife in the Twentieth Century.* Vancouver: UBC Press, 2006.

Lower, Joseph Arthur. "The Grand Trunk Pacific Railway and British Columbia." Master's thesis, University of British Columbia, 1939.

MacCallum, Todd. "The Great Depression's First History? The Vancouver Archives of Major J.S. Matthews and the Writing of Hobo History." *Canadian Historical Review* 87, 1 (March 2006): 79–107.

Macleod, R.C. *The North-West Mounted Police and Law Enforcement, 1873–1905.* Toronto: University of Toronto Press, 1976.

Makowsky, Tom. "Prince George at War." In *Sa ts'e: Historical Perspectives on Northern British Columbia,* edited by Thomas Thorner, 441–59. Prince George: College of New Caledonia Press, 1989.

Mar, Lisa Rose. *Brokering Belonging: Chinese in Canada's Exclusion Era, 1885–1945.* Toronto: Oxford University Press, 2010.

Marks, Lynne. *Infidels and the Damn Churches: Irreligion and Religion in Settler British Columbia.* Vancouver: UBC Press, 2017.

Marquis, Greg. "The History of Policing in the Maritime Provinces." *Urban History Review* 19, 2 (October 1990): 84–99.

—. *Policing Canada's Century: A History of the Canadian Association of Chiefs of Police.* Toronto: Osgoode Society for Canadian Legal History and University of Toronto Press, 1993.

—. "Vancouver Vice: The Police and the Negotiation of Morality, 1904–35." In *Essays in the History of Canadian Law: BC and Yukon,* edited by Hamar Foster and John McLaren, 242–73. Toronto: Osgoode Society for Canadian Legal History, 1995.

Mathieu, Sarah-Jane. *North of the Color Line: Migration and Black Resistance in Canada, 1870–1955.* Chapel Hill: University of North Carolina Press, 2010.

Mawani, Renisa. "In Between and Out of Place: Mixed-Race Identity, Liquor, and the Law in British Columbia, 1850–1913." In *Race, Space, and the Law: Unmapping a White Settler Society,* edited by Sherene H. Razack, 47–70. Toronto: Between the Lines, 2002.

—. *Colonial Proximities: Crossracial Encounters and Juridical Truths in British Columbia, 1871–1921.* Vancouver: UBC Press, 2009.

McLaren, Angus. "Males, Migrants, and Murder in British Columbia, 1900–1923." In *On the Case: Explorations in Social History,* edited by Franca Iacovetta and Wendy Mitchinson, 159–80. Toronto: University of Toronto Press, 1998.

—. *The Trials of Masculinity: Policing Sexual Boundaries, 1870–1930.* Chicago: University of Chicago Press, 1997.

McQueen, Ken, and Patricia Treble. "Canada's Most Dangerous City: Prince George." *Maclean's,* 15 December 2011. https://www.macleans.ca/news/canada/crime-most-dangerous-cities.

Mickleburgh, Rod. *On the Line: A History of the British Columbia Labour Movement.* Madeira Park, BC: Harbour Publishing, 2018.

Miller, Wilbur R. *Cops and Bobbies: Police Authority in New York and London, 1830–1870.* Chicago: University of Chicago Press, 1973.

Moore, Christopher. *The British Columbia Court of Appeal: The First Hundred Years.* Vancouver: UBC Press and the Osgoode Society for Canadian Legal History, 2010.

Morrison, William. *Showing the Flag: The Mounted Police and Canadian Sovereignty in the North, 1894–1925.* Vancouver: UBC Press, 1985.

Morton, Suzanne. *At Odds: Gambling and Canadians, 1919–1969.* Toronto: University of Toronto Press, 2003.

Mullins, Christine, and Arthur E. Harvey. *Russell & DuMoulin: The First Century, 1889–1989.* Vancouver: Russell & DuMoulin, Barristers and Solicitors, 1989.

Murphy, Emily. *The Black Candle.* Toronto: Thomas Allen, 1922.

–. "The Grave Drug Menace." *Maclean's* 33, 3 (15 February 1920): 9–11.

–. "The Underground System: Some Secrets of the Sale and Distribution of Drugs." *Maclean's* 33, 5 (15 March 1920): 12–13 and 55.

Neufeld, Andrew, and Andrew Parnaby. *The IWA in Canada: The Life and Times of an Industrial Union.* Vancouver: New Star Books, 2000.

Newell, G.R. "Cox, William George." *Dictionary of Canadian Biography.* Vol. 10. http://www.biographi.ca/en/bio/cox_william_george_10E.html.

Owram, Douglas. *Promise of Eden: The Canadian Expansionist Movement and the Idea of the West, 1856–1900.* Toronto: University of Toronto Press, 1992.

Parker, C.W., ed. *Who's Who and Why: A Biographical Dictionary of Notable Men and Women of Western Canada.* Vol. 2. Vancouver: Canadian Press, 1912.

Patrias, Carmela, and Larry Savage. *Union Power: Solidarity and Struggle in Niagara.* Edmonton: Athabasca University Press, 2012.

Peebles, Frank. "Hard Time: When Your Attacker Is the Judge." *Prince George Citizen,* 1 March 2008, 13.

Perry, Adele. *On the Edge of Empire: Gender, Race, and the Making of British Columbia, 1849–1871.* Vancouver: UBC Press, 2001.

Petersen, Bernard L., Jr. *A Century of Musicals in Black and White: An Encyclopedia of Musical Stage Works by, about, or Involving African Americans.* Westport, CT: Greenwood Press, 1993.

Pugh, Rhys. "The Newspaper Wars in Prince George, BC, 1909–1918." Master's thesis, University of Northern British Columbia, 2004.

Reclaiming Power and Place: The Final Report of the National Inquiry into Missing and Murdered Indigenous Women and Girls. N.d. https://www.mmiwg-ffada.ca/final-report/.

Reimers, Mia. "The Glamour and the Horror: A Social History of Wartime in Northwest British Columbia, 1939–1945." Master's thesis, University of Northern British Columbia, 1999.

Roy, Patricia, E. *Boundless Optimism: Richard McBride's British Columbia.* Vancouver: UBC Press, 2012.

–. *The Oriental Question: Consolidating a White Man's Province, 1914–41.* Vancouver: UBC Press, 2003.

–. *A White Man's Province: British Columbian Politicians and Chinese and Japanese Immigrants, 1858–1914.* Vancouver: UBC Press, 1989.

F.R. Runnalls, "Boom Days in Prince George, 1906–1913." *British Columbia Historical Quarterly* 8, 4 (October 1944): 281–306.

—. *The History of the Knox United Church, Prince George, British Columbia.* Prince George: Prince George Printers, 1986.

—. *A History of Prince George.* Vancouver: Wrigley Printing Co., 1946.

Sager, Ed, and Mike Frye. *The Bootlegger's Lady.* Surrey, BC: Hancock House Publishers, 1993.

Sangster, Joan. "'Pardon Tales' from Magistrate's Court: Women, Crime, and the Court in Peterborough County, 1920–50." *Canadian Historical Review* 74 (June 1993): 161–97.

Scholefield, E.O.S., ed. *British Columbia from Earliest Times to the Present.* Vol. 3. Vancouver: S.J. Clarke Publishing Co., 1914.

Sharpe, Robert, and Patricia McMahon. *The Persons Case: The Origins and Legacy of the Fight for Legal Personhood.* Toronto: Osgoode Society for Canadian Legal History, 2007.

Shorten, Rebecca. "The Shapeliest Legs under the Table: Defining the Feminist Influence on Women in British Columbia Municipal Politics, 1950–1980." Master's thesis, University of Northern British Columbia, 2008.

Shpayer-Makov, Haia. *The Ascent of the Detective: Police Sleuths in Victorian and Edwardian England.* Oxford: Oxford University Press, 2011.

Silver, Allan. "The Demand for Order in Civil Society: A Review of Some Themes in the History of Urban Crime, Police, and Riot." In *The Police: Six Sociological Essays,* edited by David J. Bordua, 1–24. New York: John Wiley and Sons, 1967.

Smith, Charleen P. "Boomtown Brothels in the Kootenays, 1895–1905." In *People and Place: Historical Influences on Legal Culture,* edited by Jonathan Swainger and Constance Backhouse, 120–52. Vancouver: UBC Press, 2003.

Stanley, Timothy J. *Contesting White Supremacy: School Segregation, Anti-Racism, and the Making of Chinese Canadians.* Vancouver: UBC Press, 2011.

Stenning, Philip C. *Police Commissions and Boards in Canada.* Toronto: University of Toronto Centre of Criminology, 1981.

Stonier-Newman, Lynne. *Policing a Pioneer Province: The BC Provincial Police, 1858–1950.* Madeira Park, BC: Harbour Publishing, 1991.

Storey, Kenton. *Settler Anxiety at the Outposts of Empire: Colonial Relations, Humanitarian Discourses, and the Imperial Press.* Vancouver: UBC Press, 2016.

Strange, Carolyn. *The Death Penalty and Sex Murder in Canadian History.* Toronto: Osgoode Society for Canadian Legal History and University of Toronto Press, 2020.

—. "Determining the Punishment of Sex Criminals in Confederation-Era Canada: A Matter of National Policy." *Canadian Historical Review* 99, 4 (December 2018): 541–62.

—. "The Lottery of Death: Capital Punishment, 1867–1976." *Manitoba Law Journal* 23, 3 (January 1996): 594–619.

Strong-Boag, Veronica. *Liberal-Labour Lady: The Life and Times of Mary Ellen Spear Smith.* Vancouver: UBC Press, 2021.

Sussman, Robert Wald. *The Myth of Race: The Troubling Persistence of an Unscientific Idea.* Cambridge, MA: Harvard University Press, 2014.

Swainger, Jonathan. "Anxiety at the Gates of Hell: Community Reputation in the Georges, 1908–15." *BC Studies* 205 (Spring 2020): 57–78.

—. "Breaking the Peace: Fictions of the Law-Abiding Peace River Country, 1930–50." *BC Studies* 119 (Autumn 1998): 5–25.

–. "'Not in Keeping with the Tradition of the Cariboo Courts': Courts and Community Identity in Northeastern British Columbia, 1920–50." In *The Grand Experiment: Law and Legal Culture in British Settler Societies,* edited by Hamar Foster, Benjamin L. Berger, and A.R. Buck, 176–92. Vancouver: UBC Press for the Osgoode Society for Canadian Legal History, 2008.

–. "Police Culture in British Columbia and 'Ordinary Duty.'" In *People and Place: Historical Influences on Legal Culture,* edited by Jonathan Swainger and Constance Backhouse, 198–223. Vancouver: UBC Press, 2003.

–. "Teen Trouble and Community Identity in Post–Second World War Northern British Columbia." *Journal of Canadian Studies* 47, 2 (Spring 2013): 150–79.

Talbot, F.A. *The New Garden of Canada: By Packhorse and Canoe through Undeveloped New British Columbia.* London: Cassell and Co., 1912.

Thorner, Tom, and Neil Watson. "Patterns of Prairie Crime: Calgary, 1875–1939." In *Crime and Criminal Justice in Europe and Canada,* edited by Louis A. Knafla, 219–55. Waterloo: Wilfrid Laurier University Press, 1985.

Trachtenberg, Alan. *The Incorporation of America: Culture and Society in the Gilded Age.* New York: Hill and Wang, 1982.

Valverde, Marianna. *The Age of Light, Soap, and Water: Moral Reform in English Canada, 1885–1925.* Toronto: McClelland and Stewart, 1991.

Van Orden, Kate, ed. *Music and the Cultures of Print.* New York: Routledge, 2000.

Verchere, David R. *A Progression of Judges: A History of the Supreme Court of British Columbia.* Vancouver: UBC Press, 1988.

Vogt, David, and David Alexander Gamble. "'You Don't Suppose the Dominion Government Wants to Cheat the Indians?' The Grand Trunk Pacific Railway and the Fort George Reserve, 1908–12." *BC Studies* 166 (Summer 2010): 55–72.

Voisey, Paul. *Vulcan: The Making of a Prairie Community.* Toronto: University of Toronto Press, 1988.

Walker, Barrington. *Race on Trial: Black Defendants in Ontario's Criminal Courts, 1858–1958.* Toronto: Osgoode Society for Canadian Legal History, 2010.

–, ed. *The African Canadian Legal Odyssey: Historical Essays.* Toronto: Osgoode Society for Canadian Legal History, 2012.

Walker, Russell R. *Bacon, Beans 'n' Brave Hearts.* Lillooet: Lillooet Publishers, 1972.

Ward, W. Peter. *White Canada Forever: Popular Attitudes and Public Policy towards Orientals in British Columbia.* Montreal and Kingston: McGill-Queen's University Press, 1978.

Watts, Alfred. "County Court of British Columbia." *Advocate* 27 (1969): 76–77.

Weaver, John C. *Crimes, Constables, and Courts: Order and Transgression in a Canadian City, 1816–1970.* Montreal and Kingston: McGill-Queen's University Press, 1995.

West, Willis J. "The 'BX' and the Rush to Fort George." *British Columbia Historical Quarterly* 13, 3/4 (July–October 1949): 129–229.

White, Kimberley. *Negotiating Responsibility: Law, Murder, and States of Mind.* Vancouver: UBC Press, 2008.

Williams, David Ricardo. "O'Reilly, Peter." *Dictionary of Canadian Biography.* http://www.biographi.ca/en/bio/o_reilly_peter_13E.html.

–. *Trapline Outlaw.* Victoria: Sono Nis Press, 1982.

Williams. Kristian. "The Demand for Order and the Birth of Modern Policing." *Monthly Review* 55, 7 (December 2003). https://monthlyreview.org/2003/12/01/the-demand-for-order-and-the-birth-of-modern-policing/.

Wing, Chung Ng. *The Chinese in Vancouver, 1945–90: The Pursuit of Identity and Power.* Vancouver: UBC Press, 1999.

Winks, Robin W. *The Blacks in Canada: A History.* 2nd ed. Montreal and Kingston: McGill-Queen's University Press, 1997.

Wolfe, Patrick. "Tramp Printer Extraordinary: British Columbia's John 'Truth' Houston." *BC Studies* 40 (Winter 1978–79): 5–31.

York, Lillian, ed. *Lure of the South Peace: Tales of the Early Pioneers to 1945.* Dawson Creek, BC: Peace River Block News, 1981.

Index

Note: "(f)" after a page number indicates a photo or map.

PUBLICATIONS OF THE OSGOODE SOCIETY
FOR CANADIAN LEGAL HISTORY

G. BLAINE BAKER and DONALD FYSON, eds., *Essays in the History of Canadian Law. Volume 11: Quebec and the Canadas*

2012 R. BLAKE BROWN, *Arming and Disarming: A History of Gun Control in Canada*

ERIC TUCKER, JAMES MUIR, and BRUCE ZIFF, eds., *Property on Trial: Canadian Cases in Context*

SHELLEY A.M. GAVIGAN, *Hunger, Horses, and Government Men: Criminal Law on the Aboriginal Plains, 1870-1905*

BARRINGTON WALKER, ed., *The African-Canadian Legal Odyssey: Historical Essays*

2011 ROBERT J. SHARPE, *The Lazier Murder: Prince Edward County, 1884*

PHILIP GIRARD, *Lawyers and Legal Culture in British North America: Beamish Murdoch of Halifax*

JOHN MCLAREN, *Dewigged, Bothered and Bewildered: British Colonial Judges on Trial*

LESLEY ERICKSON, *Westward Bound: Sex, Violence, the Law, and the Making of a Settler Society*

2010 JUDY FUDGE and ERIC TUCKER, eds., *Work on Trial: Canadian Labour Law Struggles*

CHRISTOPHER MOORE, *The British Columbia Court of Appeal: The First Hundred Years*

FREDERICK VAUGHAN, *Viscount Haldane: The Wicked Step-father of the Canadian Constitution*

BARRINGTON WALKER, *Race on Trial: Black Defendants in Ontario's Criminal Courts, 1850-1950*

2009 WILLIAM KAPLAN, *Canadian Maverick: The Life and Times of Ivan C. Rand*

R. BLAKE BROWN, *A Trying Question: The Jury in Nineteenth-Century Canada*

BARRY WRIGHT and SUSAN BINNIE, eds., *Canadian State Trials. Volume 3: Political Trials and Security Measures, 1840-1914*

ROBERT J. SHARPE, *The Last Day, the Last Hour: The Currie Libel Trial*

2008 CONSTANCE BACKHOUSE, *Carnal Crimes: Sexual Assault Law in Canada, 1900-1975*

JIM PHILLIPS, R. ROY MCMURTRY, and JOHN SAYWELL, eds., *Essays in the History of Canadian Law. Volume 10: A Tribute to Peter N. Oliver*

GREGORY TAYLOR, *The Law of the Land: Canada's Receptions of the Torrens System*

HAMAR FOSTER, BENJAMIN BERGER, and A.R. BUCK, eds., *The Grand Experiment: Law and Legal Culture in British Settler Societies*

2007 ROBERT SHARPE and PATRICIA MCMAHON, *The Persons Case: The Origins and Legacy of the Fight for Legal Personhood*
LORI CHAMBERS, *Misconceptions: Unmarried Motherhood and the Ontario Children of Unmarried Parents Act, 1921-1969*
JONATHAN SWAINGER, ed., *The Alberta Supreme Court at 100: History and Authority*
MARTIN FRIEDLAND, *My Life in Crime and Other Academic Adventures*

2006 DONALD FYSON, *Magistrates, Police and People: Everyday Criminal Justice in Quebec and Lower Canada, 1764-1837*
DALE BRAWN, *The Court of Queen's Bench of Manitoba 1870-1950: A Biographical History*
R.C.B. RISK, *A History of Canadian Legal Thought: Collected Essays*, edited and introduced by G. Blaine Baker and Jim Phillips

2005 PHILIP GIRARD, *Bora Laskin: Bringing Law to Life*
CHRISTOPHER ENGLISH, ed., *Essays in the History of Canadian Law. Volume 9: Two Islands, Newfoundland and Prince Edward Island*
FRED KAUFMAN, *Searching for Justice: An Autobiography*

2004 JOHN D. HONSBERGER, *Osgoode Hall: An Illustrated History*
FREDERICK VAUGHAN, *Aggressive in Pursuit: The Life of Justice Emmett Hall*
CONSTANCE BACKHOUSE and NANCY BACKHOUSE, *The Heiress versus the Establishment: Mrs. Campbell's Campaign for Legal Justice*
PHILIP GIRARD, JIM PHILLIPS, and BARRY CAHILL, eds., *The Supreme Court of Nova Scotia, 1754-2004: From Imperial Bastion to Provincial Oracle*

2003 ROBERT SHARPE and KENT ROACH, *Brian Dickson: A Judge's Journey*
GEORGE FINLAYSON, *John J. Robinette: Peerless Mentor*
PETER OLIVER, *The Conventional Man: The Diaries of Ontario Chief Justice Robert A. Harrison, 1856-1878*
JERRY BANNISTER, *The Rule of the Admirals: Law, Custom and Naval Government in Newfoundland, 1699-1832*

2002 JOHN T. SAYWELL, *The Law Makers: Judicial Power and the Shaping of Canadian Federalism*
DAVID MURRAY, *Colonial Justice: Justice, Morality and Crime in the Niagara District, 1791-1849*

F. Murray Greenwood and Barry Wright, eds., *Canadian State Trials. Volume 2: Rebellion and Invasion in the Canadas, 1837-38*
Patrick Brode, *Courted and Abandoned: Seduction in Canadian Law*

2001 Ellen Anderson, *Judging Bertha Wilson: Law as Large as Life*
Judy Fudge and Eric Tucker, *Labour before the Law: Collective Action in Canada, 1900-1948*
Laurel Sefton MacDowell, *Renegade Lawyer: The Life of J.L. Cohen*

2000 Barry Cahill, *"The Thousandth Man": A Biography of James McGregor Stewart*
A.B. McKillop, *The Spinster and the Prophet: Florence Deeks, H.G. Wells, and the Mystery of the Purloined Past*
Beverley Boissery and F. Murray Greenwood, *Uncertain Justice: Canadian Women and Capital Punishment*
Bruce Ziff, *Unforeseen Legacies: Reuben Wells Leonard and the Leonard Foundation Trust*

1999 Constance Backhouse, *Colour-Coded: A Legal History of Racism in Canada, 1900-1950*
G. Blaine Baker and Jim Phillips, eds., *Essays in the History of Canadian Law. Volume 8: In Honour of R.C.B. Risk*
Richard W. Pound, *Chief Justice W.R. Jackett: By the Law of the Land*
David Vanek, *Fulfilment: Memoirs of a Criminal Court Judge*

1998 Sidney Harring, *White Man's Law: Native People in Nineteenth-Century Canadian Jurisprudence*
Peter Oliver, *"Terror to Evil-Doers": Prisons and Punishments in Nineteenth-Century Ontario*

1997 James W. St. G. Walker, *"Race," Rights and the Law in the Supreme Court of Canada: Historical Case Studies*
Lori Chambers, *Married Women and Property Law in Victorian Ontario*
Patrick Brode, *Casual Slaughters and Accidental Judgments: Canadian War Crimes and Prosecutions, 1944-1948*
Ian Bushnell, *The Federal Court of Canada: A History, 1875-1992*

1996 Carol Wilton, ed., *Essays in the History of Canadian Law. Volume 7: Inside the Law – Canadian Law Firms in Historical Perspective*
William Kaplan, *Bad Judgment: The Case of Mr. Justice Leo A. Landreville*
Murray Greenwood and Barry Wright, eds., *Canadian State Trials. Volume 1: Law, Politics and Security Measures, 1608-1837*

1995   DAVID WILLIAMS, *Just Lawyers: Seven Portraits*
HAMAR FOSTER and JOHN MCLAREN, eds., *Essays in the History of Canadian Law. Volume 6: British Columbia and the Yukon*
W.H. MORROW, ed., *Northern Justice: The Memoirs of Mr. Justice William G. Morrow*
BEVERLEY BOISSERY, *A Deep Sense of Wrong: The Treason, Trials and Transportation to New South Wales of Lower Canadian Rebels after the 1838 Rebellion*

1994   PATRICK BOYER, *A Passion for Justice: The Legacy of James Chalmers McRuer*
CHARLES PULLEN, *The Life and Times of Arthur Maloney: The Last of the Tribunes*
JIM PHILLIPS, TINA LOO, and SUSAN LEWTHWAITE, eds., *Essays in the History of Canadian Law. Volume 5: Crime and Criminal Justice*
BRIAN YOUNG, *The Politics of Codification: The Lower Canadian Civil Code of 1866*

1993   GREG MARQUIS, *Policing Canada's Century: A History of the Canadian Association of Chiefs of Police*
MURRAY GREENWOOD, *Legacies of Fear: Law and Politics in Quebec in the Era of the French Revolution*

1992   BRENDAN O'BRIEN, *Speedy Justice: The Tragic Last Voyage of His Majesty's Vessel* Speedy
ROBERT FRASER, ed., *Provincial Justice: Upper Canadian Legal Portraits from the* Dictionary of Canadian Biography

1991   CONSTANCE BACKHOUSE, *Petticoats and Prejudice: Women and Law in Nineteenth-Century Canada*

1990   PHILIP GIRARD and JIM PHILLIPS, eds., *Essays in the History of Canadian Law. Volume 3: Nova Scotia*
CAROL WILTON, ed., *Essays in the History of Canadian Law. Volume 4: Beyond the Law – Lawyers and Business in Canada 1830-1930*

1989   DESMOND BROWN, *The Genesis of the Canadian Criminal Code of 1892*
PATRICK BRODE, *The Odyssey of John Anderson*

1988   ROBERT SHARPE, *The Last Day, the Last Hour: The Currie Libel Trial*
JOHN D. ARNUP, *Middleton: The Beloved Judge*

1987   C. Ian Kyer and Jerome Bickenbach, *The Fiercest Debate: Cecil A. Wright, the Benchers and Legal Education in Ontario, 1923-1957*

1986   Paul Romney, *Mr. Attorney: The Attorney General for Ontario in Court, Cabinet and Legislature, 1791-1899*
        Martin Friedland, *The Case of Valentine Shortis: A True Story of Crime and Politics in Canada*

1985   James Snell and Frederick Vaughan, *The Supreme Court of Canada: History of the Institution*

1984   Patrick Brode, *Sir John Beverley Robinson: Bone and Sinew of the Compact*
        David Williams, *Duff: A Life in the Law*

1983   David H. Flaherty, ed., *Essays in the History of Canadian Law. Volume 2*

1982   Marion MacRae and Anthony Adamson, *Cornerstones of Order: Courthouses and Town Halls of Ontario, 1784-1914*

1981   David H. Flaherty, ed., *Essays in the History of Canadian Law. Volume 1*

Printed and bound in Canada by Friesens
Set in Garamond by Artegraphica Design Co.
Copy editor: Barbara Tessman
Proofreader: Judith Earnshaw
Indexer: Noeline Bridge
Cartographer: Eric Leinberger
Cover designer: Alexa Love
Cover image: Arcade Café riot aftermath, 1919. Courtesy BCA